# READING THE
# TWENTIETH CENTURY

# READING THE TWENTIETH CENTURY
## Documents in American History

Donald W. Whisenhunt

ROWMAN & LITTLEFIELD PUBLISHERS, INC.
*Lanham • Boulder • New York • Toronto • Plymouth, UK*

Published by Rowman & Littlefield Publishers, Inc.
A wholly owned subsidiary of The Rowman & Littlefield Publishing Group, Inc.
4501 Forbes Boulevard, Suite 200, Lanham, Maryland 20706
http://www.rowmanlittlefield.com

Estover Road, Plymouth PL6 7PY, United Kingdom

British Library Cataloguing in Publication Information Available

**Library of Congress Cataloging-in-Publication Data**

Reading the twentieth century : documents in American history / [compiled and edited by] Donald W. Whisenhunt.
    p. cm.
  Includes bibliographical references.
  ISBN 978-0-7425-6476-3 (cloth : alk. paper) — ISBN 978-0-7425-6477-0 (pbk. : alk. paper) — ISBN 978-0-7425-6478-7 (electronic)
  1. United States—History—20th century—Sources. 2. United States—History—Study and teaching. I. Whisenhunt, Donald W.
  E740.5.R43 2009
  973.91—dc22                                      2009015659

Printed in the United States of America

To my sons, Donald, Jr. (chemist) and William Benton "Ben" (historian)
Who have never ceased to make me proud.
Now they are my inspiration.
Again and always

# Contents

# Preface

SOME HAVE CALLED THE TWENTIETH century "the American Century." Whether or not the United States dominated the world, as that phrase suggests, the United States was clearly a major player on the world scene and was particularly important after the end of World War II in 1945.

The twentieth century for the United States was bracketed by two significant events, the acquisition of an empire following the Spanish-American War after 1898 and the attack on the World Trade Center in New York in 2001.

At the beginning of the century, the United States had become a world power after the war with Spain that resulted in the freeing of Cuba and the acquisition of foreign territory for the United States. This was not the first time the United States had acquired territory beyond the nation's contiguous boundaries. Following the Civil War, the United States purchased Alaska and had made overtures at annexing other areas. But with the Spanish-American War, the United States gained title to Puerto Rico, Guam, and the Philippine Islands.

The United States could now be classified as an imperial power, although not everyone agreed with the direction the country was taking. The Industrial Revolution was reaching maturity, and America now had a large manufacturing surplus that needed markets. In addition, many Americans believed, as they had for many years, that the American system of government and democracy should be carried to other parts of the world. They were especially concerned about areas of the world they considered racially and culturally inferior. The goal of taking Christianity to other parts of the world played a part in this "New Manifest Destiny."

Throughout the century, the United States continued, with some interruptions, its growth and strength so that by the time of World War II, the actions of the United States were the determining factor in who won that war.

Despite the growth in world power, a significant portion of Americans were suspicious of the outside world and held to older isolationist tendencies. This was due, in part, to the size and location of the United States, which contributed to a sense of isolation and geographic protection. Much of the reaction against the rest of the world had to do with the belief that Europe was old and decadent, a major reason immigrants to America had left there in the first place. The other parts of the world were considered racially, socially, and politically inferior. Much of America's energy was devoted to protecting itself from being tainted by the Old World. World War I, the Russian Revolution, and turmoil in various parts of the world contributed to this feeling. To be sure, Americans were conflicted in the twentieth century as to their role in the world.

Tensions and growing pains inside the United States contributed to the ambivalent feelings toward the larger world. The United States was a growing and dynamic economy and culture, but the changes constantly occurring caused internal problems. The issues of immigration, race, gender, poverty, wealth, and social change all contributed to defining America in the twentieth century. Clearly, issues such as these had both domestic and international ramifications.

By the end of the century, the Cold War had ended, and the United States was the sole remaining "superpower." This development is a good symbol of the status of the United States at the end of the twentieth century. It stands as a good bookend to the acquisition of the Philippines and other possessions that occurred in the last years of the nineteenth century.

The relief felt at the collapse of the Soviet Union was soon replaced by anxiety regarding small conflicts all around the world. The United States had replaced Great Britain as the world's most powerful country and often found itself in a situation similar to ones faced by the British—trying to maintain world peace and the balance of power.

Because of the dependence of the world on the oil reserves of the Middle East, Americans became more involved in the affairs of that part of the world. Since the Middle East, with the exception of Israel, is predominantly Muslim in religion and culture, one would think that Americans would become more knowledgeable about that culture, but that was not the case. The rise of radical Islamic groups puzzled Americans, many of whom saw no way of dealing with them.

The twenty-first century opened dramatically when a group of Islamic suicide bombers attacked the World Trade Center towers in New York and the

Pentagon in Washington. Americans' shock and anger were understandable. Except for the attack by the Japanese on Pearl Harbor in 1941, the nation had been invincible to attack at home since the British invaded and burned Washington, D.C., during the War of 1812. The century that began with the acquisition of the Philippines and great optimism for the future had ended with a feeling of euphoria as the Cold War came to an end without violence. That feeling of well-being was short-lived, however, with September 11, 2001, and the fear and uncertainty it brought to the average American.

This volume is intended to show the growing influence of the United States upon world affairs and the impact of the rest of the world on the United States during the twentieth century. That story would be incomplete and one sided if the social and cultural changes occurring in the United States are ignored. Therefore, this book focuses on both the domestic development of the United States and the role of the United States in the world. Technological developments—many of them originating in the United States—are ubiquitous in the world. Television, computers, and cable news stations have made American music, television programming, social and cultural changes, and religious developments well known around the world. This American influence has had positive and negative results. Americans as individuals are often welcome in many parts of the world, while America as a nation and a government is often resented. The impact of technological changes have also made Americans suspicious of the motives of other countries and other cultures.

This book uses selected documents from key events—some well known and others less so—to illustrate both the role of America in the world and the growing pains and social tensions occurring within the United States. These developments are revealed through selected documents—from government documents, personal memoirs, and the popular press—that illustrate the way the United States developed, despite stops and starts and detours along the way. Included in the volume are documents that may already be familiar, such as Wilson's war message, the Kellogg-Briand treaty, the Truman Doctrine, and the Marshall Plan. It also includes lesser-known documents such as those relating to the student antiwar and pacifist movement in the 1930s, and the "constitution" of the Ku Klux Klan.

These documents illuminate aspects of the United States in the twentieth century. Clearly, I had to make choices regarding the documents to include; some vital events in American history were considered for inclusion, but I had to make choices and eliminate some excellent documents that could have been included. That was painful for me, but it was necessary. The documents that survived scrutiny and are included give the reader an excellent overview of major events of the twentieth century. I hope that reading these documents will stimulate interest and cause the reader to read more deeply in some topics.

# Acknowledgments

I WOULD LIKE TO ACKNOWLEDGE THE invaluable help of one of my former students, Edward Chatterton, who was both an undergraduate and graduate student of mine at Western Washington University. He was instrumental in assisting me in searching for and collecting documents for this book. My editors, Niels Aaboe, Elaine McGarraugh, and especially Michelle Cassidy, at Rowman & Littlefield have been supportive and patient through this process. Thanks, Niels, Michelle, and Elaine. I will forever be grateful for the libraries and librarians at Western Washington University, Murray State University, and Northern Illinois University. Not least, to be sure, are those people (too many to name) who allowed me free use of documents they produced.

# Prologue

# Dawning of the Twentieth Century— Acquisition of an Empire

## Background

*A*t THE BEGINNING OF THE TWENTIETH *century, the United States had become a world power after the war with Spain in 1898 that resulted in the freeing of Cuba and the acquisition of foreign territory for the United States.*

*This was not the first time the United States had acquired territory beyond the nation's contiguous boundaries. Following the Civil War, the United States purchased Alaska and had made overtures at annexing other areas. But with the Spanish-American War, the United States gained title to Puerto Rico, Guam, and the Philippine Islands.*

*The United States could now be classified as an imperial power, although not everyone agreed with the direction the country was taking. The Industrial Revolution was reaching maturity, and America now had a large manufacturing surplus that needed markets. In addition, many Americans believed, as they had for many years, that the American system of government and democracy should be carried to other parts of the world. They were especially concerned about areas of the world they considered racially and culturally inferior. The goal of taking Christianity to other parts of the world played a part in this "New Manifest Destiny."*

*When the war with Spain began, the anti-imperialists had been able to get the Teller Resolution through Congress, stating that the United States had no intention of annexing Cuba; instead, its motives in fighting Spain were to free Cuba from Spanish oppression and to set the island free. Imperialists were not happy about this development, but they had to accept it. Not mentioned in the Teller*

*Resolution* were the other colonial possessions still owned by Spain, especially Puerto Rico, Guam, and the Philippines.

The United States moved quickly to integrate these territories under American control, despite objections from the anti-imperialists and the people of these territories, especially the Filipinos. The United States did not expect resistance from the Filipinos. The result was a period of vicious guerilla warfare known as the "Philippine Insurrection." This native uprising lasted far longer and cost more in casualties and money than the war against Spain. When the war became more prolonged and brutal, the opponents of annexation in America tried to reverse the tide, but to no effect. At the time of the peace with Spain, few expected the events that occurred within the next three years.

## Questions

In reading these documents, the student should contemplate several questions to put these activities in the proper context.

1. Why did Americans expect the subjects of the Spanish empire to accept American control in place of Spanish?
2. What do the documents reflect about American attitudes regarding race?
3. Were Americans worried about world opinion regarding the takeover of parts of the world quite unfamiliar to Americans and very different from the United States?
4. Are the Filipino arguments against American control convincing?
5. Were the American imperialists honest and sincere in their wishes to bring the benefits of American democracy to these people?

## Document 1: Peace Is Established; President McKinley Tries to Reassure the Filipinos[1]

*Following the end of hostilities in August 1898, American officials moved to make peace and to establish control in the Philippines. Before the end of 1898, President McKinley issued a statement that has become known as the "Benevolent Assimilation" proclamation, reassuring the world, and the Filipinos especially, that American intentions were of the highest order.*

In performing this duty [the extension of American sovereignty throughout the Philippines by means of force] the military commander of the United States is enjoined to make known to the inhabitants of the Philippine Islands that in succeeding to the sovereignty of Spain, in severing the former political relations, and in establishing a new political power, the authority of the United States is to be exerted for the securing of the persons and property of the people of the Islands and for the confirmation of all private rights and relations. It will be the duty of the commander of the forces of occupation to announce and proclaim in the most public manner that we come not as invaders or conquerors, but as friends, to protect the natives in their homes, in their employment, and in their personal and religious rights. All persons who, either by active aid or by honest submission, cooperate with the Government of the United States to give effect to these beneficent purposes will receive the reward of its support and protection. All others will be brought within the lawful rule we have assumed, with firmness if need be, but without severity, so far as may be possible. . . .

Finally, it should be the earnest and paramount aim of the military administration to win the confidence, respect, and affection of the inhabitants of the Philippines by assuring them in every possible way that full measure of individual rights and liberties which is the heritage of a free people, and by proving to them that the mission of the United States is one of the benevolent assimilation, substituting the mild sway of justice and right for arbitrary rule. In the fulfillment of this high mission, supporting the temperate administration of affairs for the greatest good of the governed, there must be sedulously maintained the strong arm of authority, to repress disturbance and to overcome all obstacles to the bestowal of the blessings of good and stable government upon the people of the Philippine Islands under the flag of the United States.

## Documents 2–4: Filipinos Resist American Control to No Avail

*Filipinos, who had been in revolt against Spain before the American war with Spain, were not happy about the American takeover of their islands. Filipinos tried to resist American control, but eventually they were forced to surrender and accept American hegemony.*

### Document 2: Aguinaldo protests the U.S. claim of sovereignty[2]

*Emilio Aguinaldo, a leader in the Philippines, had been in exile, but he returned to Manila during the war, expecting the United States to defeat Spain and set the Philippines free. He proclaimed the Philippines independent on June 12, 1898. He was chosen as president of the Philippine Republic on January 1, 1899, following a constitutional convention. Because of McKinley's "Benevolent Assimilation" statement and General Otis's proclamation, Aguinaldo responded as a Filipino nationalist by protesting the American claim of sovereignty.*

General Otis styles himself Military Governor of these Islands, and I protest one and a thousand times and with all the energy of my soul against such authority. I proclaim solemnly that I have not recognized . . . the sovereignty of America over this beloved soil. On the contrary, I say that I returned to these Islands on an American warship on the 19th of May last for the express purpose of making war on the Spaniards to regain our liberty and independence. I stated this in my proclamation of the 24th of May last, and I publish it in my Manifesto addressed to the Philippine people on the 12th of June. Lastly, all this was confirmed by the American General Merritt himself, predecessor of General Otis, in his Manifesto to the Philippine people some days before he demanded the surrender of Manila from the Spanish General Jaudenes. In that Manifesto it is distinctly stated that the naval and field forces of the United States had come to give us our liberty, by subverting the bad Spanish Government, And I hereby protest against this unexpected act of the United States claiming sovereignty over these Islands. My relations with the United States did not bring me over here from Hong Kong to make war on the Spaniards for their benefit, but for the purpose of our own liberty and independence. . . .

*The resistance from the residents to the American occupation of the Philippines was much more serious than anyone expected, and the casualty rate among both Americans and Filipinos was high. Here is a photo of an American soldier standing near corpses of Filipino rebels. Courtesy of the Library of Congress, LC-USZ62-100490.*

### Document 3: Aquinaldo surrenders[3]

*Emilio Aguinaldo led the Filipino forces against the United States for more than four years, but he was eventually captured on March 31, 1901. The following month he issued a statement of surrender explaining his position.*

To the Filipino People:

I believe that I am not in error in presuming that the unhappy fate to which my adverse fortune has led me is not a surprise to those who have been familiar day to day with the progress of the war. The lessons thus taught, the full meaning of which has recently come to my knowledge, suggested to me with irresistible force that the complete termination of hostilities and a lasting peace are not only desirable but absolutely essential to the welfare of the Philippines.

The Filipinos have never been dismayed by their weakness, nor have they faltered in following the path pointed out by their fortitude and courage. The time has come, however, in which they find their advance along the path impeded by an irresistible force—a force which, while it restrains them, yet enlightens the mind and opens another course by presenting to them the cause of peace. This cause has been joyfully embraced around the glorious and sovereign banner of the United States. In this manner they repose their trust in the belief that under its protection our people will attain all the promised liberties which they are even now beginning to enjoy.

The country has declared unmistakably in favor of peace; so be it. Enough of blood; enough of tears and desolation. This wish cannot be ignored by the men still in arms if they are animated by no other desire than to serve this noble people which has clearly manifested its will.

So also do I respect this will now that it is known to me, and after mature deliberation resolutely proclaim to the world that I cannot refuse to heed the voice of a people longing for peace, nor the lamentations of thousands of families yearning to see their dear ones in the enjoyment of the liberty promised by the generosity of the great American nation.

By acknowledging and accepting the sovereignty of the United States throughout the entire Archipelago, as I now do without any reservations whatsoever, I believe that I am serving thee, my beloved country. May happiness be thine!

### Document 4: The war ends[4]

*Even though Aguinaldo surrendered in March 1901, more than a year passed before the war was considered over. By that time, Theodore Roosevelt had become president after the assassination of President McKinley. Finally on July 4, 1902, Roosevelt issued his proclamation ending the conflict.*

Whereas, many of the inhabitants of the Philippine Archipelago were in insurrection against the authority and sovereignty of the Kingdom of Spain at divers [*sic*] times from August, eighteen hundred and ninety-six, until the cession of the archipelago by that Kingdom to the United States of America, and since such cession many of the persons so engaged in insurrection have until recently resisted the authority and sovereignty of the United States; and

Whereas, the insurrection against the authority and sovereignty of the United States is now at an end, and peace has been established in all parts of the archipelago except in the country inhabited by the Moro tribes, to which this proclamation does not apply; and

Whereas, during the course of the insurrection against the Kingdom of Spain and against the Government of the United States, persons engaged therein, or those in sympathy with and abetting them, committed many acts in violation of the laws of civilized warfare, but it is believed that such acts were generally committed in ignorance of those laws, and under orders issued by the civil or insurrectionary leaders; and

Whereas, it is deemed to be wise and humane, in accordance with the beneficent purposes of the Government of the United States towards the Filipino people, and conducive to peace, order, and loyalty among them, that the doers of such acts who have not already suffered punishment shall not be held criminally responsible, but shall be relieved from punishment for participation in these insurrections, and for unlawful acts committed during the course thereof, by a general amnesty and pardon:

Now, therefore, be it known that I, Theodore Roosevelt, President of the United States of America, by virtue of the power and authority vested in me by the Constitution, do hereby proclaim and declare, without reservation or condition, except as hereinafter provided, a full and complete pardon and amnesty to all persons in the Philippine Archipelago who have participated in the insurrections aforesaid, or who have given aid and comfort to persons participating in said insurrections, for the offenses of treason or sedition and for all offenses political in their character committed in the course of such insurrections pursuant to orders issued by the civil or military insurrectionary authorities, or which grew out of internal political feuds or dissension between Filipinos and Spaniards or the Spanish authorities, or which resulted from internal political feuds or dissension among the Filipinos themselves, during either of said insurrections. . . .

### Documents 5–8: The Question of Empire

*When the United States was confronted with whether it should annex the Philippines or set the islands free, there was much agonizing as to the correct*

*course. Various critics argued that the acquisition of colonies was not in the American tradition, while the supporters argued for it on various grounds.*

## Document 5: Rudyard Kipling checks in[5]

*Rudyard Kipling, the British poet who had spent much time in India, published a poem in* McClure's Magazine *that became famous through the years. Some Americans embraced it heartily, while others were horrified, especially by its title, "The White Man's Burden."*

> Take up the White Man's burden—
>     Send forth the best ye breed—
> Go, bind your sons to exile
>     To serve your captives' need;
> To wait, in heavy harness,
>     On fluttered folk and wild—
> Your new-caught sullen peoples,
>     Half devil and half child.
>
> . . .
>
> Take up the White Man's burden—
>     No iron rule of kings,
> But toil of serf and sweeper—
>     The tale of common things.
> The ports ye shall not enter,
>     The roads ye shall not tread,
> Go, make them with your living
>     And mark them with your dead.
>
> . . .
>
> Take up the White Man's burden—
>     Ye dare not stoop to less—
> Nor call too loud on Freedom
>     To cloak your weariness.
> By all ye will or whisper,
>     By all ye leave or do,
> The silent sullen peoples
>     Shall weigh your God and you. . . .

## Document 6: McKinley explains his dilemma[6]

*President McKinley explained to a group of ministers of the Methodist Episcopal Church the dilemma he found himself in when the United States took control of the Philippines. As he explains in this short excerpt, he resolved the moral conflict. This article was published about two years after McKinley's death.*

I have been criticized a good deal about the Philippines, but I don't deserve it. The truth is I didn't want the Philippines, and when they came to us as a gift from the gods, I did not know what to do with them. When the Spanish War broke out, Dewey was at Hong-kong, and I ordered him to go to Manila and to capture or destroy the Spanish fleet, and he had to; because, if defeated, he had no place to refit on that side of the globe, and if the Dons were victorious, they would likely cross the Pacific and ravage our Oregon and California coasts. And so he had to destroy the Spanish fleet, and did it! But that was as far as I thought then.

When next I realized that the Philippines had dropped into our laps I confess I did not know what to do with them. I sought counsel from all sides—Democrats as well as Republicans—but got little help. I thought first we would take only Manila; then Luzon; then other islands, perhaps, also. I walked the floor of the White House night after night until midnight; and I am not ashamed to tell you gentlemen, that I went down on my knees and prayed to Almighty God for light and guidance more than one night. And one night late it came to me this way—I don't know how it was, but it came: (1) That we could not give them back to Spain—that would be cowardly and dishonorable; (2) that we could not turn them over to France or Germany—our commercial rivals in the Orient—that would be bad business and discreditable; (3) that we could not leave them to themselves—they were unfit for self-government—and they would soon have anarchy and misrule there worse than Spain's was; and (4) that there was nothing left for us to do but to take them all, and to educate the Filipinos, and uplift and civilize and Christianize them, and by God's grace do the very best we could by them, as our fellow men for whom Christ also died. And then I went to bed, and went to sleep, and slept soundly, and the next morning I sent for the chief engineer of the War Department (our map-maker), and I told him to put the Philippines on the map of the United States [pointing to a large map on the wall of his office], and there they are, and there they will stay while I am president!

### Document 7: Senator Lodge provides justification for taking the Philippines[7]

*Senator Henry Cabot Lodge of Massachusetts, later to become famous for his opposition to the treaty that ended World War I and for his opposition to American entry into the League of Nations, was a leading expansionist at the turn of the century. In March 1900 in a speech in the Senate (excerpted here), he explained the benefits for the United States and for the Philippines for American acquisition of the islands.*

I shall not argue our title to the [Philippine] islands by the law of nations; for it is perfect. No other nation has ever questioned it. . . . Equally plain is our right under the Constitution, by a treaty which is the supreme law of the land, to hold those islands, . . . The opposition . . . rests its weight on grounds widely different from these. They assert that on moral grounds we have no right to take or retain the Philippines, and that as a matter of expediency our whole Eastern policy is a costly mistake. . . . I deny both propositions. I believe we are in the Philippines as righteously as we are there rightly and legally. I believe that to abandon the islands, or to leave them now, would be a wrong to humanity, a dereliction of duty, a base betrayal of the Filipinos who have supported us . . . and in the highest degree contrary to sound morals. As to expediency, the arguments in favor of the retention of the Philippines seem to me so overwhelming that I should regard their loss as a calamity to our trade and commerce and to all our business interests so great that no man can measure it. . . .

Our opponents put forward as their chief objection that we have robbed these people of their liberty, and have taken them and hold them in defiance of the doctrine of the Declaration of Independence in regard to the consent of the governed. As to liberty, they have never had it, and have none now, except when we give it to them protected by the flag and the armies of the United States. . . .

The second objection, as to the consent of the governed, requires more careful examination, because of the persistency with which it has been made the subject of heated declamation. . . . If the arguments which have been offered against our taking the Philippine Islands because we have not the consent of the inhabitants be just, then our whole record of expansion is a crime. . . . Does anyone really believe it? Then let us be honest and look at this whole question as it really is. I am not ashamed of that long record of American expansion. I am proud of it. . . . The taking of the Philippines does not violate the principles of the Declaration of Independence, but will spread them among a people who have never known liberty, and, who in a few years will be as unwilling to leave the shelter of the American flag as those of any other territory we ever brought beneath its folds.

The next argument of the opponents of the Republican policy is that we are denying self-government to the Filipinos. Our reply is that to give independent self-government at once, as we understand it, to a people who have no just conception of it and no fitness for it, is to dower them with a curse instead of a blessing. . . .

The Filipinos are not now fit for self-government. . . . The form of government natural to the Asiatic has always been a despotism. . . . You can not change race tendencies in a moment. . . .

I come now to a consideration of the advantages to the United States involved in our acquisition of the Philippine Islands. . . . When these arguments are offered in behalf of our Philippine policy, the opponents of policy stigmatize them as sordid. . . . I do not myself consider them sordid, for anything which involves the material interests and the general welfare the United States seems to me of the highest merit and the greatest importance. Whatever duty to others might seem to demand, I should pause long before supporting any policy if there were the slightest suspicion that it was not for the benefit of the people of the United States. I conceive my first duty to be always to the people of the United States, and most particularly for the advantage of our farmers and our workingmen, upon whose well-being, and upon whose full employment at the highest wages, our entire fabric of society and government rests. In a policy which gives us a foothold in the East, which will open a new market in the Philippines, and enable us to increase our commerce with China, I see great advantages to all our people, and more especially to our farmers and our workingmen. . . .

There is no reason to doubt that in a comparatively short time peace and order will be restored, and when we are considering what burden the possession of the islands will impose upon us we must proceed upon the normal conditions of peace. . . . The islands themselves are abundantly able to pay for the establishment there, both civil and military. . . . In a word, the Philippine Islands, as we should govern and administer them, would throw no burden of expense at all on the people of the United States after peace and order were once restored and business was again flowing in its normal channels.

. . . Let us now look at the other side, and there, I believe, we shall find arguments in favor of the retention of the Philippines as possessions of great value and a source of profit to the people of the United States which cannot be overthrown. . . .

A much more important point is to be found in the markets which they furnish. The total value of exports and imports for 1896 amounted in round numbers to $29,000,000. . . . We took from the Philippines exports to the value of $4,308,000, next in amount to the exports to Great Britain; but the Philippine Islands took from us imports to the value of only $94,000. There can be no doubt that the islands in our peaceful possession would take from us a very large proportion of their imports. Even as the islands are to-day there is opportunity for a large absorption of products of the United States, but it must not be forgotten that the islands are entirely undeveloped. The people consume foreign imports at the rate of only a trifle more than $1 per capita. With the development of the islands and the increase of commerce and of business activity the consumption of foreign imports would rapidly advance, of this increase we should reap the chief benefit. We shall also find great profit in the work of developing islands. They require railroads every-where. Those railroads would be planned by American engineers, the rails and the bridges would come from American mills, the locomotives and cars from American workshops. The same would hold true in regard to electric railways, electric lighting, telegraphs, telephones, and steamships for the local business. . . .

Thus . . . duty and interest alike, duty of the highest kind and interest of the highest and best kind, impose upon us the retention of the Philippines, the de-velopment of the islands, and the expansion of our Eastern commerce.

*Document 8: William Jennings Bryan rebuts and provides another point of view[8]*

*William Jennings Bryan, the young firebrand who had startled the country in 1896 by capturing the presidential nomination of the Democratic Party, was nominated in 1900 to run against President McKinley again. In his acceptance speech to the Democratic National Convention, a part of his speech dealt with imperialism and the acquisition of the Philippines.*

. . . Instead of meeting the issue boldly and submitting a clear and positive plan for dealing with the Philippine question, the Republican convention adopted a platform the larger part of which was devoted to boasting and self-congratulation. . . .

But they shall not be permitted to evade the stupendous and far-reaching issue which they have deliberately brought into the arena of politics. When the president, supported by a practically unanimous vote of the House and Sen-ate, entered upon a war with Spain for the purpose of aiding the struggling pa-triots of Cuba, the country, without regard to party, applauded. . . .

When the President finally laid before the Senate a treaty which recognized the independence of Cuba, but provided for the cession of the Philippine Is-lands to the United States, the menace of imperialism became so apparent that many preferred to reject the treaty and risk the ills that might follow rather than take the chance of correcting the errors of the treaty by the independent action of this country.

I was among the number of those who believed it better to ratify the treaty and end the war, release the volunteers, remove the excuse for war expendi-tures and then give the Filipinos the independence which might be forced from Spain by a new treaty. . . .

When hostilities broke out at Manila Republican speakers and Republican editors at once sought to lay the blame upon those who had delayed the ratifi-cation of the treaty, and, during the progress of the war, the same Republicans have accused the opponents of imperialism of giving encouragement to the Filipinos. This is a cowardly evasion of responsibility.

If it is right for the United States to hold the Philippine Islands permanently and imitate European empires in the government of colonies, the Republican party ought to state its position and defend it, but it must expect the subject races to protest against such a policy and to resist to the extent of their ability. . . .

. . . The Republican platform assumes that the Philippine Islands will be retained under American sovereignty, and we have a right to demand of the Republican leaders a discussion of the future status of the Filipino. Is he to be a citizen or a subject? Are we to bring into the body politic eight or ten million Asiatics so different from us in race and history that amalgamation is impossible? Are they to share with us in making the laws and shaping the destiny of this nation? No Republican of prominence has been bold enough to advocate such a proposition. . . .

The Republican platform promises that some measure of self-government is to be given the Filipinos by law; but even this pledge is not fulfilled. Nearly sixteen months elapsed after the ratification of the treaty before the adjournment of congress last June and yet no law was passed dealing with the Philippine situation. The will of the president has been the only law in the Philippine islands wherever the American authority extends. . . .

What is our title to the Philippine islands? Do we hold them by treaty or by conquest? Did we buy them or did we take them? Did we purchase the people? . . . If governments derive their just powers from the consent of the governed, it is impossible to secure title to people, either by force or by purchase. We could extinguish Spain's title by treaty, but if we hold title we must hold it by some method consistent with our ideas of government. . . .

It is argued by some that the Filipinos are incapable of self-government and that therefore, we owe it to the world to take control of them. Admiral Dewey, in an official report to the navy department, declared the Filipinos more capable of self-government than the Cubans and said that he based his opinion upon a knowledge of both races. . . .

"Can we not govern colonies?" we are asked. The question is not what we can do, but what we ought to do. This nation can do whatever it desires to do, but it must accept responsibility for what it does. If the constitution stands in the way, the people can amend the constitution. I repeat, the nation can do whatever it desires to do, but it cannot avoid the natural and legitimate results of its own conduct. . . .

There is an easy, honest, honorable solution of the Philippine question. It is set forth in the democratic platform and it is submitted with confidence to the American people. This plan I unreservedly indorse. If elected, I will convene congress in extraordinary session as soon as inaugurated and recommend an immediate declaration of the nation's purpose, first, to establish a stable form of government in the Philippine islands, just as we are now establishing a stable form of government in Cuba; second, to give independence to the Cubans; third, to protect the Filipinos from outside interference while they work out their destiny, just as we have protected the republics of Central and South America, and are, by the Monroe doctrine, pledged to protect Cuba....

## Document 9: African American Soldiers Report from the Philippines[9]

*Following the end of the Civil War, former slaves were inducted into the armed forces and served admirably on the Western frontier against Native Americans. They were in segregated units led by white officers. When the war against Spain began, they were sent to the battlefront, again in segregated units with white officers. When the war was over, American black soldiers served in putting down the insurrection in the Philippines, and some stayed there as occupation forces.*

*Quite a number of these black troops wrote letters to African American newspapers in the United States. Most white Americans never knew they existed or that they had been published, and would have been angered if they had. The letters describe the conditions of African American troops in the Philippines, attitudes and treatment of white soldiers toward the Filipinos, and the quality of white officers, among many other topics.*

*The following excerpts from letters give a flavor of the conditions in the Philippines and the activities of American soldiers there. The following documents are excerpts from four of these letters.*

John W. Galloway to *Richmond Planet*, December 30, 1899.

I felt it worth the while to probe the Filipino as to his knowledge and view of the American colored man that we might know our position intelligently. What follows is a condensed account of the results. The questions were put to the intelligent, well-educated Filipinos so you may know the opinions are those of the sort who represent the feelings of the race, and may be taken as solid.

Ques. Do the Filipinos hold a different feeling toward the colored American from that of the white?

Ans. "Before American occupation of the islands and before the colored troops came to the Philippines, Filipinos knew little if anything of the colored people of America. We had read American history in the general, but knew nothing of the different races there. All were simply Americans to us. This view was held up to the time of the arrival of the colored regiments in Manila, when the white troops, seeing your acceptance on a social plane by the Filipino and Spaniard was equal to, if not better than theirs, (for you know under Spanish rule we never knew there was a difference between men on account of racial identity. Our differences were political.) began to tell us of the inferiority of the American blacks—of your brutal natures, your cannibal tendencies—how you would rape our senioritas, [*sic*] etc. Of course, at first we were a little shy of you, after being told of the difference between you and them; but we studied you, as results have shown. Between you and him, we look upon you as the angel and him as the devil. . . ."

Interview of Senor Tordorica Santos, a Filipino physician. By the difference in "dealing with us" expressed is meant that the colored soldiers do not push them off the streets, spit at them, call them damned "niggers," abuse them in all manner of ways, and connect race hatred with duty, for the colored soldier has none such for them.

The future of the Filipino, I fear, is that of the Negro in the South. Matters are almost to that condition in Manila now. No one (white) has any scruples as regards respecting the rights of a Filipino. He is kicked and cuffed at will and he dare not remonstrate. . . .

Ques. How would the Filipinos view immigration to any extent of American colored people to their country? How about conditions between them, living side by side?

Ans. "Of what I have seen of American colored people, as exemplified in their soldiers, I am very much impressed with them. This in the light of present conditions, when they have little opportunity to show themselves to us in a social way . . . is very encouraging.

"I have very little knowledge of what the American government will do with us in case they elect to hold us as a colony. I have heard that all confiscated lands will be opened for American colonization under some homestead law . . . but I had not counted the effect it would have upon us. We are accustomed to look upon American relations on any basis, other than that of Filipino independence, as inimical to us. But since American sovereignty is inevitable and American colonization is a probability, I unreservedly believe that all my people would look very kindly upon your people as neighbors. What we are resisting is effacement. Contact with whites to any extent in whatever way we accept them means that to us. The colored people, being of like complexion to our own, the evolution that would come to us through contact would not be so radical, can be viewed in an entirely different light from contact with white people. In your country you are used to moulding all nations and races of white men into one—white Americans—that forms an example of what I mean. The same condition would obtain between you and my people, they would become good Filipinos.

"I wish you would say to your young men that we want occidental ideas but we want them taught to us by colored people. In the reconstruction of our country new ideas will obtain. In American political and industrial ideas we will be infants. We ask your educated, practical men to come and teach us them. We have a beautiful country and a hospitable people to repay them for their trouble. Our country needs development. Unless an unselfish people come to our assistance we are doomed." Interview of Senor Tomas Consunji, a wealthy Filipino planter. . . .

Yours truly, John
W. Galloway
Sgt. Major,
24th U.S. Infant

Unsigned letter to *Wisconsin Weekly Advocate*, reprinted in *New York Age*, May 17, 1900.

I have mingled freely with the natives and have had talks with American colored men here in business and who have lived here for years, in order to learn of them the cause of their (Filipino) dissatisfaction and the reason for this insurrection, and I must confess they have a just grievance. All this never would have occurred if the army of occupation would have treated them as people. The Spaniards, even if their laws were hard, were polite and treated them with some consideration; but the Americans, as soon as they saw that the native troops were desirous of sharing in the glories as well as the hardships of the hard-won battles with the Americans, began to apply home treatment for colored peoples: cursed them as damned niggers, steal [from] and ravish them, rob them on the street of their small change, take from the fruit vendors whatever suited their fancy, and kick the poor unfortunate if he complained, desecrate their church property, and after fighting began, looted everything in sight, burning, robbing the graves.

This may seem a little tall—but I have seen with my own eyes carcasses lying bare in the boiling sun, the results of raids on receptacles for the dead in search of diamonds. The [white] troops, thinking we would be proud to emulate their conduct, have made bold of telling their exploits to us. One fellow, member of the 13th Minnesota, told me how some fellows he knew had cut off a native woman's arm in order to get a fine inlaid bracelet. On upbraiding some fellows one morning, whom I met while out for a walk (I think they belong to a Nebraska or Minnesota regiment, and they were stationed on the Malabon road) for the conduct of the American troops toward the natives and especially as to raiding, etc., the reply was: "Do you think we could stay over here and fight these damn niggers without making it pay all it's worth? The government only pays us $13 per month: that's starvation wages. White men can't stand it." Meaning they could not live on such small pay. In saying this they never dreamed that Negro soldiers would never countenance such conduct. They talked with impunity of "niggers" to our soldiers, never once thinking that they were talking to home "niggers" and should they be brought to remember that at home this is the same vile epithet they hurl at us, they beg pardon and make some effiminate [*sic*] excuse about what the Filipino is called.

I want to say right here that if it were not for the sake of the 10,000,000 black people in the United States, God alone knows on which side of the subject I would be. And for the sake of the black men who carry arms and pioneer for them as their representatives, ask them to not forget the present administration at the next election. Party be damned! We don't want these islands, not in the way we are to get them, and for Heaven's sake, put the party [Democratic] in power that pledged itself against this highway robbery. Expansion is too clean a name for it.

Walter E. Merchant to *Richmond Planet,* July 28, 1900

Sir:

Allow me space in your valuable paper to say a few words about the 48th Infantry, U.S.V. (colored) that is doing such brilliant work in the Philippines. I must say brilliant work, for when regular army officers day after day, send out circulars congratulating colored officers of the volunteer service, that is enough to tell the world that somebody is doing noble work. For it is well known that the white officers . . . are deadly opposed to Negro men wearing the bars. It matters not how soon the war will end (of course after the war is over the commissions will be taken from the noble blacks as was done after the close of the Spanish-American War) the Negro captains and lieutenants of the 48th are by their bravery and daring vindicating the race and stamping the lie to those rumors that the Negro makes poor officers and for Negroes to accomplish anything in battle must be commanded by white officers.

The men of our regiments are proud of our black officers and will follow them where ever they lead. . . .

Very truly yours,
Corp'l. Walter E. Merchant
Co. D, 48th Inf., U.S.V.

James Booker to *Richmond Planet,* December 22, 1900

. . . I have read a good many accounts, by discharged volunteers and regulars through the American newspapers, of depredations committed upon Filipinos by our men in the field, which reports are false. . . . The prisoners as well as the peaceable [natives] are treated with great consideration. Our officers take great pride in protecting [the natives]. . . .

If a person were to search the roots of these reports they could easily see where they originate. Some men came into the army for pleasure and some for adventure, but when they enlist and are presented their field equipment and commence camp life, their expectation of feather mattresses . . . ham and eggs, quail on toast and other such delicacies are not realized, they commence to cry to go home; they generally turn [out] to be chronic kickers and newspaper correspondents.

It seems as if they expect to campaign in a Pullman Palace Car. The American Army is better off without such men. . . . They should all be corralled up and fed on beef tea and chicken broth until they can be given back to their parents. . . .

Our doctors exercise the greatest precaution against contagious diseases and they see that a strict sanitary law is observed by soldiers as well as natives. All of the 25th are quartered in good barracks. Duty has been reduced 50 per cent and everything is going on in harmony.

I hope to write you again soon. Co. H as well as myself extend to you our best wishes for the success of your paper and the betterment of the condition of the Southern Negro. I remain

Respectfully yours
James Booker
Co. H, 25th Infantry

## Notes

1. "Benevolent Assimilation" Proclamation of President William McKinley, December 21, 1898, *The Statutes At Large of the United States of America from March 1897 to March 1899* XXX (Washington, D.C.: Government Printing Office, 1899).

2. "Aguinaldo's Manifesto Protesting the United States' Claim of Sovereignty Over the Philippines," January 5, 1899, *The Statutes At Large of the United States of America from March 1897 to March 1899* XXX (Washington, D.C.: Government Printing Office, 1899).

3. "Aguinaldo's Proclamation of Formal Surrender to the United States," April 19, 1901, *The Statutes At Large of the United States of America from March 1897 to March 1899* XXX (Washington, D.C.: Government Printing Office, 1899).

4. "President Theodore Roosevelt's Proclamation Formally Ending the Philippine 'Insurrection' and Granting of Pardon and Amnesty," July 4, 1902, U.S. Senate, 57th Congress, 2nd Session, Doc. No. 111 (January 26, 1903).

5. Rudyard Kipling, "The White Man's Burden," *McClure's Magazine* 12 (February 1899).

6. *Christian Advocate*, January 22, 1903; reprinted in C. S. Olcott, *The Life of William McKinley* (Boston: Houghton Mifflin Co., 1916), II, 109–11.

7. Henry Cabot Lodge speech, *Congressional Record*, 56th Congress, 1st Session, 2618–21, 2627–29, March 7, 1900.

8. "Speech delivered by Mr. William Jennings Bryan in response to the Committee appointed to notify him of his nomination to the presidency, at Indianapolis, August 8, 1900," William Jennings Bryan, *Speeches of William Jennings Bryan*, 2 vols. (New York: Funk & Wagnalls, 1909).

9. Willard B. Gatewood, Jr., *"Smoked Yankees" and the Struggle for Empire: Letters from Negro Soldiers, 1898–1902* (Fayetteville: University of Arkansas Press, 1987), 252–54, 279–82, 287–88, 304–6. Used by permission of the University of Arkansas Press, www.uapress.com.

# 1

# War and Peace

*A* MERICA'S ROLE IN WORLD AFFAIRS *continued to grow after the acquisition of the Philippines. In 1914, the position of the United States was questioned when Europe went to war—a war that eventually was known as a "world war." The United States tried to stay out of the conflict, but that proved to be impossible in the long run. After America became a participant in the war, the power and influence of the United States grew even more. What happened in North America became more important than ever before to the other nations of the world, especially in Europe where the power rested at the time.*

*Following the war, Americans tried to return to a type of isolation, but that eventually proved impossible. During the 1920s, despite efforts to remain uninvolved, the United States did participate in several peace efforts. One of the more interesting was the Kellogg-Briand Peace Pact.*

### Part A: World War I—Neutrality, Propaganda, and Civil Liberties

### Background

*A war that eventually engulfed most of the world and became known as a "world war" began in Europe in 1914. President Woodrow Wilson immediately declared the United States neutral in this struggle; he even asked Americans to be "neutral in thought as well as in deed." As the years passed and the fighting became more intense and bloody, maintaining neutrality was more difficult. For the United States, the greatest challenge was on the sea. The German use of the submarine, a relatively new weapon of war, was considered barbaric and inhumane. Germany regularly violated the rights of neutral nations, especially the United States. By this time the importance of the United States in the world was clear as each side in the conflict was determined to convince the United States to enter on its side. British and German propaganda became a major factor in the years between 1914 and 1917.*

*Finally, in 1917, Wilson decided that the United States could no longer stay out of the war. He went to Congress and asked for a declaration of war on Germany. This was the first international war that had the qualities of "total war," a war that involved civilians as well as the military. It was also the world's first industrial war in that the ability to produce weapons of war and other materiel was crucial to determining the outcome of the conflict.*

*The United States went into the war with determination to "win" it at all costs. This meant, to Wilson and his staff, that certain civil liberties would have to be curtailed in order to protect America against an enemy the likes of which it had never seen before. This also meant that the government would engage in propaganda to promote the war among the American people—and to tell the American story around the world.*

## Questions

In reading these documents, the student should ask and answer several questions to put these activities in the proper context.

1. Why did Wilson think that mobilization of public opinion was so important?
2. Were the Espionage and Sedition acts necessary?
3. Did the government go overboard in its insistence that everyone follow the government's dictates and that no one criticize the government?
4. Were the news reports of the violation of civil liberties reliable?
5. Was George Creel honest in his assessment of the public relations campaign during the war?

## Document 1: Wilson Declares Neutrality[1]

*When war began in Europe in 1914, President Woodrow Wilson moved quickly to keep the United States out of it. He issued a short statement of neutrality on August 19, 1914, that reflected his idealism about the world.*

The effect of the war upon the United States will depend upon what American citizens say and do. Every man who really loves America will act and speak in the true spirit of neutrality, which is the spirit of impartiality and fairness and friendliness to all concerned. The spirit of the nation in this critical matter will be determined largely by what individuals and society and those gathered in public meetings do and say, upon what newspapers and magazines contain, upon what ministers utter in their pulpits, and men proclaim as their opinions upon the street.

The people of the United States are drawn from many nations, and chiefly from the nations now at war. It is natural and inevitable that there should be the utmost variety of sympathy and desire among them with regard to the issues and circumstances of the conflict. Some will wish one nation, others another, to succeed in the momentous struggle. It will be easy to excite passion and difficult to allay it. Those responsible for exciting it will assume a heavy responsibility, responsibility for no less a thing than that the people of the United States, whose love of their country and whose loyalty to its government should unite them as Americans all, bound in honor and affection to think first of her and her interests, may be divided in camps of hostile opinion, hot against each other, involved in the war itself in impulse and opinion if not in action.

Such divisions amongst us would be fatal to our peace of mind and might seriously stand in the way of the proper performance of our duty as the one great nation at peace, the one people holding itself ready to play a part of impartial mediation and speak the counsels of peace and accommodation, not as a partisan, but as a friend.

I venture, therefore, my fellow countrymen, to speak a solemn word of warning to you against that deepest, most subtle, most essential breach of neutrality which may spring out of partisanship, out of passionately taking sides. The United States must be neutral in fact, as well as in name, during these days that are to try men's souls. We must be impartial in thought, as well as action, must put a curb upon our sentiments, as well as upon every transaction that might be construed as a preference of one party to the struggle before another.

## Document 2: Wilson's War Message[2]

*Finally, after intense propaganda and repeated violations of American neutrality, Wilson decided he could not maintain the previous policy. He spoke to Congress on April 2, 1917, asking for a declaration of war against Germany. In this speech, he outlined some of the idealistic goals he was setting for America. A portion of the speech is reprinted below.*

. . . But armed neutrality, it now appears, is impracticable. Because submarines are in effect outlaws when used as the German submarines have been used against merchant shipping, it is impossible to defend ships against their attacks as the law of nations has assumed that merchantmen would defend themselves against privateers or cruisers, visible craft giving chase upon the open sea. It is common prudence in such circumstances, grim necessity indeed, to endeavor to destroy them before they have shown their own intention. . . .

There is one choice we cannot make, we are incapable of making; we will not choose the path of submission and suffer the most sacred rights of our nation and our people to be ignored or violated. The wrongs against which we now array ourselves are not common wrongs; they cut to the very roots of human life.

With a profound sense of the solemn and even tragical character of the step I am taking and of the grave responsibilities which it involves, but in unhesitating obedience to what I deem my constitutional duty, I advise that the Congress declare the recent course of the Imperial German Government to be in fact nothing less than war against the government and people of the United States; that it formally accept the status of belligerent which has thus been thrust upon it; and that it take immediate steps not only to put the country in a more thorough state of defense but also to exert all its power and employ all its resources to bring the Government of the German Empire to terms and end the war. . . .

Our object now, as then, is to vindicate the principles of peace and justice in the life of the world as against selfish and autocratic power and to set up among the really free and self-governed peoples of the world such a concert of purpose and of action as will henceforth insure the observance of those principles. Neutrality is no longer feasible or desirable where the peace of the world is involved and the freedom of its people, and the menace to that peace and freedom lies in the existence of autocratic governments backed by organized force which is controlled wholly by their will, not by the will of their people. . . .

We have no quarrel with the German people. We have no feeling towards them but one of sympathy and friendship. It was not upon their impulse that their government acted in entering this war. It was not with their previous knowledge or approval. . . .

It was a war determined upon as wars used to be determined upon in the old, unhappy days when peoples were nowhere consulted by their rulers and wars were provoked and waged in the interest of dynasties or of little groups of ambitious men who were accustomed to use their fellow men as pawns and tools. . . .

We are accepting this challenge of hostile purpose because we know that in such a Government, following such methods, we can never have a friend; and that in the presence of its organized power, always lying in wait to accomplish we know not what purpose, there can be no assured security for the democratic Governments of the world.

We are now about to accept the gauge of battle with this natural foe to liberty and shall, if necessary, spend the whole force of the nation to check and nullify its pretensions and its power. We are glad, now that we see the facts with no veil of false pretence [*sic*] about them, to fight thus for the ultimate peace of the world and for the liberation of its peoples, the German peoples included: for the rights of nations great and small and the privilege of men everywhere to choose their way of life and of obedience.

The world must be made safe for democracy. Its peace must be planted upon the tested foundations of political liberty. We have no selfish ends to serve. We desire no conquest, no dominion. We seek no indemnities for ourselves, no material compensation for the sacrifices we shall freely make. We are but one of the champions of the rights of mankind. We shall be satisfied when those rights have been made as secure as the faith and the freedom of nations can make them.

*The extent and the fierceness of World War I were a shock to most participants. When the United States entered the war, it was not well prepared. One of the major areas of concern was in health care. This is an American field hospital in a wrecked French church. Courtesy of the Library of Congress, LC-USZ62-51354.*

Just because we fight without rancor and without selfish object, seeking nothing for ourselves but what we shall wish to share with all free peoples, we shall, I feel confident, conduct our operations as belligerents without passion and ourselves observe with proud punctilio the principles of right and of fair play we profess to be fighting for. . . .

We shall, happily, still have an opportunity to prove that friendship in our daily attitude and actions towards the millions of men and women of German birth and native sympathy who live among us and share our life, and we shall be proud to prove it towards all who are in fact loyal to their neighbors and to the Government in the hour of test.

They are, most of them, as true and loyal Americans as if they had never known any other fealty or allegiance. They will be prompt to stand with us in rebuking and restraining the few who may be of a different mind and purpose. If there should be disloyalty, it will be dealt with with a firm hand of stern repression; but, if it lifts its head at all, it will lift it only here and there and without countenance except from a lawless and malignant few. . . .

## Documents 3–4 Espionage and Sedition Acts

*Despite Wilson's statements to the contrary in his war message, the government was concerned about the loyalty of Americans during the war. Some of this may have been due to the large number of German Americans in the country. There was fear that they might be more loyal to their families' homelands than they were to the United States. It may have also been due to the fact that the large number of Irish Americans in the United States were very anti-British. During the two and a half years of the war before America entered, the country had been bombarded by propaganda from both the British and the Germans. Now the United States entered on the side of the British and French, against the Germans and their allies. Loyalty became paramount.*

### Document 3: Espionage Act[3]

*Shortly after the American entry into World War I, Congress passed the Espionage Act to identify and specify punishments for people committing espionage. The law enabled the Justice Department to prosecute individuals who spoke or wrote against the government. More than 2,000 people were prosecuted under this law. A small portion of the Espionage Act follows.*

Whoever, with intent or reason to believe that it is to be used to the injury or the United States or to the advantage of a foreign nation, communicated, delivers, or transmits, or attempts to, or aids, or induces another to, communicate, deliver or transmit, to any foreign government, or to any faction or party or military or naval force within a foreign country, whether recognized or unrecognized by the United States, or to any representative, officer, agent, employee, subject, or citizen thereof, either directly or indirectly and document, writing, code book, signal book, sketch, photograph, photographic negative, blue print, plan, map, model, note, instrument, appliance, or information relating to the national defence [*sic*], shall be punished by imprisonment for not more than twenty years: Provided, That whoever shall violate the provisions of subsection:

(a) of this section in time of war shall be punished by death or by imprisonment for not more than thirty years; and

(b) whoever, in time of war, with intent that the same shall be communicated to the enemy, shall collect, record, publish or communicate, or attempt to elicit any information with respect to the movement, numbers, description, condition, or disposition of any of the armed forces, ships, aircraft, or war materials of the United States, or with respect to the plans or conduct, or supposed plans or conduct of any naval of military operations, or with respect to any works or measures undertaken for or connected with, or intended for the fortification of any place, or any other information relating to the public defence[*sic*], which might be useful to the enemy, shall be punished by death or by imprisonment for not more than thirty years.
Section 3

Whoever, when the United States is at war, shall willfully [*sic*] make or convey false reports or false statements with intent to interfere with the operation or success of the military or naval forces of the United States or to promote the success of its enemies and whoever when the United States is at war, shall willfully cause or attempt to cause insubordination, disloyalty, mutiny, refusal of duty, in the military or naval forces of the United States, or shall wilfully [*sic*] obstruct the recruiting or enlistment service of the United States, to the injury of the service or of the United States, shall be punished by a fine of not more than $10,000 or imprisonment for not more than twenty years, or both. . . .

### Document 4: Sedition Act[4]

*Most of the prosecutions under the Espionage Act were successful, but there were a few acquittals that frustrated Attorney General Thomas Gregory. He was able to convince Congress in 1918 to amend the Espionage Act with a sedition clause. This change is commonly referred to as the Sedition Act. Under this amendment, free speech was essentially squelched. Following is the amendment known as the Sedition Act; compare Section 3 of this amendment with the original Section 3 of the Espionage Act.*

Sec. 3. Whoever, when the United States is at war, shall willfully make or convey false reports or false statements with intent to interfere with the operation or success of the military or naval forces of the United States, or to promote the success of its enemies, or shall willfully make or convey false reports or false statements, or say or do anything except by way of bona fide and not disloyal advice to an investor or investors, with intent to obstruct the sale by the United States of bonds or other securities of the United States or the making of loans by or to the United States, and whoever when the United States is at war, shall willfully cause or attempt to cause, or incite or attempt to incite, insubordination, disloyalty, mutiny, or refusal of duty, in the military or naval forces of the United States, or shall willfully obstruct or attempt to obstruct the recruiting or enlistment services of the United States, and whoever, when the United States is at war, shall willfully utter, print, write or publish any disloyal, profane, scurrilous, or abusive language about the form of government of the United States or the Constitution of the United States, or the military or naval forces of the United States, or the flag of the United States, or the uniform of the Army or Navy of the United States into contempt, scorn, contumely, or disrepute, or shall willfully utter, print, write, or publish any language intended to incite, provoke, or encourage resistance to the United States, or to promote the cause of its enemies, or shall willfully display the flag of any foreign enemy, or shall willfully by utterance, writing, printing, publication, or language spoken, urge, incite, or advocate any curtailment of production in this country of any thing or things, product or products, necessary or essential to the prosecution of the war in which the United States may be engaged, with intent by such curtailment to cripple or hinder the United States in the prosecution of war, and whoever shall willfully advocate, teach, defend, or suggest the doing of any of the acts or things in this section enumerated, and whoever shall by word or act support or favor the cause of any country with which the United States is at war or by word or act oppose the cause of the United States therein, shall be punished by a fine of not more than $10,000 or the imprisonment for not more than twenty years, or both: Provided, That any employee or official of the United States Government who commits any disloyal act or utters any unpatriotic or disloyal language, or who, in an abusive and violent manner criticizes the Army or Navy or the flag of the United States shall be at once dismissed from the service. . . .

Sec. 4. When the United States is at war, the Postmaster General may, upon evidence satisfactory to him that any person or concern is using the mails in violation of any of the provisions of this Act, instruct the postmaster at any post office at which mail is received addressed to such person or concern to return to the postmaster at the office at which they were originally mailed all letters or other matter so addressed, with the words "Mail to this address un-deliverable under Espionage Act" plainly written or stamped upon the outside thereof, and all such letters or other matter so returned to such postmasters shall be by them returned to the senders thereof under such regulations as the Postmaster General may prescribe.

### Document 5: The Committee on Public Information[5]

*A novel departure during the war was the creation of the Committee on Public Information. More commonly referred to as the Creel Committee, for George Creel, the head of the committee, it was sometimes called the Department of Censorship. It was not just a public relations effort. Some people believed that it, in conjunction with the Espionage and Sedition acts, helped to silence criticism of the government during the war. After the war, in 1920, Creel wrote a book about the activities of the committee. The following includes extracts from his comments about the committee's actions.*

As Secretary Baker points out, the war was not fought in France alone. Back of the firing-line, back of armies and navies, back of the great supply-depots, another struggle waged with the same intensity and with almost equal significance attaching to its victories and defeats. It was the fight for the *minds* of men, for the "conquest of their convictions," and the battle-line ran through every home in every country.

It was in this recognition of Public Opinion as a major force that the Great War differed most essentially from all previous conflicts. The trial of strength was not only between massed bodies of armed men, but between opposed ideals, and moral verdicts took on all the value of military decisions. Other wars went no deeper than the physical aspects, but German *Kultur* raised issues that had to be fought out in the hearts and minds of people as well as on the actual firing-line. The approval of the world meant the steady flow of inspiration into the trenches; it meant the strengthened resolve and the renewed determination of the civilian population that is a nation's second line. The condemnation of the world meant the destruction of morale and the surrender of that conviction of justice which is the very heart of courage.

The Committee on Public Information was called into existence to make this fight for the "verdict of mankind," the voice created to plead the justice of America's cause before the jury of Public Opinion. . . . *In no degree was the Committee an agency of censorship, a machinery of concealment or repression. Its emphasis throughout was on the open and the positive. At no point did it seek or exercise authorities under those war laws that limited the freedom of speech and press.* In all things, from first to last, without halt or change, it was a plain publicity proposition, a vast enterprise in salesmanship, the world's greatest adventure in advertising. . . .

There was no part of the great war machinery that we did not touch, no medium of appeal that we did not employ. The printed word, the spoken word, the motion picture, the telegraph, the cable, the wireless, the poster, the sign-board—all these were used in our campaign to make our own people and all other peoples understand the causes that compelled America to take arms. All that was fine and ardent in the civilian population came at our call until more than one hundred and fifty thousand men and women were devoting highly specialized abilities to the work of the Committee, as faithful and devoted in their service as though they wore the khaki. . . .

Starting with the initial conviction that the war was not the war of an administration, but the war of one hundred million people, and believing that public support was a matter of public understanding, we opened up the activities of government to the inspection of the citizenship. A voluntary censorship agreement safeguarded military information of obvious value to the enemy, but in all else the rights of the press were recognized and furthered. . . .

As swiftly as might be, there were put into pamphlet form America's reasons for entering the war, the meaning of America, the nature of our free institutions, our war aims, likewise analyses of the Prussian system, the purposes of the imperial German government, and full exposure of the enemy's misrepresentations, aggressions, and barbarities. . . .

The importance of the spoken word was not underestimated. A speaking division toured great groups like the Blue Devils, Pershing's Veterans, and the Belgians, arranged mass-meetings in the communities, conducted forty-five war conferences from coast to coast, co-ordinated the entire speaking activities of the nation, and assured consideration to the crossroads hamlet as well as to the city.

The Four Minute Men, an organization that will live in history by reason of its originality and effectiveness, commanded the volunteer services of 75,000 speakers, operating in 5,200 communities, and making a total of 755,190 speeches, every one having the carry of shrapnel.

With the aid of a volunteer staff of several hundred translators, the Committee kept in direct touch with the foreign-language press, supplying selected articles designed to combat ignorance and disaffection. . . .

The Committee mobilized the advertising forces of the country—press, periodical, car, and outdoor—for the patriotic campaign that gave millions of dollars' worth of free space to the national service.

It assembled the artists of America on a volunteer basis for the production of posters, window-cards, and similar material of pictorial publicity for the use of various government departments and patriotic societies. A total of 1,438 drawings was used.

It issued an official daily newspaper, serving every department of government, with a circulation of one hundred thousand copies a day. For official use only, its value was such that private citizens ignored the supposedly prohibitive subscription price, subscribing to the amount of $77,622.58. . . .

It gathered together the leading novelists, essayists, and publicists of the land, and these men and women, without payment, worked faithfully in the production of brilliant, comprehensive articles that went to the press as syndicate features. . . .

Through the medium of the motion picture, America's war progress, as well as the meanings and purposes of democracy, were carried to every community in the United States and to every corner of the world. . . .

## Documents 6–9: Press Criticism of the Restriction of Civil Liberties

*During the war, many of the left-leaning magazines of the time criticized the actions of the government. Some of them believed that freedom of speech had been severely curtailed, and others were critical of the government's actions regarding any kind of dissent. There were magazines that defended the government's actions, but they were still critical.*

### Document 6: The Creel Committee is criticized[6]

*The Creel Committee generated much comment, as this magazine article indicates. This article recognizes that the committee did valuable things that were long overdue.*

With a shrewd appreciation of the average American's ingrowing antipathy to anything like dictation, or abridgment of his rights as a citizen of the United States, George Creel, when he assumed control of Uncle Sam's new departure, the department of censorship, decided upon a less objectionable name, and a method entirely the reverse of all previous Government efforts in the line of "news control." He started off by calling his bureau the Committee on Public Information, which conveys an impression of expression rather than suppression.

And Mr. Creel carried this idea further by actually making it a news-bureau. He had some novel ideas connected with the "suppression" of news, and strangely enough they were not at all objectionable to the correspondents in Washington, for while his plan gave him absolute control of the information that went out of the various departments at the capital, it also saw to it that nothing that was "printable" was withheld. Instead of breeding trouble with the correspondents, as was at first predicted, the newspaper men's confidence was quickly won. Mr. Creel's censorship plans met their most active opponents in Government officials.

David Lawrence, in the New York *Evening Post*, says of the new organization:

> The Committee on Public Information (which is too long a name to say in these busy times, and therefore Washington christens it "The Creel Committee") has already done some constructive things which the Government has sorely needed for many years, and which surely will survive the war and be a permanent part of the executive departments. For example, it has been manifestly impossible hitherto for the correspondents to know all that the Government was doing, even tho [*sic*] no particular restriction of secrecy attached to many acts of public policy. The United States Government is an immense thing, and most of the officials are too busy doing things to sit down and tell newspaper men about them or to write outlines or sketches of their work. The need of a publicity man for each Government department has always been obvious.

Ten experienced newspaper men—one in each of the executive departments of the Government—constitute a staff whose daily duty it is to obtain from the officials of the respective departments the information which their news instinct tells them the people of the country would be interested to know about. . . .

Then there is a division for the foreign-language press, and the sending of authorized statements of the United States Government for publication in neutral countries. . . . The division is obtaining constantly digests of what the newspapers of foreign countries are saying about the United States, and watching carefully enemy propaganda, so that, if erroneous impressions or distorted versions of the American position on any important question are being circulated anywhere, officials of the United States Government can make reply, and those replies carried to the points where the misunderstanding exists. Central- and South-American countries are handled by a subdivision of this bureau. What the United States is doing is not spreading a propaganda, but seeing to it that the facts about the United States are widely disseminated.

There is an Art Committee, . . . which prepares posters and drawings for advertising the Government's needs. Already the Army and Navy recruiting has been helped considerably by cartoons and sketches that have attracted the eyes of American youth and stirred their patriotism. . . .

Another division of the Committee on Public Information is that which is mobilizing the "four-minute men." Good speakers have been selected in nearly every city and town of importance in this country who will appear at theaters, moving-picture shows, and other entertainments and speak just four minutes on various subjects that have to do with an effective prosecution of the war—enlistments, for the Navy or National Guard or regular Army, or the conservation of food, agricultural improvement, the Liberty Loan, and kindred questions.

A moving-picture bureau has been established in cooperation with the Creel Committee. . . . Moving-picture reels showing the making of a sailor or a soldier, or demonstrating various phases of the war for the benefit of the American people, will be sent to moving-picture companies throughout the country for display in all theaters.

Then there is the censoring of cables to Central and South America and Asia, and telephone and telegraph on the Mexican border. The Navy is using its men to handle the former, and the Army is at work on the latter, but the Creel Committee is supervising the whole thing.

"And that's about half the number of things we expect to do," remarked a member of the Committee on Public Information.

### Document 7: Charges of treason are questioned[7]

The Nation *was one of the most prominent left-leaning magazines in the war years—as it is today—and it was critical of actions taken during the war to stifle dissent. "Treason" was the subject of this article in 1917.*

. . . there is but one way of appraising the peril arising from the preachment of "treason" and "sedition"; and that is by its results. In New York no evidence has been forthcoming that anti-war utterances have eventuated in unlawful opposition to the Government. What we have been beholding since the declaration of war against Germany has been the steady functioning of the machinery of preparation for war without popular hindrance. The registration under the Draft law was carried out without a hitch. The selection of the new armies is now being made without a single instance, in this great community, of attempted resistance. The Irish enemies of Great Britain on the Broadway corners have been working under full steam, but at the same time the young Americans of Irish birth have been answering the call of the Exemption Boards, and an Irish regiment of the National Guard is among the first to be designated for service abroad.

What makes the problem of the street forum peculiarly one to be handled with discrimination is that the corner propagandist represents the right of free speech in its most obvious and elemental form, and at the same time in its least dangerous form. "Treason" and "sedition" call up the vision of subterranean forces and midnight conspiracies, of wicked subornations and corruptions, of organized menace against the safety of these United States. But there is nothing secret, nothing subtly perilous, in the loud utterances of ancient animosities against Great Britain in Broadway and its environs. Given the existence of an anti-war sentiment in New York which it would be idle to overlook, given the existence of a very strong anti-British feeling among certain sections of the population, it is best perhaps to let such feeling vent itself frankly under the open sky. This is no time to discard from democracy the safety-valve of free criticism. But more than that, any policy of repression directed against the Lenines [*sic*] of the soap-box is discrimination against the plain citizen, while tolerating the utterance of just the same sentiments in certain press organs under the very thinnest of disguises. Postmaster-General Burleson has come down on the *Masses* for preaching very much the same doctrine that appears in widely circulated newspapers under a very obvious *camouflage* of patriotic mottoes and American flags scattered over the editorial page. There can be no comparison between the street orator and such press propaganda in its capacity for mischief; and the merit of frankness is all one way.

Essentially, the problem of anti-war criticism in the open is one to be dealt with according to the specific fact. Congress and the country rejected the attempt to establish a censorship in the absence of any demonstrated need. We believe that no need has been proved of a Federal law against "seditious" utterances such as Commissioner Woods mentions as the preliminary to proceeding against the corner orators. The perils of abuse inherent in such a law are so manifest that a much more serious case must be made out of the effective lending of aid and comfort to the enemy. . . .

### Document 8: The *Nation* Protests Arrests[8]

*In 1918, toward the end of World War I, The* Nation *continued to report on and protest the arrests of citizens for speaking their minds.*

It is estimated that in New York and near-by towns 75,000 men have been "arrested" in the last two days by the agents of the Department of Justice, assisted by soldiers, sailors, and patriotic organizations impressed for that purpose, and that fewer than 3 per cent. of those arrested were found to be "slackers" in fact. This means that over 70,000 citizens who had faithfully discharged their self-imposed obligations in the first selective draft were rudely seized in their goings to and fro, bundled into trucks and improvised patrol wagons, exposed in a helpless manner to the hoots and jeers of the populace, detained for hours in barracks and armories, and at last released without any possibility of redress. . . .

Thus speaks no pacifist or anti-war newspaper, but the Republican, intensely pro-war, "bitter-ender" New York *Tribune*. It errs on the side of mildness. Senator Johnson likened these raids to the application of the "Law of Suspects" during the Reign of Terror of the French Revolution. Senator Calder and other pro-war Senators were unrestrained in their denunciation, and even Senator Sherman asked: "Is there any material difference between this militarism and Kaiserism in Berlin and the bayonetting [*sic*] of innocent men about the streets of New York?" No more disgraceful or more lawless happening has occurred in the metropolis. These arrests without warrants, mostly by striplings in uniform and irresponsible agents of a volunteer, self-appointed protective (!) league, were an offense against the historic spirit of the nation, as they were a deadly insult to the men who had submitted to the draft, either joyfully or with patriotic resignation. It was Prussian militarism pure and simple, even if it emanated from the Department of Justice.

No wonder the President has ordered an inquiry. Men were torn from their wives' sides in the theatres, yanked out of street cars, pulled off milk-wagons and trucks of all kinds, which vehicles were left to stand where they were abandoned. Men from up-State and New Jersey—and there were thousands of them—who had no warning of the raid and had left their cards at home—were first taken to police stations and then to an armory, where everything was in utter confusion and where many spent the entire night upon their feet. Numbers were held by the police who showed their registration cards, but were without their classification cards, which have never been issued by the draft boards of many up-State towns. And always there was this Prussian spectacle of men with rifles in their hands surrounding groups like the curb-market brokers in Broad Street as if they were criminals. This not in Russia nor in the home of the "Beast of Berlin," but in America, the home of democracy, the land of the free. . . .

But, after all, the worst feature of the affair is not the official anarchy. It is the fact that personal liberty and freedom have disappeared in America, and that the bulk of our vocal patriots thoughtlessly approve of it in the earnestness of their desire to win the war. . . . Senator Johnson did not exaggerate when on Friday last he declared that the only place in the United States, in which there is free speech to-day is the Senate in which he spoke. Both Democrats and Republicans denounced the New York outrage irrespective of party lines. . . . If the American people could realize what has been done and is being done throughout the country in the name of liberty, they would emphatically demand and support an organized Opposition to the end that this government may again be a government of laws and not of men.

. . . Why is it that a democracy that ought to be infinitely more jealous of its constitutional rights and prerogatives than a limited monarchy can thus in a year's time knuckle under to official bureaucracy and autocracy—without protest? What is the psychological explanation? Is it terrorism? Is it the all-embracing Espionage act, under which a man may go to jail for expressing an unfavorable opinion about the principle of a draft, or for saying that this is a capitalistic war? Is it the result of official propaganda, or of an over-cultivation of the narrowly nationalistic spirit? We cannot answer. But we are certain that if the war goes on much longer and Mr. Wilson wishes to retain such leadership of the world of liberalism as he has obviously won in the last eighteen months and to shape the outcome or the war, he has no time to lose in examining what is being done to make democracy unsafe in America.

### Document 9: Palmer's Case Against the Reds[9]

*The activities of the government against wartime dissent evolved into what has become known as the "Red Scare" in the two or three years immediately following the end of World War I. The fall of Russia to the Bolshevik revolution in 1917 brought a new dimension to the war because it added an ideological element to world affairs and awakened the latent fear of Americans that others wanted to destroy their system. The attorney general of the United States, A. Mitchell Palmer, is commonly credited with starting and carrying out the Red Scare. In 1920, he made his case against the "Reds" in the magazine,* Forum.

In this brief review of the work which the Department of Justice has undertaken, to tear out the radical seeds that have entangled American ideas in their poisonous theories, I desire not merely to explain what the real menace of communism is, but also to tell how we have been compelled to clean up the country almost unaided by any virile legislation. Though I have not been embarrassed by political opposition, I have been materially delayed because the present sweeping processes of arrests and deportation of seditious aliens should have been vigorously pushed by Congress last spring. The failure of this is a matter of record in the Congressional files.

The anxiety of that period in our responsibility when Congress, ignoring the seriousness of these vast organizations that were plotting to overthrow the Government, failed to act, has passed. The time came when it was obviously hopeless to expect the hearty cooperation of Congress in the only way to stamp out these seditious societies in their open defiance of law by various forms of propaganda.

Like a prairie-fire, the blaze of revolution was sweeping over every American institution of law and order a year ago. It was eating its way into the homes of the American workmen, its sharp tongues of revolutionary heat were licking the altars of the churches, leaping into the belfry of the school bell, crawling into the sacred corners of American homes, seeking to replace marriage vows with libertine laws, burning up the foundations of society.

Robbery, not war, is the ideal of communism. This has been demonstrated in Russia, Germany, and in America. As a foe, the anarchist is fearless of his own life, for his creed is a fanaticism that admits no respect of any other creed. Obviously it is the creed of any criminal mind, which reasons always from motives impossible to clean thought. Crime is the degenerate factor in society.

Upon these two basic certainties, first that the "Reds" were criminal aliens and secondly that the American Government must prevent crime, it was decided that there could be no nice distinctions drawn between the theoretical ideals of the radicals and their actual violations of our national laws. An assassin may have brilliant intellectuality, he may be able to excuse his murder or robbery with fine oratory, but any theory which excuses crime is not wanted in America. This is no place for the criminal to flourish, nor will he do so so long as the rights of common citizenship can be exerted to prevent him. . . .

. . . If the Department of Justice could succeed in attracting the attention of our optimistic citizens to the issue of internal revolution in this country, we felt sure there would be no revolution. The Government was in jeopardy; our private information of what was being done by the organization known as the Communist Party of America, with headquarters in Chicago, of what was being done by the Communist Internationale under their manifesto planned at Moscow last March by Trotzky, Lenin and others addressed "To the Proletariats of All Countries," of what strides the Communist Labor Party was making, removed all doubt. In this conclusion we did not ignore the definite standards of personal liberty, of free speech, which is the very temperament and heart of the people. The evidence was examined with the utmost care, with a personal leaning toward freedom of thought and word on all questions. . . .

My information showed that communism in this country was an organization of thousands of aliens who were direct allies of Trotzky. Aliens of the same misshapen caste of mind and indecencies of character, and it showed that they were making the same glittering promises of lawlessness, of criminal autocracy to Americans, that they had made to the Russian peasants. How the Department of Justice discovered upwards of 60,000 of these organized agitators of the Trotzky doctrine in the United States is the confidential information upon which the Government is now sweeping the nation clean of such alien filth. . . .

. . . In the confused information that sometimes reaches the people they are compelled to ask questions which involve the reasons for my acts against the "Reds." I have been asked, for instance, to what extent deportation will check radicalism in this country. Why not ask what will become of the United States

Government if these alien radicals are permitted to carry out the principles of the Communist Party as embodied in its so-called laws, aims and regulations?

There wouldn't be any such thing left. In place of the United States Government we should have the horror and terrorism of bolsheviki tyranny such as is destroying Russia now. Every scrap of radical literature demands the overthrow of our existing government. All of it demands obedience to the instincts of criminal minds, that is, to the lower appetites, material and moral. The whole purpose of communism appears to be a mass formation of the criminals of the world to overthrow the decencies of private life, to usurp property that they have not earned, to disrupt the present order of life regardless of health, sex or religious rights. By a literature that promises the wildest dreams of such low aspirations, that can occur to only the criminal minds, communism distorts our social law. . . .

## Part B: Kellogg-Briand Pact—A Search for Peace

### Background

*Because World War I was such a devastating event that shocked the whole world, the postwar period witnessed many initiatives from various countries seeking to prevent a repeat of the horrors of that conflict. By the end of the war, the United States could not be denied its place as a leading power of the world. Within fifty years, the United States had risen from a third- or fourth-rate power to become one of the most powerful and wealthy nations in the world.*

*The American president, Woodrow Wilson, proposed the League of Nations as a medium for maintaining peace and preventing disputes that could lead to conflict. Even though the United States Senate rejected his idea and did not join the league, the American government cooperated with the organization when it could, and it undertook several initiatives on its own. For example, President Warren G. Harding called the Washington Naval Conference to try to limit the growth of navies and thus prevent conflict.*

*One of the more unusual peace initiatives was officially known as the Pact of Paris (1928), but it became commonly known as the Kellogg-Briand Peace Pact. This pact has been mostly forgotten, but those who do know about it scorn, even ridicule, its idealistic tone. In common discussion, the Kellogg-Briand Pact, signed in 1928, is known as the treaty that outlawed war. But within only a few years, the threat to peace was greater than it had ever been. Many called the pact naïve, idealistic, and unrealistic. Should a nation violate the treaty, the only recourse— other than accepting the aggression—was to use force to stop the violation. Therefore, the treaty to end war would culminate in war.*

The pact was based on the concept of moral persuasion and world condemnation for any nation that violated it. There was no mechanism for enforcement; in fact, that would have violated the spirit of the agreement. Today, few people take it seriously, especially after a second world war and numerous other smaller wars in the years since 1939.

Despite its failure and idealistic tone, the Kellogg-Briand Pact was embraced by many countries and by Americans in large number. They saw it as an alternative to conflict and probably believed that world opinion would keep aggressor nations at bay. An analysis of the pact reflects the temper of the times. It also indicates the growing status of the United States, since the treaty originated when France approached America with an idea for a bilateral treaty to renounce war between France and the United States.

## Questions

In reading these documents, the student should ask and answer several questions to put these activities in the proper context.

1. Why was the Kellogg-Briand Pact so vague? Why didn't it spell out the types of aggression and the methods of enforcement?
2. Were the supporters of the pact naïve, or were they convinced that the power of world opinion could keep the peace?
3. Why did France initiate the discussions that led to this treaty? Did France have ulterior motives for becoming involved in these diplomatic negotiations?
4. Did the pact have any successes during its short life?
5. Were there any actions that the signer nations could have taken to prevent the aggression that developed in the 1930s and led to the second war?

## Document 1: The Text of the Treaty[10]

On July 24, 1929, President Herbert Hoover, who had succeeded Calvin Coolidge in office, announced that the treaty had been ratified by all the major countries and was now in effect. The significant portion of the text of the treaty follows.

## BY THE PRESIDENT OF THE UNITED STATES OF AMERICA.
## A PROCLAMATION.
... Deeply sensible of their solemn duty to promote the welfare of mankind; Persuaded that the time has come when a frank renunciation of war as an

instrument of national policy should be made to the end that the peaceful and friendly relations now existing between their peoples may be perpetuated;

Convinced that all changes in their relations with one another should be sought only by pacific means and be the result of a peaceful and orderly process, and that any signatory Power which shall hereafter seek to promote its national interests by resort to war a should be denied the benefits furnished by this Treaty;

Hopeful that, encouraged by their example, all the other nations of the world will join in this humane endeavor and by adhering to the present Treaty as soon as it comes into force bring their peoples within the scope of its beneficent provisions, thus uniting the civilized nations of the world in a common renunciation of war as an instrument of their national policy;

Have decided to conclude a Treaty and for that purpose have appointed as their respective Plenipotentiaries:

[Here are listed the countries and their delegates who signed the treaty.] having communicated to one another their full powers found in good and due form [they] have agreed upon the following articles:

ARTICLE I

The High Contracting Parties solemly [*sic*] declare in the names of their respective peoples that they condemn recourse to war for the solution of international controversies, and renounce it, as an instrument of national policy in their relations with one another.

ARTICLE II

The High Contracting Parties agree that the settlement or solution of all disputes or conflicts of whatever nature or of whatever origin they may be, which may arise among them, shall never be sought except by pacific means.

ARTICLE III

The present Treaty shall be ratified by the High Contracting Parties named in the Preamble in accordance with their respective constitutional requirements, and shall take effect as between them as soon as all their several instruments of ratification shall have been deposited at Washington.

This Treaty shall, when it has come into effect as prescribed in the preceding paragraph, remain open as long as may be necessary for adherence by all the other Powers of the world. . . .

DONE at Paris, the twenty seventh day of August in the year one thousand nine hundred and twenty-eight.

[Here is the list of the original signers.]

FRANK B. KELLOGG

Secretary of State of the United States of America . . .

NOW THEREFORE, be it known that I, Herbert Hoover, President of the United States of America, have caused the said Treaty to be made public, to the end that the same and every article and clause thereof may be observed and fulfilled with good faith by the United States and the citizens thereof.

IN TESTIMONY WHEREOF, I have hereunto set my hand and caused the seal of the United States to be affixed.

DONE at the city of Washington this twenty-fourth day of July in the year of our Lord one thousand nine hundred and twenty-nine, and of the Independence of the United States of America the one hundred and fifty-fourth.

HERBERT HOOVER
By the President:
HENRY L STIMSON
Secretary of State

## Document 2: The Origin of the Treaty[11]

*The Kellogg-Briand Pact came about rather suddenly, based upon a suggestion by French foreign minister Aristide Briand. In a speech delivered in August 1928, Edwin Borchard explained the origin of the proposal. The first portion of his speech follows. One can see the convoluted nature of the negotiations and the reservations and exceptions that were discussed, making one wonder how the treaty was ever finalized. One can also see the fatal weaknesses.*

The origin of the negotiations between the United States and other powers leading to the conclusion of the so-called Briand-Kellogg Pact for the renunciation of war is well known. Beginning with an expression of good-will in M. Briand's note of April 6, 1927, commemorating the entry of the United States into the war [World War I] and expressing France's willingness to conclude a treaty renouncing war between France and the United States, the negotiations developed rapidly. On June 20, 1927, the French Foreign Minister presented the draft of a treaty embodying his proposal, providing for a condemnation of "recourse to war" and renouncing war as between France and the United States as an "instrument of their national policy." The settlement of all disputes was never to be sought "except by pacific means."

On December 28, 1927, Mr. Kellogg proposed to the French ambassador the extension of the proposed declaration to all the principal Powers. It was argued in the United States that, if the treaty were signed by the United States and France alone, it would be a treaty of alliance. In his accompanying draft of a treaty, Mr. Kellogg recommended the outright and unconditional renunciation of war and the solution of disputes by pacific means only. . . .

Considerable correspondence took place in the early part of 1928 as to the construction to be given to the proposed treaty. In his note of February 27,

1928, in explaining his objection to qualifications on the obligation to renounce war, Mr. Kellogg stated:

The ideal which inspires the effort so sincerely and so hopefully put forward by your [the French] Government and mine is arresting and appealing just because of its purity and simplicity; . . .

The same thought was expressed in Mr. Kellogg's speech to the Council on Foreign Relations on March 15, 1928, in which he said:

It seems to me that any attempt to define the word "aggression," and by exceptions and qualifications to stipulate when nations are justified in going to war with one another, would greatly weaken the effect of any treaty such as that under consideration and virtually destroy its positive value as a "guaranty of peace."

The subsequent negotiations, however, disclose the unfortunate fact that these very exceptions and qualifications to which Mr. Kellogg objected as so nullifying in effect have, in fact, found their way into the treaty as now universally construed.

The French Government maintained that the treaties must be construed so as not to bar the right of legitimate defense, the performance of obligations under the Covenant of the League of Nations, under the treaties of Locarno, under its treaties of alliance with its allies—now for some unexplainable reason called treaties of neutrality—that the treaty was to become ineffective if violated by one nation, and that it was to be signed by every state before it became effective as to any state. . . .

In his note of May 19, 1928, accepting the American proposition in principle, Sir Austen Chamberlain for Great Britain expressed his assent to the reservations made by France and added a new one in the following paragraph:

There are certain regions of the world, the welfare and integrity of which constitute a special and vital interest for our peace and safety. His Majesty's Government have been at pains to make it clear in the past that interference with these regions cannot be suffered. Their protection against attack is to the British Empire a measure of self-defense. It must be clearly understood that *His Majesty's Government in Great Britain accept the new treaty upon the distinct understanding that it does not prejudice their freedom of action in this respect.* The Government of the United States have comparable interests, any disregard of which by a foreign Power they have declared they would regard as an unfriendly act." (Italics are the author's.)

The words in italics were repeated in the British note of July 18, 1928, undertaking to sign the treaty only on the understanding that the British Government maintained this freedom of action with respect to those regions of the world in which it had "a special and vital interest."

## Document 3: Questions Are Raised[12]

*During the time the treaty was being considered by the Senate Foreign Relations Committee, serious questions were raised about whether the United States would be required to go to war against any country violating the pact, the same question that had been so controversial at the time the United States was considering joining the League of Nations. In addition, some people were concerned about the right to use force in self-defense. When Secretary Kellogg appeared before the committee, these two questions were paramount. Following is a brief selection from the testimony and questions from senators.*

Senator SWANSON. As I understand from what you say, if this multilateral treaty is violated by any other nation, there is no obligation, moral or legal, for us to go to war against any nation violating it?

Secretary KELLOGG. That is thoroughly understood. It is understood by our Government; and no other government made any suggestion of any such thing. I knew, from the attitude of many governments, that they would not sign any treaty if there was any moral obligation or any kind of obligation to go to war. In fact, Canada stated that. The other governments never suggested any such obligation. . . .

The question was raised by some governments, does this take away the right of self-defense? It seemed to me incomprehensible that anybody could say that any nation would sign a treaty which could be construed as taking away the right of self-defense if a country was attacked. That is an inherent right of every sovereign, as it is of every individual, and it is implicit in every treaty. . . .

Senator SWANSON. The term "self-defense" is not confined to defense of any territory, but any nation may send troops into any territory where it may be necessary for its self-defense.

Secretary KELLOGG. Certainly; the right of self-defense is not limited to territory in the continental United States, for example. It means that this Government has a right to take such measures as it believes necessary to the defense of the country, or to prevent things that might endanger the country; but the United States must be the judge of that, and it is answerable to the public opinion of the world if it is not an honest defense; that is all.

Senator REED of Missouri. The whole of that rule would apply equally to every other country.

Secretary KELLOGG. Certainly; nor do I think it is practicable to do anything else; although there are idealists who say that it is practicable. It is entirely impracticable, in my judgment. . . .

The CHAIRMAN. Suppose you take up the English note. . . .

Secretary KELLOGG. Very well. This is on page 28 of the treaty pamphlet, the tenth subdivision. The British Government said:

10. The language of article 1, as to the renunciation of war as an instrument of national policy, renders it desirable that I should remind your excellency that there are certain regions of the world the welfare and integrity of which constitute a special and vital interest for our peace and safety. His Majesty's Government have been at pains to make it clear in the past that interference with these regions can not be suffered. Their protection against attack is to the British Empire a measure of self-defense.

Now, then, they did not say, "We reserve the right to make war against anybody in the world that we want to because we want peace in the country." The British Government put it solely on the ground of self-defense. I apprehend that the United States has got interests, the peace and security of which are necessary to the defense of the United States. Take the Canal Zone. Self-defense, as I said, is not limited to the mere defense, when attacked, of continental United States. It covers all our possessions, all our rights; the right to take such steps as will prevent danger to the United States. . . .

Secretary KELLOGG. . . . Here is what I said [reading]:

Since, however, the purpose of the United States is so far as possible to eliminate war as a factor in international relations, I can not state too emphatically that it will not become a party to any agreement which directly or indirectly, expressly or by implication, is a military alliance. The United States can not obligate itself in advance to use its armed forces against any other nation of the world. It does not believe that the peace of the world or of Europe depends upon or can be assured by treaties of military alliance, the futility of which as guarantors of peace is repeatedly demonstrated in the pages of history.

Every nation had that speech.

### Document 4: The Issue of Self-Defense[13]

*While the Kellogg-Briand Pact was under consideration, numerous people analyzed it and tried to explain its meaning, advantages, and pitfalls to the American people. During its several years of debate, many people tried to make it work, but concerns remained about the matter of fighting wars of self-defense. George Wickersham had been the attorney general in the cabinet of President Taft. In this excerpt from an article in* The Century Magazine *in June 1929, he discusses this question.*

In his inaugural address, President Hoover said: "The whole world is at peace. The dangers to a continuation of this peace to-day are largely the fear and suspicion which still haunt the world. No suspicion or fear can be rightly directed toward our country."

Every lover of his country must wish this to be a correct statement. The President's words surely will carry some relief to many anxious minds in our own and in other lands. But those who have followed the recent expressions of members of our Government are justified in a feeling of apprehension that there is a different sentiment among a certain class of Americans; one which is less friendly and which affords ground for a reasonable fear that American influence may not be wholly exerted for the stabilization of the peace of the world.

The Chairman of the Committee on Foreign Relations of the United States Senate, Mr. Borah, . . . stated that we are on the eve of a race for naval supremacy with Great Britain, and likened the situation between the two great English-speaking nations to that existing between England and Germany in 1914.

This alarming statement was made at a singularly infelicitous moment. The Senate had just given its approval, virtually its unanimous approval, to the Multilateral Treaty for the Renunciation of War—a treaty which President Coolidge described as "one of the most important treaties ever laid before the Senate of the United States." By this treaty, to which our Government has invited all the nations of the world to become parties, the high contracting parties "in the names of their respective peoples" condemn "recourse to war for the solution of international controversies, renounce it as an instrument of national policy in their relations with one another"; and "agree that the settlement or solution of all disputes or conflicts *of whatever nature* or *of whatever origin* they may be, which may arise among them, shall never be sought *except by pacific means.*" . . .

"The observance of this covenant, so simple and so straightforward," wrote President Coolidge to the Senate, "promises more for the peace of the world than any other agreement ever negotiated among the nations." Great words these. Their justification lies in the predicate "observance." If this treaty be honestly observed, it would seem that the clouds of war never again should darken the lives of men. But in the very process of negotiation, a notion was born and allowed to grow, which became a veritable upastree, casting its shadow over the whole fair flowering plant of peace, with doubt whether even those who propounded the treaty intended its actual and unqualified observance.

"What about the right of self-defense?" governments began to inquire, when confronted with Mr. Kellogg's proposal, to extend the proposed agreement to all nations and to embrace within its provisions not merely *aggressive* war, but *all* war. Nothing in the proposed treaty, was the reply, restricts or impairs the right of self-defense, a right which "is inherent in every sovereign state and implicit in every treaty." "Every nation," wrote Secretary Kellogg, "is free at all times and regardless of treaty provisions to defend its territory from attack or invasion and it alone is competent to decide whether circumstances require recourse to war in self-defense." . . .

As a matter of fact, the votes necessary for its ratification could not be procured until a report of the Committee on Foreign Relations was submitted to the Senate and spread upon its records, which emphasized the Senate's understanding that "the right of self-defense is in no way curtailed or impaired by the terms or conditions of the treaty." "Each nation," the report declared, "is free, at all times and regardless of the treaty provisions, to defend itself and is the sole judge of what constitutes the right of self-defense and the necessity and extent of the same."

### Document 5: Opposition to the Pact Appears[14]

*Edwin Borchard, who provided a good history of the development of the pact (excerpted earlier), was also an opponent of it. He saw it as dangerous for the United States, especially since the United States was not a member of the League of Nations and had no voice in shaping world policy. He thought the pact paved the way for war, and that the United States should join the League of Nations. The second part of his speech, reprinted here, shows his opposition.*

The original proposition of Mr. Kellogg was an unconditional renunciation of war. The treaty note qualified by the French and British reservations constitutes no renunciation or outlawry of war, . . . When we look at the exceptions we observe that they include wars of self-defense, each party being free to make its own interpretation as to when self-defense is involved, . . . If self-defense could be limited to the terms "to defend its territory from attack or invasion," as suggested by Mr. Kellogg, it would be of some value, but it is understood that no specific definition of self-defense is necessarily accepted.

Considering these reservations, it would be difficult to conceive of any wars that nations have fought within the last century, or are likely to fight in the future, that cannot be accommodated under these exceptions. Far from constituting an outlawry of war, they constitute the most definite sanction of specific wars that has ever been promulgated. . . .

Again it will be noticed that we recognize a British claim to use war as an instrument of national policy in certain undefined "regions of the world," any "interference" with which by anybody, including the United States, will be regarded by Great Britain as a cause of war. To this we subscribe. When the United States at the first Hague Conference secured recognition by our cosignatories for the Monroe Doctrine, it was regarded as an achievement of American diplomacy. But the Monroe Doctrine has geographical limits known to everybody. To this new British claim there are no geographical limits. The vague and expansive terms of the British claim to make war, now recognized by us, covers any part of the world in which Britain has "a special and vital interest." No such broad claim of the right to make war has ever before been recognized.

But the most extraordinary feature of this treaty still remains to be mentioned. . . . We indeed recognize by this treaty the legal right of the League to make war even against us, and it will be observed that Sir Austen Chamberlain in his note of May 19, 1928, frankly admits that respect for the obligations arising out of the Covenant is "the foundation of the policy" of Great Britain. Whether the further European claim that we are bound to *support* League conclusions as to "aggressor" nations, and other political conclusions, either by joining with the League or by refusing to trade with the League-declared pariah, is sustainable or not, at the very best it places us in the uncomfortable position either of being bound by decisions in the making of which we had no part or of having recriminations leveled against us for refusing to support our treaty.

. . . Far better and safer would it be had we openly joined the League of Nations and been privileged to take part in deliberations which may lead to most important consequences. We might have been able to prevent undesirable conclusions and use our bargaining power to obtain occasional benefits and advantages instead of disadvantages only. We are now about to sign a treaty in which we expressly recognize the right of the other signatories to make war upon anybody, including ourselves, for the purpose of enforcing, even against us, their mutual obligations under the Covenant of the League of Nations, not to mention individual undefined national interests in any part of the world. They alone will determine the occasion of such action, without our participation. . . .

## Documents 6–7: The Kellogg-Briand Pact Faces Challenges

*The ink was hardly dry on the Kellogg-Briand Pact ratification before it faced its first challenge, a potential conflict between Russia and China. The pact seemed to prevail in this situation, but the peace could not be maintained. Throughout the 1930s, much of the world hoped fervently for peace, but the rise of dictators— especially Hitler and Mussolini—threatened that peace as never before. The following documents show how the pact was challenged until it finally collapsed in the face of continued aggression.*

### Document 6: The pact prevails[15]

*In 1929, a potential conflict between Russia and China emerged. The United States responded by reminding the two countries of their obligations under the*

*Kellogg-Briand agreement. Conflict was averted for a short time, but it was not long before other challenges to the peace emerged. When Herbert Hoover became president in 1929, Frank Kellogg stayed on as secretary of state for a few months until Henry Stimson could take office. Shortly after Stimson came into office, the Pact of Paris faced the challenge of the conflict between Russia and China. Diplomacy continued apace as documents of diplomatic correspondence reveal. Two memos dealing with the Russia-China issue show this.*

## AIDE MEMOIRE

A week ago when the issues which had arisen in Manchuria between China and Russia were causing anxiety throughout the world, I took the liberty of pointing out, through you to your governments, the immeasurable harm which would be done to the cause of world peace should a clash between those great nations occur at the very moment when the nations of the world were assembling to celebrate a solemn covenant between themselves never to resort to war but to settle all disputes by pacific means. I suggested that, inasmuch as both Russia and China had signed this covenant, it could not be inappropriate to bring to their attention the seriousness of this situation and to urge upon them that they find some way of settling their disputes by pacific means.

The response of your governments has been most cordial and unanimous. Friendly representations have been made to both China and Russia and each of these nations has averred that it did not intend to resort to war.

Unfortunately, the situation between them still remains difficult and gives rise to much apprehension in respect to an ultimate peaceful solution of their controversy. Diplomatic relations having been severed, the normal bridge by which they might approach each other for that purpose no longer exists. Popular feelings of intensity upon each side have been excited and an ill-considered act of even a subordinate commander upon either side of the boundary might easily precipitate a situation fraught with serious consequences to the entire world.

Under these circumstances, if a road with honor out of their difficulties can be suggested to these sister nations, who have joined with us in this solemn compact of Peace and who have just signified their desire to maintain it, even in the perplexities which confront them at the present time, it seems that it should be done.

I do not suggest mediation by any nation or group of nations. Such a course would have its difficulties and might excite unfounded suspicion. I suggest a way by which Russia and China themselves in the exercise of their own sovereign action may create the machinery for conciliation and thus bring about an ultimate settlement of their present dispute, based upon the only foundation upon which such a lasting settlement can be constructed, namely, a full and impartial investigation of the facts. It is not a new suggestion. Even today two of our sister nations of South America are in that way working out their own solution of a serious controversy into which they drifted nearly two years ago. In their case this method of solution was suggested to them by a conference of American nations meeting under the auspices of the Pan American Union.

I have therefore, taken the liberty of putting into writing a suggestion of such a step for Russia and China. I should be glad if you would refer it to your governments. If, after carefully considering it and suggesting any criticisms, they will join my Government in suggesting it to China and Russia as a possible way in which they may start on the road to a settlement by themselves of their own difficulties, I should be most happy.

The press despatches [*sic*] this morning have reported a meeting between consular representatives of China and Russia which it is hoped may possibly lead to a resumption of diplomatic relations between them. I hope sincerely that these reports may prove to be correct. But until such a solution is more definitely hopeful, I venture to present these suggestions for your consideration, since I am sure that the nations which you represent, all earnestly desirous of peace, will wish to be prepared to take any helpful initiative should this prove necessary in the maintenance of peace between China and Russia.

WASHINGTON JULY 25, 1929.

[enclosure]

### SUGGESTIONS FOR A COMMISSION OF CONCILIATION

Pending the investigation mentioned below both countries agree to commit no act of hostility against the other country or its nationals and to prevent their armed forces from crossing the boundaries of their respective countries.

Pending such investigation the regular operation of the Chinese Eastern Railway will be restored and carried on, the interests of both Russia and China in said Railway being guarded by the appointment as President and General Manager with full powers, of a prominent national of some neutral country approved by both China and Russia, and by the recognition and continuance in their respective positions as directors under the agreement of May 31, 1924 of the five Russian and the five Chinese appointees.

Pending such investigation the obligations upon both China and Russia of the treaty of 1924, including particularly the obligation of the mutual covenants contained in said treaty "not to permit within their respective territories the existence and/or activities of any organizations or groups whose aim is to struggle by acts of violence against the governments of either contracting party" and "not to engage in propaganda directed against the political and social systems of either contracting party" will continue in full force and effect.

The grievances and claims of both countries shall be investigated by an impartial commission of conciliation the membership of which shall be agreed upon by Russia and China and which shall have full power to investigate all the facts concerning such grievances and claims and to render to both countries and make public its conclusions both as to the facts and as to any suggested remedies for the future.

[Washington,] October 10, 1929

The French Ambassador came in to say that the French Government was very warmly pleased with the visit of Mr. MacDonald and that they considered it a great success. I thanked him and told him that I was especially glad to see him because of the confidential note which he had sent me a few days ago. I told him that that represented just the line of thought which I had been following, particularly the suggestion of the extension of the Pacific Treaty of the four powers to other parts of the world. I then reminded him of the difficulties which we found under the Kellogg-Briand Pact when we reminded China and Russia of their obligations thereunder, in that there was no machinery for investigation and for enlightening the public opinion of the world as to the controversy.

I pointed out that in the Kellogg-Briand Pact, unlike the League of Nations, we had no sanction except the public opinion of the world and that I felt from my experience both in China and Russia and in regard to Bolivia and Paraguay, the importance of machinery which should be invokable by the parties themselves and also by outsiders when they would not invoke it. He said he agreed with me, recalling Mr. Coolidge's analogy of plague in which outsiders were interested that it should not spread. I suggested that he ascertain Mr. Briand's views on this subject and as to the possibility of taking further steps to achieve such machinery for arousing public opinion. He manifested great interest and said he would be glad to do so.

He asked me if I would give him an *aide memoire*. I told him I would be glad to draw one up as soon as possible and give it to him, but that I felt that the initiative in this really belonged to Mr. Briand because he was one of the authors of the Kellogg-Briand Pact and this was so closely related to the purpose of that Pact. The Ambassador asked whether I thought it should take the form of the extension of the Pacific Treaty or of the Kellogg-Briand Pact. I told him I had no conclusive views but that I thought that the latter pact was more in the thoughts of the world today and more popular than the Pacific Treaty; that, however, I should like to have Mr. Briand's views on it. He asked whether I thought that such a treaty would not meet opposition in the Senate. I told him I could not go so far as to say that, but I thought it would be less likely to meet opposition than any other treaty because the MacDonald visit had stimulated great interest in the Kellogg-Briand Treaty.

In the course of his felicitations on the success of the MacDonald visit I said we should be very glad to welcome Mr. Briand in a similar manner and asked him whether he thought there would be any chance of Mr. Briand making such a visit. He seemed quite interested and said he thought there would.

### Document 7: Kellogg still has hopes for the treaty[16]

*In 1935, the former secretary of state who crafted the Pact of Paris, Frank Kellogg, spoke over the CBS Radio Network in response to the Italian invasion of Ethiopia. He still had hope for the pact, but he also reminded the American people that the violation of the treaty by Mussolini was a violation of American policy.*

The right thinking American citizens desire that our country keep out of war; but at the present time the most superficial observer as well as the person who is doing the cause of peace the most harm is he who says that the situation in the world today is the same as that which prevailed in 1914. A small but vociferous group of isolationists have created for themselves an unreal world based upon the conditions of 1914. They fail to realize how different is the world of 1935.

Let us compare: The Pact of Paris, the League of Nations and many treaties for the prevention of war are the symbols of a very different world. In 1914 war was an accepted method for the settlement of international disputes with which no nation other than the belligerents had a right to interfere. The nations who went to war in that fateful year violated no general principle of international law in so doing. International law was to a great extent a code under which a duel between nations could be carried on. While many enlightened individuals opposed war upon principle, there was then no general public opinion against it as a nation's legal right, nor had there been any organization of a community of nations to outlaw it.

On the other hand, today we have the Pact of Paris, by which all nations in language simple and emphatic, first renounced war as an instrument of national policy in their relations with one another, and secondly agreed that the settlement of disputes of whatever nature which might arise among them should never be sought except by pacific means. Today 51 nations are taking positive action to stop a nation that is invading the territory of another signatory of the Pact of Paris.

## Notes

1. Woodrow Wilson, *Message to Congress*, 63rd Congress, 2nd Session, Senate Doc. No. 566 (Washington, D.C., 1914), 3–4.

2. Woodrow Wilson, "Address Delivered at the Joint Session of the Two Houses of Congress, April 2, 1917," reprinted in Charles F. Horne, ed., *Source Records of the Great War* (n.p., National Alumni, 1923), vol. 5, 107–17.

3. "The Espionage Act of 1917," *The United States Statutes at Large* (Washington, D.C.: Government Printing Office, 1919), v. 40.

4. "The Sedition Act of 1918," *The United States Statutes at Large* (Washington, D.C.: Government Printing Office, 1919), v. 40.

5. George Creel, *How We Advertised America* (New York: Harper & Brothers, 1920), 3–9.

6. "Uncle Sam's Press-Agent," *The Literary Digest* (June 16, 1917): 1867–68.

7. "'Treason' on the Street Corners," *The Nation* (August 30, 1917): 214–15.

8. "Civil Liberty Dead," *The Nation* (September 14, 1918): 282.

9. A. Mitchell Palmer, "The Case against the 'Reds,'" *Forum* 63 (1920): 173–85.

10. *The United States Statutes at Large*, 46, part 2, 2343.

11. Edwin Borchard, "The Multilateral Pact for the 'Renunciation of War,'" an address delivered at the Williamstown Institute of Politics, August 22, 1928, Lillian Goldman Law Library, Yale University Law School.

12. Hearings Before the Committee on Foreign Relations, United States Senate, Seventieth Congress, Second Session, on the General Pact For the Renunciation of War, Signed at Paris August 27, 1928, held on December 7 and 11, 1928 (Washington, D.C.: Government Printing Office, 1928).

13. George W. Wickersham, "Making Real the Pact of Paris," *The Century Magazine*, June 1929. Reprinted with permission of Scribner, a Division of Simon & Schuster Adult Publishing Group, from THE CENTURY MAGAZINE, June 1929 issue. Copyright © 1929 by The Century Magazine. Copyright renewed © 1957 by Charles Scribner's Sons. All rights reserved.

14. Edwin Borchard, "The Multilateral Pact for the 'Renunciation of War.'"

15. Department of State, *Papers Relating to the Foreign Relations of the United States, 1929* (Washington, D.C.: Government Printing Office, 1943), v. 1.

16. Frank B. Kellogg, "The Pact of Paris and the Relationship of the United States to the World Community," An Address Delivered over the Columbia Broadcasting System October 30, 1935, Frank B. Kellogg Papers, Minnesota Historical Society. Reprinted by permission of the Minnesota Historical Society.

# 2

# Affluence, Anxiety, and Hard Times

*B*ETWEEN THE WORLD WARS, THE *people of the United States focused on domestic issues and hoped to avoid entanglement in another foreign war. Even with this attitude, the United States was still influenced by events around the world. After World War I and the Bolshevik Revolution of 1917, many Americans were concerned about the possibility of communist subversion. An extremist organization of the 1920s, the revived Ku Klux Klan, was attempting to preserve "America for Americans" and to reject things, many of which were foreign, that would change the nature of American society. In the 1930s, the concern about communist influence in America surfaced again after the Communist Party became more active in the United States. This was reflected in the Bonus March on Washington in 1932.*

## Part A: Resurgence of the Ku Klux Klan

### Background

*World War I forever changed the United States, especially with regard to its status in the world. America's participation in the war, including the wealth and manufacturing capacity it contributed, showed that it could no longer be ignored by the older European powers. The United States had become a player on the world stage whether it wanted to be or not.*

*For many Americans, the best thing the country could do was to return to the nineteenth-century model of "Fortress America." According to this interpretation, the United States should rely on its own initiative and resources, staying completely out of the affairs of the rest of the world, especially Europe. For this sizable portion of America, world power and leadership should be avoided rather than welcomed.*

*Other events of the war caused concern in the United States. American soldiers fighting in Europe returned to America with alien ideas. The Bolshevik Revolution in Russia frightened Americans, not because they had any particular sympathy for the Russian tsar, but because the Bolsheviks were openly saying that the Marxist revolution had to be taken to the rest of the world. According to Marx, industrialized countries were most susceptible to turmoil and revolution. That meant that England and the United States were prime targets for the worldwide Marxist revolution.*

*Americans responded to the changed world by trying to avoid being part of the international community. In addition, "foreign" or "alien" ideas—especially from Europe—were resisted as they became more prevalent in America. The new goal was to promote patriotism, which usually meant anti-Bolshevism or anticommunism. But the new patriotism—the 100% Americanism—reacted against all things considered foreign whether they be Marxist ideas, the Catholic Church of Rome, foreign immigrants, Jews, or black people (who failed to be effectively assimilated into America, even after several centuries of being here).*

*The newly revived Ku Klux Klan achieved prominence in the 1920s by embodying the anti-foreign ideas so prevalent at the time. The Klan originally developed in the Reconstruction period following the Civil War when Southern men organized into various terrorist organizations—the most important being the Ku Klux Klan—as a way to intimidate former slaves to keep them from voting or trying to participate in society in other ways. The original Klan was known for burning crosses on the lawns of freedmen as a warning of what could happen to them if they did not do as the Klan demanded. Burnings, lynching, and other forms of violence effectively intimidated targets, whether black or white. One hallmark of the Klan was secrecy. Members wore white robes and masks to hide their identity and to strike fear in their targets.*

*By the end of the nineteenth century, the Klan had mostly withered away. Occasional episodes of Klan activity occurred, but, for the most part, the organization was defunct by the end of the century.*

*The second Klan was founded in 1915 by William J. Simmons. He was a preacher strongly influenced by D. W. Griffith's film* Birth of a Nation, *one of the first full-length silent motion pictures. The new Klan was anti-black, as was the first one, but it was also anti-Semitic, anti-foreign, and anti-Catholic. It developed a new motto, "One Hundred Percent Americanism."*

*Through the 1920s, the Klan grew in membership and in political influence. It enrolled as many as four million members, and elected many public officials,* even to the point of controlling a few states through their governors and legis-latures. It continued to use the symbols of the old Klan—the robe, the mask, the burning cross. It also participated in occasional violence. It developed a wide range of titles that made it seem ridiculous to some and more impressive to others.

It seems logical to assume that the Klan would not have been reborn had it not been for the new status of the United States in the world and the impact of the massive immigration that crested just before the war.

## Questions

In reading these documents, the student should ask and answer several questions to put these activities in the proper context.

1. What conditions in America made it possible for an organization such as the Klan to develop and thrive?
2. Why did the new Klan find so many more enemies and threats to worry about than the original Klan did?
3. What features of the new Klan made it so attractive to so many people?
4. How significant was the political influence of the Klan? Were the elected officials honest in their beliefs or were they merely playing on the pop-ularity of the organization to get elected?
5. How important was the new Klan to long-range American develop-ment?

## Document 1: The Klan's Constitution[1]

*In 1925, the Ku Klux Klan issued a document known popularly as its consti-tution. It is long and detailed, but it gives the essence of what the Klan was at-tempting to do. A small portion of the document is excerpted here. Several of the points here show the fear of foreign ideas and the impact of foreign influences on the United States.*

### THE ORDER

*III. Its Nature*

*1. Patriotic.* One of the paramount purposes of this order is to "exemplify a pure patriotism toward our country." . . .

*2. Military.* This characteristic feature applies to its form of organization and its method of operations. It is so organized on a military plan that the whole power of the whole order, or of any part of it, may be used in quick, united action for the execution of the purposes of the order.

*3. Benevolent.* This means that the movement is also committed to a program of sacrificial service for the benefit of others. . . .

*4. Ritualistic.* In common with other orders, the Knights of the Ku Klux Klan confers ritualistic degrees and obligations, and commits its grips, signs, words, and other secret work to those persons who so meet its requirements as to find membership in the order. The ritualistic devices become the ceremonial ties that bind Klansmen to one another.

*5. Social.* The Knights of the Ku Klux Klan endeavors to unite in companionable relationship and congenial association those men who possess the essential qualifications for membership. It is so designed that kinship of race, belief, spirit, character, and purpose will engender a real, vital, and enduring fellowship among Klansmen.

*6. Fraternal.* The order is designed to be a real brotherhood. Klansmen have committed themselves to the practice of Klannishness toward fellow-Klansmen. By this commitment they have agreed to treat one another as brothers. . . .

*V. Its Authority*

Is "Vested primarily in the Imperial Wizard." The organization of the Knights of the Ku Klux Klan provides, and its principle of government demands, that there shall always be one individual, senior in rank to all other Klansmen of whatever rank, on whom shall rest the responsibility of command, and whose leadership will be recognized and accepted by all other loyal Klansmen.

*To be recognized by all Klansmen.* The Constitution is very explicit: "And whose decisions, decrees, edicts, mandates, rulings, and instructions shall be of full authority and unquestionably recognized and respected by each and every citizen of the Invisible Empire." The whole movement, fraught with its tremendous responsibilities and rich in its magnificent possibilities, makes stirring appeal to red-blooded American manhood. Every Klansman is an important, necessary, and vital factor in the movement. In this crusade there are few occasions for "individual plays." Success is possible only through the most unselfish "playing for the team."

## OBJECTS AND PURPOSES (ARTICLE II, THE CONSTITUTION)

*I. Mobilization*

*This is its primary purpose:* "To unite white male persons, native-born, Gentile citizens of the United States of America, who owe no allegiance of any nature or degree to any foreign government, nation, institution, sect, ruler, person, or people; whose morals are good; whose reputations and vocations are respectable; whose habits are exemplary; who are of sound minds and eighteen years or more of age, under a common oath into a brotherhood of strict regulations."

## II. Cultural

The Knights of the Ku Klux Klan is a movement devoting itself to the needed task of developing a genuine spirit of American patriotism. Klansmen are to be examples of pure patriotism. . . . Klansmen are dedicated to the principle that America shall be made American through the promulgation of American doctrines, the dissemination of American ideals, the creation of wholesome American sentiment, the preservation of American institutions.

## III. Fraternal

The movement is designed to create a real brotherhood among men who are akin in race, belief, spirit, character, interest, and purpose. . . .

## V. Protective

*1. The Home.* "*To shield the sanctity of the home.*" The American home is fundamental to all that is best in life, in society, in church, and in the nation. . . .

*2. Womanhood.* The Knights of the Ku Klux Klan declares that it is committed to "the sacred duty of protecting womanhood"; and announces that one of its purposes is "to shield . . . the chastity of womanhood." . . .

*3. The Helpless.* "To protect the weak, the innocent, and the defenseless from the indignities, wrongs, and outrages of the lawless, the violent, and the brutal." . . .

*4. American Interests.* "To protect and defend the Constitution of the United States of America, and all laws passed in conformity thereto, and to protect the states and the people thereof from all invasion of their rights from any source whatsoever."

## VI. Racial

"To maintain forever the God-given supremacy of the white race."

## Document 2: The Klan in Politics and Scandal[2]

*The Ku Klux Klan's influence spread throughout the country, including to Northern and Midwestern states, unlike the original Klan which was largely Southern-based. One of the strongholds of the Klan was the state of Indiana. There the leader was David C. Stephenson, the Grand Dragon of the Klan. According to contemporary sources, Stephenson controlled the state of Indiana almost completely. His downfall came when he kidnapped a young woman who eventually died. The coroner said she was subject to cannibalism, but others believed that she committed suicide by taking poison. Stephenson was convicted of murder and sentenced to life in prison. He was paroled in 1950 after twenty-five years, but he was accused of rape and was again sent to prison. Had these legal matters not disrupted Stephenson's political career, one can only wonder how far he would have taken the Klan in dominating Indiana. In the following excerpts from an article in the* New Republic, *one can see the influence of the Klan in the*

*state. One can also see how the Klan used the fear of foreign influences in gain-*
*ing its position of strength.*

The story of Indiana's undoing centers in the amazing story of Stephenson.
. . . But he would have had no career had it not been for the Ku Klux Klan, for
religious fundamentalism and its concomitant, 100 percent Americanism, for
the provincialism both of the honest ruralists and the city business men, for
the dominance of a political party whose major prophet has won the sobri-
quet, "Slippery Jim." Even the ingenious King Kleagle could not have har-
vested from sterile soil.

The biography of the "Old Man," told by one of his klavern partners and
confidants, begins in Houston, Texas, where he was born in 1891. He went to
a parochial school (!), moved to Oklahoma, became a tramp printer at sixteen,
married a prize-winning beauty, played Governor Jack Walton's brand of politics, deserted his wife upon the birth of a daughter, sowed plenty of wild oats,
made Socialist stump speeches, went to Iowa for a while to get away from his
family, managed to avoid going to France with the army, married again, deserted the new wife, and wound up in Evansville, in the coal business, just
when the high-pressure Ku-Klux salesmen began to invade Indiana. Hitherto
he had been variously a Democrat and a Socialist. He now joined the Klan and
became a Republican. His uncanny ability in the manipulation of a crowd became the Klan's chief asset, and his rise to the highest authority was rapid.

In an amazingly short time, he had more than a quarter of a million dues-
paying members. He acquired a city mansion, a summer home, a beautiful
yacht on Lake Erie. The fiery cross was lifted high all over the state—and highest, strange to say, where Jews, Catholics and Negroes were fewest. Churches
went Ku Klux. Many pastors joined the hooded ranks, and from their number
organizers and promoters were selected; a fee of $25 per speech looked good,
when you had been won to Anglo-Saxon, Protestant, 100 percent principles
and convinced of the God-ordained supremacy of the Nordic.

Stephenson was strong on "pure Americanism." Like his illustrious mentor,
Mussolini, he turned from Socialism to a crusade against the "reds."
Napoleon's image always graced his desk, and Mussolini's methods were, to
his mind, the model for men of action like himself. Alien baiting was even
more popular with him than mere crusades against Jews and Catholics; it was
more comprehensive and more popular, and it included many of the Jews and
Catholics, anyhow. It was popular everywhere, all the way from the hill-billies
of southern Indiana to the business men of the cities. . . .

The hooded order was out to save Indiana from all alien powers, whether
deriving from Rome, Russia, or Africa. The crisis, it was clear, demanded that
type of action which only a trusted leadership could supply. To the honest

church folk, the bootlegger was attacked. The fundamentalist was shown the fiery cross, the 100 percenter was promised the scalps of aliens, and the politician, sure election if he lined up and took orders. . . .

When the 1924 primary came on, the "Old Man" had it sewed up in his pillowcase. . . . He had elected a legislature and a state administration. If you "wanted anything," you went to Stephenson first, and afterward or not at all to those who had official power to grant it. His boast, "I am the law," was not altogether idle. . . .

While many honest men, narrow and prejudiced, to be sure, but sincere, had been helping Stephenson to lead the white-clad crusaders, he had been in the habit of retiring from the front of the procession to indulge in private orgies of dissipation. . . . Seeking new thrills, he invited a worthy young woman who was promoting some educational measures before the legislature to come to his home and "talk things over." The final result was her committing suicide, dying after an accusation of forcible rape. Responsible toxicologists swore that teeth wounds on her person were sufficient to have caused death, independently of the poison she took. Public indignation waxed hot, the revulsion among thousands of sincere Klansmen was complete, and all his highpowered attorneys could not save the culprit from a life sentence for "malicious mayhem" and murder. . . .

## Document 3: The Klan Gets New Leadership[3]

*In the early 1920s, Hiram W. Evans took control of the national Klan and began to promote it with new vigor. In 1926, he accepted an invitation from the* North American Review *to write about his organization, its benefits, and its programs. The magazine followed it in later issues with similar articles from other points of view. This was an extensive article that explained the Klan very well. This short excerpt gives a flavor of what he said, especially his emphasis on "old-stock Americans," which can be read as white, Protestant, and Northern European.*

. . . We have won the leadership in the movement for Americanism. Except for a few lonesome voices, almost drowned by the clamor of the alien and alien-minded "Liberal," the Klan alone faces the invader. This is not to say that the Klan has gathered into its membership all who are ready to fight for America. The Klan is the champion, but it is not merely an organization. It is an idea, a faith, a purpose, an organized crusade. No recruit to the cause have ever been really lost. Though men and women drop from the ranks they remain with us in purpose, and can be depended on fully in any crisis. Also, there are many millions who have never joined, but who think and feel and—when called on—fight with us. This is our real strength, and no one who ignores it can hope to understand America today.

. . . The Klan, therefore, has now come to speak for the great mass of Americans of the old pioneer stock. We believe that it does fairly and faithfully represent them, and our proof lies in their support. To understand the Klan, then, it is necessary to understand the character and present mind of the mass of old-stock Americans. The mass, it must be remembered, as distinguished from the intellectually mongrelized "Liberals."

These are the first place, a blend of various peoples of the so-called Nordic race, the race which, with all its faults, has given the world almost the whole of modern civilization. The Klan does not try to represent any people but these. . . .

These Nordic Americans for the last generation have found themselves increasingly uncomfortable, and finally deeply distressed. . . . Presently we began to find that we were dealing with strange ideas; policies that always sounded well but somehow always made us still more uncomfortable.

Finally came the moral breakdown that has been going on for two decades. One by one all our traditional moral standards went by the boards or were so disregarded that they ceased to be binding. The sacredness of our Sabbath, of our homes, of chastity, and finally even of our right to teach our own children in our own schools fundamental facts and truths were torn away from us. Those who maintained the old standards did so only in the face of constant ridicule. . . .

The old-stock Americans are learning, however. They have begun to arm themselves for this new type of warfare. Most important, they have broken away from the fetters of the false ideals and philanthropy which put aliens ahead of their own children and their own race.

. . . The first and immediate cause of the break with Liberalism was that it had provided no defense against the alien invasion, but instead excused it—even defended it against Americanism. Liberalism is today charged in the mind of most Americans with nothing less than national, racial and spiritual treason. . . .

One more point about the present attitude of the old-stock American: he has revived and increased his long-standing distrust of the Roman Catholic Church. It is for this that the native Americans, and the Klan as their leader, are most often denounced as intolerant and prejudiced. . . .

The real indictment against the Roman Church is that it is, fundamentally and irredeemably, in its leadership, in politics, in thought, and largely in membership, actually and actively alien, un-American and usually anti-American. . . . By no stretch of the imagination can it fairly be called religious prejudice, though, now that the hostility has become active, it does derive some strength from the religious schism. . . .

The Ku Klux Klan, in short, is an organization which gives expression, direction and purpose to the most vital instincts, hopes, and resentments of the old-stock Americans, provides them with leadership, and is enlisting and preparing them for militant, constructive action toward fulfilling their racial and national destiny. . . . The Klan literally is once more the embattled American farmer and artisan, coordinated into a disciplined and growing army, and launched upon a definite crusade for Americanism! . . .

There are three of these great racial instincts, vital elements in both the historic and the present attempts to build an America which shall fulfill the aspirations and justify the heroism of the men who made the nation. These are the instincts of loyalty to the white race, to the traditions of America, and to the spirit of Protestantism, which has been an essential part of Americanism ever since the days of Roanoke and Plymouth Rock. They are condensed into the Klan slogan: "Native, white, Protestant supremacy." . . .

## Documents 4–5: The Press Comments

*From the moment of its founding, the new Klan was the subject of intense scrutiny. Few, other than its own leaders and members, said anything favorable about the organization. Yet, it continued to grow for a number of years. The following two documents provided information and revealed doubts about the Klan.*

### Document 4: A popular writer weighs in[4]

*Frederick Lewis Allen was a popular writer of the time who is still read today. In his seminal book,* Only Yesterday: An Informal History of the 1920s, *his comments on the Klan are revealing.*

In practice the "pure Americanism" varied with the locality. At first, in the South, white supremacy was the Klan's chief objective, but as time went on and the organization grew and spread, opposition to the Jew and above all to the Catholic proved the best talking point for Kleagles in most localities. Nor did the methods of the local Klan organizations usually suggest the possession of a "high spiritual philosophy." These local organizations were largely autonomous and beyond control from Atlanta. They were drawn, as a rule, mostly from the less educated and less disciplined elements of the white Protestant community. . . .

If a white girl reported that a colored man had made improper advances to her—even if the charge were unsupported and based on nothing more than a neurotic imagination—a white-sheeted band might spirit the Negro off to the woods and "teach him a lesson" with tar and feathers or with the whip. If a white man stood up for a Negro in a race quarrel, he might be kidnapped and beaten up. If a colored woman refused to sell her land at an arbitrary price which she considered too low, and a Klansman wanted the land, she might receive the K.K.K. ultimatum—sell or be thrown out. Klan members would boycott Jewish merchants, refuse to hire Catholic boys, refuse to rent their houses to Catholics. A hideous tragedy in Louisiana, where five men were kidnapped and later found bound with wire and drowned in a lake, was laid to Klansmen. R. A. Patton, writing in *Current History*, reported a grim series of brutalities from Alabama: "A lad whipped with branches until his back was ribboned flesh; a Negress beaten and left helpless to contract pneumonia from exposure and die; a white girl, divorceé, beaten into unconsciousness in her own home; a naturalized foreigner flogged until his back was a pulp because he married an American woman; a Negro lashed until he sold his land to a white man for a fraction of its value."

Even where there were no such outrages, there was at least the threat of them. The white-robed army paraded, the burning cross glowed across the valley, people whispered to one another in the darkness and wondered "who they were after this time," and fear and suspicion ran from house to house. Furthermore, criminals and gangs of hoodlums quickly learned to take advantage of the Klan's existence; if they wanted to burn someone's barn or raid the slums beyond the railroad tracks, they could do it with impunity now: would not the Klan be held responsible? Anyone could chalk the letters K.K.K. on a fence and be sure that the sheriff would move warily. Thus, as in the case of the Red hysteria, a movement conceived in fear perpetuated fear and brought with it all manner of cruelties and crimes.

Slowly, as the years passed and the war-time emotions ebbed, the power of the Klan waned, until in many districts it was dead and in others it had become merely a political faction dominated by spoilsmen: but not until it had become a thing of terror to millions of men and women.

*Document 5:* The New Republic *explains some of the origin of the Klan*

*In an article in 1921, one of the most reliable of the left-leaning publications in the United States took a sober, yet humorous, look at the origin of the Klan.*

Thanks to the New York World, we have now in full view one of the most grotesque and at the same time one of the most horribly revealing exposures of a debauched and exploited, public mind. If some enemy of America, some infuriated German, had invented the World's story of the Ku Klux Klan, people would have thrown it away contemptuous and bored. Those oaths? Those rituals? Those insignia and declarations and regalia? No satirist could have got people to believe them. But they are true, and the outrages that have sprung from them are real. It is fantastic, but it is the outcome of a long preparation to which America has been subjected by creatures who have been permitted to usurp the name of America.

. . . At a bound Colonel Simmons of Atlanta has surpassed every one of his timid forerunners. As the Imperial Wizard of the Ku Klux Klan he has gone into the business of invisible empire with a terminology that no modern Kingdom can emulate. What is a Knight Commander of the Bath or a Knight of the Garter compared to a Grand Goblin or an Exalted Cyclops? What is a Goldstick-Waiting alongside a Klaliff or a Klarogo or a Klexter? What are recruiting sergeants compared to Kleagles? This man Simmons has not hesitated to lavish honorific titles: he has laid them on thick and in a short period he has, he boasts, enrolled 650,000 native-born white American citizens. Protestant gentiles, from whom he himself and the Kleagles have collected $6,500,000 in dues not to mention the profits on "literature" and on their fool's caps, and the white sheets in which the Knights wrap themselves. (The regalia costs $1.25 to make and sells for $6.50.) In every state in the Union except three, in the north and west rather than the south, Emperor Simmons has found his ripe fruit waiting merely to be plucked. He and his Kleagles have been extremely busy picking plums. . . .

What prepared the United States for this eruption of primitive superstition? Mr. Lusk and Mr. Stevenson and their secret paid spies and secret volunteer agents are in part entitled to the credit. This is plainly an outcropping in final idiocy of the many tyrannical manifestations with which this country has been afflicted since Woodrow Wilson as President yielded completely to the illiberalism and gave Burleson and Palmer carte blanche. It is not so many months since the National Security League paved the way for the Ku Klux Klan. In the activities of that and similar organizations, in the intolerances of the American Legion, in the attacks on civil liberty that culminated in such events as the Albany expulsions, the more jungle-minded Americans have naturally been led to believe that 100-per cent Americanism really calls for an "invisible empire" on the lines of imperial wizardry. . . . All the balderdash in which native-born Americans have indulged in recent years seems to have coagulated in this cesspool of the Ku Klux Klan, to be ladled out by its Kludds, its Klokards and its Kleagles, as a poison, which the feeble-minded cannot distinguish from anything but normal "loyalty." . . .

## Document 6: The African American Press Speaks[6]

*Many African American newspapers professed worry about the Klan. The one comment below is representative of this segment of the press.*

The Klu [*sic*] Klux made a big spurt here Sunday and show a membership of over 1000 in a single lodge. Our colored people had better wake up. It will be a little late wehn [*sic*] their outrages begin. In times of peace, prepare for war. While the order is opposed also to Catholics and Jeews [*sic*] it will not dare to touch them publicly. they are too strong. But everybody and everything lands on the Negro, because they know he is not ready for anything but heaven and so certain of our white friends use every means to send him there as quickly as possible.

### Document 7: What Was Wrong with the Klan?[7]

*A progressive magazine,* The Nation, *also wanted to know what was wrong with the Klan.*

Earl Mayfield, Ku Klux Klan candidate for United States Senator from Texas, apparently is to retain his seat in the Senate. Ed Jackson, Ku Klux Klan candidate for the Republican nomination for governor of Indiana won the primary election in that State, hands down. Klan candidates have won local elections in Ohio, and the New York State delegation to the Republican convention at Cleveland is reported to be opposed to a stringent anti-Klan plank in the Republican platform. Oregon has a Klan governor, and in Georgia and other Southern States the Klan dominates the courts. What is behind this Klan which builds fiery crosses in every State of the Union, which dominates elections, and sways millions?

The New York *World*, which has been waging a vigorous campaign against the Klan, has conducted an interesting poll of Democrats and Republicans on the question whether the political conventions should go on record against "all groups, open or secret, which attempt to take the law into their own hands;" against prejudice or discrimination on account of race, color, or creed; and, specifically, against the Ku Klux Klan. The answers are various; most of the politicians declare in vague, general terms against race prejudice but prefer to avoid mention of the word "Klan." The most pithy comes from the Republican national committeeman from Oklahoma, Jim A. Harris. "All this hullabaloo about the Klan and the anti-Klan," says Mr. Harris, "reminds me of a statement once made by Josh Billings: 'Thur hez bin a heep sed consarnin' the wether, but nuthin' hes ever bin dun about it yet.'"

There has been too much said about the Klan, and too little done about Klannishness. The organization is not as important as its spirit. As the Klan has spread through the North and entered politics as it has acquired an increasing restraint without changing its inner nature. The atrocities with which the early history of the Klan was punctuated seem to have been declining while the bitter, intolerant spirit of the Klan has been spreading. To kill the organization today would mean little if its spirit persisted. . . .

To assume that all Klansmen are reprobates is to adopt the habit of mind exemplified in the ridiculous campaign posters distributed by the Klan in Indiana, reading:

Every criminal, every gambler, every thug, every libertine, every girl-ruiner, every home-wrecker, every wife-beater, every dope-peddler, every moonshiner, every crooked politician, every pagan Papist priest, every shyster lawyer, every K. of C., every white slaver, every brothel madam, every Rome-controlled newspaper, every black-spider—is fighting the Klan. Think it over. Which side are you on?

Well, we are on the side of those who fight Klannishness, although sometimes the fight against the Klan seems to borrow its evils. . . . It will certainly help if the Klan is forced into the open—made to unmask, and to act, when it acts, publicly. It might help if it were proved that Mayfield was elected to the Senate by Klan money and that some of the officials who collected the money knew of crimes committed by Klansmen. . . . The Klan has invented no new crimes. Anti-Catholic sentiment is an old story in American political life; it had its greatest success in the fifties and was active again in the nineties. The Klan has revived an old intolerance, which will still be an evil when the passions now stirred by the three K's have been forgotten. The fight against the Klan will make most headway when it abandons personalities and vague principles. The worst sample of Klannishness in recent American history was the immigration law, and with that, as far as we know, the Ku Klux Klan had nothing to do.

## Document 8: The Klan and Politics[8]

*In 1924, the Klan was a major issue for both major parties as well as 1924's third party, the Progressive Party of Senator Robert La Follette. The various candidates were careful about what they said about the Klan. The Democratic Party was almost torn apart by the issue of the Klan, which another leading journal of the time commented on. By this time, the hysteria about foreign influences in America that had motivated Americans at the end of World War I had dissipated, but the Klan was still going strong.*

Every presidential and vice presidential candidate has now had at least one say—some of them more. So far, not a single new thought has been evolved nor a new issue thrown into the arena that had not been heralded by the three conventions. The next two months will probably see nothing but a restatement of these same ideas with varying emphasis in different parts of the country, and the candidates will have to count on their choice of words or personalities to win such votes as are still undetermined.

The Ku-Klux Klan issue alone bids fair to lend fireworks to the proceedings. Senator La Follette may ignite some unexpected high explosive in his promised revelations, but for the moment, the Knights of the Fiery Cross hold the center of the stage. Republicans stood by and laughed while this issue almost shattered the Democratic Convention. La Follette discreetly avoided the topic at Cleveland. Yet, in the past month, both Davis and La Follette have recognized the desirability of removing the question once and for all time from national politics, have exorcised the Klan in forceful language, and have challenged President Coolidge to do the same. The President hesitates, and by this hesitation alone proves that the curse has now swung from the Democrats to the Republicans.

The President probably has more to win than to lose by maintaining silence. In Maine, Indiana, Kansas, and Oklahoma, the Klan issue is being fought on party lines with Klan support behind the Republican nominees. Dawes' Augusta speech is a sufficient repudiation to satisfy many Republicans who despise the Klan, while silence on the part of the President allows Klansmen to derive comfort as they may. At the same time, silence is an obvious attempt to carry water on both shoulders. The courageous course for the President would be a denunciation so explicit as to leave the Klan completely outlawed by all the political parties. Unless and until he does this, he will be heckled continuously his opponents, and a major issue will be created that has no place in our national life.

## Part B: Bonus March

### Background

*In 1932, the Great Depression was reaching its lowest point. During this period, the Communist Party of America was making strong efforts to bring upheaval to the United States. There was much talk of revolution and overthrow of the government. Most historians do not believe there was much chance of violent upheaval, but the talk of it was widespread. The "Red Scare" of 1919 had dissipated through the years, but the concern was still strong that America was the target of the Marxist revolutionary movement. While most Americans were concerned about daily life and how to get from one meal to another, international events kept intruding on American affairs. A good example is the way the communists in America tried to insinuate themselves into the "Bonus March" in the summer of 1932.*

*The economic depression was the most pressing issue, to be sure. President Herbert Hoover was being savaged for his programs—or lack of programs—to deal with the economic crisis. During the summer, the presidential campaign between Hoover, who was running for reelection, and the governor of New York, Franklin D. Roosevelt, was gearing up. Probably nothing could have happened to harm Hoover's image and reputation more than the march on Washington of some 20,000 or more World War I veterans who were demanding early payment of an annuity—or bonus—they had been promised for their service in the war. They were scheduled to receive the bonus of approximately $1,000 per person in 1945. In desperate need, the veterans were demanding that it be paid in advance. In addition, some of them argued that early payment would stimulate the economy enough to end the depression.*

*The leader of the former soldiers was W. W. Waters, a veteran from Oregon. The veterans organized themselves into the Bonus Expeditionary Force (BEF), a play on the title of the American army that went to Europe during the war—the American Expeditionary Force (AEF).*

*Hoover was opposed to the bonus, as was the majority of the members of Congress. When Congress refused to pay the bonus early, Hoover and Congress tried to encourage the veterans to leave Washington and return to their homes.*

*The removal of the veterans, which involved the U.S. Army, and the destruction of their shack town at Anacostia Flats in the District of Columbia was quite controversial. This controversy was complicated by the fact that the commander of the force, General Douglas MacArthur, disobeyed Hoover's orders and took actions considered extreme—actions for which he was never punished. MacArthur, along with a number of others, believed that the Bonus Army was a revolutionary group led by communists who were determined to overthrow the American government. Hoover agreed with this, and for the rest of his life contended that the unemployed veterans were a threat to the future of the American government. The issue of communist influence and the revolutionary nature of the BEF has been a matter of contention since 1932. The documents selected here show both sides of the issue.*

## Questions

In reading these documents, the student should ask and answer several questions to put these activities in the proper context.

1. How do you assess the BEF as a protest vehicle? Make a list of arguments for and against the contentions that it was a native-grown revolutionary force or a group of gullible veterans influenced by communists.

2. Why did President Hoover continue to discuss this issue in the years following the Great Depression? Why didn't he just put the event behind him?
3. How strong was communist influence in this event?
4. Is the question of communist influence exaggerated, distracting the student from the other key points of this issue—e.g., deficit financing, the power of veterans, "raids" on the treasury? Why does the historian still focus on the expulsion of the veterans from the District of Columbia?

## Document 1: From the Military Point of View[9]

*The national press gave what appears to be an inordinate amount of coverage to the Bonus March. For example, the* New York Times *covered the bonus issue in detail. An interested researcher can trace the development of the march quite easily by following the almost daily reports in the* Times. *The* Times *and other newspapers and magazines were especially concerned about communist influence among the veterans. One of the best accounts of the entire incident came from the memoirs of a soldier who was stationed at Fort Myer and who participated in the entire episode. He explains the origin and development of the Bonus Army as well as the way the military dispersed the veterans from the District of Columbia.*

During the winter of 1931/32, the gloom of the Great Depression was settling over the nation, despite presidential assurance that "prosperity was just around the corner." The words had a hollow ring to the increasing millions of unemployed who could find no work. Desperation drove many of these unfortunate people into "hunger marches" in their demand for employment or other assistance in their hour of need. Press and radio reflected an atmosphere of unrest in the land, and there were occasional clashes with police. It was expected that groups would descend on Washington to petition Congress or the president for aid. Recognizing that disorder was always possible, as a precautionary measure, the commanding general of the Third Corps Area directed that all officers be given a thorough review course in officers' schools in "The Military in Domestic Disturbances." Accordingly, the legal and tactical aspects involved in the use of federal troops to assist civil authorities in maintaining or restoring order in riot conditions were thoroughly reviewed in schools during the month of January. No one dreamed during the instruction the circumstances under which the knowledge would be put to use.

Among the millions of unemployed in the nation, there was one group that considered it had a just claim which the government should settle and thereby afford them direly needed economic assistance. This group, the veterans of the World War, held "Adjusted Service Certificates," which represented the bonus that Congress had voted as partial recompense for their wartime service. The certificates were actually bonds, which were to mature in twenty years, or about the year 1945. To the veterans in need, it seemed only just and reasonable that the Congress should authorize the immediate payment of these certificates in this period of distress. In fact, most veterans believed that the bonus should have been paid in cash in the first place.

So, as winter passed, press and radio began reporting groups here and there across the country heading for Washington, with the avowed purpose of petitioning the Congress for the immediate payment of the bonus. The first veterans that came to the notice of the troops at Fort Myer, however, were not members of these organized groups, but rather were indigent individual veterans seeking food, shelter, and work. As was to be expected, the soldiers were very sympathetic toward these unfortunate men. As a relief measure, the troops employed a few of them as kitchen police and stable police, each man in the troop contributing a small sum each month to afford them a very modest wage. The arrangement was popular with the men, for each would willingly contribute a dollar a month to escape the drudgery of the kitchen and stable-police duties. Besides, they felt they were helping unfortunate comrades. Troop commanders were pleased because the arrangement provided more soldiers for training. But it was not to last.

Early in May, veterans began arriving in Washington, at first in individual driblets, and then in more or less organized groups in ever increasing numbers. Almost spontaneously, or so it seemed, movements began in various parts of the country, all converging on Washington, reminding one of "Coxey's Army" of an earlier period of national economic distress. Like other movements of the sort, it gathered momentum as it was widely publicized in press and radio, as agitators redoubled their efforts, and as economic efforts continued to worsen. And there were a few Communist and radical elements which sought to exploit the movement to their own ends.

Municipal and state authorities met these veterans with sympathy as they crossed the country in bands of varying sizes. However, they presented problems beyond the capabilities of the local authorities. Thus, they hurried the groups on their way, often providing trucks to transport them to the boundary of whatever town, city, or state was involved. Thousands more rode freight trains, without interference on the part of the railroad authorities—in fact, with their acquiescence. The people of the nation sympathized deeply with the veterans.

The trickle that began flowing into Washington in May, then a city of a little more than 450,000, soon swelled into a flood that reached an estimated 20,000 or 25,000 at its peak. And many of these men had their families with them. The civilian authorities in the District of Columbia were not prepared to handle any such influx of indigent persons, even though there was great sympathy for them. In fact, the policy of the administration was not to accord official recognition to the movement or to provide any official assistance in the way of housing, food, or other conveniences, lest by doing so, Washington should become the mecca for floods of other unemployed throughout the nation and thus impose an intolerable burden upon the community.

Gen. Pelham D. Glassford, US. Army, Retired, the chief of police, on his own responsibility and against the wishes of the District's commissioners, made valiant efforts to assist these veterans as a measure of preserving public order. He was even elected treasurer of the initial organization of veterans in Washington. The veterans took over and occupied numerous empty buildings scattered about the downtown area, some that were already condemned and awaiting demolition as a part of the development of the Mall project. They also established camps in various parks and open areas in the city. The largest of these was in the Anacostia Flats, on the east bank of the Anacostia River north of the Naval Air Station. At the height of this veterans' movement, this camp housed some twelve to fourteen thousand persons—men, women and children—in a shantytown of nondescript tents, shacks, and hovels of the most primitive kind, constructed from scrap lumber, packing cases, and tin salvaged from various dumps.

The veterans organized themselves along military lines into the Bonus Expeditionary Force (BEF) and elected a commander, Walter W. Waters, the leader of the California contingent. The BEF was further divided into regiments to facilitate administration and control. It adopted regulations for conduct and control, and it organized its own "military police" to enforce them. The vast majority of the veterans belonged to this organization, but there were two or three groups, totaling several hundred, led by two well-known Communists from Detroit, who remained outside the major organization and pursued their own reactionary and obstructionist course.

Benefits were staged to assist the veterans, and private donations from the sympathetic citizenry of Washington and other parts of the country also aided in sustaining them. The veterans themselves resorted to all sorts of money-raising devices, from selling apples to staging exhibitions. As Camp Marks—the name given to the huge camp on the Anacostia Flats—grew in size, it attracted many sightseers and curious persons. One of the favorite money-raising schemes was to bury an individual who was to remain underground presumably until Congress authorized payment of the bonus, but actually for periods of a few days. The coffin had an aperture through which the buried individual could be seen, and curious spectators paid a fee to see him!

One of the special attractions in this "buried-veteran act" was Joe Angelo. During the war he had been the orderly of Maj. George S. Patton, Jr. When

Major Patton was seriously wounded while on a patrol, Joe Angelo had dragged him into a shell hole, sheltered him under heavy fire, and had then got him back to the American lines. For this heroic deed, Angelo had been decorated. The fact that Major Patton and the Patton family had done everything possible for Angelo during the years following the war did not prevent others from exploiting him and his heroic deed.

For the most part, this mass of veterans was disciplined and law-abiding even though the Communist-led groups sought to create dissension and discord. Nevertheless, thousands of idle men, roaming the streets of Washington, trying to force neckties, shoe laces, pencils, apples, gimcracks of various kinds on passers-by, were never pleasant to experience, and unescorted women soon avoided downtown streets. Then the thousands of veterans, living in half-demolished buildings, rude tents, huts, and hovels under the most primitive of conditions, presented city with a sanitary problem of great magnitude.

As the number of veterans increased in the various camps, pressures on Congress intensified. Thousands of veterans thronged the Capitol grounds almost daily when Congress was in session, and there they heard pathetic addresses by various members of Congress. Bills introduced to appropriate funds to assist in feeding and caring for the veterans were opposed by the District's commissioners and the administration for fear encouraging further "marches" on the city. And the Congress took no action on the legislation that was introduced, nor did it act to authorize payment of the Adjusted Service Certificates, which the veterans advocated. Waters, the commander of the BEF, was violently anti-Communist, as were the vast majority of the many thousands of veterans. The Pace and Stembler communistic groups, however, increased their agitation. Tempers flared now and then, and there were occasional clashes with the police, although the District police were most sympathetic and sought to aid the veterans in every way possible. There was a feeling of unease in official circles, and a restless, troubled feeling throughout the city. No one knew what to expect.

This feeling of uneasiness was reflected at Fort Myer, for the officers and men of the garrison were soon restricted to the limits of the post. Individual officers and men could leave only with permission of the commanding officer, and then only for brief periods for urgent reasons. Meanwhile, troops were being thoroughly trained in the tactics of riot duty and the techniques of handling riotous crowds. Day after day, one troop, equipped with pick handles, slickers, blankets, and noise-making implements of various kinds, would take position behind a shoulder-high corral fence. Another troop would ride its horses up against the fence in the face of waving slickers and blankets, shouting and noise of all kinds, and the beating of sticks—all possible actions of a disorderly mob. These exercises were repeated day after day, until horses and men were thoroughly accustomed to the sound and fury and would advance into any crowd, regardless of any action it might take.

These activities did not escape the notice of the veterans, for while the garrison was confined to post, there was no restriction on access to it. People came to and from the post as usual. One indication of the notice that the Communist agitators were taking of the training in progress was the handbills that were surreptitiously distributed on the post during this time. They were found in barracks, stables, and other places frequented by the soldiers, but none of the distributors was ever apprehended. Practically all of the papers immediately found their way to the desks of the troop commanders, for the soldiers were irritated by such clandestine activities. One of the handbills on ordinary newsprint about eight and a half by eleven inches read as follows:

TO ALL MARINES ON DUTY IN WASHINGTON
TO ALL ENLISTED MEN AT FORT MYERS, [sic] VA.
SOLDIERS AND MARINES:

The higher Army and Navy authorities, acting for the Wall Street-Hoover government are taking steps to use you against the Ex-servicemen who are now in Washington. Your officers expect you, if the government considers it necessary to club or shoot down the Veterans to prevent them from carrying on their struggle and getting the bonus.

The veterans demand their bonus which is due them. The "heroes" of 1917 are now facing unemployment and starvation together with the rest of the 15,000,000 unemployed workers. The vets are fighting not only for the bonus but for unemployment insurance for all the workers. Only unemployment insurance will give proper relief to all the workers. The bonus is but a drop in the bucket. The unemployed workers are tired of starving. Your folks back home are getting tired of slowly starving to death.

The government has billions for the bankers but not one cent for the unemployed or for the Vets. It has not done anything to increase the miserable pay in the service. It has even cut the ration allowance.

Only a few weeks ago you marched in memory of the dead. Now the bosses want you to club and shoot these same ex-Servicemen who fought in the last war. Did you ever stop to think how many of you will be killed in the next war? The last war was fought for the bankers, for Morgan and Rockefeller, and the veterans got nothing but promises and police clubs. Now preparations are going on for a new war project to protect the bankers' interests, to destroy the only country where unemployment has been abolished by its workers' and farmers' government—The Soviet Union (Russia). You servicemen will be among the first to go. What will you get when you get out of the service? You will be treated the same way they are treating Vets today.

The bosses want you to do their dirty work for them. They want you workers and farmers in uniform to protect their profits for them. Soldiers! Marines! You are workers! No real red-blooded American soldier will allow himself to be used to shoot down fellow workers,—his wartime buddies,—his father or brothers who are unemployed.

Servicemen—Fraternize with the Vets! Help them get their bonus! Tell your officers en mass [*sic*] that you will not be used against the Vets! Organize Committees in every single company to support the Bonus! Refuse duty if you are ordered out against the bonus marchers and the unemployed!

SUPPORT THE FIGHT FOR UNEMPLOYMENT INSURANCE!
JOIN THE YOUNG COMMUNIST LEAGUE,
P.O. BOX 28, STATION D,
NEW YORK, NEW YORK

WRITE TO THE YOUNG COMMUNIST LEAGUE,
P.O. BOX 28, STATION D,
NEW YORK, NEW YORK
(All names will be strictly confidential)

YOUNG COMMUNIST LEAGUE OF THE
UNITED STATES OF AMERICA
PO. Box 28, Station D                                      New York City

Another of these handbills, about ten by thirteen inches in size, also printed on ordinary newsprint, was headed: "Refuse Duty against your People!" It was addressed: "To all men in the U.S. Army, Navy, Marines, and national Guard; Workers and Workers in Uniform!' This sheet had a small cartoon in the upper left entitled "Heroes of 1917" and another in the lower right entitled "Bums of 1932!' The text was an appeal along the lines similar to the one quoted above. This one ended:

"REFUSE DUTY AGAINST WORKERS AND FARMERS!"
FIGHT FOR UNEMPLOYMENT RELIEF!
ORGANIZE ENLISTED MENS COMMITTEES
IN EVERY OUTFIT!
"(Printed by Union Labor) Issued by a group of servicemen"

There were many more of these handbills, but their only effect on enlisted personnel was to create a feeling of anger and impatience with those responsible for distributing such crude appeals.

Congress adjourned on July 16 without authorizing payment of bonus. Before adjournment, however, it did authorize veterans to borrow against their Adjusted Service Certificates for funds for transportation to return to their homes. Several thousand availed themselves of authorization, and several thousand others departed as they had come. But the hard core of veterans, some ten thousand or so, refused to depart, insisting they would "stay till 1945 to get the bonus!" Their chant was "Bonus or a job!" This group was of course symbolic of the vast army of the unemployed throughout the country. But it presented a special problem for the Administration and the District authorities.

As numbers of veterans departed during the ten days following the adjournment of Congress, tensions of the past weeks appeared to lessen, and the dangers seemed to recede. On July 27 the restriction on post personnel was lifted, and officers and men were permitted to leave the post for the first time in a number of weeks. A day or so before this, the District's commissioners ordered that a group of condemned buildings on Pennsylvania Avenue at Third Street be cleared for demolition, so that development on the Mall could be continued. Veterans who were occupying the buildings refused to vacate them, assaulted police with bricks and pieces of concrete, tossed General Glassford down a flight of stairs, and took away his pistol. In the course of this rioting, two veterans were killed by the police. Then the commissioners appealed for federal troops to quell the rioting and restore order. Their use was authorized by the president.

About two o'clock on the afternoon of July 28, Maj. George S. Patton, the regimental executive officer, telephoned the troop commanders at their headquarters, saying the squadron was ordered into Washington to quell riots and that the troops were being alerted by the sergeant major. He also dispatched a messenger for Major Surles, who was absent from the post for first time since the restriction was originally imposed. Troop commanders hurried to join their troops, which were soon saddled and formed along the stable line. Major Surles joined shortly, and the squadron then pounded down through Arlington National Cemetery, over the recently completed Memorial Bridge, and halted on the Ellipse south of the White House at about half past two o'clock. Then there was a long delay while the squadron waited for the arrival of the infantry battalion, coming by steamer on the Potomac from Fort Washington. Eventually the battalion docked near the War College and joined the squadron on the Ellipse by truck. Then we formed the column.

The squadron moved out in a column of platoons, followed by the infantry battalion with a few of their old World War tanks, and swept down Pennsylvania Avenue from the Treasury Building at Fifteenth Street toward Capitol— the reverse of the direction normally followed by parades. Simultaneously, so it seemed, every office building and business establishment in downtown Washington discharged its occupants onto the streets. This parade was indeed witnessed by thousands, and a tense atmosphere of excitement pervaded the scene.

At Third Street and Pennsylvania Avenue, opposite the half-demolished buildings where the rioting had occurred earlier and which were still held by the veterans, there was another delay. Cavalry troops isolated the building, for thousands were converging on the scene—both veterans from other camps and spectators. The spectators often caused more difficulty than the veterans and provided some incidents more amusing in retrospect than the soldiers appreciated at the time. For example, one cavalry corporal kept applying the flat side of his saber to the rear of a pompous, stout individual who kept maintaining loudly that he was a member of Congress. Since the corporal was denying permission to cross Third Street, he won the argument.

General MacArthur, the chief of staff of the army, conferred with military, civilian, and police authorities on the scene. Eventually, the infantry moved into the building and asked the veterans to disperse. They were met with ribald refusal and some opposition. However, a few tear-gas grenades soon emptied the premises of hundreds of veterans. The cavalry troops pushed them along Third and Fourth streets to Missouri Avenue, about a block from the vacated buildings where they halted to permit the veterans to disperse and to await further orders.

Spread out in a single thin line for several blocks, faced with the veterans just expelled from the emptied buildings and thousands of others who were now pouring into the area from other camps, the situation became more and more tense by the moment. One group of veterans gathered in front of Troop E, where they recognized 1st Sgt. William Lawrence and some of the other noncommissioned officers they had served with during the war. The group began baiting Sergeant Lawrence and the other non-commissioned officers as only men who have also been soldiers can do. But Sergeant Lawrence and the other soldiers sat like statues and answered back not a word. Their only action was to apply the flat of a saber when individuals tried to slip through the thin lines. Theirs was a magnificent illustration of Regular Army discipline.

But the tensions increased, and eventually the mob became bolder in the face of seeming inaction on the part of the cavalry. A few bricks and stones from the rubble heaps were thrown. Several soldiers were struck, and at least two were knocked unconscious. Then word came to disperse the mob. The cavalry troops moved forward, with drawn sabers in hand. There was a hail of bricks and stones. But not one drop of veterans' blood was shed, although many felt the flat of troopers' sabers and some few were threatened with the point. Many veterans sought refuge in shacks they had built along the Mall or in trucks parked along the streets. A few blows with the pommel of a saber on the tin roofs or the thrust of a saber through cracks soon emptied the shacks and trucks, though, and the veterans continued their flight.

It went on across the Mall to the vicinity of Twelfth and D streets, where the communistic-led veterans were housed in vacant buildings. These were soon emptied. Then, after some delay to allow the veterans time to disperse, the troops turned toward the big camps on the Anocostia [*sic*] Flats.

Shortly after nightfall, they crossed the Anacostia Bridge and were on the flats on the edge of the camp by about half past ten. The squadron halted, to allow the veterans time to vacate the area. The Infantry Battalion moved in to clear it. It was soon a mass of flames. By morning, the veterans were gone, and the huge primitive camp was a smoldering mass. No one knew who set off the first fires, but it was the complete answer from both a sanitary and disciplinary point of view.

About nine o'clock on the morning of July 19, while the now-almost-vacant camp was still smoldering, trucks arrived from Fort Myer with forage for the animals, much needed picket lines, and kitchens for the troops. Horses were soon fed and groomed. Kitchens were set up, and the aroma of coffee soon contended with the smell of the smoldering ruins. Once fed, the troops waited patiently—and waiting is not at all unusual in the army.

While waiting, the senior officers of the squadron gathered around one end of the picket lines. There, seated on bales of hay, they gossiped over events of the afternoon and night and wondered what the next move would be. Time passed, and a tall sergeant of the Twelfth Infantry approached, with a small civilian in tow, and asked for Major Patton, saying that the man claimed to be a friend of the major's. When Major Patton saw them, his face flushed with anger: "Sergeant, I do not know this man. Take him away, and under no circumstances permit him to return!" The sergeant led the downcast man away.

Then Major Patton turned to the small group of officers and said: "That was my orderly during the war. When I was wounded, he dragged me from a shell hole under fire. I got him a decoration for it. Since the war my mother and I have more than supported him. We have given him money. We have set him up in business several times. Can you imagine headlines if the papers got wind of our meeting here this morning!" Then he added, "Of course, we'll take care of him anyway!"

The only duties performed by the squadron that night were rescuing some army tentage from fires set by the veterans. Troops bivouacked on the ground until nearly four o'clock in the afternoon of July 29, except for the detachments of Headquarters and Machine Gun Troops which were guarding the Eleventh Street and Pennsylvania Avenue bridges. They kept busy. About four o'clock, the squadron and the Infantry Battalion assembled and marched back into the city, visiting areas on Pennsylvania Avenue at Second and A streets northeast, the area between Maine and Maryland avenues, a small part of which had not burned the preceding day, and finally back to the vicinity of Twelfth and D streets southwest, with the mission of mopping up stragglers. Almost none were found.

At Twelfth and D, word came that the emergency was over. Troops were to return to their stations. The squadron was back at Fort Myer, with horses and equipment cared for, by half past five o'clock, ready for the evening meal. The emergency indeed was over. The remnants of the BEF were streaming out of Washington, as one correspondent described it: "The bonus army, bedraggled,

*During the bonus struggle, several thousand veterans came to Washington, D.C., many with their families, to petition Congress for payment of the bonus. When Congress refused, President Hoover became concerned about public safety. General MacArthur was ordered to evacuate the shack town the veterans had built; many of their shacks were burned. U.S. Army Signal Corps Photo.*

hungry, shabby, moved out along the roads that led away from the Nation's Capital. . . . The BEF had died in the same confusion in which it was born."

For a few days, news reports in the papers followed the progress of these remnants. But the great Bonus March was ended. And never again would such a movement be repeated in Washington. Cavalry training and special training for riot duty had paid off. The unruly mob had been dispersed, without bloodshed, without animosity, and with comparatively little trouble. For the troops, the following day was duty as usual.

### Document 2: Hoover Responds to the Marchers[10]

*Eventually President Hoover concluded that he could not allow such a large group of unemployed people to remain in the District of Columbia. During the dispersal of the marchers, he issued two statements giving his reasons for the action. Hoover mentioned that Congress appropriated money to assist the veterans in getting home, but he neglected to say that the amount they received would be deducted from their bonus when it was eventually paid. The first statement was issued on July 28 after Hoover ordered the army to act, and the second was on July 29 reporting what had happened.*

### Statement of July 28, 1932

For some days police authorities and Treasury officials have been endeavoring to persuade the so-called bonus marchers to evacuate certain buildings which they were occupying without permission.

These buildings are on sites where government construction is in progress and their demolition was necessary in order to extend employment in the district and to carry forward the government's construction program.

This morning the occupants of these buildings were notified to evacuate and at the request of the police did evacuate the buildings concerned. Thereafter, however, several thousand men from different camps marched in and attacked the police with brickbats and otherwise injuring several policemen, one probably fatally.

I have received the attached letter from the Commissioners of the District of Columbia [letter not reprinted], stating that they can no longer preserve law and order in the district.

In order to put an end to the rioting and defiance of civil authority, I have asked the army to assist the District authorities to restore order.

Congress made provision for the return home of the so-called bonus marchers, who have for many weeks been given every opportunity of free assembly, free speech and free petition to the Congress. Some 5,000 took advantage of this arrangement and have returned to their homes. An examination of a large number of names discloses the fact that a considerable part of those remaining are not veterans; many are Communists and persons with criminal records.

The veterans amongst these numbers are no doubt unaware of the character of their companions and are being led into violence which no government can tolerate.

I have asked the Attorney General to investigate the whole incident and to cooperate with the District civil authorities in such measures against leaders and rioters as may be necessary.

Statement of July 29, 1932

A challenge to the authority of the United States Government has been met, swiftly and firmly.

After months of patient indulgence, the Government met overt lawlessness as it always must be met if the cherished processes of self-government are to be preserved. We cannot tolerate the abuse of constitutional rights by those who would destroy all government, no matter who they may be. Government cannot be coerced by mob rule.

The Department of Justice is pressing its investigation into the violence which forced the call for Army detachments, and it is my sincere hope that those agitators who inspired yesterday's attack upon the Federal authority may be brought speedily to trial in the civil courts. There can be no safe harbor in the United States of America for violence.

Order and civil tranquility are the first requisites in the great task of economic reconstruction to which our whole people now are devoting their heroic and noble energies. This national effort must not be retarded in even the slightest degree by organized lawlessness. The first obligation of my office is to uphold and defend the Constitution and the authority of the law. This I propose always to do.

## Document 3: An Eye Witness Account[11]

*Bera Roberts (Mrs. Elbridge C. Purdy), a native of Kentucky, was in Washington, D.C., during the time of the Bonus March. In 1976, she recorded her memories of the dispersal of the veterans and donated it to the MacArthur Archives in Norfolk, Virginia. Although her reflections are brief, they give a "civilian" point of view to the eviction of the war veterans.*

The evening was still and calm as the Potomac River moonlight excursion boat was returning from Fort Washington [on Maryland side of Potomac, across from Mt. Vernon] on the night of [late July 1932]. The decorated boat with an outline of bright lights was a familiar nightly sight on the Potomac

River. It left tiny dancing diamond-like reflections in its path as it churned along and pulled steadily upstream. The ride down was smooth and easy because the boat drifted with the current. It was a pleasure trip and an escape from the sweltering Washington heat. Especially since there was a cool steady breeze. It had been a perfect evening as the boat neared its landing dock on Water Street in Southeast Washington, D.C. The strains of the last music for dancing were nearing its end.

Near the mouth of the Anacostia River a red haze appeared becoming brighter with a mass of flames. The section on the right side of the boat beyond Bolling Air Force Base seemed to be on fire. The whole bank seemed to be burning. All of the occupants of the boat rushed to the right side to see the spectacle.

Immediately the excursion crew began pushing the passengers on board back as the boat began to list to the right side.

"Move back, or the boat will capsize!

Move back please, the boat is listing.

Please move to the other side."

Everyone became extremely excited. Immediately it became known that General Douglas MacArthur had been given orders [by the President] to drive the Veteran Bonus Marchers out. These were the marchers who had come to Washington, D.C. and camped on the flats at Anacostia and stayed on.

My sister was with a young Army Captain by the name of Bender. Captain Bender had reported to Washington, D.C. for duty in case MacArthur had to drive the veterans away. He would be there to help General MacArthur. Captain Bender had been waiting for several months when MacArthur was finally given orders to drive the Bonus Marchers away. Public sympathy lay with the Bonus Marchers. General opinion felt that the veterans were due the bonus they marched for.

After the boat had docked, we immediately took the shortest route to Anacostia so the Captain could report to General MacArthur as soon as possible. At the old Eleventh Street Bridge, soldiers and police were on patrol cutting off all traffic across to the area of the flats where the Bonus Marchers were encamped. After a brief conversation and identification had been presented, we were permitted to cross to the fiery riverside flats so that we could hurriedly drive the Captain to join General MacArthur. My date knew the area well, and maneuvered his way through the rough roadways.

There were continuous flames. Veterans were packing and rushing about. Tear gas, which was being used to drive them out, made it difficult to see. We went winding about the crowded pathways inquiring as to where General MacArthur's headquarters was so that the Captain could report immediately for duty. On this drive we witnessed unforgettable sights—rough looking dirty ruffians with unkempt clothing and shabby shoes. Then they saw the Captain's uniform. Quickly, a mad rush of men began throwing rocks and pieces of brick at our car. One veteran hurled a brick at our car that just missed the top by a few inches. I recall my sister scrunching down in the back of the car. My younger sister was so frightened that she ducked below the front seat. Clouds of dust and tear gas appeared over the winding dirt roadways. Clouds resembling cumulus clouds reflected the glowing red of the fires. It was like riding through the steam of a teakettle.

The tents and lean-tos were set on fire by fire being carried from one to another. Some must have caught fire from torches made of rolls of paper. There were dilapidated old cars, with lean-tos attached as living quarters. Huts were built of blankets and quilts for protection. There were some pregnant women and some babies. These were the veteran's [*sic*] families. They were grabbing and packing their meager belonging, rolling them up in bundles and swinging them over their shoulders. They stuffed them into wagon beds and cars. There were old-fashioned washtubs and outdoor cooking utensils being hurriedly packed. These hot sultry wagons were serving as homes and sleeping quarters. The odor was vile all along the way. Horses and mules lived alongside of the lean-tos and tents. The stench was great as we passed through the streets full of garbage. No wonder the residents of Anacostia were making so many complaints. As we arrived at MacArthur's Headquarters, I will always remember the staunch outline, the erect figure of MacArthur in the middle of the melee as he gave orders. Captain Bender walked up and saluted. As MacArthur returned the salute, he turned and glanced about to see how the Captain had arrived. We were motioned on and directed by soldiers to the quickest and easiest route out of there. Our eyes were still red, blurry, and wet from the tear gas, dust, and filth.

## Document 4: President Hoover Tells His Side of the Story[12]

*When President Hoover published his memoirs in 1952, twenty years after the Bonus March, he was bothered—one might say obsessed—by that event. In another part of his memoirs, he goes to great length to explain his strong support of veterans. In this selection, he is determined to convince the American people that the march was dominated by communists and that he was right in his response to it. Clearly, he was trying to justify his actions and improve his standing in history. When he discusses his actions to get Congress to appropriate money for tickets for the veterans to return home, he neglects to mention that the amount received would be deducted from the bonus when it was eventually paid. General Douglas MacArthur, later the hero of the American army in the Pacific Theater in World War II, was a major player in the bonus issue, and Hoover uses him to justify his actions. In his own memoirs published after his death in the 1960s, MacArthur maintains and emphasizes his conviction about the role of communists and other radicals among the veterans.*

Probably the greatest coup of all was the distortion of the story of the Bonus March on Washington in July, 1932. About 11,000 supposed veterans congregated in Washington to urge action by Congress to pay a deferred war bonus in cash instead of over a period of years.

The Democratic leaders did not organize the Bonus March nor conduct the ensuing riots. But the Democratic organization seized upon the incident with great avidity. Many Democratic speakers in the campaign of 1932 implied that I had murdered veterans on the streets of Washington.

The story was kept alive for twenty years. I, therefore, deal with it at greater length than would otherwise be warranted. As abundantly proved later on, the march was in considerable part organized and promoted by the Communists and included a large number of hoodlums and ex-convicts determined to raise a public disturbance. They were frequently addressed by Democratic Congressmen seeking to inflame them against me for my opposition to the bonus legislation. They were given financial support by some of the publishers of the sensational press. It was of interest to learn in after years from the Communist confessions that they also had put on a special battery of speakers to help Roosevelt in his campaign, by the use of the incident.

When it was evident that no legislation on the bonus would be passed by the Congress, I asked the chairmen of the Congressional committees to appropriate funds to buy tickets home for the legitimate veterans. This was done and some 6,000 availed themselves of its aid, leaving about 5,000 mixed hoodlums, ex-convicts, Communists, and a minority of veterans in Washington. Through government agencies we obtained the names of upwards of 2,000 of those remaining and found that fewer than a third of them had ever served in the armies, and that over 900 on the basis of this sampling were ex-convicts and Communists.

Some old buildings on Pennsylvania Avenue had been occupied by about 50 marchers. These buildings stood in the way of construction work going on as an aid to employment in Washington. On July 28th the Treasury officials, through the police, requested these marchers to move to other quarters. Whereupon more than 1,000 of the disturbers marched from camps outside of the city armed with clubs and made an organized attack upon the police. In the melee Police Commissioner Glassford failed to organize his men. Several were surrounded by the mob and beaten up; two policemen, beaten to the ground, fired to protect their lives and killed two marchers. Many policemen were injured.

In the midst of this riot the District Commissioners, upon Glassford's urging, appealed to me. They declared that they could not preserve order in the Capital, that the police were greatly outnumbered, and were being overwhelmed. With the same right of call on me as municipalities have on the governor of any state, they asked military assistance to restore order. At my direction to Secretary of War Hurley, General Douglas MacArthur was directed to take charge. General Eisenhower (then Colonel) was second in command. Without firing a shot or injuring a single person, they cleaned up the situation. Certain of my directions to the Secretary of War, however, were not carried out. Those directions limited action to seeing to it that the disturbing factions returned to their camps outside the business district. I did not wish them driven from their camps, as I proposed that the next day we would surround the camps and determine more accurately the number of Communists and ex-convicts among the marchers. Our military officers, however, having them on the move, pushed them outside the District of Columbia. . . .

General MacArthur issued his own statement on September 28th, saying:

I sent word by General Glassford to the various camps that I was going to clear Government property and that I hoped that they would not be humiliated by being forced out. I hoped that they would take advantage of the time element and evacuate without trouble. We moved down Pennsylvania to the Avenue area. . . . That mob . . . was a bad looking mob. It was animated by the essence of revolution. The gentleness, the consideration, with which they had been treated had been mistaken for weakness and they had come to the conclusion, beyond the shadow of a doubt, that they were about to take over in some arbitrary way either the direct control of the Government or else to control it by indirect methods. It is my opinion that had the President not acted today, had he permitted this thing to go for 24 hours more, he would have been faced with a grave situation which would have caused a real battle. Had he let it go on another week I believe that the institutions of our Government would have been very severely threatened. . . .

I have never seen greater relief on the part of the distressed populace than I saw today. I have released in my day more than one community which had been held in the grip of a foreign enemy. I have gone into villages that for three and one half years had been under the domination of the soldiers of a foreign nation. I know what gratitude means along that line. I have never seen, even in those days, such expression of gratitude as I heard from the crowds today. At least a dozen people told me, especially in the Negro section, that a regular system of tribute was being levied on them by this insurrectionist group; a reign of terror was being started which may have led to a system of Caponeism, and I believe later to insurgency and insurrection. . . .

That the Bonus March was largely organized and managed by Communists became clear with the passage of time, through disclosures by Congressional committees and repentant Communist leaders who participated in it. Benjamin Gitlow, who was a leader in the Communist party, later published a full account of the movement in which he described the organization of the march and its direction in Washington by a Russian Communist agent from a safe hotel room, and the anger of the director when the attempt failed after the troops took charge without hurting a single veteran.

An acknowledged Communist who actually led in the march—John T. Pace—made a complete confession which is worth partial reproduction as it shows the activities of the Communists in opposing my election in 1932. Pace stated:

> I feel responsible in part for this often-repeated lie about President Hoover and General MacArthur. . . .
>
> I led the left-wing or Communist section of the bonus march. I was ordered by my Red superiors to provoke riots. I was told to use every trick to bring about bloodshed in the hopes that President Hoover would be forced to call out the Army. The Communists didn't care how many veterans were killed. I was told Moscow had ordered riots and bloodshed in the hopes that this might set off the revolution. My Communist bosses were jumping for joy on July 28 when the Washington police killed one veteran. The Army was called out next day by President Hoover and didn't fire a shot or kill a man. General MacArthur put down a Moscow-directed revolution without bloodshed, and that's why the Communists hate him even today. . . .
>
> But MacArthur did the job without firing a shot and acting under Mr. Hoover's instructions, prevented any violence.
>
> I was told . . . [after the riots] . . . to come to an address near Union Square (New York). It was a highly secret meeting and plenty of the big-shot Communists were there, including Browder, Foster, and Stachel.
>
> Levine and I made reports on the bonus march and our work in Washington. Then a squat, dark-haired man was introduced to us as the "C.I. Rep" (Communist International representative). This man complimented me for my work. Speaking with a thick Russian accent, he said Moscow was pleased with my "working class leadership." He told me that Moscow wanted me to make a national tour speaking in every State to agitate against President Hoover and General MacArthur.
>
> This Moscow agent said I was to refer to Mr. Hoover as "the murderer of American veterans" and to MacArthur as "the tool of the Fascists."
>
> I knew that MacArthur's men didn't fire a shot, but I had at least one "commissar" with me during all my speaking tour to see that I followed instructions.
>
> The "C.I. Rep" also told the party leaders to arrange my speaking tour under the auspices of the Workers' Ex-Servicemen's League, a Communist-front group.

Communist leaders told me the smear campaign was successful. They were happy when the parlor pinks took up the smear against the two great Americans and even today the Reds boast that the propaganda drive of 1932 carried on by the Communists turned the Nation against Mr. Hoover.

On the basis of my personal experience, I want to repeat again and again that Mr. Hoover took the only step he could have taken to avert a bloody revolution right there in Washington. . . .

## Document 5: A Democrat Recalls the Bonus March[13]

*Rexford Tugwell, while not directly involved in the bonus issue, was nonetheless an interested observer since he was working for Governor Franklin Roosevelt who was challenging President Hoover for the presidency. Tugwell went on to be a member of the "Brain Trust" of Roosevelt and to serve in numerous positions during the New Deal. He later wrote his memories of how the Roosevelt camp viewed the bonus debacle.*

Americans were uneasy, but they were not ready to concede imminent overthrow of the government by a few thousand indigents who, not long ago, had been its defenders. People might be having it hard; but they were not persuaded that their veterans were about to storm the White House or the Capitol.

There were, however, mutterings from both Right and Left that tougher treatment was called for. The rightists had taken to praising Mussolini for making the notoriously inefficient Italian railways meet their schedules, and leftists were pointing out that there was no unemployment in the Soviet Union. Fascist and Communist alike offered order and security to those who were being made to bear the risks of a free economy. Mention of the accompanying regimentation was omitted, usually.

Glassford thought something more humane was called for than seemed to be contemplated by federal authorities and the District commissioners, and he conceived the idea of reconditioning an abandoned army camp not far from the city where some sort of life could be organized for those who were homeless. Before he could make much progress, however, the inevitable infiltration of real radicals began, and when John Pace of Detroit, a notorious agitator, persuaded some two hundred like-minded fellows to gather outside the White House, Washingtonians became as hysterical as Chicagoans had been in 1895 when Cleveland and Olney had chosen to regard railway strikers as rebels.

Armed guards were posted to watch the White House and hasty high-level conferences were held. The imaginary threat to the government became front-page news. Within a few days the whole country was watching the president. What would he do?

## Notes

1. The Ku Klux Klan Constitution, excerpted from the Original Electronic Text as archived at the Center for History and New Media. Online at: http://history.hanover .edu/courses/excerpts/227kkkmanual.html.

2. Alva W. Taylor, "What the Klan Did in Indiana," *The New Republic* (November 16, 1927).

3. Hiram W. Evans, "The Klan's Fight for Americanism," *North American Review* (March 1926): 38–39.

4. Frederick Lewis Allen, *Only Yesterday: An Informal History of the 1920's* (New York: Harper and Row, 1931), 49–50. Copyright 1931 by Frederick Lewis Allen, renewed © 1959 by Agnes Rogers Allen. Reprinted by permission of HarperCollins Publishers.

5. "The K.K.K.," *The New Republic* (September 21, 1921).

6. *The Union* (an African-American newspaper published in Cincinnati, Ohio), February 18, 1922. Online at: http://dbs.ohiohistory.org/africanam/nwspaper/ union.cfm.

7. "What Is Wrong with the Klan?" *The Nation* (June 18, 1924): 698.

8. "Casting Out the Klan," *The Independent* (September 13, 1924).

9. General Lucian K. Truscott, Jr. *The Twilight of the U.S. Cavalry: Life in the Old Army, 1917–1942* (Lawrence: University of Kansas Press, 1989), 120–30. Edited and with a preface by Colonel Lucian K. Truscott III. Foreword by Edward M. Coffman. Modern War Series. Reprinted by permission of the University of Kansas Press.

10. *Public Papers of the Presidents of the United States: Herbert Hoover, 1932–1933*, (Washington, D.C.: Government Printing Office, 1977), 339–45, 348–50.

11. "Eye Witness Account of the Bonus Incident, including the burning of the Camp at Anacostia, 1932." Courtesy of MacArthur Memorial Archives, Norfolk, VA, RG-15, Elbridge Purdy Collection.

12. Herbert Hoover, *The Memoirs of Herbert Hoover. The Great Depression, 1929–1941* (New York: Macmillan, 1952), 225–32.

13. Rexford G. Tugwell, "Roosevelt and the Bonus Marchers of 1932." Reprinted by permission from *Political Science Quarterly* 87 (September 1972), 363–76.

# 3

# The New Deal

*D*URING THE 1930s, THE UNITED *States suffered through the Great Depression, but this was not something that affected the United States alone. Most of the industrialized world endured an economic decline as great or greater than that in the United States. There has been some debate in the past whether the depression in America was the result of European events or whether the wider depression in the world originated in the United States. Whatever the answer may be, it is certainly true to say that the hard times were worldwide. At the same time, a serious antiwar movement existed throughout the world. The European pacifist movement had a strong influence in America while, at the same time, the student movement in America had its influence abroad.*

## Part A: Security for the Elderly

### Background

*The Great Depression that dominated American society during the 1930s was a worldwide economic crisis, even if the average American thought first only of himself and his family. The world had become interdependent enough by the 1930s that an economic collapse in one part of the world would inevitably have an impact elsewhere.*

*In the United States, two groups were especially hard-hit by the economic decline. The young, especially children, were at serious risk, as were elderly people. Even in good times, older people were at risk if they were not wealthy to begin with. If they had worked all their lives and had few resources for old age, they had to rely on family or on public charity. Too many times, the children or other relatives of the elderly were not able to provide much, if any, assistance. Charity, whether public or private, was limited at best, but these agencies were overwhelmed by people needing relief in a time of depression.*

*The concept of social insurance—old age assistance—was an established system in some parts of Europe. In Germany, it went back to the period of German unification under Otto von Bismarck. Social insurance recognized that the agrarian method of caring for the old in the homes of children and relatives did not work in an urban, industrialized economy. People had difficulty saving for old age, and there were few resources to turn to for help when that time came. By the beginning of the twentieth century, most of these countries had recognized a government responsibility to assist the elderly.*

*Social insurance was a new idea for America. Traditionally, Americans had believed in small government and had been imbued with the concept of "rugged individualism," in which all people took care of themselves. Clearly, that was a flawed concept and never had been true, but the idea of taking care of oneself had become a part of American way of thinking. With the coming of a depression of unprecedented proportions, people began to question the idea of rugged individualism and to ask if the government had any responsibility for people after they reached a certain age. There was no universal answer to that question, but it was raised more often in the 1930s. The number of people who believed the government did have a responsibility grew quickly during hard times. The European experience with social insurance began to impact Americans in positions of influence.*

*The federal government eventually devised the Social Security plan, which was enacted in 1935. When Roosevelt became president in 1933, old age assistance was not one of his priorities. But as the depression worsened and more people began to demand aid for the elderly, numerous plans for old-age pensions emerged throughout the country. When that happened, Roosevelt's advisors convinced him that if the government did not do something, he would be co-opted by some of the other plans—some quite bizarre—that were circulating around the country and garnering support. The result was the passage of the Social Security Act.*

## Questions

In reading these documents, the student should ask and answer several questions to put these activities in the proper context.

1. Did the Sinclair and Long plans provide workable answers to the problems?

2. Why was Townsend's plan taken so much more seriously than the others were?

3. Could the Townsend plan have been enacted? What economic repercussions would it have had?

4. What were the major arguments against the Townsend plan?

5. Was the Social Security plan of Roosevelt's a serious attack on the depression?

6. Did the Social Security program alleviate the needs of the elderly?

## Documents 1–2: Plans Proliferate

*As the depression worsened month after month and year after year, many plans to care for the elderly were proposed, but two of them stand out, although they were not the main tenets of the promoters' programs. These two plans are excerpted here.*

### Document 1: Huey Long supports pensions[1]

*Senator Huey Long of Louisiana was a flamboyant politician who angered many people, but who seemed to have unlimited support from his base in Louisiana. He was in the U.S. Senate for only three years before he was assassinated in Baton Rouge, Louisiana. Long became famous for his "Share Our Wealth" program, sometimes called "Soak the Rich." His program was basically a redistribution-of-wealth scheme, but he did include pensions for older people as a part of it. In four repetitive speeches in the Senate in 1934 and 1935, Long mentioned the pension plan while he was promoting his larger program. The following excerpts are examples. Long probably was reacting mostly to his own political base in Louisiana, which was one of the poorer states in the country. Elderly people there were suffering very much.*

3. Old-age pensions:

Everyone has begun to realize something must be done for our old people who work out their lives, feed and clothe children and are left penniless in their declining years. They should be made to look forward to their mature years for comfort rather than fear. We propose that, at the age of 60, every person should begin to draw a pension from our Government of $30 per month, unless the person of 60 or over has an income of over $1,000 per year or is worth $10,000, which is two thirds of the average wealth in America, even figured on a basis of it being frozen into a few hands. Such a pension would retire from labor those persons who keep the rising generations from finding employment.

\* \* \*

Ladies and gentlemen, the only means by which any practical relief may be given to the people is in taking the money with which to give such relief from the big fortunes at the top. . . .

### *Document 2: EPIC includes pensions*[2]

*Upton Sinclair became famous at the turn of the century for his muckraking novel,* The Jungle. *He always took a radical, socialist view of the world, and that was just as true during the Great Depression as it had been before. Sinclair developed a program called End Poverty in California (EPIC). It became popular enough that he was convinced to change his party registration to Democrat so that he could run for governor of California in 1934 with a better chance of winning. EPIC was a 12-point program that included issuing scrip currency, taxing idle land, and creating a large state-run bartering system. Point 10 was a plan to give pensions of $50 per month to all needy persons older than sixty. The existing pension program in the state was much lower and was difficult for most people to qualify for. This part of EPIC was very popular in California. The following excerpt comes from a pamphlet issued by EPIC.*

### THE PROBLEM OF PENSIONS

The last three planks of the EPIC platform provide pensions for the aged, the blind, the disabled, and the widowed mothers of dependent children. The law provides inadequate pensions at present, and they are so hedged around with red tape that few persons get them. We have in mind pensions which will be paid, and opponents of the EPIC Plan estimate the cost of such pensions and ask us where we are going to get the money; having done this, they go ahead and list pensions plans of their own, and don't tell us where they are going to get the money! Even Governor Merriam has not been able to refrain from promising old age pensions. The most reactionary Republican in the State of California had to say something to get him some votes! . . .

### Documents 3–5: Townsend Steps Forward

*The most popular and widely debated pension program was proposed by an elderly doctor in California, Dr. Francis E. Townsend. He was unsophisticated in the political world and, despite the popularity of his plan among average persons, he soon ran into questions he could not answer and opposition from people who saw it, not as a pension plan, but as a plan to redistribute wealth. The documents available about the Townsend plan are numerous; those excerpted here are a sampling.*

*Document 3: The Plan in brief*[3]

*During the debate over Townsend's proposals, his organization put out a one-page flyer with the tenets of the program listed.*

The Townsend Plan
—in Brief

Have the National Government enact legislation to the effect that all citizens of the United States—man or woman—over the age of 60 years may retire on a pension of $200 per month on the following conditions:

1. That they engage in no further labor, business or profession for gain.
2. That their past life is free from habitual criminality.
3. That they take oath to, and actually do spend, within the confines of the United States, the entire amount of their pension within thirty days after receiving same.

Have the National Government create the revolving fund by levying a general sales tax; have the rate just high enough to produce the amount necessary to keep the Old Age Revolving Pensions Fund adequate to pay the monthly pensions.

Have the act so drawn that such sales tax can only be used for Old Age Revolving Pension Fund.

OLD AGE REVOLVING PENSIONS, INC.

148 American Avenue             Long Beach, California

*Document 4: The Plan analyzed*[4]

*The Townsend Plan generated so much interest that the organization produced many publications explaining and justifying the proposed program. One of these was an analysis that was widely circulated.*

. . . Approximately 8,000,000 people will be eligible to apply for the pension. Economists estimate that each person spending $200.00 per month creates a job for one additional worker. The retirement of all citizens of 60 and over from all productive industry and gainful occupation, will thereby create jobs for 8,000,000 workers which will solve our national labor problem.

RETIREMENT ON A MONTHLY PENSION OF $200

The spending of $200 per month is for a constructive purpose. First, to place an adequate amount of buying power in the hands of the citizens which will permit them to satisfy their wants that have been so restricted for the past four years. Second, to create such a demand for new goods of all descriptions that all manufacturing plants in the country will be called upon to start their wheels of production at full speed and provide jobs for all workers.

This money made suddenly available to the channels of trade will immediately start a tremendous flood of buying, since the country has been on short commodity rations for the past four years, and since all sections of the country will be affected alike (the old are everywhere) and the poorest sections will at once become important buying centers.

All factories and avenues of production may be expected to start producing at full capacity and all workers called into activity at high wages, since there will be infinitely more jobs available and many less workers to fill the jobs, the old folks having retired from competition for places as producers. . . .

### PENSIONERS TO RETIRE WITHOUT FURTHER GAIN FROM LABOR OR PROFESSION

This is an important feature of the plan since the idea is to create jobs for the young and able, eliminating competition for such jobs and positions on the part of elderly people.

Consumption of the products of farm and factory is the vital problem now facing our nation. The success of this plan is based entirely on the creation of jobs of production and by retiring all those pensioned, with adequate spending power, that they may consume for all their need in comforts, necessities and pleasure. . . .

### COSTS OF MAINTAINING THE HUGE REVOLVING FUND

The unthinking see a great increase in the cost of living due to the necessity for the retailer to raise his prices to meet the government tax for maintaining the pension roll. He fails to take into consideration the fact that the elimination of poor houses, organized state and county relief agencies, public and private pension systems, community chests, etc., are now costing the country many millions of dollars per month that the Townsend plan would eliminate. And, too, would not the cost of crime and insane asylums be greatly reduced after the public became assured of the permanency of our prosperity? Further, the tremendous increase in the volume of retail business which this huge revolving fund would insure makes certain that bigger profits would be possible to the retailer through his old rates than ever before and make unnecessary the advance in prices on any articles except those classified as luxuries. Estimated from the sources available a tax of 10% will be ample to raise this fund and the tax can be materially lowered as the volume of trade increases. . . .

## SALES TAX TO BE USED EXCLUSIVELY FOR THE PENSIONS

It is the intent of the plan to apply the sales tax solely to the one purpose of maintaining the pensions roll until such time as the public becomes fully assured of the beneficent and fair system of taxation involved in a universal retail tax. Here is the only fair system of taxation for all that can be devised. Every individual who enjoys the benefits of the numerous social agencies maintained for his benefit, such as schools, police protection, sanitation, public health supervision and the thousand and one functions of government, should be compelled to carry his share of the costs just in proportion to his ability to do so; that is, in proportion to his ability to spend money. This compels the child to become a taxpayer at an early age and accustoms him to the idea that he must do his share throughout his life.

## NO CHANGE IN FORM OF GOVERNMENT

This plan of Old Age Revolving Pensions interferes in no way with out present form of government, profit system of business or change of specie in our economic setup. . . .

## THE MEANING OF SECURITY TO HUMANITY

Here lies the true value in the Townsend Plan. Humanity will be forever relieved from the fear of destitution and want. The seeming need for sharp practices and greedy accumulation will disappear. Benevolence and kindly consideration for others will displace suspicion and avarice, brotherly love and tolerance will blossom into full flower and the genial sun of human happiness will dissipate the dark clouds of distrust and gloom and despair.

*Document 5: Townsend defends himself*[5]

*As the Townsend Plan grew in popularity, it could not be ignored. Even after Roosevelt proposed his version of old-age assistance, support for Townsend's ideas continued to grow. It was such a generous program that many elderly people continued to hope that it could be enacted. To receive $200 per month with only the conditions that the person over sixty retire and that the money had to be spent within thirty days was truly "pie in the sky." Townsend was no economist, and he was a naïve and simple man. When Congress held hearings on his proposal in 1935, he had to defend his ideas. The following are excerpts from Townsend's Congressional testimony.*

(The Committee challenged Dr. Townsend relentlessly about the practicality of his plan, resulting in this admission.)

*Dr. Townsend.* "It has been very obvious to all of us that it would be quite impossible to start pensioning all of the old folks who have attained the age of 60 at one particular time, but it is also very obvious that it will take several years even to register them—a good many months. Now, if we were to start at the age of 75, we will say, and register these old folks as rapidly as possible and place them upon a $200 per month basis of pensioning, by the time we got down to the 60-year-olds, all the way through, time enough would have elapsed and the new amount of money put into circulation would so stimulate the productive ability of America, that we could easily take care of these classes as they came along on a $200 a month basis. . . . Nobody has been fool enough to expect that we could take 10 millions of old folk and put them immediately on a $200 a month basis without putting this country into debt considerably to carry it. There has never been any idea that 10 millions would be retired immediately. But we can eventually do it by starting at a certain age, and the productive increase due to this power of buying which these elderly people would have would un-questionably so stimulate the productivity of America that the taxes of 2 per cent would be ample to eventually retire them at that age."

*The Chairman.* "We are not going to prolong the hearing by debating the ques-tion further, but evidently you must know that the people who are writing these letters, inundating Congress with letters by the carload, must have had it sold to them on the theory that just as soon as this law is enacted they will immediately go on the pay roll. That is evidently the way they understand it, and you are bound to know they understand it that way."

*Dr. Townsend.* "I cannot help that. We all expect to go on that pay roll." . . .

*   *   *

*(This exchange concerns the potential impact of the Townsend Plan's taxes on the value of the dollar.)*

*Mr. Hill.* "Dr. Townsend, I understood you to say that in 1929 the dollar turned over 132 times."

*Dr. Townsend.* "Yes, sir."

*Mr. Hill.* "What do you estimate would be the turn-over under the provisions of this bill?"

*Dr. Townsend.* "It should be vastly increased."

*Mr. Hill.* "About how much?"

*Dr. Townsend.* "Over anything we have ever known. I do not know that there is any particular way of making a definite estimate. I figure that under this system of taxation whereby everybody gets his shoulder under the load, making it so light that no one will feel it, particularly, seeing to it that a sufficient amount of money is in circulation constantly, forced there by the strength of the National Government, we shall be able to create a state of business that will quadruple anything we have ever known."

*Mr. Hill.* "Quadruple? That is multiplied four times?"

*Dr. Townsend.* "Yes, sir."

*Mr. Hill.* "Say, 528 times under the plan of this bill; $1 would turn over 528 times."

*Dr. Townsend.* "Approximately."

*Mr. Hill.* "That is, in a year?"

*Dr. Townsend.* "Yes."

*Mr. Hill.* "That would be 528 transactions on the average for a dollar?"

*Dr. Townsend.* "Yes, sir."

*Mr. Hill.* "Each transaction would bear a 2 per cent tax. The burden of tax that each dollar would carry would be twice 528, or $10.56."

*Dr. Townsend.* "Then we will easily reduce the tax, the rate of tax that is provided for in the bill. It can be reduced until no one will know that he is paying a tax. It will be insignificant—a half of 1 per cent will carry the entire pension roll, once we get fairly going under this system." . . .

\* \* \*

*(This exchange concerns potential adverse impacts from the taxes of the Townsend Plan.)*

*Dr. Townsend.* "May I speak a word in reply to that?" "Gentlemen, think back a little bit. We had a war 20 years ago."

*Mr. Knutson.* "Yes."

*Dr. Townsend.* "If an increase in price means a tax, we paid a 100 per cent tax at that time and liked it. It was the best period of prosperity this country ever saw."

*Mr. Knutson.* "And what followed it?"

*Dr. Townsend.* "What followed it? Never mind what followed. We are not going to have any such thing as that follow. We propose a prosperity based on the turn-over of money such as we had in that day, and we are going to keep it up."

*Mr. Knutson.* "As I understand it, then, this is a bill to abolish the morning after the night before, speaking in terms of economics."

*Dr. Townsend.* "This is going to abolish the morning after, certainly."

\* \* \*

*(This exchange concerns one of the key flaws in the Townsend Plan, i.e., how to determine that the pensioner has in fact spent the monthly allotment in the month received.)*

*Senator Barkley.* "How are you going to determine that he has spent it for commodities at the end of the month?"

*Dr. Townsend.* "The banker will be in a position to know."

*Senator Barkley.* "How?"

*Dr. Townsend.* "It will be a very difficult thing to ascertain."

*Senator Barkley.* "The banker has got to be the inspector for every one of the pensioners who has an account in his bank?"

*Dr. Townsend.* "Not necessarily the banker."

*Senator Barkley.* "Somebody will have to do the inspecting."

*Dr. Townsend.* "But not necessarily the banker. Everyone who is spending the money, who is known to be the recipient of it, is going to have neighbors immediately about him."

*Senator Barkley.* "So the neighbors are going to watch him?"

*Dr. Townsend.* "The neighbors are going to watch him, certainly."

## Documents 6–8: The Social Security Program Prevails

*By 1934, President Roosevelt had recognized the threat of the Townsend Movement, and he moved to add an old-age pension program to his New Deal program. He appointed a special committee with Frances Perkins, the secretary of labor, to head it. The committee's proposal included much more than just a pension program, but that is the popular perception of it. The unemployment assistance and aid to dependent mothers and children are known to most people today, but most people do not realize that they were part of the original Social Security Act.*

*In the following documents, one can see how the committee operated and some of the major issues as the plan was developed. Also included is an article from the popular press about the bill.*

### Document 6: Secretary Perkins explains[6]

*In February 1935, Secretary of Labor Frances Perkins gave a radio address on the committee's report and the proposal made by President Roosevelt. Her broadcast included the whole scope of the program, but the section here deals primarily with the old-age portion of the proposal.*

. . . The program now under consideration represents, I believe, a most significant step in our National development, a milestone in our progress toward the better-ordered society. . . .

The process of recovery is not a simple one. . . . The task of recovery is inseparable from the fundamental task of social reconstruction.

Among the objectives of that reconstruction, President Roosevelt in his message of June 8, 1934, to the Congress placed "the security of the men, women and children of the Nation first." He went on to suggest the social insurances with which European countries have had a long and favorable experience as one means of providing safeguards against "misfortunes which cannot be wholly eliminated in this man-made world of ours."

Subsequent to this message he created the Committee on Economic Security, of which I have the honor to be the chairman, . . . The recommendations of that committee are embodied in the economic security bill, now pending in Congress. The measures we propose do not by any means provide a complete and permanent solution of our difficulties. If put into effect, however, they will provide a greater degree of security for the American citizen and his family than he has heretofore known. . . .

It may come as a surprise to many of us that we in this country should be so far behind Europe in providing our citizens with those safeguards which assure a decent standard of living in both good times and bad, but the reasons are not far to seek. We are much younger than our European neighbors. Our abundant pioneer days are not very far behind us. With unlimited opportunities, in those days, for the individual who wished to take advantage of them, dependency seemed a reflection on the individual himself, rather than the result of social or economic conditions. There seemed little need for any systematic organized plan, such as has now become necessary.

It has taken the rapid industrialization of the last few decades, with its mass-production methods, to teach us that a man might become a victim of circumstances far beyond his control, and finally it "took a depression to dramatize for us the appalling insecurity of the great mass of the population, and to stimulate interest in social insurance in the United States." . . .

The American program for economic security now before our Congress follows no single pattern. It is broader than social insurance, and does not attempt merely to copy a European model. . . .

I come now to the other major phase of our program. The plan for providing against need and dependency in old age is divided into three separate and distinct parts. We advocate, first, free Federally-aided pensions for those now old and in need; second, a system of compulsory contributory old-age insurance for workers in the lower income brackets, and third, a voluntary system of low-cost annuities purchasable by those who do not come under the compulsory system.

Enlightened opinion has long since discarded the old poor-house method of caring for the indigent aged, and 28 States already have old-age pension laws. Due to financial difficulties, many of these laws are now far less effective than they were intended to be. Public sentiment in this country is strongly in favor of providing these old people with a decent and dignified subsistence in their declining years. Exploiting that very creditable sentiment, impossible, hare-brained schemes for providing for the aged have sprung into existence and attracted misguided supporters. But the administration is confident that its plan for meeting the situation is both humane and practical and will receive the enthusiastic support of the people.

We propose that the Federal Government shall come to the aid of the State pension systems already in existence and stimulate the enactment of similar legislation elsewhere by grants-in-aid equal to one-half the State expenditures for such purposes but not exceeding $15 per month. This does not necessarily mean that State pensions would not anywhere exceed $30 per month. Progressive States may find it possible to grant more than $15 per month as their share. The size of the pension would, of course, be proportionate to the need of the applicant and would quite likely vary with conditions in different States. A larger pension would, for example, be necessary in certain industrial States than in communities where living conditions are easier.

For those now young or even middle-aged, a system of compulsory old-age insurance will enable them to build up, with matching contributions from their employers, an annuity from which they can draw as a right upon reaching old age. These workers will be able to care for themselves in their old age, not merely on a subsistence basis, which is all that gratuitous pensions have anywhere provided, but with a modest comfort and security. Such a system will greatly lessen the hazards of old age to the many workers who could not, unaided, provide for themselves and would greatly lessen the enormous burden of caring for the aged of future generations from public funds. The voluntary system of old-age annuities is designed to cover the same income groups as does the compulsory system, but will afford those who for many reasons cannot be included in a compulsory system an opportunity to provide for themselves.

Many of you will be interested to know that the two proposed annuity systems in no way infringe on the commercial annuity markets. . . .

This, in broad outlines, is the program now before us. We feel that it is a sound and reasonable plan and framed with due regard for the present state of economic recovery. I can do no better than to pass on to you the words with which President Roosevelt closed his letter submitting these recommendations to the Congress now in session:

*"The establishment of sound means toward a greater future economic security of the American people is dictated by a prudent consideration of the hazards involved in our national life. No one can guarantee this country against the dan-*

gers of future depressions, but we can reduce these dangers. We can eliminate many of the factors that cause economic depressions, and we can provide the means of mitigating their results. This plan for economic security is at once a measure of prevention and a method of alleviation.

"We pay now for the dreadful consequence of economic insecurity—and dearly. This plan presents a more equitable and infinitely less expensive means of meeting these costs. We cannot afford to neglect the plain duty before us. I strongly recommend action to attain the objectives sought in this report."

### Document 7: How the Committee operated[7]

*Thomas H. Eliot was one of the young men who went to Washington during the days of the New Deal to do what he could to make a difference. Although he had other jobs, he was appointed a staff member to the Committee on Economic Security. His memoirs were published in 1992 shortly after his death. His book illuminates the environment in Washington during the heady days of the early New Deal. He and the other staff members were clearly aware of the European social insurance programs, especially the idea that the programs would be partially paid for by employer and employee, but also that a major share of the cost was a part of the government's regular budget. The section below gives a glimpse into what the committee attempted and how it operated. As with the case of the Perkins document shown earlier, this deals only with the old-age part of the Social Security Act.*

Today the phrase "social security" has come to mean old age insurance, perhaps with Medicare thrown in. But the bill that became law in 1935 included many other things: grants to the states for the needy aged and the needy blind, for child welfare and public health programs, and for aid to families with dependent children, plus a payroll tax with offset provisions to induce the states to establish unemployment insurance systems. I think it was only after World War II that "social security" came to connote old age insurance, not too surprisingly, because by that time most of us had social security cards and numbers to evidence our participation in the old age insurance program.

Still, it was social insurance, not "welfare," that the president specifically mentioned when, in a message to Congress on June 15, 1934, he said: "Among our objectives I place the security of the men, women, and children of the nation first. . . security against the hazards and vicissitudes of life. . . . Next winter we may well undertake the great task of furthering the security of the citizen and his family, through social insurance. . . . I am looking for a sound means which I can recommend to provide at once security against several of the great disturbing factors in life—especially those which relate to unemployment and old age." . . .

There were other compelling political reasons for promising to take action. In increasing numbers, people—especially the elderly—were flocking to the banner of Dr. Francis Townsend, who was advocating handouts of $200 a month to everybody sixty or older, to be financed by something he called a transactions tax. The zeal of the good doctor's converts was intense, and Townsend Clubs were blossoming all over the place. Meanwhile, in the wings was Senator Huey Long, the self-styled Kingfish, recently the autocratic governor of Louisiana. Unlike most despots, Huey Long was not only smart and vulgar but funny, and hence more appealing and more dangerous. His slogans were "Share the Wealth" and "Every man a King," and it was pretty generally assumed that he had his eye on the presidency in 1936. The economy was improving somewhat, but there was a chance that in 1936 times would still be so hard that either the Democrats would dump Roosevelt or both of the old parties could be defeated by an independent candidate shouting populist slogans.

Times were indeed hard, especially for those whom Roosevelt targeted as objects of social insurance: the unemployed and the aged. Many millions were unemployed. Millions more were old and destitute. In the previous decade most states, often spurred on by the Fraternal Order of Eagles, had enacted old age pension laws, under which monthly grants to the needy aged enabled them to live at home rather than be herded into public poorhouses. Alas, the Depression had depleted every state's resources, and those monthly payments had shrunk and shrunk again, from $30 down to a national average of $16.28, and, in thirteen states, less than ten dollars. Starvation was a reality in the Great Depression. . . .

But in one respect—and this is what impressed me as I sought to learn more about the subject I was grappling with—all the European systems were alike. All were "contributory," but in everyone of them the "contributions" from employers and employees were not enough to meet the full cost of the program. The government, out of its general funds, made up the difference. I knew that the president was intent on having a contributory system here: I could only hope that this was the kind he would prefer. . . .

On August 12, 1934, before the committee had had its first meeting, Miss Perkins invited Witte, Altmeyer, and me to accompany her to the White House. We were with the president for nearly an hour, in the course of which one of us mentioned that some people were suggesting that unemployment insurance should be a federal function. "Oh no," said Roosevelt quickly, "we've got to leave all that we can to the states. All the power shouldn't be in the hands of the federal government. Look—just think what would happen if all the power *was* concentrated here, and *Huey Long* became president!" . . .

The committee had agreed on recommending a national old age insurance system based primarily on payroll taxes on employers and taxes on employees' wages and salaries. Miss Perkins and Harry Hopkins had spent an evening with the president and left believing that they had his full approval of the comprehensive bill they were discussing, including its old age insurance provisions. In that belief they had a Committee Report drafted, and on January 17 the White House issued a statement summarizing that report.

. . . Late the same day word came from the White House that the bill that was supposedly ready for introduction would have to be changed; the taxes for old age insurance would have to be increased, so that ultimately the reserve fund would be nearly six times greater than the committee had contemplated and no "government contribution" would be necessary, ever. . . .

Some newspapers were off the beam, too, in their criticism of the bill after it was introduced and its contents were made public. They assailed the new bill as a hodgepodge, an ill-drafted legislative monstrosity. Their criticisms on this score were uninformed. The chief complaint was that various subjects were scattered throughout the measure: thus, one chapter or "title" imposed a tax for old age insurance, while the provisions for old age benefits appeared in a separate title many pages distant. The critics did not know—or perhaps they did—that this awkward arrangement was deliberate. It was designed to make it easier for the Supreme Court to sustain the measure's validity—not to fool the Court, but to give the justices a technical peg on which to hang their hats if they so desired. Meanwhile, some social security experts joined the chorus, citing other examples of bad draftsmanship; again, their examples did not prove their point. They objected to substance, not form; they preferred ways of promoting unemployment compensation different from the tax-offset device included in the bill.

Yet the original bill was certainly not well drafted. It was indeed a hodgepodge—not of unrelated subjects, but of drafts prepared by various people, drafts that I either accepted in *toto* . . . or edited far too hastily. . . .

. . . Once, on a Friday, several members expressed dismay that, in the bill, the old age benefits stopped at the recipient's death; no provision was made for his widow. (It was assumed that the recipient would be male!) The chairman then directed Mr. Beaman and me to draft new sections to include benefits for widows. Over the weekend Mr. Beaman, Alanson Willcox and I worked late into the night, even getting an actuary to advise us. On Monday, when we presented our draft to the committee, the members discussed it for five minutes and then voted to drop the whole subject. Not until the law was amended in 1939 did old age insurance become the "Old Age and Survivors' Insurance" that we know today. . . .

As for old age insurance, I still had doubts about its constitutionality, and regretted the absence of "government contributions" and the consequent high rate of the regressive tax on wages (the employee half of the payroll tax); but it was an awful lot better than nothing, and did put a quietus on such movements as the Townsend Plan. Furthermore, it could be amended to rectify what I thought were its chief shortcomings—as, indeed, it was in 1939.

### Document 8: The press comments[8]

*In the fall of 1935,* The Nation *provided its view of the Social Security Act, giving both the pros and cons of the law.*

. . . The subject of social insurance, in which economics, politics, statistics, social policy, trade unionism, wages, and industrial production are intertwined, was barely discussed in the United States prior to the President's message to Congress in June, 1934, when he promised to undertake "the great task of furthering the security of the citizen and his family through social insurance." For more than half a century social-insurance programs have been keen political issues throughout Europe, but here there has not been even academic interest; our newspapers gave the subject no notice until a year ago and have given it very little since. Everywhere abroad social-insurance measures have been championed chiefly by organized labor. Our labor movement has either opposed them or given half-hearted and uninformed support.

No wonder, therefore, that the President's speech of June 8, 1934, fell like a bombshell on the country. The most ardent advocates of social insurance in America were bewildered by its boldness and political audacity. Even more deluding was the almost universal approval which greeted the speech. Everybody jumped on the social-security bandwagon. Governors made it their campaign issues. Congressmen spoke for it. Candidates for state legislatures made it a plank in their platforms. Even candidates for city councils and sheriff's offices felt compelled to declare themselves in favor of social security. And when, on November 6, 1934, the American electorate gave the President the most Democratic Congress in two generations, hopes were raised sky-high.

Like all nine days' wonders, it was too good to be true. The President spoke of "social security," and who could be against that? True, he did mention "social insurance," but why bother to discover the meaning of so strange a term? Of several hundred articles and newspaper stories on social security appearing during the past year, less than a score attempted an analysis of social insurance. Social security was identified with old-age pensions, for an ardent twenty-year campaign for old-age security had brought about a tremendous popular demand for old-age protection. More than half the states had actually adopted pension laws. This movement had gained such popularity that it attracted a galaxy of nondescript promoters ranging from the Fraternal Order of Eagles to the messianic Dr. Townsend. The country was thus clamoring for old-age pensions. But the Administration, symbolized by Madame Secretary Perkins, seemed for a while almost totally unaware of this uproar. Miss Perkins had been principally concerned with the problem of unemployment insurance. . . .

Although handicapped by a total lack of information on a subject requiring years of study, the staff did draft a reasonable plan, which was approved by the Cabinet committee and incorporated in the original bill.

This plan provided for payroll contributions from employers and employees to reach 2½ per cent each within the next twenty years. Pensions to all insured were to begin in 1942 out of money borrowed from the accumulated fund. After thirty or thirty-five years the federal government was to reimburse the loan. But when the President learned that the federal government would owe the fund more than a billion dollars by 1970 he ordered his Secretary of the Treasury—a member of the Cabinet committee, who apparently had approved this scheme before it was introduced—to insist that under no circumstances would the federal government assume any financial responsibility. The plan must be made self-sustaining.

Under White House pressure the House committee stepped up the contributions to a total of 6 per cent within twelve years, This transfers the entire burden of old-age dependency after 1942 to the backs of the young workers and their employers, to the exclusion of the well-to-do, who have shared in the maintenance of the aged poor since the establishment of the Elizabethan poor-law system three centuries ago. Since industry will make every effort to pass on its levy to the consumers, it means that the young employees—in their dual role of workers and consumers—will bear the major cost of the accumulated problem of old-age dependency. No other nation has ever put into operation a plan of this nature without government contributions derived from the higher-income groups. . . .

. . . The federal grants for pensions in old age, to dependent mothers, to the blind, and to varied child-welfare and public-health activities are sound and constitutional. They mark truly advanced steps and genuine progress. The unemployment-insurance and old-age contributory insurance plans, however, are administratively and socially unwise.

The effect this bill may have on the American social-insurance movement is of vital importance. Social insurance is recognized today as offering the only practicable instrument for meeting the problem of insecurity arising from modern industrial development. It is used in communist as well as capitalist and fascist countries. Its chief asset lies in its power to distribute the cost over all groups in society—the rich as well as the poor. But in placing the entire burden of insecurity upon the workers and industry, to the exclusion of the well-to-do in the nation, the present social-security bill violates the most essential modern principles of social insurance. There is also grave danger that the administrative perplexities inherent in the bill, to say nothing of possible court nullification, may deal a death blow to the entire movement in the United States.

## Part B: Isolation and Antiwar Sentiment

### Background

*As mentioned earlier, World War I was a devastating event that scarred the American public for many years to come. Even before the war ended, but especially in the aftermath, people began to question why the United States had entered the war, what the country's goals had been, and what the war had achieved. They questioned President Wilson's statements that this was a "war to end wars" and "a war to make the world safe for democracy." For them, these were promises that rang hollow soon after the war ended.*

*American casualties and costs in the war were very small compared to the rest of the world, but were shocking, nonetheless, especially the massive destruction of property and the loss of life on a scale never seen before.*

*Soon after the war, Americans took various paths to try to guarantee that nothing like this could happen again. The Kellogg-Briand Pact was one international example in which the United States took a leading role. But various other actions were taken to try to prevent such destruction in the future. The United States, by its refusal to join the League of Nations and other actions, retreated to its traditional policy of isolation from international diplomacy. By the 1930s, efforts were made in Congress to impose legal restraints on the president from taking actions that would drag America into another foreign war. These Neutrality Acts were popular with the public, but they were also controversial. Average Americans began to say that war had to be ended and that they would not participate in any future wars. The antiwar sentiment was strong among the young people, especially college students.*

### Questions

In reading these documents, the student should ask and answer several questions to put these activities in the proper context.

1. Why did Congress take the lead in passing neutrality legislation?
2. From reading his comments and the documents, do you see any special motivation in the actions of Senator Nye?
3. How realistic do you see the neutrality laws to be?

4. Why did the student antiwar movements receive such an enthusiastic response?
5. Why was the Veterans of Future Wars organization misunderstood to be a peace or antiwar movement?

## Documents 1–5: The Move for Neutrality

*By the 1930s, the threat to peace in Europe was apparent once again. Mussolini came to power in Italy, and Hitler assumed power in Germany in 1933. Fascism seemed on the rise around the world, including in Japan. In this situation, more people wanted to know why the United States entered the Great War in 1917, and they wanted ways to avoid getting involved again in that kind of struggle.*

### Document 1: The Nye Report[9]

*In 1934, a special Senate committee was created to investigate the role the munitions industry and American financial institutions played in American entry into World War I. There was a widespread feeling in the country that these businesses had unduly influenced American entry. The Democratic majority of the Senate selected a Midwestern Republican senator known for his isolationist sentiments, Gerald Nye of North Dakota, to head the committee.*

*Officially known as the Senate Munitions Committee, it was more commonly called the Nye Committee. The committee issued its reports in 1936, but the hearings stopped abruptly in 1936 because the Democrats, angry over Nye's attacks on former President Woodrow Wilson, cut off funding. But the Nye Committee made a dramatic splash in the country. A small portion of its report follows.*

### FINDINGS
### II. THE SALES METHODS OF THE MUNITIONS COMPANIES

The Committee finds, . . . that almost without exception, the American munitions companies investigated have at times resorted to such unusual approaches, questionable favors and commissions, and methods of "doing the needful" as to constitute, in effect, a form of bribery of foreign governmental officials or of their close friends in order to secure business. . . .

The committee finds such practices on the part of any munitions company, domestic or foreign, to be highly unethical, a discredit to American business, and an unavoidable reflection upon those American governmental agencies which have unwittingly aided in the transactions so contaminated. . . .

The committee finds, further, that not only are such transactions highly unethical, but that they carry within themselves the seeds of disturbance to the peace and stability of those nations in which they take place. . . .

The committee finds, further, that the intense competition among European and American munitions companies with the attendant bribery of governmental officials tends to create a corrupt officialdom, and thereby weaken the remaining democracies of the world at their head. . . .

### III. THEIR ACTIVITIES CONCERNING PEACE EFFORTS

. . . The committee finds, further, that munitions companies engaged in bribery find themselves involved in the civil and military politics of other nations, and that this is an unwarranted form of intrusion into the affairs of other nations and undesirable representation of the character and methods of the people of the United States. . . .

### V. THEIR RELATIONS WITH THE UNITED STATES GOVERNMENT

. . . The committee finds that by their aid and assistance to munitions companies the War, Navy, and Commerce Departments condone, in effect, in the eyes of those foreign officials cognizant of the details of the transactions the unethical practices of the companies which characterize their foreign sales efforts. . . .

The committee finds that the War Department encourages the sale of modern equipment abroad in order that the munitions companies may stay in business and be available in the event of another war, and that this consideration outranks the protection of secrets. . . .

The committee finds that as improvements are developed here, often with the cooperation of the military services, and these improvements presumably give the United States a military advantage, we are in the anomalous position of being forced to let the other nations have the advantages which we have obtained for ourselves, in order to keep the munitions manufacturers going, so that the United States can take advantage of the same improvements which its companies have sold abroad.

### Document 2: Defense of the Nye Committee[10]

*The initial report of the Nye Committee brought a storm of controversy, especially regarding the committee's comments about President Wilson. An editorial in the* Christian Century *discusses the reaction of Congress in cutting funds for the committee.*

Seldom has the nation witnessed a more puerile or uncalled for performance than the uproar over the Nye committee which has burst forth in Washington. Senator Nye is open to a certain amount of blame for having afforded the pretext for the hullaballoo. But those democratic senators who have seized on this pretext to start beating their chests, tearing their hair, and shouting that they will vote no more funds for the arms inquiry are putting themselves in a position where the country should, and probably will, call them sharply to account. Voting no more funds for the inquiry means, in plain language, stopping the investigation at this point. And this is an extremely bad point, from the standpoint of the national welfare, at which to stop; just as it is an extremely good point from the standpoint of the principal financial interests now under scrutiny—the so-called "international bankers." In a few weeks, after the initial outburst has died down, hosts of plain Americans will begin to ask why the explosion should have come just at this point: why senators who had been in favor of the investigation so long as it stuck to munition makers should so quickly have had this spectacular change of heart when it began to penetrate to the citadels of financial interest and power. As has been said, it was poor strategy on the part of Senator Nye and Senator Clark to hand these senators the pretext for outrage which they seized upon so avidly. For while the senatorial inquisitors would doubtlessly defend an investigation of the relation of this country to the secret treaties in 1917 as having an important bearing on the justification of the United States in entering the war, yet it is hard to see why a dispute over the veracity of President Wilson had to be dragged in. However, the fact that it was dragged in offers no excuse whatever for refusing to investigate further the processes by which the United States became involved in the war.

### Document 3: Nye indicts international bankers[11]

*In June 1936, Senator Nye issued his committee's supplemental report, which took on the financial institutions, especially the loans they made during the first World War before America joined the Allies. This, along with the report on munitions makers, further heightened the interest in neutrality and isolation.*

The Committee finds that:

1. It is most important for the Nation and Congress to have full and exact information concerning all the changes in neutrality policy made by the administration and the reasons for these changes. Congress was not kept accurately informed during the neutrality years of 1914-17. . . .

2. Loans to belligerents militate against neutrality, for when only one group of belligerents can purchase and transport commodities the loans act in favor of that belligerent. They are especially unneutral when used to convert this country into an auxiliary arsenal for that belligerent who happens to control the seas, for that arsenal then becomes the subject of the military strategy of the other belligerent.

3. Such loans cannot but profoundly affect the neutrality of mind and spirit of those holding them. . . .

4. Loans extended to the Allies in 1915 and 1916, led to a very considerable war boom and inflation. . . .

5. The nature of such a war-boom inflation is that, like all inflations, an administration is almost powerless to check it, once the movement is well started. . . .

6. The foreign policy of the United States from 1914 to 1917 was, in fact, affected by our growing trade with the Allies as well as by natural sympathies. The neutral rights we claimed were simply not enforced against our largest customers. . . .

7. It is not desirable for the Nation that any foreign belligerent or any bankers representing them be allowed to get into a position as they did in 1915, when sudden stoppage of the support of sterling (or any other foreign exchange) can influence an administration into a reversal of our neutrality policy. . . .

### Document 4: Neutrality Act of 1937[12]

*Congress passed neutrality acts in 1935, 1936, and 1937 as the rise of fascism in Europe became more serious. These laws were designed to prevent a situation from developing like the one before World War I in 1914. This excerpt includes the significant portions of the 1937 revision.*

JOINT RESOLUTION . . .
EXPORT OF ARMS, AMMUNITION, AND IMPLEMENTS OF WAR
SECTION 1. (a) Whenever the President shall find that there exists a state of war between, or among, two or more foreign states, the President shall proclaim such fact, and it shall be unlawful to export, or attempt to export, or cause to be exported, arms, ammunition, or implements of war from any place in the United States to any belligerent state named in such proclamation, or to any neutral state for transshipment to, or for the use of, any such belligerent state.
(b) The President shall, from time to time, by proclamation, extend such embargo upon the export of arms, ammunition, or implements of war to other states as and when they may become involved in such war.
(c) Whenever the President shall find that a state of civil strife exists in a foreign state and that such civil strife is of a magnitude or is being conducted under such conditions that the export of arms, ammunition, or implements of war from the United foreign state would threaten or endanger the peace of the United States, the President shall proclaim such fact, and it shall thereafter be unlawful to export, or attempt to export, or cause to be exported, arms, ammunition, or implements of war from any place in the United States to

such foreign state, or to any neutral state for transshipment to, or for the use of, such foreign state. . . .

EXPORT OF OTHER ARTICLES AND MATERIALS

SEC. 2. (a) Whenever the President shall have issued a proclamation under the authority of section 1 of this Act . . . he shall so proclaim, and it shall thereafter be unlawful, except under such limitations and exceptions as the President may prescribe as to lakes, rivers, and inland waters bordering on the United States, and as to transportation on or over lands bordering on the United States, for any American vessel to carry such articles or materials to any belligerent state, or to any state wherein civil strife exists, . . . The President shall by proclamation from time to time definitely enumerate the articles and materials which it shall be unlawful for American vessels to so transport. . . .

FINANCIAL TRANSACTIONS

SEC. 3. (a) Whenever the President shall have issued a proclamation under the authority of section 1 of this Act, it shall thereafter be unlawful for any person within the United States to purchase, sell, or exchange bonds, securities, or other obligations of the government of any belligerent state or of any state wherein civil strife exists, named in such proclamation, . . .

(b) The provisions of this section shall not apply to a renewal or adjustment of such indebtedness as may exist on the date of the President's proclamation. . . .

AMERICAN VESSELS PROHIBITED FROM CARRYING ARMS TO BELLIGERENT STATES

SEC. 6. (a) Whenever the President shall have issued a proclamation under the authority of section 1 of this Act, it shall thereafter be unlawful, until such proclamation is revoked, for any American vessel to carry any arms, ammunition, or implements of war to any belligerent state, or to any state wherein civil strife exists, named in such proclamation, or to any neutral state for transshipment to, or for the use of, any such belligerent state or any such state wherein civil strife exists. . . .

SUBMARINES AND ARMED MERCHANT VESSELS

SEC. 8. Whenever, during any war in which the United States is neutral, the President shall find that special restrictions placed on the use of the ports and territorial waters of the United States by the submarines or armed merchant vessels of a foreign state, will serve to maintain peace between the United States and foreign states, or to protect the commercial interests of the United States and its citizens, or to promote the security of the United States, and shall make proclamation thereof, it shall thereafter be unlawful for any such submarine or armed merchant vessel to enter a port or the territorial waters of the United States or to depart therefrom, except under such conditions and subject to such limitations as the President may prescribe. . . .

TRAVEL ON VESSELS OF BELLIGERENT STATES

SEC. 9. Whenever the President shall have issued a proclamation under the authority of section 1 of this Act it shall thereafter be unlawful for any citizen of the United States to travel on any vessel of the state or states named in such proclamation, except in accordance with such rules and regulations as the President shall prescribe: . . .

ARMING OF AMERICAN MERCHANT VESSELS PROHIBITED

SEC. 10. Whenever the President shall have issued a proclamation under the authority of section 1, it shall thereafter be unlawful, until such proclamation is revoked, for any American vessel engaged in commerce with any belligerent state, or any state wherein civil strife exists, named in such proclamation, to be armed or to carry any armament, arms, ammunition, or implements of war, except small arms and ammunition therefor which the President may deem necessary and shall publicly designate for the preservation of discipline aboard such vessels. . . .

### Document 5: Senator Nye continues his struggle[13]

*Senator Nye continued his battle to keep America out of war. As late as 1941, after World War II had been under way in Europe for two years, Congress debated a proposal to arm American merchant ships for their protection against the Germans. By this time, only Great Britain in Europe was holding out against the Axis forces. This is a portion of a speech Nye gave in the Senate in 1941.*

The resolution provides for the arming of American merchant ships, and removes any and all restrictions upon the movement of American ships. A surer way to get into war is not known than that of going out and looking and asking for war. That way invites incidents—not lone incidents, but incidents by wholesale. . . .

We are now told that the proposal pending here, constituting what amounts to a repealer of the largest part of what remains of our neutrality laws, is in no sense a declaration of war; that it is not necessarily taking a chance on leading to a declaration of war. . . .

The pending legislation, Mr. President, asking for a setting aside of more of our law of neutrality, is nothing more than one step to get rid of every bit of fortification America afforded herself against involvement in another foreign war. . . .

The nasty looking claws of war, with all of war's meanings, were overlooked as the ears were charmed with the gentle purrs that repealing the arms embargo and adopting a lend-lease program of aid to Britain and her allies were by no means acts of war, but really designed to preserve America's neutrality while at the same time helping a gallant people.

The idea had charm. It had sufficient charm to make it possible for many who are definitely against actual involvement in war to believe that we could really go for a stroll with the leper of war and come back without having caught leprosy. . . .

Well, the gloves are off now. The claws are out. The point and purpose of it all is clear to anyone who can read or think. The mouse, the American people, has been played with long enough. Now is the time to gobble it. . . .

The pending question is this and bluntly this and no less than this:

Shall America, deliberately and consciously, go all the way into a shooting war, perhaps upon two oceans, or shall it not?

That question has no trimmings and no qualifying phrases to go along with it. It is a question of war or no war, war with its inevitable A.E.F. and its inevitable slaughter, or no war with an America pursuing the independent destiny which it can so readily achieve, beholden to no one, afraid of nothing. . . .

Certainly if we get actively into the war—as the present program would lead us into it—it is going to be our war all the way, and no longer a proposition of holding Stalin's coat and handing up the sponge and water bucket to England. It is going to be our war to a point where every American voice will demand we keep our weapons at home and our dollars at home for American purposes instead of sending them into somebody else's war. . . .

Under the Neutrality Act, how many American lives have been lost on American merchant ships? None.

There is no proof that the Neutrality Act has been a failure. Indeed, there is evidence to the contrary.

To arm merchant ships invites attack.

To arm merchant ships strips them of whatever possible immunity they might enjoy as unarmed craft.

To arm merchant ships in no way strengthens them and is a deliberate jeopardizing of American lives.

Such jeopardizing of American lives with its inevitable loss of American life is the final key to war.

It cannot be forgotten that such men as will handle the guns aboard such merchant ships would be gun crews from the United States Navy, and the Navy is under orders to shoot on sight.

This is war. Whether honestly desired here, it is what I oppose. Let the proponents of shooting on sight and of arming ships to do it be honest with us and tell us that is what they want. If it is not what they want, at least it is what is guaranteed by this program.

**Documents 6–9: Isolation and Anti-war Sentiment among the People**

*During the 1930s, while the debate about neutrality raged in Congress, various people in the country became more determined to keep America out of another war. Students were particularly active in the 1930s through a number of organizations.*

*Document 6: National Committee for the Student Congress Against War[14]*

*Various student groups emerged in the 1930s to protest war and to prevent America from entering another war. As early as 1932, an organization called the Student Congress Against War conducted a program at the University of Chicago and released its broadside, "Fight War!" The document is reproduced here in part.*

National Committee for the Student Congress Against War
Students, Give Us Your Answer!
WHAT WILL YOU BE DOING IN THE NEXT WAR? Will you, too, serve as a lever in the destructive war machine?
IF YOU ARE A STUDENT IN THE R.O.T.C., YOU CANNOT IGNORE THIS QUESTION. Because the War Department is now preparing you for the dying and killing of the next war. You cannot point to the standing army and say, "they will bear the burden, the problem of war is theirs." . . . The Annual Report of the Secretary of War for 1929 tells us: "This important element of our national defense continues to supply the life blood for the Organized Reserves, furnishing, as it does, approximately 5,000 young officers each year." YOU WILL FIGHT THE WAR. THE DANGER OF WAR IS YOUR DANGER. You cannot ignore it.
**Students of science and technology,** your part in a war was clearly revealed in the events of 1917. Scientists and engineers then became adjuncts of the army and figured out methods for bigger and better destruction. Massachusetts Institute of Technology led with the establishment of a Chemical Warfare unit and with instruction in the use of poison gas. Will these events repeat themselves? You who seek to devote your lives to the conquest of nature, will you become tools for the conquest of men? You too cannot ignore the question.
**Students of the Humanities,** concerned with the progress of human thought and behavior: In 1917 all your aims were destroyed and your achievements defiled. The country was swept by a wave of hysteria deliberately provoked by the imperialists and their press. Culture that was not stifled under the weight of military propaganda appeared in hideous caricature as a part of that prop-

aganda. Men trusted as intellectual leaders of the nation betrayed that trust. Even the schools became instruments of incitement to hatred and war, manipulated by the "Committee on Public Information." . . . Can you permit a recurrence of these shameful acts of intellectual prostitution? How will you safeguard your progressive aims and achievements? Where will you stand when a new war threatens to engulf us all? The question confronts you as well as those who will handle the guns of the next war. . . .

Even now there are wars raging on both sides of the Pacific. In Manchuria, Japanese soldiers are fighting Chinese peasants, and are provoking Soviet Russia on the Siberian border. . . . In South America, students and workers are killing one another to decide whether British or American companies shall control the oil deposits of the Chaco region. The United States is involved in both disputes and has its entire navy in the Pacific Ocean, ready for action. THE DANGER OF WAR IS IMMEDIATE, AND THREATENS EVERY COUNTRY IN THE WORLD.

OUR QUESTION THEREFORE REQUIRES AN ANSWER NOW! All students should join in that answer at THE STUDENT CONGRESS AGAINST WAR. Immediate steps must be taken to formulate a program of effective opposition to war. . . .

The Students Must Answer! Act Now!

### Document 7: The American Youth Congress[15]

*One of the most successful student groups was the American Youth Congress. It promoted the "Oxford Pledge," a pledge adopted at Oxford University in England which stated that the students would not fight in any future war that Britain might fight. The pledge was brought to America where the wording was adjusted to fit the American audience. How many students took the pledge is not known, but it was popular for a while. The most successful effort of the American Youth Congress was the strike against war in April 1936 that produced the largest demonstration of any kind ever held in America. At the designated time, students walked out of classes to protest war. Numbers are not precise, but the fairly reliable estimate is that 400,000 students participated in the strike. The organization produced a manifesto called "The Declaration of the Rights of American Youth."*

On the Fourth of July one hundred and sixty years ago our forefathers declared their independence from despotic rule in order to realize their inalienable rights to life, liberty, and the pursuit of happiness.—Today our lives are threatened by war; our liberties threatened by reactionary legislation; and our right to happiness remains illusory in a world of insecurity.—Therefore, on this Fourth day of July, 1936, we, the young People of America, in Congress assembled, announce our own declaration—A Declaration of the Rights of American Youth.

We declare that our generation is rightfully entitled to a useful, creative, and happy life, the guarantees of which are: full educational opportunities, steady employment at adequate wages, security in time of need, civil rights, religious freedom, and peace.

We have a right to life! Yet we are threatened by wars that are even now being prepared by those who profit by destruction, wars from which we can reap nothing but misery, mutilation and death. We oppose this war and its trappings of militarized youth and mounting armaments. We do not want to die! We assert our right to peace and our determination to maintain peace.

We have a right to liberty! In song and legend America has been exalted as a land of the free, a haven for the oppressed. Yet on every hand we see this freedom limited or destroyed. Progressive forces are persecuted. Minority nationalities are exposed to arbitrary deportation. The Negro people are subjected to constant abuse, discrimination and lynch laws. Workers who strike for a living wage are met with increasing violence.—These we affirm to be the omens of that modern tyranny, fascism. More brutal, more vicious and reactionary than even that against which our forefathers rebelled in 1776.—We are determined to realize in actuality the ideals of a free America. We demand not only the maintenance but the extension of our elementary rights of free speech, press and assemblage. We oppose company unions and affirm the right of workers to join labor unions of their own choosing in order to advance their economic interests. We consider full academic freedom essential to progress and enlightenment. We strongly oppose fascism, with its accompanying demagogy, as a complete negation of our right to liberty.

We have a right to happiness! Our country with its natural resources and mighty industries can more than provide a life of security and comfort for all. But today we are not provided with this security, are not permitted to enjoy its comforts. We want to work, to produce, to build, but millions of us are forced to be idle. We graduate from schools and colleges, equipped for careers and professions, but there are no jobs. You can find us along the highways, or in army-supervised camps, isolated from friends and family. We refuse to be the lost generation.—We urge a system of unemployment and social insurance as an immediate improvement in the condition of unemployed youth and we affirm our right to be employed on all relief projects at equal wages for equal work.—We who are employed express our dissatisfaction with the prevailing low wages, long hours and the intense speed-up which destroys health and stunts our development. We insist upon our right to higher wages and shorter hours. For the youth on the farms, the right to work means the right to security in the possession of their farms, free from the burden of debts. We stand unalterably opposed to any program which destroys crops and livestock while millions remain unfed and undernourished.—While we proclaim the right to work for ourselves, we also proclaim the right of freedom from toil for all children for whom labor can only mean physical and mental harm. We therefore demand the abolition of child labor with full and adequate maintenance for needy children.—Our right to work includes the right of proper preparation for work. Education must be available to everyone without discrimination, poor as well as rich, Negroes as well as white, through free scholarships and government aid to needy students. Our educational system should provide for vocational training at adequate wages, under trade union supervision.—We declare that the workers of hand and brain, the producers of our wealth, the builders of our country are the decisive force with which all true friends of peace, freedom and progress must ally themselves. We recognize that we young people do not constitute a separate social group, but that our problems and aspirations are intimately bound up with those of all the people. We extend our hand in fraternal brotherhood to the youth of other lands who also strive for peace, freedom and progress. We look at this country of ours. We love it dearly; we are its flesh and marrow. We have roamed its roads; we have camped in its mountains and forests; we have smelled its rich earth; we have tended its fields and dug its earthly treasures. We have toiled in it. Because we know it so well, we know that it could be a haven of peace, security and abundance for all.

Therefore, we the young people of America, reaffirm our right to life, liberty and the pursuit of happiness. With confidence we look forward to a better life, a larger liberty and freedom. To those ends we dedicate our lives, our intelligence and our unified strength.

## Document 8: The Veterans of Future Wars manifesto[16]

*Among the most interesting, yet most unknown, student organizations of the 1930s was the Veterans of Future Wars (VFW). Begun by a small group of men at Princeton University in March 1936, it mushroomed to between 200,000 and 400,000 members two months later. In the summer, the organization was dismantled and fell into the dustbin of history. This student group was not a pacifist or antiwar group, even though it was widely perceived as such. It was, in fact, an organization of conservative young men who disliked the veterans of World War I getting pensions or bonuses for their war service. Despite the insistence of the leaders that it was not an antiwar movement, large numbers of the people who joined it believed that it actually was. Many of the chapters on various college campuses used it as an antiwar vehicle. The founder of the VFW, Lewis J. Gorin, Jr., wrote about the organization and included two documents in his book. The manifesto of the VFW follows.*

MANIFESTO OF THE VETERANS OF FUTURE WARS

WHEREAS it is inevitable that this country will be engaged in war within the next thirty years, and WHEREAS it is by all accounts likely that every man of military age will have a part in this war,

WE, THEREFORE, demand that the Government make known its intention to pay an adjusted service compensation, sometimes called a bonus, of $1,000 to every male citizen between the ages of 18 and 36, said bonus to be payable the first of June, 1965. Furthermore, we believe a study of history demonstrates that it is customary to pay all bonuses before they are due. Therefore we demand immediate cash payment, plus three per cent interest compounded annually and retroactively from the first of June, 1965, to the first of June, 1935. It is but common right that this bonus be paid now, for many will be killed or wounded in the next war, and hence they, the most deserving, will not otherwise get the full benefit of their country's gratitude;

AND WHEREAS the women of America will suffer no less than the men in the coming strife,

WE, THEREFORE, offer to the American women the following subsidiary organization: The Home Fire Division of the Veterans of Future Wars which shall be open to all mothers and future mothers of male children, and to future wives of Veterans of Future Wars. The purpose of this organization shall be to obtain for all aforementioned mothers an immediate trip to Europe in holy pilgrimage to view the future battlefields of their present and future children, and to obtain for the future wives a pension of fifty dollars per month during the remainder of their natural life.

WE REITERATE that the immediacy of our cause is twofold: (a) inasmuch as the coming war will otherwise deprive the most deserving bloc of Veterans of Future Wars of its bonus by causing its sudden and complete demise, the bonus must be paid *now*; (b) inasmuch as the coming war will both obliterate the future battlefields of our noble future dead and will deprive many American women of their subsequent means of support, the holy pilgrimage must be made *now* and the pension to the Home Fire Division, as a partial compensation for inevitable loss, must commence *immediately*.

WE HOLD THIS to be entirely in keeping with the ideals and precedents of American government; we hold it to be logical and sound; we call upon all the manhood and womanhood of America to respond to our cause. For the realization of these just demands, we shall mutually pledge our undivided and supreme efforts.

    *AMERICA FOR AMERICANS*
    THE VETERANS OF FUTURE WARS
    THE NATIONAL COUNCIL OF THE
    VETERANS OF FUTURE WARS

In the 1930s, the matter of veterans' bonuses continued as a major issue. After Congress finally voted to pay the bonus in 1936, a group of students at Princeton University started an organization called the Veterans of Future Wars to protest this payment. Here the leaders gather on the steps of one of the Princeton buildings. Veterans of Future Wars Collection. Princeton University Archives. Department of Rare Books and Special Collections. Princeton University Library.

*Document 9: The amateur Poets speak out[17]*

*Students were not the only ones to promote pacifism and to support antiwar movements. Amateur poets wrote to Presidents Hoover and Roosevelt to express similar views. These are just a few selections from the many poems written during this time, as collected by the author of this book.*

> Over Here, we'll fight to keep our freedom,
> Over Here, we'll fight for what is fair,
> Over Here, we'll fight to keep out isms,
> But will never fight over there
> Over Here, we'll gladly give our life's blood
> To defend the land we love so dear
> Over Here, we'll fight to keep our honor
> But we'll never fight over there
> We will build our defense
> To withhold all attempts
> We will unify the western hemisphere
> And our boys will be, well prepared and free
> To protect our democracy.
> And we all should be,

Proud that we are free,
And we'll keep our boys Over Here.


Dig up the corpses
Of the, oh so glorious dead.
Scatter their ashes over this
Chaotic world
So that those preparing
May breath in the
Sufferings of the
Already dead.

Exhume the bodies
From beneath their
Six foot blankets
Of bloody soil.
Bring out their skulls
Grinning at a world not yet
Satisfied.

Show them well fed rats
And rounded worms
Fat from feeding on
The stinking flesh
Of your son
And mine.

Show them youths
Unpracticed at the
Arts of being men,
Lying dead. Baited
By a new uniform
And a loud brass band
Playing "Over There."

Strip all glory
From the dead.
Show them
Medals fit not well
Upon a bony skeleton,
That praises sound so hollow
To ears that cannot hear.

We want no war—To Hell with it.
We're not raising cannon fodder;
We'll not send our sons to be killed by guns,
But we'll strive for a better tomorrow.

We want no bombs—To Hell with them,
Why wreck our home and cities;
We struggled hard and labored long,
Not to be crushed to ashes.

We want no ghastly germs or gas,
Or subs' 'neath silent seas creeping;
Wantonly taking the lives we love,
Our gallant ships secretly sinking.

These devilish implements of war,
Make vast wealth for financiers;
But if they're willing to face the fray,
We're willing to be good bankers.

Let's pray that the day be not far away,
When our City—Town or Country;
Will ring with the Joy of Brotherhood,
With Happiness Peace and Plenty.

And we'll strive for Peace a Lasting Peace,
Which nothing shall ever sever;
We'll endeavor to live as brothers all,
And blast all wars forever.

Oh, pause for awhile
And think' ere you act,
Makers of War.
Hear the cries of the wounded and dying,
Makers of War!
O'er the beat of the drums and the roar of the guns
The tears of a million mothers come
Oh, whose is the victory when fighting is done?
Makers of War?
The gain is not theirs
Whom ye send to their deaths,
Makers of War!
Oh, the power and the gold, they are yours,
Makers of War!

And ye make them wreaths and medals gay,
But turn the world into Hell to pay!!!
God grant that we learn a more righteous way,
Makers of War!

Let them fight over there,
Let them fight anywhere,
Fight in England, In Germany, France or Spain.
While other lands share
In the battle's red glare,
Our Nation will neutral remain.
Let us shout,
Let us cheer,
There's no war over here;
Let us stand by our leader in every way,
Our comrade and friend
Will protect and defend,
The Peace of the U.S.A.

## Notes

1. *Congressional Record*, 73rd Congress, v. 78, pt. 3, February 5, 1934, 1920–21; 74th Cong., 1st Session, v. 79, pt. 1, January 23, 1935, 790–92; 74th Cong., 1st Session, v. 79, pt. 2, March 12, 1935, 11516–19; 74th Congress, 1st Session, v. 79, pt. 2, July 22, 1935, 11556–57.

2. Upton Sinclair, Final EPIC: The Final Statement of the Plan, Social Security Historical Archives.

3. "The Townsend Plan—in Brief," Final EPIC: The Final Statement of the Plan, Social Security Historical Archives.

4. "The Townsend Plan: The Plan Analyzed," Final EPIC: The Final Statement of the Plan, Social Security Historical Archives.

5. Townsend Plan Hearings, Hearings before the Committee on Ways and Means of the House of Representatives, 74th Congress, First Session, on H.R. 4120 (Washington, D.C.: Government Printing Office, 1935), Testimony of Dr. F. E. Townsend, February 12, 1925, 1126–27, February 4, 1935, 735–36, 732. Hearings before the Committee on Finance of the United States Senate, 74th Congress, First Session, on S. 1130 (Washington, D.C.: Government Printing Office, 1935), Testimony of Dr. F. E. Townsend, February 16, 1935, 1024.

6. Frances Perkins, "Social Insurance for U.S.," National Radio Address delivered February 25, 1935, Social Security Administration Historical Archives.

7. Thomas H. Eliot, *Recollections of the New Deal: When the People Mattered* (Boston: Northeastern University Press, 1992), 91–95, 97–98, 101–102, 104–107, 120–21. Reprinted by permission of the Eliot estate.

8. Abraham Epstein, "Social Security Under the New Deal," *The Nation* (September 4, 1935). Reprinted by permission of *The Nation*.

9. Report of the Special Committee on Investigation of the Munitions Industry (The Nye Report), U.S. Congress, Senate, 74th Congress, 2nd session, February 24, 1936, 3–13.

10. "The Attack on the Nye Committee," *The Christian Century* (January 29, 1936). Reprinted by permission of *Christian Century*.

11. "Conclusions of the Nye Committee," Nye Committee Report, U.S. Congress, Senate, 74th Congress, 2nd session, February 24, 1936.

12. U.S. Department of State, Publication 1983, *Peace and War: United States Foreign Policy, 1931–1941* (Washington, D.C.: U.S. Government Printing Office, 1943), 355–65.

13. *Congressional Record*, 77th Congress, 1st Session, 8306–14.

14. "FIGHT WAR!" Student Congress Against War, December 27, 1932, From a December 27, 1932, pamphlet for a program held at Mandel Hall, University of Chicago. National Committee for the Student Congress Against War, Chicago Historical Society.

15. "The Declaration of the Rights of American Youth," in *Congress*, July 4, 1936, Tamiment Library, New York City. Online at Robert Cohen, "The American Student Movement of the 1930s," http://newdeal.feri.org/search_details.cfm?link=http://newdeal.feri.org/students/index.htm.

16. Veterans of Future Wars Collection, Princeton University Archives, Department of Rare Books and Special Collections, Princeton University Library.

17. Reprinted in Donald W. Whisenhunt, *Poetry of the People: Poems to the President, 1929–1945* (Bowling Green, Ohio: Popular Press, 1996), 148–49, 155–57.

# 4

# World War II

*IN 1941, FOLLOWING THE ATTACK ON Pearl Harbor, the United States entered the war that had been going on in Europe since 1939 and in Asia since the Japanese attack on China in 1937. President Franklin D. Roosevelt had resisted pressure to intervene earlier, but once America was attacked, he immediately asked for a declaration of war. The United States soon mobilized as it never had before.*

## Part A: Rosie the Riveter

### Background

*When World War II began, more military personnel were required than ever had been before. It also meant that American farms and factories had to produce as they never had in the nation's history. As more men went into military service, a shortage of workers became acute. People who had never worked in factories soon began to take the place of the men now gone to war. Some older people were called back to work to produce for the war effort. A new part of the labor scene was the number of women who took jobs in areas that had always been considered the province of men.*

*These women were nicknamed "Rosie the Riveter" because of a magazine cover by Norman Rockwell for the* Saturday Evening Post *that portrayed women factory workers, especially welders working in the shipyards producing naval vessels of all sorts. While that was a popular image, women actually pursued all types of work to further the war effort.*

*Most of the women considered themselves temporary workers who were filling in for men who were not available. A large portion of them fully intended to go back to the home when the war was over and men were back. They were doing their patriotic duty in a time of crisis.*

*The documents below reflect some of the activities of women as remembered by them in oral history projects.*

## Questions

In reading these documents, the student should ask and answer several questions to put these activities in the proper context.

1. Did women make a real contribution to the war effort?
2. How were women treated in the jobs they took that normally were considered "men's work"?
3. How were women treated in the military?
4. How serious were the shortages faced on the home front?
5. Is the image of "Rosie the Riveter" accurate?

### Documents 1–2: Rosie Remembers

*Two women who relayed stories of their work in the shipyards of California give a glimpse into how women moved into the work force. These women were typical of those who worked temporarily to help win the war. They believed they were making a contribution, but they also thought their work might bring their husbands home sooner.*

### Document 1: Katie's story[1]

*Katie, who worked in California during the war, sent her memories to the Rosie the Riveter website sponsored by the Home Front National Historical Park.*

When our daughter was six weeks old, we decided to go to California. She was so small; we carried her on a pillow. We took my baby sister, Nancy, who was fourteen years old, and that meant that all the kids had left the farm. Only Mama and Daddy were left and I don't know how they made it.

We had $25.00, but we had canned some white beans and we took those and put flour, lard, pans, and the bed in the back of the pickup. We headed out and camped and cooked by the side of the road.

It was not dangerous then, many people did it. It was July and it sure was hot. We stopped at a service station on the desert for gas and were so thirsty for a cold drink, but water was ten cents a glass. Some servicemen out on maneuvers gave us a canteen of cold water for the baby's bottle and we filled her bottle and drank the rest.

I worked the graveyard shift 12:00-8:00 a.m., in the shipyard. I took classes on how to weld. I had leather gloves, leather pants, big hood, goggles and a leather jacket. They said you weld like you crochet.

*During World War II, many women took jobs that normally were the province of men. Rosie the Riveter became an icon of the era. Numerous versions of Rosie were created, but this is one of the best known. National Archives.*

Well, I did not know how to do that, but I could sew and make a neat stitch. We held the welding rod with one hand and the torch fire in the right hand. Placed the rod in a seam and melted it down in a small bead seam and brushed it off with a steel brush.

They put me forty feet down in the bottom of the ship to be a tacker. I filled the long seams of the cracks in the ship corners full of hot lead and then brushed them good and you could see how pretty it was. The welders would come along and weld it so it would take the strong waves and deep water and heavy weight. I liked it pretty good.

I don't remember how much I got paid for working. Lots of people came to Richmond to work in the shipyards. Lots of women went to work to help with the war. I told Melvin later that I helped to make a ship for him to come home in.


### Document 2: Irene's story[2]

*Irene Carlisle came from Arkansas and worked at Moore Shipyard in Oakland, California. Her poem below was published in the* Saturday Evening Post *on February 3, 1945. Following that is her brief recollection of life in California for newcomers.*

**Welder**
*by Irene Carlisle*
Slowly upon the waves the gray ships rise,
The hammers ring on forepeak, hold and keel.
Under our gloved hands and hooded eyes
The blue arc stitches up the patterned steel.

Over the hulls, between the clanging cranes,
We climb and kneel and seam the ships together,
Women are always sewing for their men,
It tides the heart through many a bitter weather.

The chattering rivets button up the shell,
The waiting bay is laced with windy foam,
The molten stitiches [sic] glow beneath my hand,
This is the ship on which he may come home.

My dad joined the navy and was stationed here for a while, so that's why we came to live here. We came from a regular-sized house and yard, and took what we could find here for housing. Actually our apartment was okay, just very small—a studio. We finally worked up to a 1-bedroom place; housing was extremely tight, unbelievably tight. We left our Scottie with friends, and came here. We were from Fayetteville, Arkansas. Donna S. asked if shipyard workers were admired—I don't really think so. Although the attitude of the day was generally very patriotic there was a small group who resented the servicemen, the shipyard workers, "Okies and Arkies". [*sic*] Of course we fit all three groups! Some of the natives felt that we were a real inconvenience, if not an actual threat! But the general feeling was that we were all in this together, and the country was absolutely united.

Those war years were very memorable, something to treasure. Saving grease, cans, foil, toothpaste tube, I'd forgotten all those details. I remember when bananas started slowly coming back in the stores. If you were lucky enough to get one you could take it to Fenton's and they'd make you a banana split; there were not enough that Fenton's could put them back on their menu!

I was never known as a cook, but I did have one recipe that everyone liked, before the war. It was a variation of Swiss steak—round steak that had flour pounded into it, and then was simmered for a very long time, making its own gravy.

Of course meat was rationed during the war but one day word went around about horsemeat. You could buy horsemeat at a pet store and it wasn't rationed. We got some. It looked just like lean ground beef steak. I cooked it, but we didn't really feel like having any. The taste wasn't bad but we didn't really want any after all.

### Documents 3–4: Women Did Other Work

*Despite the image of Rosie the Riveter, women did not work just in shipyards. They did all kinds of work. The following two documents show some of their activities as recalled by women many years later.*

#### Document 3: Katherine worked in a factory[3]

*Katherine O'Grady lived in Rhode Island during the war. She details her life before the war and her work in a woolen mill while her husband was in the military.*

In 1939 I lived in East Providence with my aunt. I had moved from Boston where I was originally from. I worked at Gibson's, a soda fountain at the bus stop on Westminster Street. I was very busy. Servicemen from all over used to come in. I made $15 for a 48 hour week. I bought my own clothes, paid my own expenses, car-fare, whatever I wanted, and I'd go to the movies. If you had a five dollar bill then you were very wealthy.

I met my husband while I was working at Gibson's. He had a construction job building an air base up in Newfoundland. When Pearl Harbor broke out, he came back home and we got married. All the fellows had gone into the service. His brothers were all gone. All the men were leaving. My husband had a deferment because his job was considered important to the defense, and we had a nine month old son. But he wanted to go so badly that he quit the job. They turned his name into the draft board, and he went into the service very happily.

He was shipped out to Okinawa. He was a Seabee and worked in the construction battalion which builds bases. The Seabees would go ahead of the Marines to make the landing and do all that. He went from one island to the other across the Pacific.

After my husband went into the Seabee's I quit my job at Gibson's and went to work in a woolen mill, Lister's, which before the war was just a normal routine job. When the war started they needed wool very badly so this was considered a service job. In other words, it was important.

At the mill the government used to send out all the Purple Heart soldiers to talk to us and tell us that we couldn't take time off, and pushed all this patriotism on us. One particular day I had the day off and they went to my house. I wasn't home. It would have been embarrassing to have a soldier with a Purple Heart on asking why I wasn't at work.

Well, the wool would come in just like they sheer [sic] it off the sheep. It was dirty and they'd put it in like, they called it a carding machine, and it would be probably a hundred foot long. They took that and it would be in rolls and would go into a barrel, you know like you'd take cotton and push it into a crack. Those barrels would be brought to my aunt's machine and she would put it through, maybe eight or ten of those barrels. It would make a big ball and a roll almost like you'd have a ball of rope or twine. I think I got $27 a week, so it did pay more. The soldiers needed woolen blankets. At the time all servicemen were issued their clothing, their blanket, their bedroll, the whole bit. The blankets that came home after war had traveled all over the world.

The wool was all used for the defense; what they called a defense contract. If the factory fulfilled its contract and did good work it had an "E" for excellence. The mill had an "E"—it was on a flag that would fly over the plant. We were very proud of it, because it meant that we were doing our part.

I had a young baby and I had a place to leave him in a nursery. At the mill I worked every day and I had all my evenings off, and Saturdays and Sundays, so that I was home alone with my son. I used to take him to Bristol on the trolley and we'd have picnics on the beach.

I was lucky in that there was a Salvation Army day nursery on the street I lived on. They only charged $3 a week. After I moved to my own little apartment in East Providence, I used to have to take my son on the trolley car, bring him over to the nursery, and leave him there, and go back down the street and get on another trolley and get to work, and the same thing at night.

If he was sick I either had to stay home with him or take him up to my sister's; maybe his grandmother would take care of him. One time he had scarlet fever, and the doctor put him in the hospital. The doctor figured where I was all by myself and my husband was in the service, it would have been too much to be at home with him. This way I could come and go to work.

Beef was very short. People ate a lot of chicken, and if you could get fish, eggs. Spam was a basic commodity. Everybody ate it. I remember a place downtown that sold horse meat. My sister and I decided we would try it so we bought a couple of pounds of hamburg and a couple of steaks. We cooked the steaks for our husbands and all the while we couldn't eat them because we knew what it was, but the men thought it was great!

[Did you follow the course of the war?] Oh, yes! We would listen to the radio at night and they would tell you. One particular Sunday night the Germans sunk the Wales and the Repulse which were British ships. When you're listening to it on the radio, it was like it was actually happening. It's very profound to think this is actually happening somewhere in the world and you're sitting safe in your house. There was one particular program which made a big impression on me about a woman called the "Beast of Belsen," her name was Elsa Koch. I never forgot that name. She used to make lamp shades out of human skin.

[How did you keep in touch with your husband?] They had what you call a V-mail letter. It went through like a micro-dot, micro-film I guess it was. You wrote these letters and they went through a computer and when your husband opened it, it was like an envelope and a sheet of paper, and if anything was said that wasn't right it was just blocked out. I did get a few letters with the pieces cut out. If there was anything very interesting or important in the back of it that went too, and you couldn't just use one side of the paper because it was a premium, especially for the men overseas.

[What was it like when you heard the war had ended?] They had a big victory parade in East Providence. I allowed my son to go with all his friends and they marched in it, and he was just a toddler. At that time we were all so naive, not only young people, even adults, grandparents, the whole world was naive, until after the war.

After the war things changed because women found out they could go out and they could survive. They could really do it on their own. That's where I think women's lib really started. So the whole world has changed.

Everybody's more aware of everything. We were very sheltered up until 1941.

I think it made us more aware. It made me mature. When my husband went in the service, I often used to think if anything happened to him, our baby was my complete responsibility. At 21 that was quite an awesome thing to think that you had a small human life that you were responsible for.

*Document 4: Some had family responsibilities*[4]

*Not all women worked in factories. Many had potentially overwhelming family responsibilities. Mary Gardner in Rhode Island is a good example.*

Outside riding herd on six children, believe me, that was my job.

We had two girls and four boys. Cliff was 11. Marilyn was 10. Bill was 8, Norman was 6 and Betty Jane was 4. [She had another child, Frank, in 1941.]

We knew about the war, what was going on and everything, but it was in Europe. You know how far you're removed from that. You read about it, but it doesn't really hit home until all of a sudden it's on your own doorstep.

[Rationing] They had margarine with like a small egg in it with color in that. You'd have to squeeze that and work it in until such a time it was the color that you wanted. The kids hated that. They used to do that.

My father was an avid fisherman and we ate a lot of fish because the meat was rationed. To this day, some of them like fish and some of them don't, because they had lots of fish.

It was tight at times. You had to stop and think of what you were going to buy, and buy things that were going to stretch, maybe spaghetti, macaroni and mix it up with something else. I'd say in the summer months we were fortunate that we had fresh produce. I never did much canning because that was a concentrating job, and you were trying to watch kids and not mess up what you were doing.

[Leisure time] Well, we used to go out for a ride because when you have six kids you don't do too dog gone much, believe me. We used to go visiting and whatever, but we didn't socialize too much. The two boys, they used to set up pins at the bowling alley. Not the oldest one, but the two younger ones.

Well, we had a little difficulty keeping children in clothes. For myself, I didn't desire too much, but to keep them clothed to go to school and whatever. There was no hand-me-downs. They just wore them out. As I say about the shoes, it was rough keeping them in shoes.

Well, it was just some fun keeping track of these youngsters, making sure where they were and such things. That meant that I couldn't say to my husband, "Well, so and so did such and such a thing." I took care of that pretty well, but there were times when it should have been a man's job to do these things. I had to do it. I can't even begin to tell because these boys were something else. But it was just that they needed a firm hand to bring them back into line. But I never wrote to him and told him all of the things that went on. I figured he had job enough. It was just the every day routine, cooking and washing, which were endless jobs. I didn't have a washing machine then. No dryer. Outside was the dryer. So it kept me busy.

[Reaction at end of war] Relieved, really. Very happy that that was it because it changed a lot of people's lives, particularly if they lost somebody in the war. Well, you know, it was a little difficult getting back into the stream again when you have been away like that. Some people handle it and some people don't.

[How the war changed her life] Well, it made for better living, I guess. That's about what I would tell you. We had more after the war because the pay was better. You could do things that you couldn't do before.

## Documents 5–6: Women Also Went into the Military

*In addition to defense work and the normal day-to-day activities of life, some women served in the military. Each branch of the service created units for women. Women faced many difficulties in the military, mostly from male officers who resented their being placed in their units or on their bases. But women persisted, and the women's forces became permanent until they were eventually merged into the men's units.*

### Document 5: Some were not allowed to serve in the military[5]

*Not all women who wanted to join the military were allowed to do so. The following interview with Eileen Hughes of Narragansett, Rhode Island, reflects the frustration of one young woman at the time. She did eventually get her wish to enter the military and served during the Korean War.*

We had just finished dinner, and I think I was in the living room reading the paper. I heard my mother say, "Oh, dear God. They have bombed Pearl Harbor!" I said "What?" and she said "Pearl Harbor. That's Hawaii. Do you know how many troops we have over there?" and I said "No."

Before Pearl Harbor, I didn't realize how serious the war in Europe was. I think that it was something that seemed very, very far away. We were far away from Japan and far away from Germany. It was horrible what was going on in Europe, but I don't think I realized how close it was going to hit us, until Pearl Harbor.

In 1939, I was in junior high school. Like everyone else, I worked an after school job. I think I made $10 a week and I worked every night after school.

This was during the Depression and everyone was poor. There weren't as many distinctions between who makes this, and who's in here, and who's down at the bottom. We were all the same and it was very tough, but everybody pulled together and we managed.

I spent my money on different things: probably cigarettes that I shouldn't have smoked, movies, ice cream, candy bars. As we got involved in the war, I noticed that many of the movies I saw were geared towards the war, especially after Pearl Harbor. I liked the war movies because they always make it look like we were winning.

My brother quit high school to join the army. A lot of the boys did. A lot of the boys in my class didn't bother to graduate. Everybody was very patriotic and they quit school to enlist. There were very few boys left in my senior class when we graduated. Some of my friends' fathers were already in the service. My brother was just barely 18 and he was over in the Philippines by the time he was 19. We were angry to think that things had gone that far.

I myself was interested in joining the army from the time I was a very little girl. I don't know why, but I always felt that's what I wanted. At that time, when I was growing up, the women's army was the Women's Auxiliary Army Corps, the WAAC. You could go in at 18 with parental signature. About the time I was entering my senior year of high school that was changed to 21. I was very angry because I really, really planned on going. I wrote to the President of the United States and said I just wanted to go and I didn't think it was fair. I thought they should let me go, but they didn't.

Instead, I did Civilian Defense. We spotted airplanes. We had to go to classes to be able to recognize them. I put in over 1,500 hours spotting planes. We had air raid drills and most of us volunteered and did messenger work. It was kind of scary. We were blacked out here. All the houses in Narragansett had to be totally blacked out on the ocean side. We had to buy these special shades for our windows and every night, as soon as it turned dark, you had to draw your shades. That was regulation and they had air raid wardens. If you didn't have your shades drawn, they would come and knock on your door and make you draw them. After Pearl Harbor, a lot of troops came in here and a lot of Navy came into Quonset.

As a young person, I went to a lot of USO dances on Saturday nights. That was volunteer and kind of fun. All of these men that were stationed around here were young boys, all away from home who couldn't always get home for the holidays. So we'd invite them home for Sunday dinner and things like that. It was fun.

I didn't want to get serious about any of them because I really wanted to go into the service. Some of my girlfriends did. They were more prone to "I'd like to get married." I was still angry because I couldn't go into the service when I had wanted to. I was very firm about it. I liked a lot of them, and I loved to dance and have fun, but I did not want to get serious.

There was much fear of bombing because of the submarines rumored to be floating around nearby. I don't think most of us realized that attack was a real possibility. We had this attitude, sometimes Americans are like this, that the Americans would take care of it. I suppose we just figured because we were the U.S. of A. nothing would happen. Fortunately, nothing did, but it could have and I think some people did fear it.

After graduating from high school, I went to work at the Naval Air Station at Quonset Point. There were many jobs up there. My mother was a school teacher, and I just walked right into once-and-a-half of what she was making. It was incredible. It was because of the war, there were good jobs for us then. It's an unfortunate thing, but the war brought prosperity.

Of course, then there was rationing. We were just beginning to get used to having a few things more when we got cut back. You couldn't get sugar, and often we'd have the tickets to get the meat, but it wasn't available. It was a hardship, but you learned to live with it. Some people found ways of getting around it, but we didn't do that. We just lived with it.

When the war in Europe ended, I was here in Narragansett, working at Quonset Point. I came home from work, and my mother said, "The President is going to make an announcement at seven tonight." I remember saying "Oh, I hope this war is over." That was the first night that my mother had been able to get some lamb chops at the store. But we got so emotional that we couldn't eat because we knew my brother would be coming home. At about 7 p.m. President Harry Truman made the announcement, and it was like everything was so still. Then all of a sudden there was this huge uproar. You could here people screaming and it was nothing but one big party. My girlfriend came running up. She was yelling, "Yahoo! Yahoo!" and I went running down. Everybody went crazy. It was sad for those who lost loved ones. One of my girlfriends was crying because her brother had been killed. Still, it was a wonderful feeling when it was over.

World War II. I think that probably it gave me more opportunities to do more. It's a terrible thing to say that a war does that, but I wonder if I would ever really have left Narragansett and done what I did, which was the best thing I ever did in my life.

*Document 6: Some faced discrimination in the military[6]*

*Genevieve Chasm was allowed to serve in the military, but she faced much discrimination. Her interview many years later revealed a woman of strength and determination who was able to survive in a man's army.*

I had a big mouth—in fact, that was my downfall. I didn't care what the rank was. If I had been a man, they would have said, "Take that bum out, put him in combat, and make sure somebody shoots him the first day."

When a service was opened for women, I just felt I should join, because the men were drafted, the men were enlisting, and I was single, and I just felt it was my duty. Now, I was 25 years old, very idealistic and patriotic, so I became part of the original group of enlisted women in the Women's Army Auxiliary Corps. When we arrived at Fort Ogelthorpe, Georgia, in true army fashion, the barracks weren't complete. I mean, it was just chaotic.

Somehow or another we got through basic training. We had to get up very early in the morning, race around, and then we would be marched to the mess hall, and we'd just walk in the mess hall, get food on our tray, and we'd have to get out, they'd just throw us out.

Once the Mess Officer stopped and said [changes voice], "I can get ten companies through my mess hall in a half an hour." My big mouth—that was my downfall. So afterwards when they asked for questions I said to her, "I've been hungry ever since I've been in the army because all you think about is getting the people through, in and out, but you don't think about feeding them!"

The last week before I was commissioned, we had to fill out a form, and one of the questions was: If you could have any job in the United States Army, what would it be? So I wrote, "I would like to be a mess officer because I've been hungry as long as I've been in the army."

I was put in charge of the mess hall at Fort Leavenworth, Kansas. Well, the mess sergeant had worked for Bird's Eye Frozen Food Company in Washington. She was obsessively clean, and that's a good trait in the kitchen. We had a Polish girl from Chicago who had worked in the meat packing house, cutting meat, so we had a good meat cutter. We had another girl, we called her Cookie, she was a baker from a very fine gourmet bakery in Denver. We had another girl who was a chef from Sun Valley, Idaho. So our mess hall, now, I must say, had a wonderful kitchen. It was rated as the second best mess in the United States Army. The second best! And that was because I love to feed people. I think I was put on this earth to feed people. In fact, I would have loved to have gone into the restaurant business. Even as a kid your age. But this was something I took great pride in and we had a wonderful mess, and during the war there wasn't the food to buy, and things were rationed and everything, so boy, to get an invitation to our mess hall was something. I'm very proud of that fact.

So I was there at Fort Leavenworth, Kansas, for two years. It was the only time in my life when I and all the women there suffered from discrimination. Today, I mean, women wouldn't tolerate it, but the men there, mostly career army officers, West Pointers, did everything they could to block us.

Every morning, I had to go up to headquarters and report to the adjutant. I'd stand there at attention and he would shout at me, and he would curse and swear when I'm there knocking myself out, trying to form a company, something I had never done before. As I'd stand there, the other WAC officer with me would have the tears streaming down her face—I used to get so mad at her, and I used to get so mad at him. But I stood there and I took it until one day, one day, I took the bar off my shoulder and I threw it on his desk, and I said, "I have taken the last bit of abuse I'm going to take from you or anybody else on this post!" I said, "I'm going back to my office. I'm going to call Seventh Service Command, talk to Major Bell, and I'm going to tell her to take us out of here and send us someplace where we'll be appreciated! Because I have had nothing but . . . interference. I have had no help! People have been rude to us, we get obscene phone calls all the time, day and night, from people at the detachment, the company, and I have had it!"

As I stormed out of the room he said [changes voice], "Just a minute miss, just a minute miss, come back here!" He said, "You haven't been dismissed!" and I walked back into the room and said, "That's another thing! Nobody on this post will call me lieutenant—everybody calls me miss! I'm just as much a lieutenant as any man that graduates from West Point—you want to talk to me, you call me lieutenant!" And I walked out.

The day we reported to Fort Leavenworth General Truesdale walked in. He was six feet tall and so was I! We were right at eye level and he said, "So you're what the War Department sent us, huh? Well I want you to know you're not welcome on this post." I was absolutely speechless! So I looked at him, and said, "I hope that we are both on this post long enough that you regret that rude remark! Nobody insults me like that!" Well, General Truesdale did everything he could to make me look foolish and make our women look foolish.

So one day, I'm walking along in the headquarters, down the corridor, and the General comes along and he has all these aides, all these flunkies around him, and he says [changes voice], "Just a minute miss!" I said, "Yes, sir?" He says, "Don't you go to the hops on Saturday night?" I said, "Yes, sir. Every Saturday." He said, "So how come I don't see you in the receiving line?" I said, "Well, every time I speak to you, you embarrass me, so I avoid you!" He looked at me. There's all these guys lookin', you know? They didn't expect me to say something like that. So he said, "Well next Saturday I want you to go through the receiving line." I said, "I've never disobeyed an order yet. I'll be there."

The next Saturday night we came through the receiving line. When my time comes he says to me, "You think you're pretty good, don't you, Bowland?" (That was my maiden name.) And I looked at him and I said, "No, not pretty good—very good!" Well, they all just went sorta, "Aagh!" So he says, "Oh, you're so good, you're not good enough for the Command General School!"

which was the top school in the Army at that time. Command General Staff School was for field grade officers, majors and above. And it's battle planning. So I said, "Well, I don't ever expect to be doing that." He said, "You're just making alibis! You don't have the brains to go!" And all these guys standing around sniggerin', sniggerin'.

So I had a very fresh mouth. And I looked around at all these grinning guys and said, "They all graduated from Command General Staff School, didn't they?" He says, "Yes." I said, "Well if they could do it, anybody could!" He said, "You're going to the next class." And I said, "Well, it would be a waste of government money to send me because I would never be in a position to do this. But the army is so good at wastin' money they might just as well waste a little on me!" I went to the next class of Command General Staff School. It's called a "suicide school" because usually in every class at least one man [gestures] blows his brains out. Well, I went, and I can tell you, I could feel the wheels goin' round in my head. And you know, they might just as well have been talking in a foreign language because it was all so new to me. But then I realized— nobody could know it all. Each day they gave us a handout, and if we spent 24 hours a day, nobody could have read all of it, there was so much. They gave you a foot locker, and by the time they finished the class, it was piled full with reading matter. So I realized that you had to know where to look it up, you know, whatever it was. And if you knew where to look it up, you got the answer. I graduated from that school in the top quarter.

Now one of the things we were taught before going to Europe was that you never said "Russian"—you said "Soviet." You never said "English"—you said "UK, United Kingdom." Because you'd be surprised—now I know, I served with a lot of British officers—I'd say something about being English, they'd say, "I'm not English, "I'm [changes voice] Scottish" or "I'm from South Africa" or—I remember one, "I'm from Kenya." So it was the Commonwealth and a lot of Australians, a lot of people for New Zealand. No they were called UK, United Kingdom.

Oh! So finally, V-E Day came, and a week after I was in Germany driving a jeep with three men. And we drove into Stuttgart. There was nothing! And nothing had been cleared up—there were bodies. Yet it was a beautiful, beautiful spring day, the sky was blue, it was beautiful, and it was all so terrible.

So, anyway, on the fourth of August 1945, we went to Berlin and opened our main headquarters—this was the military government now. What had been SHAEF, Supreme Headquarters American Expeditionary Forces, was now AMG-U.S. (Allied Military Government-U.S.)

Now, I had never even thought about what the Germans were like. But I realized that they were nice people. I felt I was a patriotic American; so the Germans were patriotic Germans, you know what I'm saying? Well, we made our headquarters at E.K. Farben Industries, almost a world cartel . . . in Germany.

They made a lot of war materials. Well, that was such a big industrial area, they had a little railroad system not only to carry supplies but people too. A lot of the factory was damaged, but not a window on the main building was broken because part of the United States plan was that we were going to win the war. And when we got into Germany, we wanted this building as our head-quarters so we didn't want it . . . smashed. Well, the Germans had taken slave laborers, women mostly or older men from Holland, Belgium, Czechoslova-kia, Austria, any place you can name. They had been working as slave laborers in this big factory complex. I saw, with my own eyes—because when I came back home, people said I was a liar when I told them of the things I saw. They had built the housing for these slave laborers—that's what they were called—like a dog house. Long and narrow with a pitched roof. In order to get in, you had to get on your hands and knees and crawl. And then at night, a board was dropped down. There were no windows, no nothing in there, and the people couldn't stand up in there. On one side there was a wooden shelf. And that's where the people lay down to sleep. There was no bedding provided, no sani-tation—nothing. And it gets mighty cold in Germany during the winter time. That's the way those people had to live.

I was eating dinner in the Rathskellar, the officer's mess in Berlin, and somebody came in and said, "They dropped the bomb." And they cheered. But I just sat there and said, "This is one of the worst mistakes the United States could make!" But they said, "Oh, well, this is shortening the war." And I've heard that and I've read that. But you see, we had this Manhattan Project where we were trying to find the atomic bomb. And what we wanted to do was drop it on Germany. See, the Germans had missiles. So we raced and raced to get the Atomic Bomb completed, and V-E day came. See, it's just like—you're a young fellow and somebody gives you a sports car and they say, "Hey, you can do 125 in this car!" You'd want to see if it could do it. You'd just step on it and try to make 125. So we had the bomb and we wanted to see if it would work. And I think that was a terrible, terrible thing—a terrible, terrible thing.

## Part B: Americans on the Battlefront

### Background

*Americans went off to war as never before in 1941. The government did what it could to accommodate the needs of the fighting men and women, while keep-ing in mind the greater objective of defeating the enemy. The war was an effort in production to provide the means to conduct the war, but there was also an effort to keep people at home as informed as possible without giving away secrets of what was going on in the various theaters of war.*

*Mail services were provided to allow service members to receive messages and parcels from home on a regular basis. Communication was vital to the morale needed to win the war. The government provided free mail service to the military sending letters home, and intense efforts were made to get the mail delivered to the various fronts without unnecessary delays.*

*Despite efforts to accommodate both the home front and the battle front, the government was also concerned about security. Government censors read all out-going mail from the battle areas. Americans with loved ones scattered around the world were quite familiar with the censor's scissors. Censors read all mail with an eye to any service member inadvertently giving information that could be valu-able to the enemy were the mail to fall in the wrong hands. The censors did not mark out sensitive material; they actually used scissors to cut lines or parts of lines from letters deemed inappropriate. Since service personnel were expected to write on both sides of the paper to preserve paper and to keep the weight of mail lighter, when a phrase or sentence was excised, the information on the other side of the page would be deleted as well.*

*Because of censorship, service personnel were unable to give many details of what they were doing. When they were overseas, about the most they could reveal was the country in which they were located. Therefore, most war letters do not provide descriptions of battles or strategy, but they do give a flavor of what life was like for civilians who suddenly found themselves in the military and in un-familiar surroundings.*

## Questions

In reading these documents, the student should ask and answer several questions to put these activities in the proper context.

1. Does the publication of personal letters from the war years violate the privacy of the soldiers and their families?
2. Do the letters from service members give an accurate reflection of life on the battlefronts?
3. Do you think any of these letters violated the censors' regulations about revealing sensitive information?
4. How accurate were the reports from correspondents about conditions on the battlefronts?
5. How dangerous was it for civilians to report from the battlefronts?

## Documents 1–4: Correspondence to and from Soldiers in the Field

*Men in the service tried to keep their families apprised of what they were doing, but often they could not give many details because of the censorship. Still, they managed to send letters that were revealing about their lives and the suffering they went through.*

### Document 1: Military training[7]

*Pvt. Morton D. Elevitch was sent to Fort Benning, Georgia, for basic training. In the following letter, he tries to explain to his mother some of the things he was being taught. He seems to have wanted her to understand just what the future had in store for him. Following his training, he was shipped to Europe where he was in George S. Patton's Third Army. He was wounded in January 1945 when mortar fragments struck him in the chest. After six months of hospitalization, he survived the wounds and was back in the States by Christmas 1945.*

Dear Louisa:

For the Nth time, thanks for your package. Please don't send me any more underwear, socks, or candy. The Milk of Magnesia was absolutely unnecessary. I'M HAVING NO MORE BOWEL TROUBLE AND DON'T ANTICIPATE ANY.

This week they are teaching us to kill. Now you probably looked away and shuttered [*sic*]. Well, mom, I don't like the idea, either, but we all know it's for our own good. The most strenuous work we do takes place as we stand in one place—bayonet drill. We lunge about in definite movements and are required to growl, grimace, and look at each other with hate. Five hundred of us dance about, screaming, shouting and snarling.

A rifle seems to weigh a ton more with a bayonet on. Our arms feel as if they're going to drop off as the Lt. holds us in one position and talks! Our bayonets have sheaths on them so that no one has his head cut off. They teach us how to withdraw our bayonets in a certain manner, too, because steel sticks to warm human flesh. (This sounds awful bloodthirsty, but everyone keeps serious minded about it.)

We are learning jiu jitsu holds—and to put it bluntly—plain dirty fighting. This will be invaluable in case anyone ever tries to pick on me. Maybe I shouldn't put this in—in fact I know I shouldn't—but it is going on so—Our instructors emphasize that we should be quick or be dead— always try to kill a man—break his arm first—then clip him under the nose—throat, neck or kidneys to kill him.

I'm afraid I'll never be an expert at this, because I just can't bring my-self to go at this in earnest. Surprise is a very important element—I know how to break any hold, grip and throw a man flat on his face They even teach us how to scientifically stomp on a man. I've left out many gory de-tails.

By the way everything is done in double time this week. We move in place and from place to place on the double—puff puff Confidentially,

I'm tired. S'long

Mort

*Document 2: Fighting in Italy*[8]

*Private Paul Curtis of Oak Ridge, Tennessee, was one of thousands of Ameri-can soldiers who participated in the Battle of Anzio in 1944. When his younger brother wrote asking what he thought of combat, he wrote the following letter telling him how he felt during the battle.*

May 28, 1944

Italy

Dear Mitchell:

I just finished writing you a V-Mail, but it seems I had something else to say, so I attempt this air mail. I haven't had a chance to write you for the past four or five days.

As I told you in the V-Mail, I have seen some action—a few hard, hard, days in which I saw more than I imagined I ever would. I don't think any man can exactly explain combat. It's beyond words. Take a combination of fear, anger, hunger, thirst, exhaustion, disgust, loneliness, homesick-ness, and wrap that all up in one reaction and you might approach the feelings a fellow has. It makes you feel mighty small, helpless and alone. It's a comfort to know there's one who is present at all times and any-where ready to help you through. My faith in God has been steadily growing stronger all along. Without faith, I don't see how anyone could stand this. It all seems so useless, but I realize Germany must be stopped; but they will rise again for peace will be settled by men who have never known combat and naturally they will hold no bitterness nor dread of another war, for they don't know: This war could have been avoided.

I thought I had been tired before in my life, but nothing like this; but still you can and do go on. Every time you stop you dig a hole which has saved many lives. The ground is so hard and dry that digging is very hard. You don't get so very hungry, but thirst drives you crazy. I have drunk water with everything in it and liked it. You have no energy but still you go on.

The battle seems like something in a faraway land, and everything seems sad, lonely, and dark. The roar is even as bad as the movies have it. The cries of the wounded are pitiful. They seem so helpless. The dead seem forsaken, but they are out of it all as in the Masonic textbook—"The gentle breeze fans their verdant covering, they heed it not, sunshine and storm pass over them, they are neither delighted nor disturbed"—so it is in this battle, the things rage on all around them, but they are still and quiet.

You wanted to know how I felt after I saw action and I have told you all I can that will pass the censors; I imagine all new men feel about the same and I know old men feel differently and so will I, but that's for now.

Love,
Paul

## Document 3: Death in the Pacific[9]

*The fighting was terrible in all theaters, but in the Pacific, it seemed especially cruel. When the war began in the Pacific, the Japanese invaded the Philippines and eventually drove General Douglas MacArthur from the islands. Several thousand soldiers escaped to the island of Corregidor, just south of the Bataan Peninsula. After a month-long bombardment, they surrendered to the Japanese on May 6, 1942. Lt. Tommie Kennedy was one of thousands taken prisoner. He was incarcerated on a Japanese prison ship (a "hell ship"), but by January 1945, he knew that his time was just about over. Hungry, malnourished, and ill, he wanted a last message to his parents. He wrote in very small print on the back of two family photographs that he had carried through the war. The first message began with a note to whoever might find his body. A few days later, still alive but failing fast, Kennedy found another scrap of paper and wrote another message. Both of these messages follow. After his death, his medals and letters were passed from one POW to another. In late 1945, they were mailed to his parents.*

Notify: C.R. Kennedy, Box 842 Maricopa,
California. Death of Son. Lt. Thomas R. Kennedy 0-89034.

Momie & Dad: It is pretty hard to check out this way with out a fighting chance but we can't live forever. I'm not afraid to die, I just hate the thought of not seeing you again. Buy Turkey Ranch with my money and just think of me often while your there. Make liberal donations to both sisters. See that Gary has a new car his first year hi-school.

I am sending Walts medals to his mother. He gave them to me Sept 42 last time I saw him & Bud. They went to Japan. I guess you can tell Patty that fate just didn't want us to be together. Hold a nice service for me in

Bksfield & put head stone in new cematary. Take care of my nieces & nephews don't let them ever want anything as I want even warmth or water now.

Loving & waiting for you in the world beon.
Your son,
Lt. Tommie Kennedy

Enroute Japan. Jan. 18, 1945

Dearest Momie Dad,

I am writing this so that you will know exactly what happened and won't be like so many parents. I guess I really made a mistake in not listening to you & coming over here. If I could only have been killed in action, its so useless to die here from Disentry with no medicin. Walt & Bud went to Manchuria Sept '42. We have been since Dee 13 from Manila. Bombed twice from 2 ships, on the 3rd now. Use my money to buy Turkey Ranch so you will always have some place to always go. Also give both sisters liberal amounts & see Gary has Sport model auto his 1st year hi school. Also nieces are always best dressed. Write: Mary Robertson at Houtzdale, Penn. Her son Melville died of disentry on the 17th of Jan. with his head on my shoulder. We were like brothers. He was buried at sea somewhere off the China coast. Tell Patty I'm sorry, guess we just weren't meant to be happy together. I weigh about 90 lbs now so you can see how we are. I will sign off now darlings and please don't greave to much. These are my bars & collar ensigns. The medals are Walts, please see his mom gets them. I'm not afraid to go, and will be waiting for you.

All my Love,
Tommie Kennedy

*Document 4: An American Jew helps liberate Dachau[10]*

*Fritz Schnaittacher was among the first American soldiers to enter the concentration camp at Dachau. Ironically, Schnaittacher was a German-born Jew who had fled Germany for the United States in October 1933. As a young man, he had almost been imprisoned at Dachau, and, had he stayed in Germany, he undoubtedly would have ended up in one of the camps. His entrance into Dachau in 1945 gave him a first-hand view of what might have been his fate. On May 1, 1945, he sent the following letter, which describes his reactions, to his wife.*

My dearest Dottylein,

Twelve years ago to day I came to Munich—yesterday we took it—to day we were in the heart of it—another coincidence. The past few days were some of the greatest and saddest in my life. Our regiment took Dachau or should I say liberated the human wreckage which was left there. This I consider one of the most glorious pages in the history of our regiment, not because the fighting was tough, it wasn't, but because it finally opened the gates of one of the world's most hellish places.

Twelve years ago I missed it by the skin of my teeth. This time I saw it—I shall never forget it, and nobody will, who has seen it. You know that I had never doubted the truth of all the atrocities, of which we have been reading—I know they could never be exaggerated, but at the same time I could never visualize this insane cruelty until I was confronted with it now; and now I cannot comprehend it, and it almost seems more unbelievable than before I had seen the victims of Nazi German culture.

You have heard the stories over the radio—I don't want to add much more—the most striking picture I saw was the "death train"—I say picture, no not picture, but carload and carload full of corpses, once upon a time people, who were alive, who were happy and people who had convictions or were jews—then slowly but methodically they were killed. Death has an ugly face on these people—they were starved to death—the positions they were lying in show that they succumbed slowly—they made one move, fell, were too weak to make another move, and there are hundreds of such lifeless skeletons covered by some skin. I tried to find out the origin of this train. Some of the stories corresponded—whether this train was to leave Dachau or had just arrived is not essential—essential is that they were locked into these cattle cars without sanitation and without food. The SS had to take off in a hurry—we came too fast—it was too late to cover up their atrocities.

Yet there were even worse scenes at Dachau than the one I tried to describe. And still Dachau was considered only a drop in the bucket in the eyes of an experienced observer, a high ranking SS officer. He had been in a hospital in camp as a convalescent. I was called in as an interpreter, and first when I met him I was unaware of his identity, but expected him to be a political prisoner who was anxious to help us in the elimination of those who were guilty for all these crimes. I greeted him accordingly. Then I found out he was an SS officer—my hand, which had shaken his, felt as if it wanted to shrivel up. I told him so too. Then he made the following statement, take it for what it's worth "Yes I am an SS officer, not because I wanted to, but because I had to—still I am proud to have been an SS officer, only as such I was able to see the true face of Hitler and his system, and only as such I was able to help the unfortunate ones a tiny bit." Then he told us about the Concentration Camp near Katowicz—Dachau is just child's play in comparison to Katowicz.

Dottylein I hate to close this letter so abruptly—this is all dark, but there are some light aspects in all of this nightmare too—they will follow shortly.

I love you my Dottylein with all my heart and soul.

Your Fritz

## Documents 5–9: Correspondents Report from the Front

*During the war, journalists who risked their lives to report from the battle-fronts became famous. There were many of them, but some are remembered today better than others, partly because they went on to illustrious careers in journalism after the war.*

### Document 5: Ernie Pyle's report from the front[11]

*Ernie Pyle was one of the most famous frontline reporters during the war. He was a special friend to the fighting men, and he braved danger right along with them. As he said, he had a "worm's eye view" of the fighting. The most famous column he ever wrote was "The Death of Captain Waskow." This is a poignant story of the death of a beloved officer.*

AT THE FRONT LINES IN ITALY, January 10, 1944—In this war I have known a lot of officers who were loved and respected by the soldiers under them. But never have I crossed the trail of any man as beloved as Capt. Henry T. Waskow of Belton, Texas.

Capt. Waskow was a company commander in the 36th Division. He had led his company since long before it left the States. He was very young, only in his middle twenties, but he carried in him a sincerity and gentleness that made people want to be guided by him.

"After my own father, he came next," a sergeant told me.

"He always looked after us," a soldier said. "He'd go to bat for us every time."

"I've never knowed him to do anything unfair," another one said.

I was at the foot of the mule trail the night they brought Capt. Waskow's body down. The moon was nearly full at the time, and you could see far up the trail, and even part way across the valley below. Soldiers made shadows in the moonlight as they walked.

Dead men had been coming down the mountain all evening, lashed onto the backs of mules. They came lying belly-down across the wooden pack-saddles, their heads hanging down on the left side of the mule, their stiffened legs sticking out awkwardly from the other side, bobbing up and down as the mule walked.

The Italian mule-skinners were afraid to walk beside dead men, so Americans had to lead the mules down that night. Even the Americans were reluctant to unlash and lift off the bodies at the bottom, so an officer had to do it himself, and ask others to help.

The first one came early in the morning. They slid him down from the mule and stood him on his feet for a moment, while they got a new grip. In the half light he might have been merely a sick man standing there, leaning on the others. Then they laid him on the ground in the shadow of the low stone wall alongside the road.

I don't know who that first one was. You feel small in the presence of dead men, and ashamed at being alive, and you don't ask silly questions.

We left him there beside the road, that first one, and we all went back into the cowshed and sat on water cans or lay on the straw, waiting for the next batch of mules.

Somebody said the dead soldier had been dead for four days, and then nobody said anything more about it. We talked soldier talk for an hour or more. The dead man lay all alone outside in the shadow of the low stone wall.

Then a soldier came into the cowshed and said there were some more bodies outside. We went out into the road. Four mules stood there, in the moonlight, in the road where the trail came down off the mountain. The soldiers who led them stood there waiting. "This one is Captain Waskow," one of them said quietly.

Two men unlashed his body from the mule and lifted it off and laid it in the shadow beside the low stone wall. Other men took the other bodies off. Finally there were five lying end to end in a long row, alongside the road. You don't cover up dead men in the combat zone. They just lie there in the shadows until somebody else comes after them.

The unburdened mules moved off to their olive orchard. The men in the road seemed reluctant to leave. They stood around, and gradually one by one I could sense them moving close to Capt. Waskow's body. Not so much to look, I think, as to say something in finality to him, and to themselves. I stood close by and I could hear.

One soldier came and looked down, and he said out loud, "God damn it." That's all he said, and then he walked away. Another one came. He said, "God damn it to hell anyway." He looked down for a few last moments, and then he turned and left.

Another man came; I think he was an officer. It was hard to tell officers from men in the half light, for all were bearded and grimy dirty. The man looked down into the dead captain's face, and then he spoke directly to him, as though he were alive. He said: "I'm sorry, old man."

Then a soldier came and stood beside the officer, and bent over, and he too spoke to his dead captain, not in a whisper but awfully tenderly, and he said:

"I sure am sorry, sir."

Then the first man squatted down, and he reached down and took the dead hand, and he sat there for a full five minutes, holding the dead hand in his own and looking intently into the dead face, and he never uttered a sound all the time he sat there.

And finally he put the hand down, and then reached up and gently straightened the points of the captain's shirt collar, and then he sort of rearranged the tattered edges of his uniform around the wound. And then he got up and walked away down the road in the moonlight, all alone.

After that the rest of us went back into the cowshed, leaving the five dead men lying in a line, end to end, in the shadow of the low stone wall. We lay down on the straw in the cowshed, and pretty soon we were all asleep.


### Document 6: Pyle from Africa[12]

*Pyle wrote in the language of the day, and he sometimes got away with using words that normally would not appear in family newspapers. He spoke the language of the soldier, and he had a strong admiration for the men who risked their lives every day. His discussion of the infantry in the column below entitled "The God-Damned Infantry" is a good example.*


IN THE FRONT LINES BEFORE MATEUR, NORTHERN TUNISIA, May 2, 1943—We're now with an infantry outfit that has battled ceaselessly for four days and nights.

This northern warfare has been in the mountains. You don't ride much anymore. It is walking and climbing and crawling country. The mountains aren't big, but they are constant. They are largely treeless. They are easy to defend and bitter to take. But we are taking them.

The Germans lie on the back slope of every ridge, deeply dug into foxholes. In front of them the fields and pastures are hideous with thousands of hidden mines. The forward slopes are left open, untenanted, and if the Americans tried to scale these slopes they would be murdered wholesale in an inferno of machine-gun crossfire plus mortars and grenades.

Consequently we don't do it that way. We have fallen back to the old warfare of first pulverizing the enemy with artillery, then sweeping around the ends of the hill with infantry and taking them from the sides and behind.

\* \* \*

I've written before how the big guns crack and roar almost constantly throughout the day and night. They lay a screen ahead of our troops. By magnificent shooting they drop shells on the back slopes. By means of shells timed to burst in the air a few feet from the ground, they get the Germans even in their foxholes. Our troops have found that the Germans dig foxholes down and then under, trying to get cover from the shell bursts that shower death from above. Our artillery has really been sensational. For once we have enough of something and at the right time. Officers tell me they actually have more guns than they know what to do with. All the guns in any one sector can be centered to shoot at one spot. And when we lay the whole business on a German hill the whole slope seems to erupt. It becomes an unbelievable cauldron of fire and smoke and dirt. Veteran German soldiers say they have never been through anything like it.

*    *    *

Now to the infantry—the God-damned infantry, as they like to call themselves.

I love the infantry because they are the underdogs. They are the mud-rain-frost-and-wind boys. They have no comforts, and they even learn to live without the necessities. And in the end they are the guys that wars can't be won without.

I wish you could see just one of the ineradicable pictures I have in my mind today. In this particular picture I am sitting among clumps of sword-grass on a steep and rocky hillside that we have just taken. We are looking out over a vast rolling country to the rear.

A narrow path comes like a ribbon over a hill miles away, down a long slope, across a creek, up a slope and over another hill.

All along the length of this ribbon there is now a thin line of men. For four days and nights they have fought hard, eaten little, washed none, and slept hardly at all. Their nights have been violent with attack, fright, butchery, and their days sleepless and miserable with the crash of artillery.

The men are walking. They are fifty feet apart, for dispersal. Their walk is slow, for they are dead weary, as you can tell even when looking at them from behind. Every line and sag of their bodies speaks their inhuman exhaustion.

On their shoulders and backs they carry heavy steel tripods, machine-gun barrels, leaden boxes of ammunition. Their feet seem to sink into the ground from the overload they are bearing.

They don't slouch. It is the terrible deliberation of each step that spells out their appalling tiredness. Their faces are black and unshaven. They are young men, but the grime and whiskers and exhaustion make them look middle-aged.

In their eyes as they pass is not hatred, not excitement, not despair, not the tonic of their victory—there is just the simple expression of being here as though they had been here doing this forever, and nothing else.

The line moves on, but it never ends. All afternoon men keep coming round the hill and vanishing eventually over the horizon. It is one long tired line of antlike men.

*        *        *

There is an agony in your heart and you almost feel ashamed to look at them. They are just guys from Broadway and Main Street, but you wouldn't remember them. They are too far away now. They are too tired. Their world can never be known to you, but if you could see them just once, just for an instant, you would know that no matter how hard people work back home they are not keeping pace with these infantrymen in Tunisia.

### Document 7: Pyle's last column[13]

*Ernie Pyle stayed in Europe until after Paris was freed from the Germans, and then he went home for much-needed rest. Only a short time later, he accepted an assignment, but not without reservations, to cover the war in the Pacific. On April 18, 1945, he was killed by a sniper on the island of Ie Shima. The following draft of a column was found in his pocket, which reveals that his heart was really in Europe.*

And so it is over. The catastrophe on one side of the world has run its course. The day that it had so long seemed would never come has come at last.

I suppose emotions here in the Pacific are the same as they were among the Allies all over the world. First a shouting of the good news with such joyous surprise that you would think the shouter himself had brought it about.

And then an unspoken sense of gigantic relief—and then a hope that the collapse in Europe would hasten the end in the Pacific.

It has been seven months since I heard my last shot in the European war. Now I am as far away from it as it is possible to get on this globe.

This is written on a little ship laying off the coast of the Island of Okinawa, just south of Japan, on the other side of the world from Ardennes.

But my heart is still in Europe, and that's why I am writing this column.

It is to the boys who were my friends for so long. My one regret of the war is that I was not with them when it ended.

For the companionship of two-and-a-half years of death and misery is a spouse that tolerates no divorce. Such companionship finally becomes a part of one's soul, and it cannot be obliterated.

True, I am with American boys in the other war not yet ended, but I am old-fashioned and my sentiment runs to old things.

To me the European war is old, and the Pacific war is new.

Last summer I wrote that I hoped the end of the war could be a gigantic relief, but not an elation. In the joyousness of high spirits it is easy for us to forget the dead. Those who are gone would not wish themselves to be a millstone of gloom around our necks.

But there are many of the living who have had burned into their brains forever the unnatural sight of cold dead men scattered over the hillsides and in the ditches along the high rows of hedge throughout the world.

Dead men by mass production—in one country after another—month after month and year after year. Dead men in winter and dead men in summer.

Dead men in such familiar promiscuity that they become monotonous.

Dead men in such monstrous infinity that you come almost to hate them.

These are the things that you at home need not even try to understand. To you at home they are columns of figures, or he is a near one who went away and just didn't come back. You didn't see him lying so grotesque and pasty beside the gravel road in France.

We saw him, saw him by the multiple thousands. That's the difference. . . .

### Document 8: Rooney from Germany[14]

*Andy Rooney is familiar to most Americans today as the acerbic commentator every Sunday evening on the CBS television program* 60 Minutes. *Few know or remember that he got his start in journalism reporting from the front during World War II. He was a reporter for the* Stars and Stripes. *He covered almost all the theaters of war and often put himself in danger. One of his most famous columns was "How it Feels to Bomb Germany. . . ." This was in the* Stars and Stripes *on February 27, 1943.*

A U.S. BOMBER STATION, Feb. 26—From the nose of Lt. Bill Casey's Banshee, I saw American Fortresses and Liberators drop a load of destruction on Wilhelmshaven today.

We flew to Germany in the last group of a Fortress formation and Banshee was in the trailing squadron.

Soon after dawn the bombers thundered down the runway. Lt. Casey's windshield was splattered with mud on the way. It really was a blind takeoff.

Like a pickup football team on a Saturday morning, we grew in strength as we flew, until all England seemed to be covered with bombers.

Everything was quiet—almost monotonous—for an hour after we left the English coast.

Sees First Enemy Plane
Then the trouble began.

Peeling out of the sun came shining silver German fighter planes, diving at one bomber in the formation and disappearing below the cloudbanks as quickly as they had come. They seemed tiny, hardly a machine of destruction, and an impossible target.

My first glimpse of a German fighter came when the navigator, 2nd Lt. William H. Owens, of Tullahoma, Tenn., nearly knocked me into the lap of 2nd Lt. Malcolm A. Phillips Jr., the bombardier, whose home is in Coffeyville, Kan. Owens swung around at what appeared to be an Me109 as it whipped down through the clouds on our left.

From that time until three and one-half hours later, when we were half way home, no one had to look far to see a German fighter. They were all over and they were all kinds of planes—Me109s, Ju88s and Me110s. There were no FW190s, by far the best plane Jerry has to fight the Forts. Their absence strengthened Allied contentions that Germany is desperately short of fighter planes.

From a vantage point in the pilot's cabin Lt. Casey and his co-pilot, 1st Lt. Kelly G. Ross, were calmly giving information over the inter-com.

"Here comes one at 2 o'clock, Elliot. Get the son-of-a-bitch."

T/Sgt. Wilson C. Elliot, of Detroit, Lt. Casey's top turret man, is the only man from the original Banshee crew left.

Before we were very deep into Germany deadly black puffs began to appear around us. It seemed as though they were "air mines" that were touched off as we came to them. A puff would appear to our right and then in quick succession a row of five more black splotches flowered out, each one closer as they caught up to us.

Lt. Casey zigged, and the puffs appeared in the tracks of our zag. He was one jump ahead of the flak. All but once he was one jump ahead.

Thought Plane's Nose Torn Off

Lt. Phillips was leaning far forward in the nose, between his guns and bomb-sight, when suddenly the whole nose seemed to break out of the ship. My first impression was that they had given up the flak and had thrown the gun at us.

Lt. Phillips sat back on his heels and covered his eyes with his hands. Splinters of flexiglass formed coating over his helmet. It was a minute before he recovered from the shock to open his eyes and find that he could see and was unhurt.

What appeared to be the nose being ripped off actually was only a small hole the size of a man's fist.

The formation was perfect, and the German sky dotted with Forts in front of us and Liberators behind us was comforting. Below, the land seemed to be farmland for the most part. Even that was divided into aggravatingly square plots. It looked German and unfriendly. You had the feeling you would have known it was Germany even if you hadn't attended the briefing.

German flak didn't seem to bother German fighter planes. They poured in even when their own flak was thickest.

Approaching the bombing run, the doors of the ships in front of us could be seen swinging open, and not far above us the yawning bomb bay of a Fort revealed more bombs, hanging by some mechanical hairpin, waiting for the bombardier to push the tiny button that sends them to the target.

Lt. Owens was having trouble with his oxygen and Lt. Phillips' fingers were nearly frozen. I was healthy but helpless. Finally the valve of the navigator's air intake froze completely and the next thing his head had dropped to the top of his caliber .50, and his face was an unlovely greyish purple. Both of them had work to do in the nose. I was strictly cargo. The oxygen on my side was okay. We fitted the mask to Lt. Owens' face, revived him and I started back for the pilot's cockpit.

By the time I struggled back without oxygen, with a backload of equipment that would make Santa Claus look sick, I was almost out. Lt. Casey almost yawned at what I was sure was a major crisis in my life.

He fixed me up with oxygen and the remainder of my brief first glimpse at the war was from the pit behind the pilot.

As we started the bombing run I was up in the nose of the ship, standing over to the right trying to keep out of the way of the navigator and bombardier. I had a camera, and that was probably the greatest underestimation, or something or other, of the Germans anyone ever made. I definitely did not feel like taking pictures. I made an effort once or twice and I got a couple of pictures of a small bunch of six little ships down on the water, but it's elementary that you have to be able to hold a camera still to take pictures.

We were well into the run and the flak was puffing to the right and left. The boys said it was not nearly as intensive as over St. Nazaire, but there was more of it, spread out in different places, they said.

Fighter planes were always there while we were making our run. They come in so fast it's hard to tell where they're coming from, but frequently you could see a vapor trail start to form, like a cloud standing on end. You knew that was a fighter starting a run.

As the bombardier crouched low over his sight, I was just in back of him, trying to take a picture of the bombs falling from the plane ahead. They dropped theirs, and I guess we must have the next second but I couldn't feel it.

Behind the tail gunner, T/Sgt. Parley D. Small, of Packwood, Iowa, reported that he had seen a Liberator go down with one engine flaming. Although on fire he said it was under control for a crash landing. Small himself picked off one German plane as it tried to tie a stream of machine-gun bullets on our tail. He described the end of another German fighter.

### Jerry Stopped Cold

"It looked like a piece of cardboard that had been thrown out of a plane," he said. "It came up under the belly of a B24 and someone let him have it right on the nose. He stopped dead and fell away. The plane didn't seem to be burning. It must have killed the pilot."

As Nazi planes kept nipping at the formation, far away from the coast of Germany, they probably picked us up from the French coast. It is improbable that German-based fighters followed the USAAF bombers that far, even though many of them seemed to be twin-engined planes.

Almost half way home, three Ju88s could be seen diving at a B24 that had fallen out of formation and was in distress.

After 20 minutes without sign of Jerry, things began to look more pleasant.

### Song of Triumph

Lt. Casey and the crew began to sing over the intercom. Casey had the bends and was squirming in his seat—but smiling and singing. Next to him, Lt. Ross had to do most of the flying on the way home. Finally England was sighted and believe me, whatever you think, it is one of the most beautiful islands in all the world.

As Lt. Casey says, "I'm an Irishman, southern Ireland, but that is still the best looking damned little island I ever saw."

After a roof-lifting "buzz" (hedge-hopping) over the field, not orthodox, Lt. Casey brought the ship in smoothly.

Looking over the Banshee, we found that it had been hit in about ten places. The biggest hole was a gaping wound in her metal near the tail gunner. The chip of flak tore a hole through an English penny that Sgt. Small had left on the floor behind him.

With the exception of one frozen finger—Lt. Phillips'—the Banshee had what the crew called "a quiet trip."

I don't want to go on a noisy one.

*Document 9: Rooney remembers*[15]

*In remembering his wartime experiences for an oral history of war reporting, Rooney recalled what it was like to be among a group of very talented men who reported the war and made journalism history. Many of them continued to make history for years to come. He explains how he came to be on the mission described in the previous document.*

We were covering the air war in England—eight or ten reporters writing about the Eighth Air Force. I met Walter Cronkite in London, and we traveled a lot together. Another great friend was Gladwin Hill, who was with the Associated Press, later with the *New York Times*. And there was a man named Bob Post, who was the *New York Times'* reporter.

Every time there was a raid, we would split up and each go to a different bomber group. Then, when the crews came back, we would interview them. And sometimes they didn't come back. We, on the other hand, went back to our flats in London and lived quite a comfortable life. After a while, we saw so many people we had gotten to know who were shot down, taken prisoner, or killed that we all began to feel guilty about covering this war the way we were. It just seemed wrong to us. I don't know who decided to do it, but we decided we'd better go on a bombing raid ourselves. Though correspondents were never supposed to man a gun or carry any kind of a weapon, we were all forced to go to gunnery school; we practiced gunnery in case they needed us in the air.

[On each raid] they were losing 5 to 6 percent of all the bombers that went out. There were twenty-five bombers, give or take one or two, in each group, and each crew had to do twenty-five missions. Well, if you have to do twenty-five missions in a group of twenty-five planes, and you're losing 5 percent, it doesn't take any mathematical genius to know their chances of finishing were not good, and not many finished twenty-five missions. I think maybe 15 or 20 percent finished twenty-five missions successfully and were allowed to go home.

The raid we went on was only the second raid into Germany. It was on Wilhelmshaven. I got in my bomber and I thought to myself, "Why am I doing this? I'm scared to death. I mean, I don't have to risk my life"—except that I felt so bad for all the men who did have to risk their lives all those times that it just seemed like it was the honest thing to do. I remember we had these heavy flak jackets. A B-17 is not like a modern airliner. Wires and everything were all over, and getting through the bomb bay to the back—which would be the cabin in a passenger plane now—was very difficult. If you had a parachute on, it was tough to get past all the wires without getting snagged on everything. So I didn't wear my flak jacket. I stood on it. I had this feeling that I didn't want to be hit from underneath, but of course what happened was the flak exploded in the air around you and didn't necessarily come from below.

If there was flak before you got to the target, the pilot could take evasive action. But once the bombsight zeroed in on the target, you couldn't take any evasive action or the bombs would not go where they were designed to go. That plane was a perfect target for the gunners from underneath, and that was the frightening part of it—you just had to sit there.

There were seven of us [reporters] who actually went, and I was the youngest, but I ended up with the best story because my bomber was hit. I was up in the nose of the plane, and a shell came in and took a small piece of the Plexiglas nose off. The bombardier, who was in front of me, panicked and tried to stuff something in the hole. At seventeen or eighteen thousand feet, that air coming in is subzero, and he took his gloves off. His hands froze and it was terrible. I looked across at the little desk that the navigator used. His oxygen tube had been pierced and he lost his oxygen, and at eighteen thousand feet he collapsed. So I got to the pilot intercom and I asked him what to do. He said, "Well, we have emergency air in oxygen bottles up behind me. Take some deep breaths and come back up behind me and get the oxygen bottle; bring it back down and hook him up to that." Well I didn't know how to do any of this and here I was, with somebody's life at stake, and I didn't know how long you lasted once you took your oxygen mask off. But I took some deep breaths, I took my oxygen mask off, and went through this alleyway up behind the pilot. There I got an oxygen bottle and hooked up the navigator, who was a much more experienced flyer than the bombardier. He regained consciousness and got the bombardier quieted down. So I had by far the best story to tell of all the correspondents who went out that day.

## Notes

1. Statement from Katie, Rosie the Riveter Website: www.rosietheriveter.org. Reprinted by permission.

2. Statement from Irene Carlisle, Rosie the Riveter Website: www.rosietheriveter.org. Reprinted by permission.

3. Interview with Katherine O'Grady, "What Did You Do in the War Grandma?" An Oral History of Rhode Island Women during World War II, online at: www.stg .brown.edu/projects/WWII_Women/tocCS.html. Interview slightly edited. Reprinted by permission of the University of Rhode Island.

4. Interview with Mary Gardner, "What Did You Do in the War Grandma?" An Oral History of Rhode Island Women during World War II.

5. Interview with Eileen Hughes, "What Did You Do in the War Grandma?" An Oral History of Rhode Island Women during World War II.

6. Interview with Genevieve Chasm, "What Did You Do in the War Grandma?" An Oral History of Rhode Island Women during World War II.

7. Pvt. Morton D. Elevitch to his mother, in *War Letters: Extraordinary Correspondence from American Wars*, edited by Andrew Carroll, (New York: Scribner, 2001), 196. Letters by Morton D. Elevitch, Paul Curtis, Tommie Kennedy, and Fritz Schnaittacher were first published in WAR LETTERS: Extraordinary Correspondence from American Wars (Scribner, 2001), edited by Andrew Carroll. Reprinted by permission of and © by Andrew Carroll.

8. Pvt. Paul Curtis to his brother Mitchell, *War Letters*, 233.

9. Lt. Tommie Kennedy to parents, *War Letters*, 194–95.

10. 1st Lt. Fritz Schnaittacher to wife, May 1, 1945, *War Letters*, 272–74.

11. David Nichols, ed., *Ernie's War: The Best of Ernie Pyle's World War II Dispatches* (New York: Random House, 1986), 195–97. Reprinted by permission of Scripps-Howard, Inc.

12. Nichols, *Ernie's War*, 112–13.

13. Nichols, *Ernie's War*, 418–19.

14. *The Stars and Stripes*, February 27, 1943. Used with permission from the *Stars and Stripes*. © 1943, 2008 Stars and Stripes.

15. Michelle Ferrari, comp., *Reporting America at War: An Oral History* (New York: Hyperion, 2003), 53–55. From the book REPORTING AMERICA AT WAR: An Oral History compiled by Michelle Ferrari. Copyright © 2003 Goodhue Pictures, Inc. Reprinted by permission of Hyperion.

# 5

# The Cold War

THE UNITED STATES EMERGED FROM World War II as the most powerful and the wealthiest country in the world. In that situation, one might expect all to be good for Americans, but that was not the case. The peace that people had longed for came, but along with it came the threat of another war—this time with the Soviet Union. The struggle with the Soviets was not a shooting war, but the "Cold War" that developed was in some ways more nerve-wracking than an actual shooting war might be.

Before the war, Americans had never before been involved in a sustained effort to work diplomatically with the rest of the world. Now, however, America had no choice except to be involved. During the war, President Franklin Roosevelt had committed the United States to long-term world leadership. He had pledged that the United States would join and help lead the new world body, the United Nations. The development of the atomic bomb made American leadership even more necessary. Whether individual Americans wanted it or not, the United States was now an international leader, and its actions would determine the future course of the world. Americans successfully coped with the new challenges, despite the toll they took on the fabric of society.

## Part A.: The Cold War Begins

### Background

At the end of World War II, the peace and calm of victory did not last very long. Soon after Japan's surrender, the fragile alliance between the Soviet Union and *the Western powers began to unravel. Actually, tensions were clearly present before the end of the war, but they were either ignored or papered over in the interests of bringing the final peace.*

*Soon after the Japanese surrender, the Soviet Union under Josef Stalin was making territorial demands, especially in those portions of Eastern Europe that were occupied by the Red Army. It soon became clear that Stalin had no intention of removing the troops as he had promised at the Yalta Conference shortly before the end of the war and that, in fact, he had plans to expand, if possible, the boundaries of Soviet control. This situation was exacerbated by the destruction of the war and the devastation of much of Europe. People were living in rubble and did not have enough to eat. Americans were concerned that in those circumstances people would be very susceptible to the entreaties of Russian communists.*

*Soon after the end of the war, the world entered a period now called the "Cold War." A cold war was a conflict, but without the shooting. So instead of a "hot war," it was a "cold war" with the stakes possibly as great as if the powers were waging war against one another.*

*There is still debate in the United States about what caused the Cold War. The general American interpretation is that the aggressiveness of the Soviet Union caused President Truman to respond with firm American policies. The Soviets considered Truman inexperienced and weak and were testing him. In some parts of the world, people believe that Truman's aggressiveness toward the Soviet Union caused Stalin to react more strongly when, in fact, he did not want to confront the United States.*

*Wherever the truth lies, Americans were afraid of Russian expansionism, and many were certain another war—World War III—with the Soviet Union was just a matter of time. Many documents exist that chronicle this period of crisis; a few are included here.*

## Questions

In reading these documents, the student should ask and answer several questions to put these activities in the proper context.

1. How reliable was George Kennan's message to Washington in 1946?
2. Did Winston Churchill contribute to Soviet paranoia with his "Iron Curtain" speech?
3. Why was the policy of "Containment" not applicable to China and other parts of Asia?
4. Was the Truman Doctrine an appropriate policy regarding Greece and Turkey?
5. What were the purposes of the Marshall Plan?

## Document 1: Kennan's "Long Telegram"[1]

*In 1946, George Kennan, an employee in the American embassy in Moscow and an authority on Russia and its history, wrote a message to Washington alerting the State Department and others about what he thought the Soviet Union might do. It was an extremely long message—8,000 words—and one of the most significant documents of the postwar world. Kennan, who understood Russia very well, said that the Russians react to strength. If the United States made clear how far it was willing to go, most likely the Russians would back off. This approach was adopted and became known as "Containment," a policy that worked brilliantly. The following is a small portion of the telegram.*

. . . At the bottom of the Kremlin's neurotic view of world affairs is traditional and instinctive Russian sense of insecurity. Originally, this was insecurity of a peaceful agricultural people trying to live on vast exposed plain in neighborhood of fierce nomadic peoples. To this was added, as Russia came into contact with economically advanced West, fear of more competent, more powerful, more highly organized societies in that area. But this latter type of insecurity was one which afflicted rather Russian rulers than Russian people; for Russian rulers have invariably sensed that their rule was relatively archaic in form, fragile and artificial in its psychological foundation, unable to stand comparison for contact with political systems of Western countries. For this reason they have always feared foreign penetration, feared direct contact between Western world and their own, feared what would happen if Russians learned truth about world without or if foreigners learned truth about world within. And they have learned to seek security only in patient but deadly struggle for total destruction of rival power, never in compacts and compromises with it.

It was no coincidence that Marxism, which had smoldered ineffectively for half a century in Western Europe, caught hold and blazed for first time in Russia. Only in this land which had never known a friendly neighbor or indeed any tolerant equilibrium of separate powers, either internal or international, could a doctrine thrive which viewed economic conflicts of society as insoluble by peaceful means. After establishment of Bolshevist regime, Marxist dogma, rendered even more truculent and intolerant by Lenin's interpretation, became a perfect vehicle for sense of insecurity with which Bolsheviks, even more than previous Russian rulers, were afflicted. In this dogma, . . . they found justification for their instinctive fear of outside world, for the dictatorship without which they did not know how to rule, for cruelties they did not dare not to inflict, for sacrifices they felt bound to demand. In the name of Marxism they sacrificed every single ethical value in their methods and tactics. Today they cannot dispense with it. It is fig leaf of their moral and intellectual respectability. . . .

It should not be thought from above that Soviet party line is necessarily disingenuous and insincere on part of all those who put it forward. Many of them are too ignorant of outside world and mentally too dependent to question self-hypnotism, and have no difficulty making themselves believe what they find it comforting and convenient to believe. Finally we have the unsolved mystery as to who, if anyone, in this great land actually receives accurate and unbiased information about outside world. . . .

Soviet policy is conducted on two planes: (1) official plane represented by actions undertaken officially in the name of the Soviet government; and (2) subterranean plane of actions undertaken by agencies for which the Soviet government does not admit responsibility. . . .

On official plane, we must look for following:

A. Internal policy devoted to increasing in every way strength and prestige of Soviet state; intensive military-industrialization; maximum development of armed forces; great displays to impress outsiders; continued secretiveness about internal matters, designed to conceal weaknesses and to keep opponents in dark.

B. Wherever it is considered timely and promising, efforts will be made to advance official limits of Soviet power. . . .

C. Russians will participate officially in international organizations where they see opportunity of extending Soviet power or of inhibiting or diluting power of others. . . .

D. Toward colonial areas and backward or dependent peoples, Soviet policy, even on official plane, will be directed toward weakening of power and influence and contacts of advanced Western nations, on theory that insofar as this policy is successful, there will be created a vacuum which will favor communist-Soviet penetration. . . .

It may be expected that the component parts of this far-flung apparatus will be utilized, in accordance with their individual suitability, as follows:

1. To undermine general political and strategic potential of major Western powers. Efforts will be made in such countries to disrupt national self-confidence, to hamstring measures of national defense, to increase social and industrial unrest, to stimulate all forms of disunity. . . .

2. On unofficial plane particularly violent efforts will be made to weaken power and influence of Western powers over colonial, backward, or dependent peoples. On this level, no holds will be barred. . . .

3. Where individual governments stand in path of Soviet purposes pressure will be brought for their removal from office. . . .

4. In foreign countries Communists will, as a rule, work toward destruction of all forms of personal independence, economic, political, or moral. . . .

5. Everything possible will be done to set major Western powers against each other. . . . Thus, all forms of international organization not amenable to Communist penetration and control, . . . must expect to find themselves under fire. . . .

In summary, we have here a political force committed fanatically to the belief that with US there can be no permanent modus vivendi, that it is desirable and necessary that the internal harmony of our society be disrupted, our traditional way of life be destroyed, the international authority of our state be broken, if Soviet power is to be secure. . . .

(One) Soviet power, . . . is neither schematic nor adventuristic. It does not work by fixed plans. It does not take unnecessary risks. Impervious to logic of reason, and it is highly sensitive to logic of force. For this reason it can easily withdraw—and usually does—when strong resistance is encountered at any point. Thus, if the adversary has sufficient force and makes clear his readiness to use it, he rarely has to do so. If situations are properly handled there need be no prestige-engaging showdowns.

(Two) Gauged against Western world as a whole, Soviets are still by far the weaker force. Thus, their success will really depend on degree of cohesion, firmness, and vigor which Western world can muster. And this is factor which it is within our power to influence.

(Three) Success of Soviet system, as form of internal power, is not yet finally proven. . . .

(Four) All Soviet propaganda beyond Soviet security sphere is basically negative and destructive. . . .

For these reasons I think we may approach calmly and with good heart the problem of how to deal with Russia. As to how this approach should be made, I only wish to advance, by way of conclusion, the following comments:

1. Our first step must be to apprehend, and recognize for what it is, the nature of the movement with which we are dealing. . . .

2. We must see that our public is educated to realities of Russian situation. I cannot overemphasize the importance of this. Press cannot do this alone. It must be done mainly by government, which is necessarily more experienced and better informed on practical problems involved. . . .

3. Much depends on health and vigor of our own society. World communism is like malignant parasite which feeds only on diseased tissue. . . .

4. We must formulate and put forward for other nations a much more positive and constructive picture of the sort of world we would like to see than we

have put forward in the past. . . . Many foreign peoples, in Europe at least, are tired and frightened by experiences of the past, and are less interested in abstract freedom than in security. . . .

5. Finally, we must have courage and self-confidence to cling to our own methods and conceptions of human society. After all, the greatest danger that can befall us in coping with this problem of Soviet communism is that we shall allow ourselves to become like those with whom we are coping.

## Document 2: An "Iron Curtain" Falls[2]

*Shortly after the end of the war in Europe, the British people voted the Conservative Party out of power in favor of the socialist-leaning Labour Party. Winston Churchill, the inspirational leader during the war, was suddenly out of power and in the Opposition in the British Parliament. Less than a month after Kennan's "Long Telegram," Churchill spoke at Westminster College in Missouri and delivered a message that coined a phrase that became applicable for almost forty years. President Truman, who had read the speech in advance and clearly agreed with it, introduced Churchill to the audience. Churchill described what he called an "iron curtain" that had been drawn between the areas controlled by the Soviet Union and the West. The term "iron curtain" became a catchword that virtually everyone understood. The following is a small portion of the speech.*

. . . The United States stands at this time at the pinnacle of world power. It is a solemn moment for the American Democracy. For with primacy in power is also joined an awe-inspiring accountability to the future. If you look around you, you must feel not only the sense of duty done but also you must feel anxiety lest you fall below the level of achievement. Opportunity is here now, clear and shining for both our countries. To reject it or ignore it or fritter it away will bring upon us all the long reproaches of the after-time. It is necessary that constancy of mind, persistency of purpose, and the grand simplicity of decision shall guide and rule the conduct of the English-speaking peoples in peace as they did in war. We must, and I believe we shall, prove ourselves equal to this severe requirement. . . .

What then is the over-all strategic concept which we should inscribe today? It is nothing less than the safety and welfare, the freedom and progress, of all the homes and families of all the men and women in all the lands. . . .

To give security to . . . countless homes, they must be shielded from the two giant marauders, war and tyranny. We all know the frightful disturbances in which the ordinary family is plunged when the curse of war swoops down upon the bread-winner and those for whom he works and contrives. . . .

When I stand here this quiet afternoon I shudder to visualize what is actually happening to millions now and what is going to happen in this period when famine stalks the earth. . . .

Now I come to the second danger of these two marauders which threatens the cottage, the home, and the ordinary people—namely, tyranny. We cannot be blind to the fact that the liberties enjoyed by individual citizens throughout the British Empire are not valid in a considerable number of countries, some of which are very powerful. In these States control is enforced upon the common people by various kinds of all-embracing police governments. The power of the State is exercised without restraint, either by dictators or by compact oligarchies operating through a privileged party and a political police. . . .

All this means that the people of any country have the right, and should have the power by constitutional action, by free unfettered elections, with secret ballot, to choose or change the character or form of government under which they dwell; that freedom of speech and thought should reign; that courts of justice, independent of the executive, unbiased by any party, should administer laws which have received the broad assent of large majorities or are consecrated by time and custom. . . .

A shadow has fallen upon the scenes so lately lighted by the Allied victory.
. . .

From Stettin in the Baltic to Trieste in the Adriatic, an iron curtain has descended across the Continent. Behind that line lie all the capitals of the ancient states of Central and Eastern Europe. Warsaw, Berlin, Prague, Vienna, Budapest, Belgrade, Bucharest and Sofia, all these famous cities and the populations around them lie in what I must call the Soviet sphere, and all are subject in one form or another, not only to Soviet influence but to a very high and, in many cases, increasing measure of control from Moscow. Athens alone—Greece with its immortal glories—is free to decide its future at an election under British, American and French observation. . . .

The safety of the world requires a new unity in Europe, from which no nation should be permanently outcast. . . .

In front of the iron curtain which lies across Europe are other causes for anxiety . . . the future of Italy hangs in the balance. Again one cannot imagine a regenerated Europe without a strong France . . . in a great number of countries, far from the Russian frontiers and throughout the world, Communist fifth columns are established and work in complete unity and absolute obedience to the directions they receive from the Communist center. Except in the British Commonwealth and in the United States where Communism is in its infancy, the Communist parties or fifth columns constitute a growing challenge and peril to Christian civilization. These are somber facts . . . but we should be most unwise not to face them squarely while time remains. . . .

From what I have seen of our Russian friends and Allies during the war, I am convinced that there is nothing they admire so much as strength, and there is nothing for which they have less respect than for weakness, especially military weakness. For that reason the old doctrine of a balance of power is unsound. We cannot afford, if we can help it, to work on narrow margins, offering temptations to a trial of strength. If the Western Democracies stand together in strict adherence to the principles of the United Nations Charter, their influence for furthering those principles will be immense and no one is likely to molest them. If however they become divided or falter in their duty and if these all-important years are allowed to slip away then indeed catastrophe may overwhelm us all. . . .

### Document 3: Stalin Replies[3]

*Shortly after Churchill's Iron Curtain speech in Missouri, Josef Stalin of the Soviet Union replied to him. He obviously heard Churchill's message and did not want to let it go unchallenged. He commented in an interview with* Pravda, *the official newspaper of the Soviet Union. A portion of the interview follows.*

. . . In substance, Mr. Churchill now stands in the position of a firebrand of war. And Mr. Churchill is not alone here. He has friends not only in England but also in the United States of America.

In this respect, one is reminded remarkably of Hitler and his friends. Hitler began to set war loose by announcing his racial theory, declaring that only people speaking the German language represent a fully valuable nation. Mr. Churchill begins to set war loose, also by a racial theory, maintaining that only nations speaking the English language are fully valuable nations, called upon to decide the destinies of the entire world. . . .

As a result of the German invasion, the Soviet Union has irrevocably lost in battles with the Germans, and also during the German occupation and through the expulsion of Soviet citizens to German slave labor camps, about 7,000,000 people. In other words, the Soviet Union has lost in men several times more than Britain and the United States together.

It may be that some quarters are trying to push into oblivion these sacrifices of the Soviet people which insured the liberation of Europe from the Hitlerite yoke.

But the Soviet Union cannot forget them. One can ask therefore, what can be surprising in the fact that the Soviet Union, in a desire to ensure its security for the future, tries to achieve that these countries should have governments whose relations to the Soviet Union are loyal? How can one, without having lost one's reason, qualify these peaceful aspirations of the Soviet Union as "expansionist tendencies" of our Government? . . .

Mr. Churchill wanders around the truth when he speaks of the growth of the influence of the Communist parties in Eastern Europe. . . . The growth of the influence of communism cannot be considered accidental. It is a normal function. The influence of the Communists grew because during the hard years of the mastery of fascism in Europe, Communists showed themselves to be reliable, daring and self-sacrificing fighters against fascist regimes for the liberty of peoples.

Mr. Churchill sometimes recalls in his speeches the common people from small houses, patting them on the shoulder in a lordly manner and pretending to be their friend. But these people are not so simpleminded as it might appear at first sight. Common people, too, have their opinions and their own politics. And they know how to stand up for themselves.

It is they, millions of these common people, who voted Mr. Churchill and his party out in England, giving their votes to the Labor party. It is they, millions of these common people, who isolated reactionaries in Europe, collaborators with fascism, and gave preference to Left democratic parties.

## Document 4: Acheson Remembers[4]

*Dean Acheson, later to be secretary of state for Truman, was a major official in the State Department at the beginning of the Cold War. In his memoirs, he provided his interpretation about how aid to Greece and Turkey—known as the Truman Doctrine—evolved. A portion of his remarks follows.*

. . . Stalin's offensive against the United States and the West, announced in his speech of February 9, 1946, had begun in Poland in 1945 and would reach its crescendo in Korea and the "hate America" campaign of the early 1950s. This was the start of the "cold war," and was to condition the rest of my official life. The offensive was mounted on territory thought most favorable to the interior lines of the Soviets, where their military power was superior, and on political issues in international discussion, where stubborn and skillful opposition to American proposals could be successful with little cost. Geographically, therefore, the attack was concentrated along Russia's borders in Eastern Europe and the Middle East, where the Soviets' physical position was strongest and that of the United States weakest. Politically it centered against efforts to create a United Nations military force and the United States plan to put atomic energy under effective international control. Blocking tactics in the United Nations were made easy by Soviet possession of the veto. The creation

of Soviet satellites succeeded only where the Red Army was present to rein-
force it. When the attempt moved beyond the Soviet-occupied areas of Eastern Europe to West Germany, the Balkans, and the Middle East, the United
States Government gave fair warning that, if necessary, it was prepared to meet
Soviet force with American force, rather than with mere protests and resolutions in the United Nations. The first warning was given in August 1946 but
Stalin continued to probe cautiously and to receive firm but cautious responses until June 1950, when, throwing off pretense, he made an attack in
force through a satellite on the other side of the world in Korea. Here the
American response was unequivocal.

On August 15 . . . our report expressed the seriousness of the Russian moves
against Turkey and Greece, which aimed at the domination of the Balkans and
the eastern Mediterranean. They should be resisted at all costs. Our note to the
Russians should by its studied restraint impress the Russians that we meant
every word of it. . . . We recommended making very plain to the Russians,
Turks, British, and French that we were in deadly earnest. The USS *Missouri*
was already at Istanbul, where it had been sent earlier with the ashes of a former Turkish Ambassador. We urged sending a powerful naval force, including
the newly commissioned supercarrier *Franklin D. Roosevelt,* to join her. The
President listened carefully, then told us to prepare the necessary notes and orders.

The year 1946 was for the most part a year of learning that minds in the
Kremlin worked very much as George F. Kennan had predicted they would. . . .

. . . Disappointed in its direct pressure on Iran, the Soviet Union turned
with renewed vigor to the pressure it was putting on Greece and Turkey. . . .

We had the good fortune at this time, and through the war, of having a sympathetic, wise, and first-rate Ambassador to Greece, Lincoln MacVeagh. His
reports drew an increasingly gloomy and serious picture of the Greek predica-
ment. Communist bands were forming in the north, which could and did
move back and forth across the Albanian and Yugoslav borders, gaining help
and recruits from both countries. Greek economic affairs were becoming
steadily more and more chaotic and irresponsible. . . .

Ambassador MacVeagh cabled in December that the Soviet Union wanted
complete control of Greece and would interfere with all positive steps by the
Greeks to save themselves. . . .

The situation in Greece, bad at the end of December, deteriorated rapidly
during January and February 1947. All three of our scouts in Greece . . . sent
back increasingly alarming reports of imminent collapse due to mounting
guerrilla activity, supplied and directed from the outside, economic chaos, and
Greek governmental inability to meet the crisis. MacVeagh reported rumors
of impending British troop withdrawals; Waldemar J. Gallman, Minister in

London, that the British Cabinet had met to discuss Greece, and would be asking for help from the United States. All signs pointed to an impending move by the Communists to take over the country. . . .

The next day, the three secretaries concurring, the President approved the paper for action. This moved us from consideration through decision by the Executive. The President set up a meeting for the following day to begin the all-important next step of consultation with the legislative branch, now controlled by the opposite political party. . . .

These congressmen had no conception of what challenged them; it was my task to bring it home. Both my superiors, equally perturbed, gave me the floor. Never have I spoken under such a pressing sense that the issue was up to me alone. No time was left for measured appraisal. In the past eighteen months, I said, Soviet pressure on the Straits, on Iran, and on northern Greece had brought the Balkans to the point where a highly possible Soviet breakthrough might open three continents to Soviet penetration. Like apples in a barrel infected by one rotten one, the corruption of Greece would infect Iran and all to the east. It would also carry infection to Africa through Asia Minor and Egypt, and to Europe through Italy and France, already threatened by the strongest domestic Communist parties in Western Europe. The Soviet Union was playing one of the greatest gambles in history at minimal cost. It did not need to win all the possibilities. Even one or two offered immense gains. We and we alone were in a position to break up the play. These were the stakes that British withdrawal from the eastern Mediterranean offered to an eager and ruthless opponent.

A long silence followed. Then Arthur Vandenberg said solemnly, "Mr. President, if you will say that to the Congress and the country, I will support you and I believe that most of its members will do the same." Without much further talk the meeting broke up to convene again, enlarged, in a week to consider a more detailed program of action. . . .

Like all presidential messages, this one stimulated controversy within the government. George Kennan thought it too strong, since it took the line I had taken with the legislative group, and feared that it might provoke the Soviet Union to aggressive action. Clark Clifford thought it too weak and added some points that I thought unwise. Using General Marshall's great prestige, I got Clark to withdraw his additions and recommend the message as the General had approved it. The President, . . . deciding that he had no alternative but to go ahead, and realizing that this was only a beginning, he approved a request for two hundred fifty million dollars for Greece and one hundred fifty million dollars for Turkey, . . .

Two days later the Cabinet in a body went to the chamber of the House of Representatives to hear the President deliver his message. . . .

When he finished, the President received a standing ovation from both parties. This was a tribute to a brave man rather than unanimous acceptance of his
policy. As I cabled to General Marshall in Moscow, the response to the message
was not one of opposition, but it "did disclose the inevitable pain and anguish
of Congress in facing a difficult situation." For more than two months it would
undergo the anguish of its labor pains before an "Act to Provide for Assistance
to Greece and Turkey" would be delivered to the President for approval.

## Documents 5–6: Two Truman Initiatives

*Truman inaugurated many programs during his term of office that dealt with
the issue of the Cold War. Two of them are shown here.*

### Document 5: The Truman Doctrine[5]

*Truman's program to provide aid to Greece and Turkey to prevent guerilla
communist movements from taking control became known as the Truman Doctrine. Below is a portion of the speech, mentioned by Acheson, that Truman made
to Congress asking for the appropriation.*

The gravity of the situation which confronts the world today necessitates
my appearance before a joint session of the Congress. The foreign policy and
the national security of this country are involved.

One aspect of the present situation, which I wish to present to you at this
time for your consideration and decision, concerns Greece and Turkey.

The United States has received from the Greek Government an urgent appeal for financial and economic assistance. Preliminary reports from the
American Economic Mission now in Greece and reports from the American
Ambassador in Greece corroborate the statement of the Greek Government
that assistance is imperative if Greece is to survive as a free nation.

I do not believe that the American people and the Congress wish to turn a
deaf ear to the appeal of the Greek Government. . . .

When forces of liberation entered Greece they found that the retreating
Germans had destroyed virtually all the railways, roads, port facilities, communications, and merchant marine. More than a thousand villages had been
burned. Eighty-five per cent of the children were tubercular. Livestock, poul-
try, and draft animals had almost disappeared. Inflation had wiped out practically all savings.

As a result of these tragic conditions, a militant minority, exploiting human
want and misery, was able to create political chaos which, until now, has made
economic recovery impossible.

Greece is today without funds to finance the importation of those goods which are essential to bare subsistence. . . . Greece is in desperate need of financial and economic assistance to enable it to resume purchases of food, clothing, fuel and seeds. These are indispensable for the subsistence of its people and are obtainable only from abroad. Greece must have help to import the goods necessary to restore internal order and security, so essential for economic and political recovery. . . .

The very existence of the Greek state is today threatened by the terrorist activities of several thousand armed men, led by Communists, who defy the government's authority at a number of points, particularly along the northern boundaries. . . .

Meanwhile, the Greek Government is unable to cope with the situation. The Greek army is small and poorly equipped. It needs supplies and equipment if it is to restore the authority of the government throughout Greek territory. Greece must have assistance if it is to become a self-supporting and self-respecting democracy.

The United States must supply that assistance. We have already extended to Greece certain types of relief and economic aid but these are inadequate.

There is no other country to which democratic Greece can turn. . . .

Greece's neighbor, Turkey, also deserves our attention.

The future of Turkey as an independent and economically sound state is clearly no less important to the freedom-loving peoples of the world than the future of Greece. The circumstances in which Turkey finds itself today are considerably different from those of Greece. Turkey has been spared the disasters that have beset Greece. And during the war, the United States and Great Britain furnished Turkey with material aid.

Nevertheless, Turkey now needs our support. . . .

I am fully aware of the broad implications involved if the United States extends assistance to Greece and Turkey, and I shall discuss these implications with you at this time.

One of the primary objectives of the foreign policy of the United States is the creation of conditions in which we and other nations will be able to work out a way of life free from coercion. . . .

The peoples of a number of countries of the world have recently had totalitarian regimes forced upon them against their will. The Government of the United States has made frequent protests against coercion and intimidation, in violation of the Yalta agreement, in Poland, Rumania, and Bulgaria. I must also state that in a number of other countries there have been similar developments. . . .

I believe that it must be the policy of the United States to support free peoples who are resisting attempted subjugation by armed minorities or by outside pressures.

I believe that we must assist free peoples to work out their own destinies in their own way.

I believe that our help should be primarily through economic and financial aid which is essential to economic stability and orderly political processes.

The world is not static, and the status quo is not sacred. But we cannot allow changes in the status quo in violation of the Charter of the United Nations by such methods as coercion, or by such subterfuges as political infiltration. In helping free and independent nations to maintain their freedom, the United States will be giving effect to the principles of the Charter of the United Nations.

It is necessary only to glance at a map to realize that the survival and integrity of the Greek nation are of grave importance in a much wider situation. If Greece should fall under the control of an armed minority, the effect upon its neighbor, Turkey, would be immediate and serious. Confusion and disorder might well spread throughout the entire Middle East.

Moreover, the disappearance of Greece as an independent state would have a profound effect upon those countries in Europe whose peoples are struggling against great difficulties to maintain their freedoms and their independence while they repair the damages of war.

It would be an unspeakable tragedy if these countries, which have struggled so long against overwhelming odds, should lose that victory for which they sacrificed so much. Collapse of free institutions and loss of independence would be disastrous not only for them but for the world. Discouragement and possibly failure would quickly be the lot of neighboring peoples striving to maintain their freedom and independence.

Should we fail to aid Greece and Turkey in this fateful hour, the effect will be far reaching to the West as well as to the East.

We must take immediate and resolute action. . . .


### Document 6: The Marshall Plan[6]

*The program of the United States to provide massive aid to Europe for economic recovery is usually referred to as the Marshall Plan. It was introduced in a speech by George Marshall, now the secretary of state for Truman. A portion of the speech follows.*

I need not tell you gentlemen that the world situation is very serious. That must be apparent to all intelligent people. . . . [T]he people of this country are distant from the troubled areas of the earth and it is hard for them to comprehend the plight and consequent reaction of the long-suffering peoples, and the effect of those reactions on their governments in connection with our efforts to promote peace in the world.

In considering the requirements for the rehabilitation of Europe the physical loss of life, the visible destruction of cities, factories, mines, and railroads was correctly estimated, but it has become obvious during recent months that this visible destruction was probably less serious than the dislocation of the entire fabric of European economy. For the past 10 years conditions have been highly abnormal. The feverish maintenance of the war effort engulfed all aspects of national economics. Machinery has fallen into disrepair or is entirely obsolete. Under the arbitrary and destructive Nazi rule, virtually every possible enterprise was geared into the German war machine. Long-standing commercial ties, private institutions, banks, insurance companies and shipping companies disappeared, through the loss of capital, absorption through nationalization or by simple destruction. In many countries, confidence in the local currency has been severely shaken. . . .

There is a phase of this matter which is both interesting and serious. The farmer has always produced the foodstuffs to exchange with the city dweller for the other necessities of life. This division of labor is the basis of modern civilization. At the present time it is threatened with breakdown. The town and city industries are not producing adequate goods to exchange with the food-producing farmer. Raw materials and fuel are in short supply. Machinery is lacking or worn out. The farmer or the peasant cannot find the goods for sale which he desires to purchase. So the sale of his farm produce for money which he cannot use seems to him unprofitable transaction. He, therefore, has withdrawn many fields from crop cultivation and is using them for grazing. He feeds more grain to stock and finds for himself and his family an ample supply of food, however short he may be on clothing and the other ordinary gadgets of civilization. Meanwhile people in the cities are short of food and fuel. So the governments are forced to use their foreign money and credits to procure these necessities abroad. This process exhausts funds which are urgently needed for reconstruction. Thus a very serious situation is rapidly developing which bodes no good for the world. The modern system of the division of labor upon which the exchange of products is based is in danger of breaking down. . . .

Aside from the demoralizing effect on the world at large and the possibilities of disturbances arising as a result of the desperation of the people concerned, the consequences to the economy of the United States should be apparent to all. It is logical that the United States should do whatever it is able to do to assist in the return of normal economic health in the world, without which there can be no political stability and no assured peace. Our policy is

directed not against any country or doctrine but against hunger, poverty, desperation, and chaos. Its purpose should be the revival of working economy in
the world so as to permit the emergence of political and social conditions in
which free institutions can exist. Such assistance, I am convinced, must not be
on a piecemeal basis as various crises develop. Any assistance that this Government may render in the future should provide a cure rather than a mere
palliative. Any government that is willing to assist in the task of recovery will
find full cooperation, I am sure, on the part of the United States Government.
Any government which maneuvers to block the recovery of other countries
cannot expect help from us. Furthermore, governments, political parties, or
groups which seek to perpetuate human misery in order to profit therefrom
politically or otherwise will encounter the opposition of the United States.

. . . It would be neither fitting nor efficacious for this Government to undertake to draw up unilaterally a program designed to place Europe on its feet
economically. This is the business of the Europeans. The initiative, I think,
must come from Europe. The role of this country should consist of friendly
aid in the drafting of a European program so far as it may be practical for us
to do so. The program should be a joint one, agreed to by a number, if not all
European nations.

An essential part of any successful action on the part of the United States is
an understanding on the part of the people of America of the character of the
problem and the remedies to be applied. Political passion and prejudice
should have no part. With foresight, and a willingness on the part of our people to face up to the vast responsibilities which history has clearly placed upon
our country, the difficulties I have outlined can and will be overcome.

### Document 7: Truman Speaks[7]

*By 1950, the Cold War had turned hot with the outbreak of war in Korea. The
war was unpopular with many people, and Truman tried very hard to bring it to
an end. In 1950, he flew to Wake Island to confer with General Douglas
MacArthur, who essentially refused to come to Washington to talk with Truman.
On his return to the United States, he made a speech in San Francisco in which
he explained his actions and tried again to get Stalin to be reasonable. A portion
of the speech follows.*

Here, in San Francisco, five years ago, we hoped that the Soviet Union
would cooperate in this effort to build a lasting peace.

But communist imperialism would not have it so. Instead of working with
other governments in mutual respect and cooperation, the Soviet Union attempted to extend its control over other peoples. It embarked on a new colo-

nialism—Soviet style. This new colonialism has already brought under its complete control and exploitation many countries which used to be free countries. Moreover, the Soviet Union has refused to cooperate and has not allowed its satellites to cooperate with those nations it could not control.

In the United Nations, the Soviet Union has persisted in obstruction. It has refused to share in activities devoted to the great economic, social, and spiritual causes recognized in the United Nations Charter. For months on end, it even boycotted the Security Council. . . .

The Soviet Union and its colonial satellites are maintaining armed forces of great size and strength. . . . So long as they persist in maintaining these forces and in using them to intimidate other countries, the free men of the world have but one choice if they are to remain free. They must oppose strength with strength.

This is not a task for the United States alone. It is a task for the free nations to undertake together. And the free nations are undertaking it together. . . .

Now, the Soviet Union can change this situation. It has only to give concrete and positive proof of its intention to work for peace. If the Soviet Union really wants peace, it must prove it—not by glittering promises and false propaganda, but by living up to the principles the United Nations Charter.

If the Soviet Union really wants peace, it can prove it—and could have proved it on any day since last June 25—by joining the rest of the United Nations in calling upon the North Koreans to lay down their arms at once.

If the Soviet Union really wants peace, it can prove it by lifting the Iron Curtain and permitting the free exchange of information and ideas. If the Soviet Union really wants peace, it can prove it by joining in the efforts of the United Nations to establish a workable system of collective security—a system which will permit the elimination of the atomic bomb and the drastic reduction and regulation of all other arms and armed forces.

But until the Soviet Union does these things, until it gives proof of peaceful intentions, we are determined to build up the common defensive strength of the free world. This is the choice we have made. We have made it firmly and resolutely. But it is not a choice we have made gladly. We are not a militaristic nation. We have no desire for conquest or military glory. . . .

## Part B: Sputnik—The Cold War in Action

### Background

*At the end of World War II, the United States was the most powerful and the richest country in the world. Europe and much of Asia had been devastated by the war, and American allies were prostrate in the midst of destruction. In addi-tion, the United States had a monopoly on nuclear weapons as a result of the top-secret research project during the war known as the "Manhattan Project" that produced the world's first atomic bomb just before the end of the war.*

*Within a few years after the war, the world had divided into two enemy camps with a sizable number of nations unaligned with either side; they became known in popular terminology as the "third world." On one side was the United States with its allies, mostly in Western Europe, but also with significant Asian allies. On the other side was the Soviet Union, still ruled by Josef Stalin until his death in 1953, which was supported by its allies, mostly the so-called "satellite countries" of Eastern Europe that had been occupied by the Soviets at the end of the war and where the Soviets still maintained rigorous control.*

*The position of the United States was supported, in part, because of the sizable expenditures it made in Europe to restore the economies and the physical struc-tures destroyed in the war and because it had the military might to defend the world against the Soviet threat.*

*By the late 1940s, the two world powers were in a non-shooting conflict that became known as the "Cold War." The fear on both sides was that this could be-come a "hot" war at any time. Each side continued to shore up its defenses and to anticipate what the other side might do.*

*One of the first blows to American self-confidence came in 1949 when the So-viets successfully tested an atomic bomb, several years ahead of when American scientists had estimated it could be done. Immediately, many Americans sus-pected American secrets had been obtained by Soviet spies—either native or American-born—but the secret was out nonetheless.*

*The United States was also shocked when the Soviet Union placed an artificial satellite into space that orbited the earth. This appeared to be a vindication of the superiority of Soviet science rather than spying. Known as "Sputnik," the satellite gave the Soviets a significant public relations advantage. They were "ahead" of the United States in science and technology in the minds of many. The United States had become "soft" and careless because of its wealth and its consumer com-forts. The public education system, especially, came under criticism because, in the minds of many, it was not preparing enough scientists, engineers, and tech-nologists to beat the Soviet threat. Now, in the fall of 1957, the Russians, the crit-ics believed, had shown their superiority by being the first nation into space.*

*President Eisenhower had been elected because of his hero status from World War II. He was one of the oldest men to serve in the presidency, and he had had several illnesses that made many wonder about his ability to lead in perilous times. Less than two months after the launching of Sputnik, Eisenhower had a small stroke, another event that put his leadership in question and caused more anxiety in the American people.*

*Today, Sputnik has receded from memory, especially after the United States put a man on the moon, so far the only country to do so. With the collapse of the Soviet Union at the end of the 1980s and beginning of the 1990s, the United States stood supreme in space exploration, even though no humans have been sent out of the earth's atmosphere in many years. Even so, Sputnik did create a panic and near hysteria in its immediate aftermath.*

## Questions

In reading these documents, the student should ask and answer several questions to put these activities in the proper context.

1. How significant in scientific terms was the Soviet achievement of putting a satellite into space?
2. Did Sputnik mean that the Soviet Union was truly ahead of the United States, or was it merely a sign of the growing media hype in the United States?
3. Did the United States react properly to Sputnik?
4. Was the American education system as out of touch with the modern world as its critics said?
5. Should the United States have ignored this development and continued its research programs without alteration?

## Document 1: Soviets Announce Satellite[8]

*The world was stunned on October 5, 1957, when the Soviet Union announced that it had placed a man-made satellite into orbit. This was so shocking because most people had no idea what a satellite was or what this achievement meant. It did hint at serious consequences for the United States in the Cold War with the Soviet Union. On the same day that the* New York Times *announced Sputnik, the official news agency of the Soviet Union, Tass, issued a press release that was printed in* Pravda. *Sputnik, translated as "fellow traveler," was described in a restrained statement, but it did have overtones of propaganda and the Cold War.*

... As already reported in the press, the first launching of the satellites in the USSR were planned for realization in accordance with the scientific research program of the International Geophysical Year.

As a result of very intensive work by scientific research institutes and design bureaus the first artificial satellite in the world has been created. On October 4, 1957, this first satellite was successfully launched in the USSR.

According to preliminary data, the carrier rocket has imparted to the satellite the required orbital velocity of about 8000 meters per second. At the present time the satellite is describing elliptical trajectories around the earth, and its flight can be observed in the rays of the rising and setting sun with the aid of very simple optical instruments (binoculars, telescopes, etc.). . . .

Scientific stations located at various points in the Soviet Union are tracking the satellite and determining the elements of its trajectory. Since the density of the rarified upper layers of the atmosphere is not accurately known, there are no data at present for the precise determination of the satellite's lifetime and of the point of its entry into the dense layers of the atmosphere. Calculations have shown that owing to the tremendous velocity of the satellite, at the end of its existence it will burn up on reaching the dense layers of the atmosphere at an altitude of several tens of kilometers. . . .

The successful launching of the first man-made earth satellite makes a most important contribution to the treasure-house of world science and culture. The scientific experiment accomplished at such a great height is of tremendous importance for learning the properties of cosmic space and for studying the earth as a planet of our solar system. . . .

*When the Soviet Union launched Sputnik I into space in 1957, it brought a significant reaction from the United States. Americans were convinced that the Soviets were in the lead in space exploration, and the safety—as well as the superiority—of the United States was in question. The first satellite was a small device that seems, in retrospect, to be rather primitive. This model of the spacecraft shows how simple it was. NASA.*

Artificial earth satellites will pave the way to interplanetary travel and apparently our contemporaries will witness how the freed and conscientious labor of the people of the new socialist society makes the most daring dreams of mankind a reality.

## Documents 2–4: America Reacts

*Immediately upon the announcement of Sputnik's orbiting the Earth, Americans wanted to know the reason for the Soviet superiority. They were also concerned about what this event actually meant. Some believed that the Soviets now had an "eye in the sky" that could spy on the United States and eventually would be able to drop bombs (conventional or atomic) on the United States. A common impression today is that Americans panicked in the immediate aftermath of Sputnik's launching. Others believe that most Americans took a more calm or unconcerned view of the launching of Sputnik.*

### Document 2: Assorted reactions[8]

*A number of the reactions by Americans have been collected and posted online. These reactions give a flavor of the times and how people were thinking.*

The United States was shocked. Senator Lyndon Johnson said the Russians have jumped way ahead of us in the conquest of space. "Soon, they will be dropping bombs on us from space like kids dropping rocks onto cars from freeway overpasses!" [from a movie that dramatized the emotional impact of that day]. Everyone in the United States were [sic] constantly reminded that the Russians were well on the way in conquering space and newspaper headlines, "REDS ORBIT ARTIFICIAL MOON" and "SOVIET SATELLITE CIRCLES GLOBE EVERY 90 MINUTES."

### Reactions by Americans:

- Many people did not know how to think of a satellite in orbit. It was too mysterious for them, "What is a 184 pound object in orbit?" "Are they looking down at us?"
- Engineering colleges were flooded with new students the following quarter. It was as if everyone was "joining the army" to take on the Russians in the New Frontier (the govt also provided a lot of funds for engineering schools to fuel new interests in engineering).
- Everyone on Johnston Island in the Pacific was issued sidearms to carry at all times. Johnston Island is so small it only has room for a runway and a hanger for airplanes.

- Students at Case Institute immediately became "Rocket Scientists" and stayed up many late nights discussing various methods of space travel.
- Jim Dawsons, science writer for the Star Tribune, wrote about how his third grade teacher was very nervous at the time. His school at Omaha, Neb., was just a few miles from the Air Force's Strategic Air Command headquarters. A fleet of F-100 fighters appeared in the sky coming right for the school. "MiGs!" the teacher shrieked. "MiGs!" She ran, hysterical, from the classroom, convinced they were about to be nuked by Russian fighter jets. The kids, mostly Air Force brats, ran to the windows to admire the F-100s, the coolest jet of its day.
- Politicians and editorialists began attacking the U.S. educational system for having fallen behind Soviet schools in training people in the sciences and other fields.
- Former President Harry Truman was moved to comment, charging the "persecution" of prominent U.S. scientists by Sen. Joseph McCarthy during the early 1950s had been a setback to the nation's development of satellites and rockets.

### Document 3: Eisenhower reacts[10]

*Shortly after the launching of Sputnik, the event came up, quite expectedly, during the president's press conference. President Eisenhower tried to downplay the event and to allay the fears of Americans. During the press conference, he also tried to explain why the United States was not farther along in space research.*

THE PRESIDENT. Well, let's take, first, the earth satellite, as opposed to the missile, because they are related only indirectly in the physical sense, and in our case not at all.

The first mention that was made of an earth satellite that I know of, was about the spring of 1955—I mean the first mention to me—following upon a conference in Rome where plans were being laid for the working out of the things to be done in the International Geophysical Year.

Our people came back, studying a recommendation of that conference that we now undertake, the world undertake, the launching of a small earth satellite; and somewhere in I think May or June of 1955 it was recommended to me, by the Committee for the International Geophysical Year and through the National Science Foundation, that we undertake this project with a satellite to be launched somewhere during the Geophysical Year, which was from June 1957 until December 1958.

The sum asked for to launch a missile was $22 million and it was approved. . . .

Now, in the first instance they thought they would merely put up a satellite, and very quickly they found they thought they could put up a satellite with a considerable instrumentation to get, even during the Geophysical Year, the kind of information to which I have just referred. So they came back, said they needed some more money. This time they went up to $66 million, and we said, "All right; that is—'m [sic] view of the fact we are conducting this basic research, this seems logical." So we did that.

Then they came back, and I forget which one of the steps it came along, and they realized when you put this machine in the air, you had to have some very specially equipped observation stations. So the money, the sum of money, again went up to provide for these observation stations. And so the final sum approved, I think about a year ago, something of that kind, was $110,000,000, with notice that that might have to go up even still more.

There never has been one nickel asked for accelerating the program. Never has it been considered as a race; merely an engagement on our part to put up a vehicle of this kind during the period that I have already mentioned. . . .

We are still going ahead on this program to make certain that before the end of the calendar year 1958 we have put a vehicle in the air with the maximum ability that we can devise for obtaining the kind of scientific information that I have stated. . . .

Q. Charles W. Bailey, Minneapolis Star and Tribune: Sir, can you tell us, sir, whether you had any advance information that a Russian satellite launching was imminent?

THE PRESIDENT. Not imminent. For a number of months different scientists have told me, or different people—I don't know whether it was ever told to me officially—that they were working on it, they were doing something about it; but again, no one ever suggested to me as anything of a race except, of course, more than once we would say, well, there is going to be a great psychological advantage in world. . . .

Q. Hazel Markel, National Broadcasting Company: Mr. President, in light of the great faith which the American people have in your military knowledge and leadership, are you saying at this time that with the Russian satellite whirling about the world, you are not more concerned nor overly concerned about our Nation's security?

THE PRESIDENT. Well, I think I have time and again emphasized my concern about the Nation's security. I believe I just a few months back went on the television to make a special plea about this. As a matter of fact, I plead [sic] very strongly for $38 billion in new appropriations this year, and was cut quite severely in that new appropriations for next year.

Now, so far as the satellite itself is concerned, that does not raise my apprehensions, not one iota. I see nothing at this moment, at this stage of development, that is significant in that development as far as security is concerned, except, as I pointed out, it does definitely prove the possession by the Russian scientists of a very powerful thrust in their rocketry, and that is important. I can only say that I have had every group that I know anything about, to ask them is there anything more we can do in the development of our rocket program any better than it is being done? And, except for certain minor items or, you might say, almost involving administration, there has been little said. . . .

*Document 4: Eisenhower's official statement[11]*

*At the time of his press conference, President Eisenhower also issued a formal statement regarding the development of an Earth satellite by the United States. This was clearly an effort to allay American fears that the country was falling behind the Soviets.*

1. THE FIRST serious discussion of an earth satellite as a scientific experiment to be incorporated in the program for the International Geophysical Year took place at a meeting of the International Council of Scientific Unions in Rome in October 1954. At this meeting, at which Soviet scientists were present, a resolution was adopted by the scientists of the world recommending that "in view of the advanced state of present rocket techniques . . . thought be given to the launching of small satellite vehicles. . . ."

2. Following this International Council meeting, the United States National Committee for International Geophysical Year, working under the sponsorship of the National Academy of Sciences, recommended that the United States institute a scientific satellite program. It was determined by the Administration that this program would be carried out as part of the United States' contribution to the International Geophysical Year. . . .

3. On July 29, 1955, at a White House press conference, participated in by representatives of the National Science Foundation and the National Academy of Sciences, it was announced that plans "are going forward for the launching of small, unmanned earth circling satellites as part of the United States participation in the International Geophysical Year, which takes place between July 1957 and December 1958."

At this press conference it was specifically stated that the "data which will be collected from this program will be made available to all scientists throughout the world." The National Science Foundation, it was also announced, would work with the United States National Committee for the International Geophysical Year to formulate plans for the satellite and its instrumentation as well as plans for the preparation and deployment of the ground observer equipment required for the program.

4. In May of 1957, those charged with the United States satellite program determined that small satellite spheres would be launched as test vehicles during 1957 to check the rocketry, instrumentation, and ground stations and that the first fully-instrumented satellite vehicle would be launched in March of 1958. The first of these test vehicles is planned to be launched in December of this year.

As to the Soviet satellite, we congratulate Soviet scientists upon putting a satellite into orbit.

The United States satellite program has been designed from its inception for maximum results in scientific research. The scheduling of this program has been described to and closely coordinated with the International Geophysical Year scientists of all countries. As a result of passing full information on our project to the scientists of the world, immediate tracking of the United States satellite will be possible, and the world's scientists will know at once its orbit and the appropriate times for observation. . . .

### Document 5: The Secretary of State Tries to Quiet Fears[12]

*The Eisenhower administration was concerned about the Soviet satellite even though it had been anticipated. Officials were apprehensive about the public reaction, but still they were surprised by the public concern that was expressed in the immediate aftermath. In an effort to calm the public, Secretary of State John Foster Dulles sent the White House press secretary some suggestions for a press release to put the Sputnik launch in its proper context and reassure the public.*

The launching by the Soviet Union of the first earth satellite is an event of considerable technical and scientific importance. However, that importance should not be exaggerated. What has happened involves no basic discovery and the value of a satellite to mankind will for a long time be highly problematical.

That the Soviet Union was first in this project is due to the high priority which the Soviet Union gives to scientific training and to the fact that since 1945 the Soviet Union has particularly emphasized developments in the fields of missiles and of outer space. . . . Despotic societies which can command the activities and resources of all their people can often produce spectacular accomplishments. These, however, do not prove that freedom is not the best way.

While the United States has not given the same priority to outer space developments as has the Soviet Union, it has not neglected this field. It already has a capability to utilize outer space for missiles and it is expected to launch an earth satellite during the present geophysical year in accordance with a program which has been under orderly development over the past two years.

The United States welcomes the peaceful achievement of the Soviet scientists. It hopes that the acclaim which has resulted from their efforts will encourage the Soviet Union to seek development along peaceful lines and seek to enrich the spiritual and material welfare of their people.

What is happening with reference to outer space makes more than ever important the proposal made by the United States and the other free world members of the Disarmament Subcommittee. I recall my White House statement of August 28 which emphasized the proposal of the Western Powers at London to establish a study group to the end that "outer space shall be used only for peaceful, not military, purposes."

### Document 6: Soviet Beginnings of Satellites[13]

*In 1954, a Soviet scientist, Mihail K. Tikhonravov, head of a department at the Scientific Research Institute No. 4 in the Soviet Union, prepared a report that was probably the first proposal for a Soviet space program. Sent to the government on May 26, 1954, it was a formal request to establish a satellite program. At the time, Americans had no idea that the Soviets were this far along or that they were concentrating on satellite development. A portion of his report follows.*

At the present time there are real technological possibilities for rockets to achieve the velocity necessary for creating an artificial earth satellite. The most realistic and feasible option requiring the shortest possible period of time is the creation of an artificial earth satellite in the form of an automatic device which would be equipped with scientific equipment, would have radio contact with the earth, and would circle the earth at a distance on the order of 170-1,100 km from the earth's surface. This device we shall call the simplest satellite.

We conceive the simplest satellite as an unmanned vehicle, moving in an elliptical orbit and designed for scientific purposes. The weight of such a satellite could be on the order of 2–3 tons, taking into account its scientific equipment. As we shall see from what follows, at the present time the means of realizing the simplest satellite are essentially clear. Without a doubt some questions require further research, but in any case we are able to discuss the creation of a technical plan for the simplest satellite. . . .

Stated briefly, this work program could consist of the following:

The initial work stage should be the simplest satellite, mentioned above. Along with the simplest satellite this work stage should include humans' mastery of the technique of rocket travel, as well as the development of methods for securing a safe descent from the satellite to earth. We will note that the practical development of these methods is possible, even up to and including the realization of manned satellites.

Thus, by including into the first work stage the human travel in rockets and also the research and development of safe descent methods, a natural transition can be achieved from the simplest satellite to a small, experimental, manned satellite, designed in such a way that 1–2 people can remain in circular orbit for a prolonged period of time.

On this manned satellite, along with scientific tasks, the conditions arising from the prolonged existence of human beings in a state of weightlessness should be studied, and the question of the creation of a satellite-station should be resolved experimentally—this being the next work stage in this direction. . . .

It would be difficult to overestimate the importance of such a satellite. It could be in the laboratory for a whole series of scientific research and have enormous economic importance, for example, by providing long-term observation of processes taking place on earth. Finally, it could be the dispatcher station for research of the moon and other planets.

### Document 7: Massachusetts Responds[14]

*In the aftermath of the launching of Sputnik, many people asked how the Soviets could get this far ahead. Since this was a scientific achievement, schools in America came under attack for not educating enough scientists, engineers, and technologists. About a year after Sputnik, the commissioner of education for the state of Massachusetts wrote about the impact of the satellite on his state's education program.*

In the memorable lines of Ralph Waldo Emerson, the opening battle of the American Revolution was described as "the shot heard 'round the world." At approximately 5:45 p.m., on October 4, 1957, another shot—this time the blast of a rocket—was both heard and seen around the world.

The repercussions of Sputnik are still being felt in Massachusetts. Education continues to be more in the focus of public attention than at any time in our history. As was to be expected, critics of public education were recruited overnight and our schools placed under an unprecedented attack. Panaceas were no longer developed singly but by the dozen. Our sharpest critics have been well-meaning people who perhaps have discovered that reproof and sensational denunciations attain headline prominence far more readily than praise and commendation. . . .

As an example of distorted fact, one critic in Massachusetts asserted publicly that less than 12 per cent of high school students were studying algebra and geometry. Similar inaccurate information has been published about the sciences and foreign languages. What are the facts concerning high schools of Massachusetts?

Today, 64.4 per cent of our students enroll in algebra during their high school career; 50.7 per cent take plane geometry; 73.3 per cent general science; 60 per cent biology; 49.5 per cent chemistry; 33 per cent physics; and 47.4 per cent take foreign languages.

It should be pointed out that students may enroll in different curriculum offerings. Many not included above in algebra, for example, would be taking a course in general mathematics.

. . . Because state appropriating authorities sometimes are reluctant to add personnel, the recommendation to employ a state coordinator was tabled. Not until the U.S.S.R. was successful in launching the first earth satellite did legislators realize the importance of this recommendation and subsequently funds were made available. Thus, credit must be accorded Sputnik I for serving as a catalytic agent in the appointment of a much needed staff member. That sister states have experienced similar gains is evidenced from an examination of recent issues of *Scholastic Teacher*.

On the national scene, Congressional interest in the strengthening of our schools and colleges is reflected in the passage of the National Defense Education Act of 1958. Aptly described as a "third educational milestone" in this nation's history, this important legislation takes its place beside the Northwest Ordinance of 1787 and the Morrill Act of 1862. Following the pattern of the previously-established advisory committee for math and science, similar committees have been inaugurated to assist in the implementation of this Act. Leaders in the field are now serving the state in the areas of modern foreign language, guidance, and audio-visual education.

By broadening the base of participation, Massachusetts is determined to successfully meet the challenge of this day and age. In so doing, approximately [sic] 1,000,000 students will be guaranteed their rightful place in the sun.

### Documents 8–10: President Eisenhower Responds and Acts

*President Eisenhower faced severe pressure after the launching of Sputnik. About a month after the launching, on November 3, 1957, the Soviet Union placed Sputnik II into orbit. This second satellite weighed more than 1,000 pounds and carried a dog as a passenger. Later in the month, Eisenhower had a mild stroke on November 25. A period of uncertainty followed, but leadership was disrupted only temporarily. Immediately after the launching, Eisenhower discussed how to respond.*

*Document 8: Eisenhower meets with advisors[15]*

On October 9, 1957, Eisenhower met with a group of eleven people to review the situation. The meeting was summarized by General A. J. Goodpaster. Later in the day, he met with advisors again.

<u>First meeting:</u>

October 9, 1957

MEMORANDUM OF CONFERENCE WITH THE PRESIDENT

October 8, 1957, 8:30 AM

Secretary Quarles began by reviewing a memorandum prepared in Defense for the President on the subject of the earth satellite (dated October 7, 1957). He left a copy with the President. He reported that the Soviet launching on October 4th had apparently been highly successful.

The President asked Secretary Quarles about the report that had come to his attention to the effect that Redstone could have been used and could have placed a satellite in orbit many months ago. Secretary Quarles said there was no doubt that the Redstone, had it been used, could have orbited a satellite a year or more ago. The Science Advisory Committee had felt, however, that it was better to have the earth satellite proceed separately from military development. One reason was to stress the peaceful character of the effort, and a second was to avoid the inclusion of materiel, to which foreign scientists might be given access, which is used in our own military rockets. He said that the Army feels it could erect a satellite four months from now if given the order—this would still be one month prior to the estimated date for the Vanguard. The President said that when this information reaches the Congress, they are bound to ask why this action was not taken. He recalled, however, that timing was never given too much importance in our own program, which was tied to the IGY [International Geophysical Year] and confirmed that, in order for all scientists to be able to look at the instrument, it had to be kept away from military secrets. Secretary Quarles pointed out that the Army plan would require some modification of the instrumentation in the missile.

He went on to add that the Russians have in fact done us a good turn, unintentionally, in establishing the concept of freedom of international space—this seems to be generally accepted as orbital space, in which the missile is making an inoffensive passage.

The President asked what kind of information could be conveyed by the signals reaching us from the Russian satellite. Secretary Quarles said the Soviets say that it is simply a pulse to permit location of the missile through radar direction finders. Following the meeting, Dr. Waterman indicated that there is some kind of modulation on the signals, which may mean that some coding is being done, although it might conceivably be accidental.

The President asked the group to look ahead five years, and asked about a reconnaissance vehicle. Secretary Quarles said the Air Force has a research program in this area and gave a general description of the project.

Governor Adams recalled that Dr. Pusey had said that we had never thought of this as a crash program, as the Russians apparently did. We were working simply to develop and transmit scientific knowledge. The President thought that to make a sudden shift in our approach now would be to belie the attitude we had had all along. Secretary Quarles said that such a shift would create service tensions in the Pentagon. Mr. Holaday said he planned to study with the Army the back up of the Navy program with the Redstone, adapting it to the instrumentation.

There was some discussion concerning the Soviet request as to whether we would like to put instruments of ours aboard one of their satellites. He said our instruments would be ready for this. Several present pointed out that our instruments contain parts which, if made available to the Russians, would give them substantial technological information.


*Second meeting:*
MEMORANDUM OF CONFERENCE WITH THE PRESIDENT
October 8, 1957, 5 P. M.

The President said he had asked Dr. Bronk to come in and read the statement he (the president) was proposing to give out at his press conference on the ninth. His intent was not to belittle the Russian accomplishment. He would like, however, to allay hysteria and alarm, and to bring out that the Russian action is simply proof of a thrust mechanism of a certain power to be accurate and directed to the right broad purpose.

Dr. Bronk read the statement, and suggested one or two revisions in discussion with the President. He recalled that on hearing of the Soviet satellite, he had come to attend the last session of the IGY group meeting in Washington last week and had taken the line in addressing this session that competition is a powerful stimulus and the Russians deserve credit for their accomplishment, but that our own program will also make a great scientific contribution.

Governor Adams asked whether in Dr. Bronk's opinion there is anything in this achievement to alter our research and development program, particularly in the missles [sic] area. Dr. Bronk said there was not in his opinion, and that we cannot constantly change our program with every action by the Russians.

Dr. Bronk suggested that if the President were asked if the scientists had been given adequate responsibility and opportunity to develop the satellite, he should say that they had been.

*Document 9: How did Americans really react?[16]*

*A year after the launching of Sputnik, a seminar held in Washington, D.C., analyzed how seriously most Americans considered the launching at the time it occurred. One of the participants was Donald N. Michael, a social psychologist and physicist, who had been a senior research associate for a private group. He had also worked for the Joint Chiefs of Staff and had been a consultant for the National Research Council Committee on Disaster Studies. Some of his remarks evaluated the public reaction in the fall of 1957.*

Michael [Donald N. Michael] told how on the morning following the launching of the first Russian sputnik, the New York Times announced the event in an unusual three-row headline with much supplementary information, while the Milwaukee Sentinel relegated it to a small headline and short article on the third page. These two responses represented the extremes in the responses of the American public itself, but Americans generally tended toward the attitude of the Milwaukee newspaper. For the purpose of describing these responses, one might divide Americans into 1) the policy-makers in Washington, 2) the issue-makers of the mass media and other authoritative sources, and 3) the public at large. In general, the first two categories assumed that the public at large was much more aroused than it actually was. The statements of Administration and military leaders were contradictory and ambiguous. Many persons in groups 1 and 2 made use of the occasion to indulge in personal axe-grinding, and only some of them were able to appraise the situation calmly. The issue-makers used the occasion to launch their own accusations at the Administration and the military establishment. Furthermore, many in both groups responded with a ritualistic evocation of Puritan virtues, saying, for example, that we must pull in our belts and work harder. This response was similar to that of a large segment of the public at large, but the meaning for either group was unclear in the light of their ignorance about scientific and engineering matters vis-à-vis missile development.

Knowledge about earth satellites in general did not increase significantly after the first Russian sputnik, in spite of the large amount of scientific information published in popular form; and the news media regularly confused science with engineering. . . .

Reactions to the first sputnik are equally interesting. The Baltimore survey asked the public to explain how the Russians had managed such a feat. Fifty-four percent did not know at all, 25 percent said that the Russians try harder, and 10 percent that the Russians are just better at that kind of thing. A Gallup poll showed that 30 percent ascribed the Russian success to the fact that the Russians worked harder, 20 percent to the work of German scientists, and 15 percent to better organization. One-fourth of the sample had no explanation.

Gallup also found that only about half the people were surprised at the sputnik, even though many of those asked in this sample knew nothing about it previous to its launching. Two months after the launching, only an estimated 4 percent of the U.S. population had seen either sputnik.

Interpretations of the sputnik's significance likewise show that public concern was not great. Gallup found that only 50 percent of a sample taken in Washington and Chicago regarded the sputnik as a blow to our prestige. Sixty percent said that we, not the Russians, would make the next great scientific (actually technological) advance. A poll by the Minneapolis Star and Tribune found that 65 percent of a sample in that State thought we could send up a satellite within 30 days following the Russian success, a statistic which included 56 percent of the college-educated persons asked. In the sample of the Opinion Research Corporation, 13 percent believed that we had fallen behind dangerously, 36 percent that we were behind but would catch up, and 46 percent said that we were still at least abreast of Russia. . . .

If there was any trauma following the Russian sputnik, it occurred in Washington and not among the general public. Washington, for its part, took its cue from the newspapers and other issue makers. The misevaluation by leadership of the extent of public interest, as measured by the amount of news, coverage and the words of the issue makers, led to words and actions which further confused the issue. This situation points up the general problem for a democracy of: who is the public to which leadership attends and who in fact do the issue makers represent?


*Document 10: Eisenhower proposes legislation[17]*

*The Sputnik activity resulted in many actions by the United States, but two of them were especially significant. Despite his stroke and temporary disability, Eisenhower was quick to respond positively to the situation. On April 2, he proposed the creation of the National Aeronautics and Space Agency (NASA), which was created in record time later that year. He also proposed a major spending bill for education that broke the log-jam in the matter of federal aid to education. In 1958, as well, the National Defense Education Act (NDEA) was passed by Congress. The law was designed to increase the number of teachers in America's schools and put a new emphasis on science and mathematics. A portion of Eisenhower's message to Congress regarding NASA follows.*

To the Congress of the United States:

Recent developments in long-range rockets for military purposes have for the first time provided man with new machinery so powerful that it can put satellites into orbit, and eventually provide the means for space exploration.

The United States of America and the Union of Soviet Socialist Republics have already successfully placed in orbit a number of earth satellites. In fact, it is now within the means of any technologically advanced nation to embark upon practicable programs for exploring outer space. The early enactment of appropriate legislation will help assure that the United States takes full advantage of the knowledge of its scientists, the skill of its engineers and technicians, and the resourcefulness of its industry in meeting the challenges of the space age.

... In a statement which I released on March 26, 1958, the Science Advisory Committee has listed four factors which in its judgment give urgency and inevitability to advancement in space technology. These factors are: (1) the compelling urge of man to explore the unknown; (2) the need to assure that full advantage is taken of the military potential of space; (3) the effect on national prestige of accomplishment in space science and exploration; and (4) the opportunities for scientific observation and experimentation which will add to our knowledge of the earth, the solar system, and the universe.

These factors have such a direct bearing on the future progress as well as on the security of our Nation that an imaginative and well-conceived space program must be given high priority and a sound organization provided to carry it out. . . .

I recommend that aeronautical and space science activities sponsored by the United States be conducted under the direction of a civilian agency, except for those projects primarily associated with military requirements. I have reached this conclusion because space exploration holds promise of adding importantly to our knowledge of the earth, the solar system, and the universe, and because it is of great importance to have the fullest cooperation of the scientific community at home and abroad in moving forward in the fields of space science and technology. Moreover, a civilian setting for the administration of space function will emphasize the concern of our Nation that outer space be devoted to peaceful and scientific purposes.

I am, therefore, recommending that the responsibility for administering the civilian space science and exploration program be lodged in a new National Aeronautics and Space Agency, into which the National Advisory Committee for Aeronautics would be absorbed. . . .

The National Aeronautics and Space Agency should be given that authority which it will need to administer successfully the new programs under conditions that cannot now be fully foreseen. . . .

Pending enactment of legislation, it is essential that necessary work relating to space programs be continued without loss of momentum. For this reason, I have approved, as part of an interim program of space technology and exploration, the launching of a number of unmanned space vehicles under the direction of the Advanced Research Projects Agency of the Department of Defense. The projects which I have approved include both scientific earth satellites and programs to explore space. In taking this interim action, I directed the Department of Defense to coordinate these projects with the National Advisory Committee for Aeronautics, the National Science foundation, and the National Academy of Sciences. I also indicated that when a civilian space agency is created, these projects would be reviewed to determine which should continue under the direction of the Department of Defense and which should be placed under the new Agency.

It is contemplated that the Department of Defense will continue to be responsible for space activities peculiar to or primarily associated with military weapons systems or military operations. Responsibility for other programs is to be assumed by the new Agency.

## Notes

1. George Kennan, "Excerpts from Telegraphic Message from Moscow of February 22, 1946," *Foreign Relations of the United States* (Washington, D.C.: United States Government Printing Office, 1969), VI, 696–709.

2. Winston Churchill, "The Sinews of Peace," March 5, 1946, Westminster College, Fulton, Missouri. Reproduced with permission of Curtis Brown Ltd., London on behalf of the Estate of Winston Churchill. Copyright Winston S. Churchill.

3. "Stalin's Reply to Churchill," interview with *Pravda*, March 14, 1946.

4. Dean Acheson, *Present at the Creation: My Years in the State Department* (New York: W.W. Norton & Company, 1969), 194–99, 217–23. From PRESENT AT THE CREATION: My Years in the State Department by Dean Acheson. Copyright © 1969 by Dean Acheson. Used by permission of W.W. Norton & Company, Inc.

5. President Truman's Message to Congress; March 12, 1947; Document 171; 80th Congress, 1st Session; Records of the United States House of Representatives; Record Group 233; National Archives.

6. *Congressional Record*, 80th Congress, 1st session, v. 93, pt. 6, March 12, 1947.

7. Harry S. Truman, *Memoirs: Years of Trial and Hope* (Garden City, N.Y.: Doubleday & Company, Inc., 1956), 369–70. Reprinted by permission of Clifton Truman Daniel.

8. "Announcement of the First Satellite," *Pravda*, October 5, 1957.

9. American Reactions to the Launching of Sputnik, online at www.mfwright.com/sputnik.html. Used with permission of M.F. Wright.

10. Dwight D. Eisenhower, The President's News Conference, October 9, 1957, *Public Papers of the Presidents of the United States: Dwight D. Eisenhower, 1957* (Washington, D.C.: Government Printing Office, 1958), 719–21, 728, 730–31.

11. Dwight D. Eisenhower, Statement by the President Summarizing Facts in the Development of an Earth Satellite by the United States, October 9, 1957, *Public Papers*, 733–35.

12. John Foster Dulles to James C. Hagerty, October 8, 1957, with attached: "Draft Statements on the Soviet Satellite," October 5, 1957, John Foster Dulles Papers, Dwight D. Eisenhower Library, Abilene, Kansas.

13. Mikhail K. Tikhonravov in cooperation with several other designers and scientists from the defense industry and the USSR Academy of Sciences to the Soviet Government, May 26, 1954. National Aeronautics and Space Administration, Washington, D.C. Document obtained, edited, and translated by Dr. Asif Siddiqi. Reprinted with permission of Dr. Siddiqi. http://history.nasa.gov/sputnik/russ1.html.

14. Owen B. Kiernan, "Sputnik Shot Still Reverberates Here," *Senior Scholastic*, November 21, 1958. From SENIOR SCHOLASTIC, November 21, 1958. Copyright © 1958 by Scholastic Inc. Reprinted by permission of Scholastic, Inc.

15. Memo of Meeting (2 meetings) with the President, October 8, 1957, Presidential Papers, Dwight D. Eisenhower Library.

16. International Affairs Seminars of Washington, "American Reactions to the Crisis: Examples of Pre-Sputnik and Post-Sputnik Attitudes of the Reaction to other Events Perceived as Threats," October 15–16, 1958, U.S. President's Committee on Information Activities Abroad (Sprague Committee) Records, 1959–1961, Box 5, A83-10, Dwight D. Eisenhower Library, Abilene, Kansas.

17. Special Message to the Congress Relative to Space Science and Exploration. April 2, 1958, *Public Papers of the Presidents, Eisenhower, 1958*, 269.

# 6

# The Civil Rights Movement

<hr>

*I*N THE YEARS FOLLOWING THE END OF *World War II, African Americans stepped up their efforts to gain rights they had always been denied in America. Although the struggle caught most white Americans by surprise in the 1950s, African Americans had been fighting for their rights by various means for many years before that. The civil rights movement took two paths. The first was the moderate, non-violent protest approach that eventually came to be led by Rev. Martin Luther King, Jr. Under King's leadership, significant gains were made, but younger African Americans and some not within the American Protestant culture disagreed with his moderate methods. This more radical group alarmed many white Americans and caused a backlash among those not wholly committed to assisting blacks in gaining their rights. Unfortunately, the tension between the races often led to violence during the 1960s.*

### Part A: Civil Rights in the Post-War Era

### Background

*At the end of World War II, the United States stood preeminent in the world, but there was a characteristic of America that was not very flattering to forward-thinking Americans. Whereas the United States had fought to end totalitarian governments in Europe and Asia, government actions at home toward minorities were not something most Americans could praise. As the atrocities of the Holocaust became widely known, many Americans reevaluated the treatment of their own country's minorities. To be sure, the treatment of African Americans and other minorities could not compare to the Nazi treatment of Jews, but the status of black Americans and other minorities, especially the Japanese Americans who had been interned during the war, was not something of which most Americans could be proud. Yet, to improve the status of minorities in America would run counter to the ingrained racist ideas, especially in the American South. How could the United States hold itself up as a beacon to the rest of the world when its own minorities had second-class status?*

*In the post–World War II era, a stepped-up effort on the part of African Americans to gain civil rights was not very visible at the beginning. Soon, however, the momentum began to increase.*

*The National Association for the Advancement of Colored People (NAACP) had been working to increase the rights of African Americans, but for the most part, the NAACP had worked through the court system to knock down various discrimination laws. There were some significant gains, but they did not get much attention. In the post-war era, several events converged to focus attention on and speed the civil rights movement.*

*There were so many demonstrations, marches, protests, and other actions that space will allow only a few to be covered here. President Truman surprised many with his focus on civil rights, but that was only the beginning of government actions. Beginning with the Supreme Court's famous* Brown v. Board of Education of Topeka, Kansas *decision in 1954, momentum began to build until it culminated, in a sense, in the Civil Rights Act of 1964. But that was not the end of the movement, and there were more extreme actions taken by various groups. These will be covered in a later section.*

*The civil rights movement was a domestic matter, but it was watched carefully around the world. Occasionally, it became a part of the Cold War, as President Eisenhower said in his statement regarding the violence in Little Rock, Arkansas.*

## Questions

In reading these documents, the student should ask and answer several questions to put these activities in the proper context.

1. Was Truman's action significant or merely symbolic?
2. Why did the Montgomery Bus Boycott catch the public eye in such a dramatic way? Was television the catalyst?
3. Was Martin Luther King the best leader for the movement in the 1950s and 1960s, or would more progress have been made with a more radical and demanding leader?

4. Was Lyndon Johnson sincere in his support for civil rights, or did he just see how the wind was blowing and then take advantage of it?
5. Evaluate the significance of the Civil Rights Act of 1964.

## Document 1: Truman Takes Action and Orders Desegregation of the Armed Services[1]

*At the end of World War II, the incongruity of America fighting around the world for democracy and freedom compared to the status of black Americans became even more obvious. White America was not yet ready for social integration, but one area where the president had the authority to do something about the inequality was in the military.*

*In 1948, Truman took much of the country by surprise by issuing an executive order that segregation of the races would end in the military. If people had been paying attention, however, they would have known that the proposal was under consideration and was moving forward. He made his goals clear in his order. Portions of the order follow.*

*In his memoirs written in the 1950s, President Truman was obviously proud of his action regarding segregation in the military although he did not say much about it.*

### The President's Executive Order
Establishing the President's Committee on Equality of Treatment and Opportunity In the Armed Forces.
WHEREAS it is essential that there be maintained in the armed services of the United States the highest standards of democracy, with equality of treatment and opportunity for all those who serve in our country's defense:
NOW THEREFORE, by virtue of the authority vested in me as President of the United States, by the Constitution and the statutes of the United States, and as Commander in Chief of the armed services, it is hereby ordered as follows:
1. It is hereby declared to be the policy of the President that there shall be equality of treatment and opportunity for all persons in the armed services without regard to race, color, religion or national origin. . . .
2. There shall be created in the National Military Establishment an advisory committee to be known as the President's Committee on Equality of Treatment and Opportunity in the Armed Services, which shall be composed of seven members to be designated by the President.
3. The Committee is authorized on behalf of the President to examine into the rules, procedures and practices of the Armed Services in order to determine in what respect such rules, procedures and practices may be altered or improved with a view to carrying out the policy of this order. . . .

4. All executive departments and agencies of the Federal Government are authorized and directed to cooperate with the Committee in its work, and to furnish the Committee such information or the services of such persons as the Committee may require in the performance of its duties. . . .
Harry Truman
The White House
July 26, 1948

Truman Remembers
. . . The attitude which had been taken by Southerners toward the policy of integration in the armed forces was well known. Practically all of the training camps in World War II were located in the South because of climate conditions, and the idea of integration, therefore, encountered strong resistance. The Southerners were especially bothered by integration among construction workers, who were employed without discrimination as to race for the purpose of building the government's training camps, and they were not happy over the orders on fair employment. I expected trouble, and it developed promptly at the 1948 convention.

The military establishment—particularly the Navy—had been strongly opposed to my policy of integration in the armed services, but I had forced it into practice. Then they discovered that no difficulty resulted from integration after all. Integration is the best way to create an effective combat organization in which the men will stand together and fight. Experience on the front has proved that the morale of troops is strengthened where Jim Crow practices are not imposed.

I felt also that any other course would be inconsistent with international commitments and obligations. We could not endorse a color line at home and still expect to influence the immense masses that make up the Asian and African peoples. It was necessary to practice what we preached, and I tried to see that we did it.

### Document 2: *Brown v. Board of Education*[2]

*The most dramatic action regarding civil rights came in 1954 when the Supreme Court reversed the "separate but equal" doctrine set out in 1896 in the case of* Plessy v. Ferguson. *This decision was all the more remarkable because several members of the Supreme Court were Southerners who had shown no sign of supporting integration before, and the new chief justice, Earl Warren, had a record in California of supporting the internment of the Japanese during World War II. This decision began the argument that the Court was legislating from the bench rather than merely interpreting what the Constitution said. The civil rights movement was already under way, but this decision spurred it to new levels. The following document is the relevant section of that decision.*

. . . In each of the cases, minors of the Negro race, through their legal representatives, seek the aid of the courts in obtaining admission to the public schools of their community on a nonsegregated basis. In each instance, they had been denied admission to schools attended by white children under laws requiring or permitting segregation according to race. This segregation was alleged to deprive the plaintiffs of the equal protection of the laws under the Fourteenth Amendment. . . .

The plaintiffs contend that segregated public schools are not "equal" and cannot be made "equal," and that hence they are deprived of the equal protection of the laws. Because of the obvious importance of the question presented, the Court took jurisdiction. Argument was heard in the 1952 Term, and reargument was heard this Term on certain questions propounded by the Court.
. . .

In approaching this problem, . . . [we] must consider public education in the light of its full development and its present place in American life throughout the Nation. Only in this way can it be determined if segregation in public schools deprives these plaintiffs of the equal protection of the laws.

Today, education is perhaps the most important function of state and local governments. Compulsory school attendance laws and the great expenditures for education both demonstrate our recognition of the importance of education to our democratic society. It is required in the performance of our most basic public responsibilities, even service in the armed forces. It is the very foundation of good citizenship. Today it is a principal instrument in awakening the child to cultural values, in preparing him for later professional training, and in helping him to adjust normally to his environment. In these days, it is doubtful that any child may reasonably be expected to succeed in life if he is denied the opportunity of an education. Such an opportunity, where the state has undertaken to provide it, is a right which must be made available to all on equal terms.

We come then to the question presented: Does segregation of children in public schools solely on the basis of race, even though the physical facilities and other "tangible" factors may be equal, deprive the children of the minority group of equal educational opportunities? We believe that it does. . . .

We conclude that in the field of public education the doctrine of "separate but equal" has no place. Separate educational facilities are inherently unequal. Therefore, we hold that the plaintiffs and others similarly situated for whom the actions have been brought are, by reason of the segregation complained of, deprived of the equal protection of the laws guaranteed by the Fourteenth

Amendment. This disposition makes unnecessary any discussion whether such segregation also violates the Due Process Clause of the Fourteenth Amendment.

### Document 3: Violence in Little Rock[3]

*Southern resistance to school integration was swift, although there were some places where it was accepted and went somewhat smoothly. In Little Rock, Arkansas, it did not go smoothly. A white mob gathered outside Central High School in 1957 to prevent the attendance of nine black students became violent. The governor of Arkansas, Orval Faubus, used the event for political purposes and removed the National Guard from the school. President Dwight D. Eisenhower was not happy about the* Brown *decision, and he did not want to intervene in the situation. The violence and the threat of additional violence became so great that he eventually had no choice in the matter. The existence of television coverage increased the tension. On September 14, 1957, he nationalized the National Guard and took control of the situation. The tension was so great that troops remained in Little Rock for several months to prevent harm to the students who persisted in attending the school. At the time of the violence, Eisenhower made the following speech to the American public.*

My Fellow Citizens:

For a few minutes I want to speak to you about the serious situation that has arisen in Little Rock. . . .

In that city, under the leadership of demagogic extremists, disorderly mobs have deliberately prevented the carrying out of proper orders from a Federal Court. Local authorities have not eliminated that violent opposition and, under the law, I yesterday issued a Proclamation calling upon the mob to disperse.

This morning the mob again gathered in front of the Central High School of Little Rock, obviously for the purpose of again preventing the carrying out of the Court's order relating to the admission of Negro children to the school.

Whenever normal agencies prove inadequate to the task and it becomes necessary for the Executive Branch of the Federal Government to use its powers and authority to uphold Federal Courts, the President's responsibility is inescapable.

In accordance with that responsibility, I have today issued an Executive Order directing the use of troops under Federal authority to aid in the execution of Federal law at Little Rock, Arkansas. This became necessary when my Proclamation of yesterday was not observed, and the obstruction of justice still continues.

It is important that the reasons for my action be understood by all citizens.

As you know, the Supreme Court of the United States has decided that separate public educational facilities for the races are inherently unequal and therefore compulsory school segregation laws are unconstitutional. . . .

During the past several years, many communities in our Southern States have instituted public school plans for gradual progress in the enrollment and attendance of school children of all races in order to bring themselves into compliance with the law of the land.

They thus demonstrated to the world that we are a nation in which laws, not men, are supreme.

I regret to say that this truth—the cornerstone of our liberties—was not observed in this instance. . . .

The very basis of our individual rights and freedoms is the certainty that the President and the Executive Branch of Government will support and insure the carrying out of the decisions of the Federal Courts, even, when necessary with all the means at the President's command.

Unless the President did so, anarchy would result. . . .

The interest of the nation in the proper fulfillment of the law's requirements cannot yield to opposition and demonstrations by some few persons.

Mob rule cannot be allowed to override the decisions of the courts. . . .

A foundation of our American way of life is our national respect for law.

In the South, as elsewhere, citizens are keenly aware of the tremendous disservice that has been done to the people of Arkansas in the eyes of the nation, and that has been done to the nation in the eyes of the world.

At a time when we face a grave situation abroad because of the hatred that Communism bears toward a system of government based on human rights, it would be difficult to exaggerate the harm that is being done to the prestige and influence, and indeed to the safety, of our nation and the world.

Our enemies are gloating over this incident and using it everywhere to misrepresent our nation. We are portrayed as a violator of those standards of conduct which the peoples of the world united to proclaim in the Charter of the United Nations. There they affirmed "faith in fundamental human rights and in the dignity of the human person" and did so "without distinction as to race, sex, language or religion."

And so, with confidence, I call upon citizens of the State of Arkansas to assist in bringing to an immediate end all interference with the law and its processes. . . .

## Document 4: Protest in Montgomery[4]

*Prior to the school crisis in Little Rock, an earlier event occurred in Montgomery, Alabama, that riveted the nation on the issue of civil rights.*

*Mrs. Rosa Parks, a local seamstress, was arrested when she refused to give up her seat to a white man on a Montgomery city bus. African Americans in Montgomery decided to boycott the bus system while they were filing a suit they hoped the Supreme Court would hear to overturn the bus company policy. Montgomery blacks organized the Montgomery Improvement Association (MIA) to assist with the boycott, especially to provide alternate transportation for the people who used the buses to get to work. A young minister recently arrived in Montgomery, Martin Luther King, Jr., was selected to head the organization. On December 5, 1955, a mass meeting of MIA was held to get the organization off the ground. King spoke to the group. A portion of his speech follows. Included in this transcript is the resolution read by Rev. Ralph Abernathy that was adopted that night.*

*The boycott of the bus system in Montgomery went on more than a year before the bus company went bankrupt. The boycott was incredibly successful in that almost all blacks in Montgomery refused to ride the buses and regularly endured hardship to get to work. The Supreme Court vindicated MIA's activity when it declared that the policy of discrimination by the bus company was unconstitutional. The night of the victory King again spoke to the MIA about the victory and how members should return to the buses without rancor.*

### Beginning of the Protest

But we are here in a specific sense, because of the bus situation in Montgomery. We are here because we are to get the situation corrected. This situation is not at all new. The problem has existed over endless years. For many years now Negroes in Montgomery and so many other areas have been inflicted with the paralysis of crippling fears on buses in our community. On so many occasions, Negroes have been intimidated and humiliated and impressed—oppressed—because of the sheer fact that they were Negroes. . . .

Just the other day, just last Thursday to be exact, one of the finest citizens in Montgomery—not one of the finest Negro citizens but one of the finest citizens in Montgomery—was taken from a bus and carried to jail and arrested because she refused to get up to give her seat to a white person. . . .

Mrs. Rosa Parks is a fine person. And since it had to happen I'm happy that it happened to a person like Mrs. Parks, for nobody can doubt the boundless outreach of her integrity. Nobody can doubt the height of her character, nobody can doubt the depth of her Christian commitment and devotion to the teachings of Jesus. And I'm happy since it had to happen, it happened to a person that nobody can call a disturbing factor in the community. . . .

And you know, my friends, there comes a time when people get tired of being trampled over by the iron feet of oppression. There comes a time, my friends, when people get tired of being plunged across the abyss of humiliation where they experience the bleakness of nagging despair. There comes a time when people get tired of being pushed out of the glittering sunlight of life's July, and left standing amid the piercing chill of an alpine November. There comes a time.

We are here, we are here this evening because we're tired now. And I want to say, that we are not here advocating violence. We have never done that. . . .

And we are not wrong, we are not wrong in what we are doing. If we are wrong, the Supreme Court of this nation is wrong. If we are wrong, the Constitution of the United States is wrong. If we are wrong, God Almighty is wrong. If we are wrong, Jesus of Nazareth was merely a utopian dreamer that never came down to earth. If we are wrong, justice is a lie: love has no meaning. And we are determined here in Montgomery to work and fight until justice runs down like water and righteousness like a mighty stream. . . .

Now at this point, Reverend Abernathy, pastor of the First Baptist Church of Montgomery, will come to us and read the resolutions and recommendations. . . .

In light of these observations, be it therefore resolved as follows:

Number One. That the citizens of Montgomery are requesting that every citizen in Montgomery, regardless of race, color or creed, to refrain from riding buses owned and operated in the city of Montgomery by the Montgomery Lines, Incorporated, until some arrangement has been worked out between said citizens and the Montgomery City Lines, Incorporated. . . .

Be it further resolved, that we have not, I said, we have not, we are not, and we have no intentions of using any unlawful means or any intimidation to persuade persons not to ride the Montgomery City Lines buses. However, we call upon your conscience, both moral and spiritual, to give your wholehearted support to this worthy undertaking. We believe we have a just complaint and we are willing to discuss this matter with the proper authorities.

Thus ends the resolution. . . . I move that this resolution shall be adopted. . . .

But just before leaving I want to say this. I want to urge you. You have voted. And you have done it with a great deal of enthusiasm, and I want to express my appreciation to you, on behalf of everybody here. Now let us go out to stick together and stay with this thing until the end. Now it means sacrificing, yes, it means sacrificing at points. But there are some things that we've got to learn to sacrifice for. And we've got to come to the point that we are determined not to accept a lot of things that we have been accepting in the past. . . .

And we will not be content until oppression is wiped out of Montgomery, and really out of America. We won't be content until that is done. We are merely insisting on the dignity and worth of every human personality. . . .

And I won't rest, I will face intimidation, and everything else, along with these other stalwart fighters for democracy and for citizenship. We don't mind it, so long as justice comes out of it. And I've come to see now that as we struggle for our rights, maybe some of them will have to die. But somebody said, if a man doesn't have something that he'll die for, he isn't fit to live.

### End of the Protest

For more than twelve months now, we, the Negro citizens of Montgomery have been engaged in a non-violent protest against injustices and indignities experienced on city buses. We came to see that, in the long run, it is more honorable to walk in dignity than ride in humiliation. So in a quiet dignified manner, we decided to substitute tired feet for tired souls, and walk the streets of Montgomery until the sagging walls of injustice had been crushed by the battering rams of surging justice.

. . . We have never allowed ourselves to get bogged in the negative; we have always sought to accentuate the positive. Our aim has never been to put the bus company out of business, but rather to put justice in business.

These twelve months have not at all been easy. Our feet have often been tired. We have struggled against tremendous odds to maintain alternative transportation. There have been moments when roaring waters of disappointment poured upon us in staggering torrents. We can remember days when unfavorable court decisions came upon us like tidal waves, leaving us treading in the deep and confused waters of despair. But amid all of this we have kept going with the faith that as we struggle, God struggles with us, and that the arc of the moral universe, although long, is bending toward justice. . . .

Now our faith seems to be vindicated. This morning the long awaited mandate from the United States Supreme Court concerning bus segregation came to Montgomery. This mandate expresses in terms that are crystal clear that segregation in public transportation is both legally and sociologically invalid. In the light of this mandate and the unanimous vote rendered by the Montgomery Improvement Association about a month ago, the year-old protest against city buses is officially called off, and the Negro citizens of Montgomery are urged to return to the busses tomorrow morning on a non-segregated basis.

I cannot close without giving just a word of caution. Our experience and growth during this past year of united non-violent protest has been of such that we cannot be satisfied with a court "victory" over our white brothers. We must respond to the decision with an understanding of those who have oppressed us and with an appreciation of the new adjustments that the court order poses for them. We must be able to face up honestly to our own shortcomings. We must act in such a way as to make possible a coming together of white people and colored people on the basis of a real harmony of interests and understanding. We seek an integration based on mutual respect. . . .

## Document 5: John Kennedy Weighs In[5]

*Through the late 1950s and the early 1960s, the efforts to gain civil rights continued, often resulting in violence. When Kennedy came to office, he did not seem to have a definite plan regarding civil rights. Most observers believe that his brother Robert, the attorney general, was more sensitive to the issue and helped to mold the president's views. After violence during the integration of the University of Mississippi, and after George Wallace, the governor of Alabama, stood in the doorway to prevent the integration of the University of Alabama, Kennedy took action. In June 1963, he spoke on television to announce that he was introducing new civil rights legislation. Portions of his address follow.*

Good evening my fellow citizens:

This afternoon, following a series of threats and defiant statements, the presence of Alabama National Guardsmen was required on the University of Alabama to carry out the final and unequivocal order of the United States District Court of the Northern District of Alabama. That order called for the admission of two clearly qualified young Alabama residents who happened to have been born Negro.

That they were admitted peacefully on the campus is due in good measure to the conduct of the students of the University of Alabama, who met their responsibilities in a constructive way.

I hope that every American, regardless of where he lives, will stop and examine his conscience about this and other related incidents. This Nation was founded by men of many nations and backgrounds. It was founded on the principle that all men are created equal, and that the rights of every man are diminished when the rights of one man are threatened. . . .

It ought to be possible for American consumers of any color to receive equal service in places of public accommodation, such as hotels and restaurants and theaters and retail stores, without being forced to resort to demonstrations in the street, and it ought to be possible for American citizens of any color to register to vote in a free election without interference or fear of reprisal.

It ought to be possible, in short, for every American to enjoy the privileges of being American without regard to his race or his color. . . .

This is not a sectional issue. Difficulties over segregation and discrimination exist in every city, in every State of the Union, producing in many cities a rising tide of discontent that threatens the public safety. Nor is this a partisan issue. In a time of domestic crisis men of good will and generosity should be able to unite regardless of party or politics. This is not even a legal or legislative issue alone. It is better to settle these matters in the courts than on the streets, and new laws are needed at every level, but law alone cannot make men see right. . . .

The heart of the question is whether all Americans are to be afforded equal rights and equal opportunities, whether we are going to treat our fellow Americans as we want to be treated. If an American, because his skin is dark, cannot eat lunch in a restaurant open to the public, if he cannot send his children to the best public school available, if he cannot vote for the public officials who will represent him, if, in short, he cannot enjoy the full and free life which all of us want, then who among us would be content to have the color of his skin changed and stand in his place? Who among us would then be content with the counsels of patience and delay?

One hundred years of delay have passed since President Lincoln freed the slaves, yet their heirs, their grandsons, are not fully free. They are not yet freed from the bonds of injustice. They are not yet freed from social and economic oppression. And this Nation, for all its hopes and all its boasts, will not be fully free until all its citizens are free. . . .

We face, therefore, a moral crisis as a country and as a people. . . . It is time to act in the Congress, in your State and local legislative body and, above all, in all of our daily lives. . . .

Next week I shall ask the Congress of the United States to act, to make a commitment it has not fully made in this century to the proposition that race has no place in American life or law. . . .

But there are other necessary measures which only the Congress can provide, and they must be provided at this session. . . .

I am, therefore, asking the Congress to enact legislation giving all Americans the right to be served in facilities which are open to the public—hotels, restaurants, theaters, retail stores, and similar establishments. . . .

I am also asking the Congress to authorize the Federal Government to participate more fully in lawsuits designed to end segregation in public education. . . .

Other features will also be requested, including greater protection for the right to vote. But legislation, I repeat, cannot solve this problem alone. It must be solved in the homes of every American in every community across our country. . . .

My fellow Americans, this is a problem which faces us all—in every city of the North as well as the South. Today there are Negroes unemployed, two or three times as many compared to whites, inadequate in education, moving into the large cities, unable to find work, young people particularly out of work without hope, denied equal rights, denied the opportunity to eat at a restaurant or lunch counter or go to a movie theater, denied the right to a decent education, denied almost today the right to attend a State university even though qualified. . . .

We cannot say to 10 percent of the population that you can't have that right; that your children cannot have the chance to develop whatever talents they have; that the only way that they are going to get their rights is to go into the streets and demonstrate. I think we owe them and we owe ourselves a better country than that. . . .

We have a right to expect that the Negro community will be responsible, will uphold the law, but they have a right to expect that the law will be fair, that the Constitution will be color blind, as Justice Harlan said at the turn of the century.

This is what we are talking about and this is a matter which concerns this country and what it stands for, and in meeting it I ask the support of all our citizens.

Thank you very much.

### Document 6: "I Have a Dream"[6]

*A high point of the civil rights movement came in 1963 when a mass march on Washington, D.C., to promote the civil rights bill was peaceful and attracted more people than anyone had expected. Martin Luther King, Jr., spoke once again and delivered one of his most famous speeches. It was a galvanizing moment for the movement and the nation.*

I am happy to join with you today in what will go down in history as the greatest demonstration for freedom in the history of our nation.

Five score years ago, a great American, in whose symbolic shadow we stand today, signed the Emancipation Proclamation. This momentous decree came as a great beacon light of hope to millions of Negro slaves who had been seared in the flames of withering injustice. It came as a joyous daybreak to end the long night of their captivity.

But one hundred years later, the Negro still is not free. One hundred years later, the life of the Negro is still sadly crippled by the manacles of segregation and the chains of discrimination. One hundred years later, the Negro lives on a lonely island of poverty in the midst of a vast ocean of material prosperity. One hundred years later, the Negro is still languished in the corners of American society and finds himself an exile in his own land. And so we've come here today to dramatize a shameful condition. . . .

We have also come to this hallowed spot to remind America of the fierce urgency of Now. This is no time to engage in the luxury of cooling off or to take the tranquilizing drug of gradualism. Now is the time to make real the promises of democracy. Now is the time to rise from the dark and desolate valley of segregation to the sunlit path of racial justice. Now is the

The struggle of African Americans to obtain equality in America had been going on for many years. The emergence of Martin Luther King, Jr., as the leader of the Southern Christian Leadership Council gave focus to the movement. When the march on Washington occurred in 1963 to push Congress to pass a civil rights law, it was the largest crowd ever to gather in the nation's capital. This view gives an idea of the size of the march. Courtesy of the Library of Congress, LC-U9-10363-5.

time to lift our nation from the quicksands of racial injustice to the solid rock of brotherhood. Now is the time to make justice a reality for all of God's children. . . .

The marvelous new militancy which has engulfed the Negro community must not lead us to a distrust of all white people, for many of our white brothers, as evidenced by their presence here today, have come to realize that their destiny is tied up with our destiny. And they have come to realize that their freedom is inextricably bound to our freedom.

We cannot walk alone.

And as we walk, we must make the pledge that we shall always march ahead. We cannot turn back. . . .

And so even though we face the difficulties of today and tomorrow, I still have a dream. It is a dream deeply rooted in the American dream.

I have a dream that one day this nation will rise up and live out the true meaning of its creed: "We hold these truths to be self-evident, that all men are created equal."

I have a dream that one day on the red hills of Georgia, the sons of former slaves and the sons of former slave owners will be able to sit down together at the table of brotherhood.

I have a dream that one day even the state of Mississippi, a state sweltering with the heat of injustice, sweltering with the heat of oppression, will be transformed into an oasis of freedom and justice.

I have a dream that my four little children will one day live in a nation where they will not be judged by the color of their skin but by the content of their character.

I have a *dream* today!

I have a dream that one day, down in Alabama, with its vicious racists, with its governor having his lips dripping with the words of "interposition" and "nullification"—one day right there in Alabama little black boys and black girls will be able to join hands with little white boys and white girls as sisters and brothers.

I have a *dream* today!

I have a dream that one day every valley shall be exalted, and every hill and mountain shall be made low, the rough places will be made plain, and the crooked places will be made straight; "and the glory of the Lord shall be revealed and all flesh shall see it together."

This is our hope, and this is the faith that I go back to the South with.

With this faith, we will be able to hew out of the mountain of despair a stone of hope. With this faith, we will be able to transform the jangling discords of our nation into a beautiful symphony of brotherhood. With this faith, we will be able to work together, to pray together, to struggle together, to go to jail together, to stand up for freedom together, knowing that we will be free one day.

And this will be the day—this will be the day when all of God's children will be able to sing with new meaning:

> *My country 'tis of thee, sweet land of liberty, of thee I sing.*
> *Land where my fathers died, land of the Pilgrim's pride,*
> *From every mountainside, let freedom ring!*
> And if America is to be a great nation, this must become true.
> And so let freedom ring from the prodigious hilltops of New Hampshire.
> Let freedom ring from the mighty mountains of New York.
> Let freedom ring from the heightening Alleghenies of Pennsylvania.
> Let freedom ring from the snow-capped Rockies of Colorado.
> Let freedom ring from the curvaceous slopes of California.
> But not only that:
> Let freedom ring from Stone Mountain of Georgia.
> Let freedom ring from Lookout Mountain of Tennessee.
> Let freedom ring from every hill and molehill of Mississippi.
> From every mountainside, let freedom ring.

And when this happens, when we allow freedom ring, when we let it ring from every village and every hamlet, from every state and every city, we will be able to speed up that day when *all* of God's children, black men and white men, Jews and Gentiles, Protestants and Catholics, will be able to join hands and sing in the words of the old Negro spiritual:

*Free at last! Free at last!*

*Thank God Almighty, we are free at last!*

## Document 7: President Johnson Steps In[7]

*When John Kennedy was assassinated in November 1963, the civil rights bill was languishing in Congress. When Lyndon B. Johnson became president, he shocked many people with his strong stand for civil rights. In his first State of the Union Address, Johnson called for Congress to pass Kennedy's Civil Rights Act.*

*After a long struggle, with much arm-twisting on Johnson's part, Congress passed the Civil Rights Act of 1964, the first major civil rights law since Reconstruction. For many, this was the culmination of the civil rights movement, but it did not achieve everything the supporters of the movement were seeking. Johnson made appropriate remarks at the time he signed the law.*

### State of the Union Address

Mr. Speaker, Mr. President, Members of the House and Senate, my fellow Americans:

Let me make one principle of this administration abundantly clear: All of these increased opportunities—in employment, in education, in housing, and in every field—must be open to Americans of every color. As far as the writ of Federal law will run, we must abolish not some, but all racial discrimination. For this is not merely an economic issue, or a social, political, or international issue. It is a moral issue, and it must be met by the passage this session of the bill now pending in the House.

All members of the public should have equal access to facilities open to the public. All members of the public should be equally eligible for Federal benefits that are financed by the public. All members of the public should have an equal chance to vote for public officials and to send their children to good public schools and to contribute their talents to the public good.

Today, Americans of all races stand side by side in Berlin and in Viet Nam. They died side by side in Korea. Surely they can work and eat and travel side by side in their own country.

### *Johnson signs the Civil Rights Bill*

My fellow Americans:

I am about to sign into law the Civil Rights Act of 1964. I want to take this occasion to talk to you about what that law means to every American. . . .

Americans of every race and color have died in battle to protect our freedom. Americans of every race and color have worked to build a nation of widening opportunities. Now our generation of Americans has been called on to continue the unending search for justice within our own borders.

We believe that all men are created equal. Yet many are denied equal treatment.

We believe that all men have certain unalienable rights. Yet many Americans do not enjoy those rights.

We believe that all men are entitled to the blessings of liberty. Yet millions are being deprived of those blessings—not because of their own failures, but because of the color of their skin.

The reasons are deeply imbedded in history and tradition and the nature of man. We can understand—without rancor or hatred—how this all happened.

But it cannot continue. Our Constitution, the foundation of our Republic, forbids it. The principles of our freedom forbid it. Morality forbids it. And the law I will sign tonight forbids it. . . .

The purpose of the law is simple.

It does not restrict the freedom of any American, so long as he respects the rights of others.

It does not give special treatment to any citizen.

It does say the only limit to a man's hope for happiness, and for the future of his children, shall be his own ability.

It does say that there are those who are equal before God shall now also be equal in the polling booths, in the classrooms, in the factories, and in hotels, restaurants, movie theaters, and other places that provide service to the public.

I am taking steps to implement the law under my constitutional obligation to "take care that the laws are faithfully executed." . . .

We must not approach the observance and enforcement of this law in a vengeful spirit. Its purpose is not to punish. Its purpose is not to divide, but to end divisions—divisions which have all lasted too long. Its purpose is national, not regional.

Its purpose is to promote a more abiding commitment to freedom, a more constant pursuit of justice, and a deeper respect for human dignity.

We will achieve these goals because most Americans are law-abiding citizens who want to do what is right.

This is why the Civil Rights Act relies first on voluntary compliance, then on the efforts of local communities and States to secure the rights of citizens. It provides for the national authority to step in only when others cannot or will not do the job.

This Civil Rights Act is a challenge to all of us to go to work in our communities and our States, in our homes and in our hearts, to eliminate the last vestiges of injustice in our beloved country. . . .

My fellow citizens, we have come now to a time of testing. We must not fail.

Let us close the springs of racial poison. Let us pray for wise and understanding hearts. Let us lay aside irrelevant differences and make our Nation whole. Let us hasten that day when our unmeasured strength and our unbounded spirit will be free to do the great works ordained for this Nation by the just and wise God who is the Father of us all.

Thank you and good night.

## Part B: Racial Violence

### Background

*By the early 1960s, the civil rights movement was in full swing. The acknowledged leader of the movement and the spokesman for African Americans, at least as far as white America was concerned, was Rev. Martin Luther King, Jr. By the middle of the decade, a number of other black Americans were speaking out and diverging from the methods and goals of King and his followers.*

*A number of the new activists were advocating separation, black nationalism, and possibly violence to gain the rights that African Americans had been denied.*

*Americans, including a large portion of the black community, were confused and concerned about the direction the public dialogue was taking.*

*Without question, the rising opposition to America's involvement in a war in Vietnam contributed to the "radicalism" of the 1960s and early 1970s. Some people believed that a number of these divergent voices were doing what they were doing mostly for shock value or for personal gain without a true commitment to what they professed. Others feared the direction the country was taking.*

*Like the more moderate followers of Martin Luther King, Jr., the radical leaders were a part of domestic change, but their actions had international implications as well. Because of the legacy of the Cold War and the increasing corrosiveness of the Vietnam conflict, many considered the more radical black leaders to be subversive. Many whites considered these leaders agents of foreign governments and ideologies.*

*The 1960s also became known as the decade of urban violence. Some people called these outbreaks race riots, but that term does not adequately describe national events. Most riots did occur in the sections of cities that were predominantly minority in population. Most often, as well, most of the riots were attacks on property, not battles between the races. Many white Americans dreaded the arrival of summer since each one seemed more violent than the one before.*

*The riot in the Watts section of Los Angeles in 1965 is symbolic of much of the racial violence that occurred during this time.*

## Questions

In reading these documents, the student should ask and answer several questions to put these activities in the proper context.

1. How representative was Watts of the African American community in America?
2. Are Hutchinson and Moseley representative of the Watts community in 1965?
3. Was the urban violence a logical extension or outgrowth of the nonviolent Civil Rights movement?
4. Why were the riots against property rather than people?

## Document 1: Urban Violence Begins—the Watts Riot[8]

*In the year following the passage of the Civil Rights Act in 1964 and during consideration of the Voting Rights Act of 1965, violence suddenly erupted in the Watts area of Los Angeles. Its violence and its length shocked white America. For those opposed to the Civil Rights Act, this was an example of how African Americans were a threat to American well-being. To others, it was merely an example of the pent-up anger in the black community. In the aftermath of the event, Governor Edmund G. "Pat" Brown of California appointed a special task force to investigate the causes and to recommend actions that could resolve the issue and prevent future outbursts. Officially known as the Governor's Commission on the Los Angeles Riot, it was more commonly referred to as the McCone Commission, after its chairman, John McCone. The following excerpt from the report summarizes the events and lists the recommendations of the commission.*

The rioting in Los Angeles in the late, hot summer of 1965 took six days to run its full grievous course. In hindsight, the tinder-igniting incident is seen to have been the arrest of a drunken Negro youth about whose dangerous driving another Negro had complained to the Caucasian motorcycle officer who made the arrest. The arrest occurred under rather ordinary circumstances, near but not in the district known as Watts, at seven o'clock on the evening of 11 August, a Wednesday. The crisis ended in the afternoon of 17 August, a Tuesday, on Governor Brown's order to lift the curfew which had been imposed the Saturday before in an extensive area just south of the heart of the City.

In the ugliest interval, which lasted from Thursday through Saturday, perhaps as many as 10,000 Negroes took to the streets in marauding bands. They looted stores, set fires, beat up white passersby whom they hauled from stopped cars, many of which were turned upside down and burned, exchanged shots with law enforcement officers, and stoned and shot at firemen. The rioters seemed to have been caught up in an insensate rage of destruction. By Friday, the disorder spread to adjoining areas, and ultimately an area covering 46.5 square miles had to be controlled with the aid of military authority before public order was restored.

The entire Negro population of Los Angeles County, about two thirds of whom live in this area, numbers more than 650,000. Observers estimate that only about two per cent were involved in the disorder. Nevertheless, this violent fraction, however minor, has given the face of community relations in Los Angeles a sinister cast.

When the spasm passed, thirty-four persons were dead, and the wounded and hurt numbered 1,032 more. Property damage was about $40,000,000. Arrested for one crime or another were 3,952 persons, women as well as men, including over 500 youths under eighteen. The lawlessness in this one segment of the metropolitan area had terrified the entire county and its 6,000,000 citizens. . . .

### The Frye Arrests

On August 11, 1965, California Highway Patrolman Lee W. Minikus, a Caucasian, was riding his motorcycle along 122nd street, just south of the Los Angeles City boundary, when a passing Negro motorist told him he had just seen a car that was being driven recklessly. Minikus gave chase and pulled the car over at 116th and Avalon, in a predominantly Negro neighborhood, near but not in Watts. It was 7:00 p.m.

The driver was Marquette Frye, a 21-year-old Negro, and his older brother, Ronald, 22, was a passenger. Minikus asked Marquette to get out and take the standard Highway Patrol sobriety test. Frye failed the test, and at 7:05 p.m., Minikus told him he was under arrest. He radioed for his motorcycle partner, for a car to take Marquette to jail, and a tow truck to take the car away.

They were two blocks from the Frye home, in an area of two-story apartment buildings and numerous small family residences. Because it was a very warm evening, many of the residents were outside.

Ronald Frye, having been told he could not take the car when Marquette was taken to jail, went to get their mother so that she could claim the car. They returned to the scene about 7:15 p.m. as the second motorcycle patrolman, the patrol car, and tow truck arrived. The original group of 25 to 50 curious spectators had grown to 250 to 300 persons.

Mrs. Frye approached Marquette and scolded him for drinking. Marquette, who until then had been peaceful and cooperative, pushed her away and moved toward the crowd, cursing and shouting at the officers that they would have to kill him to take him to jail. The patrolmen pursued Marquette and he resisted.

The watching crowd became hostile, and one of the patrolmen radioed for more help. Within minutes, three more highway patrolmen arrived. Minikus and his partner were now struggling with both Frye brothers. Mrs. Frye, now belligerent, jumped on the back of one of the officers and ripped his shirt. In an attempt to subdue Marquette, one officer swung at his shoulder with a night stick, missed, and struck him on the forehead, inflicting a minor cut. By 7:23 p.m., all three of the Fryes were under arrest, and other California Highway Patrolmen and, for the first time, Los Angeles police officers had arrived in response to the call for help.

Officers on the scene said there were now more than 1,000 persons in the crowd. About 7:25 p.m., the patrol car with the prisoners, and the tow truck pulling the Frye car, left the scene. At 7: 31 p.m., the Fryes arrived at a nearby sheriff's substation.

Undoubtedly the situation at the scene of the arrest was tense.

Belligerence and resistance to arrest called for forceful action by the officers. This brought on hostility from Mrs. Frye and some of the bystanders, which, in turn, caused increased actions by the police. Anger at the scene escalated and, as in all such situations, bitter recriminations from both sides followed.

Considering the undisputed facts, the Commission finds that the arrest of the Fryes was handled efficiently and expeditiously. The sobriety test administered by the California Highway Patrol and its use of a transportation vehicle for the prisoner and a tow truck to remove his car are in accordance with the practices of other law enforcement agencies, including the Los Angeles Police Department. . . .

## The Grim Statistics

The final statistics are staggering. There were 34 persons killed and 1,032 reported injuries, including 90 Los Angeles police officers, 136 firemen, 10 national guardsmen, 23 persons from other governmental agencies, and 773 civilians. 118 of the injuries resulted from gunshot wounds. Of the 34 killed, one was a fireman, one was a deputy sheriff, and one a Long Beach policeman.

In the weeks following the riots, Coroner's Inquests were held regarding thirty-two of the deaths. The Coroner's jury ruled that twenty-six of the deaths were justifiable homicide, five were homicidal, and one was accidental. Of those ruled justifiable homicide, the jury found that death was caused in sixteen instances by officers of the Los Angeles Police Department and in seven instances by the National Guard.

It has been estimated that the loss of property attributable to the riots was over $40 million. More than 600 buildings were damaged by burning and looting. Of this number, more than 200 were totally destroyed by fire. The rioters concentrated primarily on food markets, liquor stores, furniture stores, clothing stores, department stores, and pawn shops. Arson arrests numbered 27 and 10 arson complaints were filed, a relatively small number considering that fire department officials say that all of the fires were incendiary in origin. Between 2,000 and 3,000 fire alarms were recorded during the riot, 1,000 of these between 7:00 a.m. on Friday and 7:00 a.m. on Saturday. We note with interest that no residences were deliberately burned, that damage to schools, libraries, churches and public buildings was minimal, and that certain types of business establishments, notably service stations and automobile dealers, were for the most part unharmed.

There were 3,438 adults arrested, 71% for burglary and theft. The number of juveniles arrested was 514, 81% for burglary and theft. Of the adults arrested, 1,232 had never been arrested before; 1,164 had a "minor" criminal record (arrest only or convictions with sentence of 90 days or less); 1,042 with "major" criminal record (convictions with sentence of more than 90 days). Of the juveniles arrested, 257 had never been arrested before; 212 had a "minor" criminal record; 43 had a "major" criminal record. Of the adults arrested, 2,057 were born in 16 southern states whereas the comparable figure for juveniles was 131. Some of the juveniles arrested extensively damaged the top two floors of an auxiliary jail which had been opened on the Saturday of the riots.

Those involved in the administration of justice—judges, prosecutors, defense counsel, and others—merit commendation for the steps they took to cope with the extraordinary responsibility thrust on the judicial system by the riots. By reorganizing calendars and making special assignments, the Los Angeles Superior and Municipal Courts have been able to meet the statutory deadlines for processing the cases of those arrested. Court statistics indicate that by November 26, the following dispositions had been made of the 2278 felony cases filed against adults: 856 were found guilty; 155 were acquitted; 641 were disposed of prior to trial, primarily by dismissal; 626 are awaiting trial. Of the 1133 misdemeanor cases filed, 733 were found guilty, 81 were acquitted, 184 dismissed and 135 are awaiting trial.

The police and Sheriff's Department have long known that many members of gangs, as well as others, in the south central area possessed weapons and knew how to use them. However, the extent to which pawn shops, each one of which possessed an inventory of weapons, were the immediate target of looters, leads to the conclusion that a substantial number of the weapons used were stolen from these shops. During the riots, law enforcement officers recovered 851 weapons. There is no evidence that the rioters made any attempt to steal narcotics from pharmacies in the riot area even though some pharmacies were looted and burned.

Overwhelming as are the grim statistics, the impact of the August rioting on the Los Angeles community has been even greater. The first weeks after the disorders brought a flood tide of charges and recriminations. Although this has now ebbed, the feeling of fear and tension persists, largely unabated, throughout the community. A certain slowness in the rebuilding of the fired structures has symbolized the difficulty in mending relationships in our community which were so severely fractured by the August nightmare. . . .

To implement our conclusions, we offer the following recommendations:

1. The Board of Police Commissioners should be strengthened.
2. Investigations of all citizen complaints should be conducted by an independent Inspector General under the authority of the Chief of Police in the implementation of procedures established by the Board of Police Commissioners.
3. The Police Department should institute expanded community relations programs.
4. The Sheriff's Department should effectuate these recommendations to the extent that they are applicable to it. . . .

In light of the foregoing considerations, we recommend:

1. There should immediately be developed in the affected area a job training and placement center through the combined efforts of Negroes, employers, labor unions, and government.
2. Federal and state governments should seek to insure, through the development of new facilities and additional means of communication, that maximum advantage is taken of government and private training programs
   and employment opportunities in our disadvantaged communities.
3. Legislation should be enacted requiring employers with more than 250
   employees and all labor unions to report annually to the State Fair Employment Practices Commission the racial composition of their work
   force and membership. . . .

Accordingly, our major recommendations are:

1. Elementary and junior high schools in the disadvantaged [areas] which
   have achievement levels substantially below the city average should be
   designated as "Emergency Schools" In each of these schools an "Emergency Literacy Program" should be established consisting of a drastic reduction class size to a maximum of 22 students and additional supportive personnel to provide special services. It is estimated that this
   program will cost at least $250 per year per student in addition to pres-
   ent per student costs and exclusive of capital expenditures, and that it
   must be continued for a minimum of six years for the elementary
   schools and three years for the junior high schools.
2. A permanent pre-school program should be established throughout the
   school year to provide education beginning at age three. Efforts should
   be focused on the development of language skills essential to prepare
   children to learn to read and write.

### Documents 2–3: Observers Remember Watts

*Many people who were in Watts at the time of the riot later were interviewed,
and some wrote their memories of that event. Two of these people recorded their
memories.*

### Document 2: Hutchinson remembers[9]

*Earl Ofari Hutchinson is an author and political commentator who is often
called upon by various television programs to comment on current affairs. He was*

*a teenager at the time of the riot. His memories from that time were published in*
*a two-part interview posted online on the* Huffington Post.

The young National Guard officer curtly and sternly ordered my high school buddies and me to keep moving down the street. He waved his bayoneted rifle menacingly at us as he barked out his orders. Behind him, a small army of white helmeted LAPD officers and battle fatigue dressed National Guardsman stood tensely with their rifles poised. I kept a wary eye on them as we nervously walked past the three-deep barricades that ringed the streets around my house.

My friends and I were on our way home from summer school classes that hot August day 40 years ago. The smoke from burning stores a few blocks away choked our eyes and seared our lungs. In the distance, we could hear the crackle of gunfire. The streets were strewn with empty liquor and cigarette cartons that had been hastily discarded by the horde of looters, who, for nearly four days, roamed the streets near my house.

A resident of the Watts curfew area that fateful summer, I remember not only the fires and the gunfire, but also the blind rage and desperation that drove the rioters as they pillaged stores and shouted, "Burn, baby, burn!" (taken from a slogan made popular by a local Black DJ). Many considered this a payback for the century of racism and violence against Blacks. When Dr. Martin Luther King visited Watts in an effort to stop the violence, young toughs shouted him down.

The orgy of violence and destruction marked the end of an era for the non-violent civil rights struggle. To many poor Blacks, non-violent marches and demonstrations seemed a worthless antidote to the cycle of poverty, violence and neglect. In the next few years, Detroit, Newark and Washington, D.C. and dozens of other cities erupted into violence and destruction. Many Blacks embraced the call by Black militants Malcolm X, Stokely Carmichael, Rap Brown, the Black Panthers and the Black Muslims for Black power, armed confrontation and separatism.

The violence in Watts also made many Whites recognize that America's ghettoes were powder kegs that could explode at any moment. The suburbs suddenly seemed less safe and secure. White fears forced politicians to scramble to find solutions to the racial crisis. The McCone Commission appointed by Governor Edmund Brown called for modest police reform and increased spending on jobs and social programs. That established an all-too-familiar pattern. When cities erupted in racial violence, hand-wringing city officials would quickly appoint a commission or blue-ribbon panel, issue a voluminous report on the causes of the riots, cobble together a few job programs, and toss out a few more dollars for social service programs.

To many Americans, that sounded like a reward for criminal behavior, and they weren't having any of that. They blamed the violence on liberal permissiveness and outside agitators, and demanded more police, heavy weaponry and tougher prison sentences. With the exception of the Martin Luther King Hospital, which was the one tangible thing that came out of the riots, the McCone Commission's recommendations were mostly ignored. The few piecemeal, badly mismanaged poverty programs, slapped together to cool out the ghetto, did little to relieve the misery of the Black poor.

When Lyndon Johnson escalated the war in Vietnam, politicians and the public became even more reluctant to spend more on domestic programs. The Black poor, lacking competitive skills and training, were shoved even further to the outer economic fringe. Their anger quickly turned to cynicism and despair. Many turned to guns, gangs and drugs to survive.

Civil rights leaders and organizations did not help. They defined the "Black Agenda" in increasingly narrow terms. Affirmative Action, economic parity, professional advancement and bussing [sic] replaced poverty, unemployment, quality education, police abuse and political empowerment as the goals that all Black people should fight for. Young, upwardly mobile Black business people and professionals fled the inner cities in droves. This further drained talent, skills, leadership and positive role models from poor communities. Economic shrinkage, government budget cuts and the elimination of job and social programs dumped more and more Blacks into the ranks of the underclass.

This pointed up a phenomenon about race and class in America that has been ignored, downplayed or denied. Speaking strictly in terms of the Black-White conflict, there are no longer two Americas, Black and White, and seemingly at permanent odds with each other. There are now three Americas, one Black, one White, and the other, Black and Black. In by-gone years, the iron curtain of segregation had blurred, but not obliterated, the class divisions between the Black well-to-do and the Black poor. When the Jim Crow signs came down and ghetto walls tumbled, more Blacks than ever marched into the corporations, onto universities, and into Congress and statehouses.

This gave the false, and misleading impression that economic deprivation was a thing of the past for all but a few unlucky Blacks. That was a pipedream, and America soon found it out.

My friend and I watched looters gleefully make mad dashes into the corner grocery store; their arms bulged with liquor bottles and cigarette cartons. Suddenly, my friend shouted out as if he was speaking to an audience, "Maybe now they'll see how rotten they treat us." The "they" was the white man. His words were angry, and bitter. Yet underneath there was a subtext of hope that the mass orgy of death and destruction that engulfed the block we lived on and the surrounding blocks during the harrowing five days and nights of the Watts riot in August 1965 might improve things for blacks. Over the years, as I returned to the block we lived on during the riot, I often thought of his bitter yet hopeful words.

Forty years after the riots, his hope remains a hope still unfulfilled. The streets that my friend and I were shooed down by the police and the National Guard forty years ago looks as if time has literally stood still. They are dotted with fast food restaurants, beauty shops, and liquor stores, and mom and pop grocery stores. The main street near my block is just as unkempt, pothole ridden, and trash littered. All the homes and stores in the area are all hermetically sealed with iron bars, security gates, and burglar alarms. Forty years ago, many of us were poor and trapped in a segregated neighborhood, but we knew, trusted, and looked out for our neighbors. We could walk the streets at night, and felt secure in our homes. That day is long past.

In the decades after the Watts riots, Watts and other inner city neighborhoods were written off as vast wastelands of violence and despair. That became a self-fulfilling prophecy. Many banks, and corporations, as well as government officials, reneged on their promises to fund and build top-notch stores, make more home and business loans, and provide massive funding for job and social service programs in ghettoes such as Watts. Business leaders had horrific visions of their banks and stores going up in smoke or being hopelessly plagued by criminal violence.

Meanwhile, L.A.'s politicians naively buried their head in the sand and pretended that all was well in the city. That was glaringly and embarrassingly evident in the rash prediction that then Mayor Tom Bradley made on the 25th anniversary of the 1965-Watts riots in 1990. When Bradley was asked whether L.A. could be racked by another riot, he confidently said that it couldn't happen again. A scant two years later, L.A. was torn by nightmarish urban violence following the acquittal in the Simi Valley trial of the four LAPD officers that beat black motorist Rodney King. When the smoke cleared the death toll and property damage far exceeded the damage and destruction of the Watts riots.

That should have been yet another wake-up call that things were still bad, and could get worse. Since then they have. Last April, the National Urban League in its annual state of Black America report grimly noted that blacks have lost ground in income education, health care, and their treatment in the criminal justice system in relation to whites. They are more likely than any other group in America to be victimized by crime and violence. In L.A., things are worse still. In July, the L.A. chapter of the National Urban League and the United Way issued an unprecedented report on the State of Black L.A. The report called the conditions in Watts and South L.A., dismal. Blacks have higher school drop out rates, greater homelessness, die younger and in greater numbers, are more likely to be jailed and serve longer sentences, and are far and away more likely to be victims of racial hate crimes than any other group in L.A. County. King hospital, once the shining symbol of change and progress in the area, is mired in bitter controversy over mismanagement, medical incompetence, and patient neglect. The threat of closure perennially hangs over the hospital.

The only significant social change in Watts is the ethnic demographic shift. Forty years ago, the area was predominantly black; it is now predominantly Latino, with growing numbers of Cambodian, Vietnamese, and Filipino residents.

The fast changing demographics have at times imploded in inter-ethnic battles between blacks and Latinos over jobs, housing, schools, and deadly clashes within the L.A. county jails. Black flight has also drastically diminished black political strength in L.A. and statewide. In the past decade, the number of blacks in the California legislature has shrunk to half the number, and there is the real possibility that blacks could lose one, possibly two, of their three city council seats in the next few years.

Watts is no longer the national and world symbol of American urban racial destruction, neglect and despair. But the poverty, violence and neglect that made it that symbol is still very much there. Forty years later that hasn't changed.

### Document 3: Mosley remembers[10]

*Walter Mosley is today a successful and famous author. He writes about many subjects, but many of his novels are set in the Watts area of Los Angeles. He was a teenager at the time of the riots. In an interview with Powell's Bookstore in Portland, Oregon, posted online, he recalled the summer of 1965.*

**Farley [interviewer from bookstore]:** You grew up in LA, correct?

**Walter Mosley:** Yes.

**Farley:** I'm curious what memories you have of the Watts riots?

**Mosley:** I was thirteen-years-old during the Watts riots. I have two memories: . . .
   The first is that I was a member of an acting group called the Afro-American Traveling Actors Association, and at the height of the riots we went down to perform our play. But nobody was going to plays because they were either rioting or fighting rioting or hiding from rioting. So we drove back to West Los Angeles right through the riots. I saw all the fighting and police and people lying unconscious or, you know, dead on the street, and all that kind of stuff.

But that had less of an impact on me than the night I came into a room and found my father drinking and sobbing. And I said, "What's wrong." And he said, "It's the riots." "Are you afraid," I said. And he goes, "No, I want to go out there and riot. I want to fight. I want to burn. I want to shoot at these people." And I was very afraid, and I said, "Are you going to?" And he went, "No, I'm not, because it's wrong to hurt people you don't know, who may not deserve it, and it's wrong to burn down your own property. But I want to," he said. And that had a really big impact on me.

**Farley:** After the '92 riots in LA following the Rodney King verdict, Dan Quayle said: "When I have been asked during these last weeks who caused the riots and the killing in LA, my answer has been direct and simple: Who is to blame for the riots? The rioters are to blame. Who is to blame for the killings? The killers are to blame." Doesn't that accurately sum up an attitude that was prevalent after the Watts riots, as well? And if so, how would you respond to that attitude?

**Mosley:** Well, you know, listen, he's not wrong, in so far as it goes. If you shoot somebody and kill them, and somebody asked, *Who killed that guy?*, I'd have to say, *Well, you killed him.*

**Farley:** But the unstated message in Quayle's comment is: *And we therefore aren't obliged to think any more about it.*

**Mosley:** Exactly. And that's the problem. For instance, after 9/11 some people asked, *Why do people around the world hate Americans?* and then answered *Because they hate freedom!* I don't think so. There are reasons people hate Americans, and these reasons have to be addressed. One of the problems that people from Dan Quayle's ilk have is that if you ask these questions, they believe you are trying to exonerate whatever actions somebody took.

Now, of course, my father answered that question *No.* He didn't riot because he couldn't exonerate himself for doing it. And I wouldn't either. If you murder somebody . . . if you get on top of a building and aim a rifle at somebody and shoot it and kill them, that's murder. And I won't stand in the way of you standing trial for murder.

But the Watts riots are a metaphor for all of the rage that existed in all of the hearts of almost every African American. And that's what you have to deal with. And that's how America responded. You know, people sitting in Atlanta, Georgia going, *You mean all those black people I see every day really hate me, to the level where they could understand taking out a gun and shooting at me?* To understand that that's the problem. . . .

**Farley:** It makes me think of the handful of prominent blacks in the country who are perceived by some members of the black community as taking sides against blacks. I think of Harry Belafonte's comment about Colin Powell. What did he call him?

**Mosley:** He called him a house nigger, or a house slave, I don't remember which one he said.

**Farley:** And Clarence Thomas, of course, is widely criticized in the black community.

**Mosley:** Yeah, well, you know Clarence and Condoleezza and Colin are like that sentry, yeah. . . .

**Farley:** Of course, it is also significant that our current president, a very conservative Republican, chose a black woman as one of his closest advisers.

**Mosley:** Which is going to make a big difference for black people in the future. Not today, but in the future. In a way, he may be working against himself by doing that.

**Farley:** How so?

**Mosley:** Because he'll open the door. Now you can have black women as powerful as Condoleezza Rice in high government.

**Farley:** Do you really think that George Bush would care to keep that door closed?

**Mosley:** George Bush himself? I don't know the answer to that question. And I don't care. I think he sees black America in general as having antipathy toward him, and therefore doesn't consider black America his constituency. And he's right about that. But whether he's trying to keep people down. . . . I think that there's a system in America where black people are kept out of the vote, kept out of the mainstream in America. There's a great deal of racism against poor black people, not necessarily so-called middle class or upper-class black people, but certainly against poor black people in America. There are great barriers erected against black Americans.

**Farley:** And often the people who aren't behind the barriers don't see them and so don't believe they exist.

**Mosley:** Especially some younger people, saying, you know, *I worked hard. I made it. How come he can't do it?*

**Farley:** Which brings to mind Bill Cosby, who recently stirred up a hornets' nest by criticizing poor blacks.

**Mosley:** Yeah, but Bill's comments are made out of love. They may be inappropriate at times, they may be critical to the level that they are not helpful, at times, but he's not saying them because of a dislike or an antipathy towards black people. He's saying it because of love. And I think most black people know that. You know, I'm critical of the way he's made some of his criticism. But I can't say that Bill doesn't like black people. Bill *loves* black people. And he has all of these great hopes and aspirations, and he feels in a way cheated by certain things that have happened. I think that the reasons these things have happened go far beyond the people he's criticizing. However, I'm not going to say he didn't have the right to say what he said. . . .

**Mosley:** . . . But the LA riots were the big riots, the most impactful. And why is that? I don't know. But, you know, most big cities experienced riots in the sixties. And when Martin Luther King was killed, there were riots everywhere.

**Farley:** Yes, well I think anyone could see why there were riots after that.

**Mosley:** You can see why there are riots any time. Four hundred years of oppression, you know, and people still want to mistreat you. Your kids are still being arrested and thrown into jail when white kids are not being arrested and thrown into jail for doing the exactly same thing. When you know for a fact that every night black men are arrested and beaten. And I'll say, for no reason because there is no reason. Once you're arrested, you shouldn't be beaten. That's not the police's job. But it happens to black people. And they have had no recourse for hundreds of years. It happened before the riots, during the riots, and after the riots.

So what are you going to do? A guy says, *I remember last week a cop grabbed me and took me down to the prison. And they beat me within an inch of my life. So why can't I riot?* And that becomes the answer. *So why can't I go out and fight and burn. Why can't I do that? Didn't they do that to me?* And, really, there's no answer. Because everybody would agree. Take some white guy living in Orange County, if the police systematically took his children and the children of other people in his neighborhood and took them down to the police station and just beat them mercilessly, and then framed them for crimes they didn't commit, kept them from their rights, kept them from all this stuff, they would be out there fighting. Anyone would be out there fighting. It's not a black thing. It's just not happening to these other people, so they don't do it.

## Document 4: Kerner Commission Report[11]

*In the wake of riots that continued after the Watts outbreak, President Lyndon Johnson formed a National Advisory Commission on Civil Disorders in July 1967. The commission's 1968 report, informally known as the Kerner Report, concluded that the nation was "moving toward two societies, one black, one white—separate and unequal." Unless conditions were remedied, the commission warned, the country faced a "system of 'apartheid'" in its major cities. The report delivered an indictment of "white society" for isolating and neglecting African Americans and urged legislation to promote racial integration and to enrich slums—primarily through the creation of jobs, job training programs, and decent housing. President Johnson, however, rejected the recommendations. In April 1968, one month after the release of the Kerner Report, rioting broke out in more than 100 cities following the assassination of civil rights leader Martin Luther King, Jr.*

### SUMMARY OF REPORT
#### INTRODUCTION
The summer of 1967 again brought racial disorders to American cities, and with them shock, fear and bewilderment to the nation.

The worst came during a two-week period in July, first in Newark and then in Detroit. Each set off a chain reaction in neighboring communities.

On July 28, 1967, the President of the United States established this Commission and directed us to answer three basic questions:

What happened? Why did it happen? What can be done to prevent it from happening again?

To respond to these questions, we have undertaken a broad range of studies and investigations. We have visited the riot cities; we have heard many witnesses; we have sought the counsel of experts across the country.

This is our basic conclusion: Our nation is moving toward two societies, one black, one white—separate and unequal.

Reaction to last summer's disorders has quickened the movement and deepened the division. Discrimination and segregation have long permeated much of American life; they now threaten the future of every American.

This deepening racial division is not inevitable. The movement apart can be reversed. Choice is still possible. Our principal task is to define that choice and to press for a national resolution.

To pursue our present course will involve the continuing polarization of the American community and, ultimately, the destruction of basic democratic values.

The alternative is not blind repression or capitulation to lawlessness. It is the realization of common opportunities for all within a single society.

This alternative will require a commitment to national action—compassionate, massive and sustained, backed by the resources of the most powerful and the richest nation on this earth. From every American it will require new attitudes, new understanding, and, above all, new will.

The vital needs of the nation must be met; hard choices must be made, and, if necessary, new taxes enacted.

Violence cannot build a better society. Disruption and disorder nourish repression, not justice. They strike at the freedom of every citizen. The community cannot—it will not—tolerate coercion and mob rule.

Violence and destruction must be ended—in the streets of the ghetto and in the lives of people.

Segregation and poverty have created in the racial ghetto a destructive environment totally unknown to most white Americans.

What white Americans have never fully understood—but what the Negro can never forget—is that white society is deeply implicated in the ghetto. White institutions created it, white institutions maintain it, and white society condones it.

It is time now to turn with all the purpose at our command to the major unfinished business of this nation. It is time to adopt strategies for action that will produce quick and visible progress. It is time to make good the promises of American democracy to all citizens—urban and rural, white and black, Spanish-surname, American Indian, and every minority group.

Our recommendations embrace three basic principles:

To mount programs on a scale equal to the dimension of the problems;

To aim these programs for high impact in the immediate future in order to close the gap between promise and performance;

To undertake new initiatives and experiments that can change the system of failure and frustration that now dominates the ghetto and weakens our society.

These programs will require unprecedented levels of funding and performance, but they neither probe deeper nor demand more than the problems which called them forth. There can be no higher priority for national action and no higher claim on the nation's conscience. . . .

## Notes

1. Executive Order 9981: Desegregation of the Armed Forces (1948) July 26, 1949, by President Harry S. Truman, Truman Presidential Library, Independence, Missouri; Harry S. Truman, *Memoirs: Years of Trial and Hope*, v. 2 (Garden City, N.Y.: Double day & Company, Inc., 1956). Reprinted by permission of Clifton Truman Daniel.

2. *Brown v. Board of Education*, 347 U.S. 483 (1954).

3. Text of the Address by the President of The United States, Delivered From His Office at the White House, Tuesday. September 24, 1957, Dwight D. Eisenhower Presidential Library, Abilene, Kansas.

4. Speech at MIA Mass Meeting at Holt Street Baptist Church, and Statement on Ending the Bus Boycott, December 20, 1956, Martin Luther King Papers. In the speech at the beginning of the protest, there were words within parentheses that were remarks made by the crowd as he spoke. They have been edited out here for clarity and brevity. Reprinted by arrangement with the Heirs to the Estate of Martin Luther King Jr., c/o Writers House as agent for the proprietor New York, NY. Copyright 1963 Dr. Martin Luther King Jr.; copyright renewed 1991 Coretta Scott King.

5. Radio and Television Report to the American People on Civil Rights, President John F. Kennedy, The White House, June 11, 1963, *Public Papers of the Presidents of the United States: John F. Kennedy: 1963* (Washington, D.C.: Government Publishing Office, 1963), 468–71.

6. Martin Luther King, Jr., "I Have a Dream" delivered August 28, 1963, at the Lincoln Memorial, Washington D.C., King Papers. Reprinted by arrangement with the Heirs to the Estate of Martin Luther King Jr., c/o Writers House as agent for the proprietor New York, NY. Copyright 1963 Dr. Martin Luther King Jr.; copyright renewed 1991 Coretta Scott King.

7. Annual Message to the Congress on the State of the Union, January 8, 1964, and President Lyndon B. Johnson's Radio and Television Remarks Upon Signing the Civil

Rights Bill, July 2, 1964, *Public Papers of the Presidents of the United States: Lyndon B. Johnson, 1963-64,* vol. 2 (Washington, D.C.: Government Printing Office, 1965), 842–44.

8. A Report by the Governor's Commission on the Los Angeles Riots, *Violence in the City—An End or a Beginning,* December 2, 1965, 1–2, 10–11, 23–25, 37, 55–56, 68–69.

9. Earl Ofari Hutchinson, interview in the *Huffington Post* online. Reprinted by permission of Hutchinson Political Report.

10. This interview was originally published on Powells.com.

11. United States. Kerner Commission, *Report of the National Advisory Commission on Civil Disorders* (Washington, D.C.: U.S. Government Printing Office, 1968), 1–2.

# 7

# A New Society

*B*<small>Y THE</small> *1960*<small>S AND BEYOND,</small> *change had become a normal part of life for Amer-icans. In the 1960s and 1970s, women began a new push for improving their legal and social position. The women's movement was widely supported, but it was also opposed by many, including, surprisingly, other women. By the late 1970s and early 1980s, a new phenomenon was the emergence of conservative Christian groups into the political arena. What became known as the "Christian Right" changed the landscape of domestic politics.*

*Both of these developments had the most impact on domestic developments, but they also had international ramifications. The women leaders believed they were a part of a worldwide movement, and the Christian Right was a part of the growing fundamentalism in religion throughout the world.*

## Part A: The New Feminism

### Background

*By the end of the 1960s, the civil rights movement had made important gains for African Americans, but the growing opposition to the war in Vietnam and the more radical black movements had shifted the focus to some extent. Throughout the 1960s, women had played a major role in all the movements for social change, but, according to their own accounts, women often played a secondary role to men in these activities. Women of the 1960s saw change all around them, yet re-alized that they were not benefiting from these changes as other groups were.*

*A new wave of feminism began to appear on the American scene. The struggle for women's rights was not new by any means. One of the first important actions taken for women's rights was in 1848 at the Seneca Falls Conference that declared for women's rights, especially the right to vote. Almost seventy-five years passed before that right was achieved in 1920 with the Nineteenth Amendment to the Constitution. Most men and a large percentage of women believed equality had been achieved, but others disagreed. Women's rights advocates had continued to work in the 1920s, but their voices were most often ignored. Then came the struggles of the Depression and then the challenge of war. In some cases, women made advances, such as the "Rosie the Riveter" symbolism. But when the war was over, many women left the workplace and went back home. The 1950s and early 1960s saw women concentrating on home and children, but many were restive. On the world scene, it was embarrassing for a nation that proclaimed democratic principles to have women—especially African American women—lacking full rights. So the stage was set for a new women's movement.*

## Questions

In reading these documents, the student should ask and answer several questions to put these activities in the proper context.

1. Why did the women's movement lag behind other reform movements of the 1960s?
2. What was the problem Betty Friedan called "the problem that has no name"?
3. How important was the founding of *MS* magazine to the women's movement? Was it merely symbolic?
4. How significant was the Equal Rights Amendment (ERA)? Was it really needed?
5. Evaluate the arguments for and against the ERA.

## Document 1: Declaration of American Women[1]

*Most movements issue statements of purpose, calling them manifestos, declarations, or other such designations. There were a number of such documents in the women's rights movement. After the modern feminist movement began in the 1960s, a National Women's Conference, held in Houston, Texas, in 1977 issued a new document called the Declaration of American Women.*

We are here to move history forward.
We are women from every State and Territory in the Nation.

We are women of different ages, beliefs and lifestyles.

We are women of many economic, social, political, racial, ethnic, cultural, educational and religious backgrounds.

We are married, single, widowed and divorced.

We are mothers and daughters.

We are sisters.

We speak in varied accents and languages but we share the common language and experience of American women who throughout our Nation's life have been denied the opportunities, rights, privileges and responsibilities accorded to men.

For the first time in more than 200 years of our democracy, we are gathered in a National Women's Conference, charged under Federal law to assess the status of women in our country, to measure the progress we have made, to identify the barriers that prevent us from participating fully and equally in all aspects of national life, and to make recommendations to the President and to the congress for means by which such barriers can be removed.

We recognize the positive changes that have occurred in the lives of women since the founding of our nation. In more than a century of struggle from Seneca Falls 1848 to Houston 1977, we have progressed from being non-persons and slaves whose work and achievements were unrecognized, whose needs were ignored, and whose rights were suppressed to being citizens with freedoms and aspirations of which our ancestors could only dream. . . .

But despite some gains made in the past 200 years, our dream of equality is still withheld from us and millions of women still face a daily reality of discrimination, limited opportunities and economic hardship. . . .

From infancy throughout life, in personal and public relationships, in the family, in the schools, in every occupation and profession, too often we find our individuality, our capabilities, our earning powers diminished by discriminatory practices and outmoded ideas of what a woman is, what a woman can do, and what a woman must be.

Increasingly, we are victims of crimes of violence in a culture that degrades us as sex objects and promotes pornography for profit.

We are poorer than men. And those of us who are minority women—blacks, Hispanic Americans, Native Americans, and Asian Americans—must overcome the double burden of discrimination based on race and sex.

We lack effective political and economic power. We have only minor and insignificant roles in making, interpreting and enforcing our laws in running our political parties, businesses, unions, schools and institutions, in directing the media, in governing our country, in deciding issues of war or peace.

We do not seek special privileges, but we demand as a human right a full voice and role for women in determining the destiny of our world, our nation, our families and our individual lives.

We seek these rights for all women, whether or not they choose as individuals to use them.

We are part of a worldwide movement of women who believe that only by bringing women into full partnership with men and respecting our rights as half the human race can we hope to achieve a world in which the whole human race—men, women and children—can live in peace and security.

Based on the views of women who have met in every State and Territory in the past year, the National Plan of Action is presented to the President and the Congress as our recommendations for implementing Public Law 94-167.

We are entitled to and expect serious attention to our proposals.

We demand immediate and continuing action on our National Plan by Federal, State, public, and private institutions so that by 1985, the end of the International Decade for Women proclaimed by the United Nations, everything possible under the law will have been done to provide American women with full equality.

The rest will be up to the hearts, minds and moral consciences of men and women and what they do to make our society truly democratic and open to all.

We pledge ourselves with all the strength of our dedication to this struggle "to form a more perfect Union."

### Document 2: Friedan Defines the "Problem"[2]

*Betty Friedan, a woman some consider the founder of the modern feminist movement, published her ground-breaking book,* The Feminine Mystique, *in 1963. This book, both hated and loved, sold millions of copies, made Friedan a household name and stimulated discussion and action as nothing had for some time. She brought to light a "problem that has no name," a phrase that caught the imagination of millions of women. In this excerpt from the first chapter, her theme is clear.*

. . . For over fifteen years there was no word of this yearning in the millions of words written about women, for women, in all the columns, books and articles by experts telling women their role was to seek fulfillment as wives and mothers. Over and over women heard in voices of tradition and of Freudian sophistication that they could desire—no greater destiny than to glory in their own femininity. . . .

The suburban housewife—she was the dream image of the young American women and the envy, it was said, of women all over the world. The American housewife—freed by science and labor-saving appliances from the drudgery, the dangers of childbirth and the illnesses of her grandmother. She was healthy, beautiful, educated, concerned only about her husband, her children, her home. She had found true feminine fulfillment. As a housewife and mother, she was respected as a full and equal partner to man in his world. She was free to choose automobiles, clothes, appliances, supermarkets; she had everything that women ever dreamed of.

In the fifteen years after World War II, this mystique of feminine fulfillment became the cherished and self-perpetuating core of contemporary American culture. Millions of women lived their lives in the image of those pretty pictures of the American suburban housewife, kissing their husbands goodbye in front of the picture window, depositing their stationwagonsful of children at school, and smiling as they ran the new electric waxer over the spotless kitchen floor. They baked their own bread, sewed their own and their children's clothes, kept their new washing machines and dryers running all day. They changed the sheets on the beds twice a week instead of once, took the rughoolag class in adult education, and pitied their poor frustrated mothers, who had dreamed of having a career. Their only dream was to be perfect wives and mothers; their highest ambition to have five children and a beautiful house, their only fight to get and keep their husbands. They had no thought for the unfeminine problems of the world outside the home; they wanted the men to make the major decisions. They gloried in their role as women, . . .

If a woman had a problem in the 1950's and 1960's, she knew that something must be wrong with her marriage, or with herself. Other women were satisfied with their lives, she thought. What kind of a woman was she if she did not feel this mysterious fulfillment waxing the kitchen floor? She was so ashamed to admit her dissatisfaction that she never knew how many other women shared it. If she tried to tell her husband, he didn't understand what she was talking about. She did not really understand it herself. . . .

But on an April morning in 1959, I heard a mother of four, having coffee with four other mothers in a suburban development fifteen miles from New York, say in a tone of quiet desperation, "the problem." And the others knew, without words, that she was not talking about a problem with her husband, or her children, or her home. Suddenly they realized they all shared the same problem, the problem that has no name. They began, hesitantly, to talk about it. Later, after they had picked up their children at nursery school and taken them home to nap, two of the women cried, in sheer relief, just to know they were not alone. . . .

The year American women's discontent boiled over, it was also reported . . . that the more than 21,000,000 American women who are single, widowed, or divorced do not cease even after fifty their frenzied, desperate search for a man. . . .

This terrible tiredness took so many women to doctors in the 1950's that one decided to investigate it. He found, surprisingly, that his patients suffering from "housewife's fatigue" slept more than an adult needed to sleep—as much as ten hours a day—and that the actual energy they expended on housework did not tax their capacity. The real problem must be something else, he decided—perhaps boredom. Some doctors told their women patients they must get out of the house for a day, treat themselves to a movie in town. Others prescribed tranquilizers. Many suburban housewives were taking tranquilizers like cough drops. "You wake up in the morning, and you feel as if there's no point in going on another day like this. So you take a tranquilizer because it makes you not care so much that it's pointless." . . .

If I am right, the problem that has no name stirring in the minds of so many American women today is not a matter of loss of femininity or too much education, or the demands of domesticity. It is far more important than anyone recognizes. It is the key to these other new and old problems which have been torturing women and their husbands and children, and puzzling their doctors and educators for years. It may well be the key to our future as a nation and a culture. We can no longer ignore that voice within women that says: "I want something more than my husband and my children and my home."

### Document 3: A New Women's Magazine[3]

*Gloria Steinem became, in some ways, the face of the new feminist movement. She was attractive, articulate, and willing to confront her opponents. In the late 1960s and early 1970s, she and a group of like-minded women decided it was time for a new type of women's magazine. Women's magazines were nothing new in America; they had been around since the early 1820s. The earlier magazines had focused how a woman could be a "better woman," how she could make a home, support her husband, and remain feminine. The women's magazines of the twentieth century were quite similar. MS, the magazine they ultimately created, was different and was seen as radical by those who did not support the women's movement. This excerpt from the first regular issue of MS in 1972 explains how the magazine came into being.*

First, there were some women writers and editors who started asking questions. Why was our work so unconnected to our lives? Why were the media, including women's magazines, so rarely or so superficially interested in the big changes happening to women? Why were we always playing the game by somebody else's (the publisher's, the advertiser's) rules?

Then, there were questions from activists, women who were trying to raise money for an information service and self-help projects, particularly for poor or isolated women, and having very little luck. Mightn't a publication—say, a newsletter—serve to link up women, and to generate income as well?

The two groups met several times early in 1971, and agreed that we all wanted a publication that was owned by and honest about women. Then we did some hard financial figuring. Newsletters that made decent profits seem confined to giving stock-market tips, or servicing big corporations. Some small but valuable ones for women were already struggling along. Besides, newsletters were a fine service for people already interested, but weren't really meant to reach out in a populist way.

So the idea of a full-fledged national magazine came up; a publication created and controlled by women that could be as serious, outrageous, satisfying, sad, funky, intimate, global, compassionate, and full of change as women's lives really are.

Of course, we knew that many national magazines were folding, or doing poorly. Rocketing production and mailing costs, plus competition from television for both advertising and subject matter, had discouraged some of the people who loved magazines most. Even those magazines still flourishing were unresponsive to the silenced majority. Women just weren't getting serious or honest coverage, and we doubted that we were the only people who felt the need for change. Besides, the Women's Movement had raised our hopes; it had given us courage.

So we had many more meetings, and we made big plans: long lists of article ideas, a mock-up of illustration and design, proposed budgets, everything. Then we spent many months making appointments, looking for backing from groups that invest in new ventures—and just as many months getting turned down. Flat. . . .

Most of all, there were the several women writers and editors, one businesswoman, and some all-purpose feminist volunteers who were willing to contribute their talents and time in return for very little except hope. "It's very simple," said one of the writers. "We all want to work for a magazine we read."

Then, two concrete things happened to bolster our hopes. First, Katharine Graham, one of the few women publishers in the country, was willing to pretend that a few shares of stock in a nonexistent magazine were worth buying, a fiction that allowed us some money for out-of-the-pocket expenses. . . . Second and even more unusual was an offer from Clay Felker, editor and publisher of *New York,* a weekly metropolitan magazine. He had thought up an ingenious way of helping *Ms.* produce the thing it needed most: a nationwide test; a sample issue to prove that we could create a new kind of magazine, and that women would buy it.

The plan was this. *New York* needed something special for its year-end double issue, and also wanted practice in producing national "one-shot" magazines (single issues devoted to a particular area or subject). *Ms.* needed the money and editorial freedom to produce a sample issue. Therefore, *New York* offered to bear the full risk of the $125,000 necessary to pay printers, binders, engravers, paper mills, distributors, writers, artists, and all the other elements vital to turning out 300,000 copies of our Preview Issue. (Plus supplying the great asset of *New York's* staff, without which the expenses would have been much higher.) In return, some of the *Ms.* articles and features would appear first as an insert in that year-end issue of *New York,* half of the newsstand profits (if any) of our own Preview Issue would go to *New York,* and so would all of the advertising proceeds. . . .

It was an odd way of introducing a magazine, but a generous and unusual offer—the first time, as far as we know, that one magazine would give birth to another without the *quid pro quo* of editorial control, or some permanent financial interest. Clay Felker made a few gruff noises about how it was strictly a business deal. After all, didn't *New York* stand to make a profit if *Ms.* did very well? (This last was generally said in earshot of his Board of Directors, who might otherwise think he was as crazy as we were.)

Several of us were regular writers for *New York,* however, and we had a different idea. Over the years, we must have convinced him, or at least worn him down. Clay had begun to believe, like us, that something deep, irresistible, and possibly historic, was happening to women.

## THE PREVIEW ISSUE

In a small office, with four people working full time and the rest of us helping when we could get away from our jobs, the Spring Preview Issue was put together, start to finish, in two months. . . .

We just chose not to do anything with which one of us strongly disagreed. And we didn't expect our more junior members to get coffee, or order lunch, or do all the typing, or hold some subordinate title. We each did as much of our own phone-answering and manuscript typing as deadlines and common sense would allow. On the masthead, we listed ourselves alphabetically, divided only by area of expertise and full- or part-time work. . . .

The crowded *Ms.* office had an atmosphere of camaraderie, of people doing what they cared about. But there was apprehension, too. Could there possibly be even 100,000 women in the country who wanted this unconventional magazine? We had been listening to doomsayers for so long that we ourselves began to doubt it.

When the insert from our Preview Issue appeared as part of *New York* in December, the issue set a newsstand sales record, more than *New York* had ever sold. Of course, said the doomsayers, women in a metropolitan area might be interested. But would we appeal to the women of Ohio or Arizona?

When the full-length Spring Preview Issue of *Ms.* was distributed nationally in January, we packed off all available authors and staff to talk to women's groups around the country, and to appear on any radio or television shows that reached women (thus changing the lives of several of us, who had never spoken in public before).

The Preview Issue was designed to stay on the newsstands for at least two months (which is why it was dated "Spring"), and we wanted to make sure women knew about it. But we got to our various assigned towns only to be met with phone calls: "Where is *Ms.?*" "We can't find a copy." "What newsstands are selling it?"

Worriedly, we called the distributor, and the truth finally dawned on us. The 300,000 copies supposed to last for at least eight weeks had virtually disappeared in eight days. *Ms.* had sold out. . . .

But the most gratifying experience was still to come. Letters came pouring into our crowded office, more than 20,000 long, literate, simple, disparate, funny, tragic and very personal letters from women all over the country, including Ohio and Arizona. . . .

We were feeling inundated by all the mail, but didn't realize how unusual it was until we asked the editor of another women's magazine—with a circulation of 7 million, compared to our 300,000—how much editorial response each issue got. "About 2,000 letters," she said, "and a lot of them not very worthwhile. Four thousand letters of any kind would be considered quite extraordinary."

Obviously, the need for and interest in a nonestablishment magazine were greater and deeper than even we had thought. More out of instinct than skill, the women of *Ms.* had tapped an emerging and deep cultural change that was happening to us, and happening to our sisters. . . .

### Document 4: The Equal Rights Amendment[4]

*Following the success in 1920 of the Nineteenth Amendment giving women the right to vote, the women's movement did not die. One of the new initiatives, proposed by Alice Paul in 1921, was to get an equal rights amendment to the Constitution. It was introduced in Congress in 1923 and every session after that. The new National Organization of Women (NOW), created as a part of the new women's movement, and other organizations stepped up support for the amendment in the 1960s and early 1970s. Congress passed the amendment in 1972 and sent it out to the states for ratification with a time limit of seven years. Even after the time was extended to 1982, the amendment failed by three states to get enough ratifications for approval. The amendment is short and simple.*

Section 1. Equality of Rights under the law shall not be denied or abridged by the United States or any state on account of sex.
Section 2. The Congress shall have the power to enforce, by appropriate legislation, the provisions of this article.
Section 3. This amendment shall take effect two years after the date of ratification.

## Documents 5–7: Support for the ERA

*When the ERA was voted out of Congress, most people seemed to believe that it would be ratified, but it generated opposition right away, some of the most vocal coming from women. Much of the opposition came from religious groups who saw the amendment as somehow lowering the status of women. Yet, some of the most impassioned support came also from religious groups. A sampling of the support follows.*

### Document 5: A Catholic magazine speaks out[5]

*The magazine* America *is a Catholic publication. In 1975, as the amendment was working its way through the states but seemed to be having trouble, a lengthy article provided support. The section below is the conclusion of this article.*

This article has focused primarily on the impact of the ERA on marriage and family because concern for family well-being seems to be the source of the misgivings about the ERA on the part of many Catholics. The ERA will have an impact in other areas as well. Increasingly, we are becoming aware that women and girls are treated quite differently from men and boys in the judicial system. Under the guise of protection, women are penalized for "crimes" men are not—prostitution, for example—and sentences for the same crime, even in the same case, are harsher. Most of the women caught up in these cases lack the financial resources to battle through the courts for justice. One can only ask why they should have to battle for justice because they are women. Should not the system be changed now that we recognize the injustices?

It is worth calling attention to the costs of the injustice of discrimination because of sex. Women are denied the right to develop the potential with which they were created. Society, in turn, is denied a valuable, essential resource. Half the population is excluded from public life, from decision making. Women must live in a world structured by men who, more often than not, overlook their needs, their values, their dreams. Women alone do not suffer—all of us do. We suffer unjustly and needlessly. Support for the ERA this year, Holy Year International Women's Year, will do much to bring about the just society that will benefit all of us.

### Document 6: Supporters appeal to women[6]

*In 1981, the amendment was bogged down and time was running out. An article in* The Christian Century *tried to bolster support.*

Opponents of the ERA, led by Phyllis Schlafly, have halted state-by-state passage of the amendment by misrepresenting what the ERA would do to women of the country. They have convinced enough legislators that the real issue is mixed bathrooms and homosexual marriages. Nothing the pro-ERA leaders have tried has been able to offset that propaganda. The reason: our culture's understanding of male-female relationships has so ingrained the subservient status of women that advances for women can be blocked if the right emotional triggers are pulled.

And Phyllis Schlafly has pulled those triggers with her skillful portrayal of the effects of ERA's passage. Women would be dragged down from a sacred pedestal. By using the Equal Rights Amendment as a major tactic to advance the women's cause, its proponents employed a strategy developed in the civil rights movement. Martin Luther King, Jr., went after state segregation laws, for example, by working to get the federal government to pass laws that relied on constitutional guarantees of equality to overrule local racist statutes. The ERA seemed a reasonable way to accomplish a similar goal for women.

But our culture's attitude toward females reaches deeper into the public psyche than even the deep-rooted racist mentality that created segregation laws. What anti-ERA proponents are able to touch is the most sensitive of all human emotions; those related to sexuality. Even males who consider themselves liberated have difficulty accepting equal pay for women, and they resist affirmative-action programs that are designed to offset generations off prejudice against women in the job market.

As one of those liberated males who all too often is aware of an emotional bias that prefers the soft and compliant to the aggressive and successful female, I want now to offer the women's movement a word of advice: give up on trying to pass the ERA, and instead begin working to change the mind-set of contemporary culture on male-female relations. This is a longer-range goal than activists like to consider, and it holds out little tangible hope of immediate success. But the ERA has lost because the battle was joined on a field that inherently assumes an inequality between the sexes. The early success of the amendment, which saw it move through the Congress and through almost enough states to make it official, came about because no one had raised emotionally loaded questions related to sex. Phyllis Schlafly, recognizing a potent political tool to supplement her hard-right militaristic anticommunist philosophy, took aim at the amendment and stopped it dead in its legislative tracks. . . .

What we face in trying to overcome generations of cultural propaganda linked with sexual self-understanding is the turning around of a national mind-set. Passage of the ERA would have helped to do this. But that amendment has been blocked. The effort must continue with new strategies so that future media propaganda will not be able to manipulate the public into believing that half of the population is inferior to the other half.

*Document 7: Attempt to revive the amendment[7]*

*In 1982, after the time limit had expired, the amendment was introduced in Congress again.* The Christian Century *was still writing about it.*

The Equal Rights Amendment has been reintroduced in Congress. If it passes both houses, and survives a possible White House veto, then we can expect the long trek through the various state legislatures to begin again. Nothing wrong with that. Chances of passage don't appear any more promising than when proponents failed to convince those final few stubborn states to give women equality under the Constitution earlier this year. But one thing is certain: the issue will continue to raise consciousness and reshape the way we think about male-female relationships.

The ERA has become a symbol not just for equality, which is still needed in our society, but for power, which is slowly being attained by the previously powerless feminine half of the population. Even the abortion issue, complex and ambiguous as it is, involves both equality and power.

Many Americans feel deeply that abortion is murder, and they base this view on a theological understanding of life as beginning at conception. Others argue that the beginning of life is not so clearly understood, either theologically or scientifically. It is hard to shake the suspicion, however, that some of the anti-abortion fervor involves something beyond a "respect for life." There may be a strong anti-female bias in the movement, a desire to punish women for sexual activity.

Fundamentalist Protestants in particular, who do not belong to a Christian tradition with strong doctrinal beliefs on abortion such as those found in Orthodox or Roman Catholic traditions, have "discovered" abortion fairly recently. Fundamentalist sermons of 25 years ago focused on adultery, not abortion. Could it be that today's heavy emphasis on this admittedly complicated problem reflects at least as much hostility to women as it does concern for a fetus?

How many men among us have problems with the new woman, that product of a consciousness-raising era who insists that she is not only equal but entitled to power over her personal and public life? . . .

We feel powerless when we are out of control. The society that existed before the rise of feminine consciousness gave men the impression that they were in control. Family structure, sexual practices and vocational patterns were predictable in a male-dominated society. But issues like the ERA and the new attitudes toward sexual freedom pose great threats to people, male and female, who were comfortable with the predictability of the old patterns.

## Documents 8–10: The Opponents Speak

*The opponents of the ERA were organized and outspoken, as these three samples show.*

### Document 8: Opponents believe the Amendment will be approved[8]

*The* National Review, *probably the most respected of the conservative magazines in America, opposed the amendment, but, as this editorial that appeared soon after Congress approved the amendment shows, the editors believed it would be ratified in short order. The sarcasm in the editorial is obvious.*

But while we are on the subject of the Constitution, Congress will be in a weak moral position to stress the precise language of Article III, considering the Senate's passage last week (84 to 8) of the Equal Rights for Women amendment (ERA).

Though easily passed and certain to be ratified in short order during this election year, the amendment deserves a prominent place in any anthology of recent constitutional frivolities. It guarantees "equality of rights under the law," which has a satisfying ring; but what, in fact, does that mean?

When the amendment becomes effective sometime in the summer of 1974, every eighteen-year-old girl will have to register for the draft. And, presumably, women will have to be drafted in proportion to their percentage population. Nor, once drafted, can exceptions be made. That means combat duty. The WAVE and WAC approach will be constitutionally impermissible.

*Even though the Equal Rights Amendment (ERA) was designed to improve the legal sta-*
*tus of women in America, a significant portion of women opposed the amendment. Peo-*
*ple such as Phyllis Schlafly believed that the amendment would have unintended conse-*
*quences that would actually harm women. This demonstration in front of the White*
*House is an example of women opposing the amendment. Courtesy of the Library of Con-*
*gress, LC-U9-33889A-31/31A.*

Under the Social Security laws, women may now retire at 62, men at sixty-five. This will be palpably unconstitutional. But lowering the male age would cause economic disruption while raising the women's age would cause a political howl.

Furthermore, as a few senators and several commentators have pointed out, the amendment would appear to render unconstitutional a whole library of state laws bearing on child support, alimony, industrial safety and inheritance. We may expect years, nay, generations of litigation where these are concerned. The ERA thus bears no resemblance to the Nineteenth Amendment, securing women the vote, or to last year's eighteen-year-old vote amendment, which could not be misinterpreted.

Well done, gentlemen. The Senate, with those eight honorable exceptions, flagitiously violated the well-known principle that constitutional amendments must be precise and specific. Even in an election year, an amendment is no place for pious velleities. Within a short time, you may expect, the cry for repeal will be loud.

*Document 9: Opponents believe the courts are implementing
the amendment*[9]

*After the amendment had been defeated,* The National Review *said that the
courts and Congress were still trying to make it the law.*

The proponents of ERA came away from the Republican Convention with
wounded feelings—only partly assuaged by Reagan's acceptance-speech ca-
ress. That they felt unsatisfied by the declaration to "eliminate, wherever it exists, discrimination against women" indicates the special symbolism with
which ERA has come to be invested. It is, in fact, *only* as a symbol that ERA re-
tains any value, since, during the protraction of the ratification process (by no
means nearing conclusion), its provisions have become largely superfluous.

While the amendment itself has been shriveling on the vine, Congress and
the courts have been conscientious in ratifying its provisions *de facto.* The
Civil Rights Act of 1964 was amended by Congress in 1972 to include Title
VII, which bans sex discrimination by institutions receiving federal funds (i.e.,
everybody but the corner grocer). The fallout from that statute has been enormous, to the point that the EEOC recently declared even an office pass to be
"sex harassment" litigable as discrimination. Title IX of the 1974 Higher Education Act prohibits sex discrimination in intercollegiate sports, etc. At the
same time, state legislatures have been grinding out statutes to "equalize"
everything from probate to pool rooms (some have adopted their own free-
lance ERAs). But what is most important, from the point of view of the fem-
inists, is the recent pattern of court decisions in which the Fifth and Fourteenth Amendments have been construed to prohibit sex discrimination
under the "equal protection" clause . . . The proposed Twenty-Eighth Amendment is moribund, but its progeny thrive. While gender-based inequities remain law in some places, the full impact of these decisions has been to make
it exceedingly uncomfortable (and in many cases illegal) to discriminate between the sexes in employment, housing, education, alimony, and a thousand
other categories tilting toward the absurd. . . .

The trouble with ERA as a symbol is that it would not remain, like a constitutional monarch, a harmless emblem. Without ERA, such inequities as
exist can be corrected by statute. But once enacted, it would hamstring the
states, the Congress, and the courts.

*Document 10: Schlafly explains her role*[10]

*Phyllis Schlafly, a woman unknown at the time on the national level, became
the most vocal and visible of the opponents of the ERA. She opposed it because she*

*thought it would make the position of women in America worse than it had been before. Probably she got much of the attention because she was a woman opposing the women's rights movement. In 2004, she was interviewed about her activities and how she and her supporters stopped the amendment from being ratified in Illinois, a key state.*

**FRAN EATON:** *How did you begin a movement that resulted in ultimately defeating the Equal Rights Amendment?*

**PHYLLIS SCHLAFLY:** The ERA came out of Congress in March of 72 and it was coming up in Illinois in late spring. The first thing we did was to ask the legislators to have a hearing. There were hearings in state legislatures all over the country, and for the most part, we got equal time. We never had that in the media. It was usually twenty to one against us in the media, but in the hearings we got equal time.

We were able to present the arguments about why the ERA was hurtful to women and what legal rights women would lose if the ERA was ratified. At the time, Henry Hyde was the Republican leader in the Illinois House. He got onto the prodigious effect of ERA right away and helped to defeat it, which gave us a little victory.

We didn't know then, of course, that we had started a 10-year battle and that the Illinois legislature would vote on it every year for the next 10 years. If we'd known that, we might not have taken up the battle in the first place, but our belief was the legislators were reasonable people, that if we presented the facts to them they would vote the right way.

A lot of them did, enough of them did that we were able to defeat it every year for 10 years, despite the opposition of all the powers that be in the state—all the media, all the television, all these women's organizations, news organizations, women's magazines.

By presenting the facts, we were able to outsmart them.

**FE:** *You're being humble about your background and the persuasive tactics you used to resist the ERA. You also developed a national grassroots network at the same time.*

**SCHLAFLY:** Well you're right, at first we thought if we just told them the facts that they would all do the right thing. For the first couple of years, we had a small group, mostly the women who had worked with me in Republican women's clubs, and we held back the avalanche for a couple of years.

Then we realized the forces against us were too powerful. We needed reinforcements. That's when I sent out the word to the churches. That was the one place we felt we could get reinforcements.

In 1976 when we prayed we could bring 1000 people to Springfield, no one had ever seen that many in Springfield before. They came that day in April of '76, and they came on buses that said "Joy" and "Jesus Saves." A lot of them were carrying their babies in their arms, and we did have 1000 people there.

The legislators were just in total shock. They didn't know there were so many like us out there. That demonstration convinced them we were there, we cared, and that we would be around at election time.

One of the problems we had was that so many of the legislators had committed to ERA before we got started and didn't want to go back on their word.

But anyway, we had a lobbying day every week. People teased me about my rotunda letters that would say, "Meet Phyllis in the rotunda at the state capitol at 11 on Wednesdays." We had people there every week, and we kept lobbying, we kept explaining how ERA would be hurtful to women.

FE: *Did you have a different focus every week? Did you have a long-range plan being there every Wednesday? Was it that organized?*

. . . I kind of laid down the party line about what arguments to use and what was going on in other states and the ERAers didn't have any argument, they were unable to show any benefit ERA would give to women. . . .

They were never able to show any benefit that ERA would give to women whereas we could show that it would draft young women, take away rights of wives, take away veterans benefits, give enormous new powers to federal government of Section 2 of ERA.

So we hung in there. It got very ugly. You talk about persuasive. We were nice to the legislators. We didn't say mean things to them but the other side got very ugly. . . .

When we got down to the very end in 1982, you remember they had the chain gang on the second floor—a lesbian chain gang. They chained themselves to the doors of Senate chambers and the senators had to step over them to get in. Then they had the hunger strike on the first floor of the capitol, led by an excommunicated Mormon, and they had some experienced hunger strikers from some Vietnam demonstrations.

And that didn't persuade anybody to vote for ERA. It's hard to see how they think it would. . . .

SCHLAFLY: . . . The ones who came out of the churches, many had never been to the capital before. They didn't understand that when ERA didn't come up, we were winning, but they learned and were very valuable. What I think we did was to invent the pro-family movement because what our stop ERA fight did was to get good people of all denominations to work together. . . .

I think we really invented the pro-family movement, which has now become a tremendous factor in national politics and was copied in other states. The crucial day was the day of 1980 when the whole national media were in Springfield and the ERAers had predicted this was the day it was going to pass. . . .

FE: *Were you surprised when you won? Or did you know there were enough votes?*

SCHLAFLY: No, I didn't know we had the votes. We had done all we could. God found a couple of votes for us in Chicago that had never voted our way before. I remember, *Nightline* put Eleanor Smeal in front of the cameras in the gallery of the House and said, "Ms. Smeal, you said you had the votes, what happened?"

She said, "There was something very powerful against us, and I don't mean people." . . .

## Part B: The Rise of the Religious Right

### Background

*Beginning in the late 1970s and growing in strength through the 1980s and on into the new century, a new phenomenon arose in the political arena—what has become popularly known as the "Religious Right." The movement said that the religious community had been silent for too long, and it was time for "people of faith" to exert their electoral muscle and do what they could to get people elected to office who shared their views.*

*Although some of the leaders wanted the world to believe that the movement embraced people of all faiths, in the popular mind, the Religious Right was composed primarily of fundamentalist and evangelical Protestants. In the popular mind of the 1980s and 1990s, the organization known as the "Moral Majority" was symbolic of the new political activism of the conservative Protestant movement.*

*This followed, somewhat, the rise of religious fundamentalism around the world, especially in the Middle East. Although many American fundamentalists denied it, the rise of intolerance in religion had an impact on political life that made governing more difficult. The move toward theocracy was not restricted to only one part of the world.*

*The fundamentalist movement was strengthened by its virulent anti-communism. Since the Soviet version of Marxism was aggressively atheist, it was a natural enemy of fundamentalist Christians. So the Religious Right had not only a social agenda but a foreign one as well.*

*The Religious Right had a number of successes. This group claimed credit for the election of Ronald Reagan as president and for the election to office of any number of religious conservatives from local communities to the U.S. Congress. The Right had a number of issues that symbolized their movement, for example opposition to abortion, homosexuality, and pornography. The strength of this political movement has been a source of disagreement, but few would deny that it was a new force to be reckoned with in any political election.*

*This section deals with the Moral Majority and its influence. Although there were many threads and influences other than the Moral Majority, space does not permit a broader review of this new political movement.*

## Questions

In reading these documents, the student should ask and answer several questions to put these activities in the proper context.

1. Did the religious movement overstep its bounds when it entered political battles?
2. Did the political movement violate the concept of the separation of church and state as embodied in the Constitution?
3. Was Jerry Falwell a good spokesman for the religious right, or could another person have done a better job.
4. Were the arguments of the critics of the religious right correct in their attempts to discredit the movement?
5. What do you foresee as the future of this religious political movement?

## Document 1: Falwell Makes His Case[11]

*The founder of the Moral Majority was Rev. Jerry Falwell. In 1981, not long after he founded the organization, he wrote in a thorough fashion about what his group was—and what it was not. The following is a small excerpt from a much longer article, but it gives a thumbnail sketch of the organization and its aims.*

These are the greatest days of the twentieth century. We have the opportunity to formulate a new beginning for America. For the first time in my lifetime, we have the opportunity to see spiritual revival and political renewal in the United States. We now have a platform to express the concerns of the majority of moral Americans who still love those things for which this country stands. We have the opportunity to rebuild America to the greatness it once had as a leader among leaders in the world.

The 1980s are certainly a decade of destiny for America. The rising tide of secularism threatens to obliterate the Judeo-Christian influence on American society. In the realm of religion, liberal clergy have seduced the average American away from the Bible and the kind of simple faith on which this country was built. We need to call America back to God, back to the Bible, and back to moral sanity.

. . . In our attempt to rally a diversity of morally conservative Americans together in the Moral Majority, we were convinced that millions of people were fed up with the fruits of liberalism, both in politics and in religion. I am well aware that it is unpopular in some circles to equate the two, but I say that they must be viewed as cousins of the same family because both rest upon the same foundational presupposition of the inherent goodness of mankind. The ultimate product of theological liberalism is a vague kind of religious humanism that is devoid of any true gospel content. . . .

As a pastor, I kept waiting for someone to come to the forefront of the American religious scene to lead the way out of the wilderness. . . . Finally, I realized that we had to act ourselves. Something had to be done. The government was encroaching upon the sovereignty of both the church and the family. The Supreme Court had legalized abortion-on-demand. The Equal Rights Amendment, with its vague language, threatened to do further damage to the traditional family, as did the rising sentiment toward so-called homosexual rights. Most Americans were shocked, but kept hoping someone would do something about all this moral chaos. . . .

Facing the desperate need in the impending crisis of the hour, several concerned pastors urged me to put together a political organization that could provide a vehicle to address these crucial issues. . . . They urged that we formulate a nonpartisan political organization to promote morality in public life and combat legislation that favored the legalization of immorality. Together we formulated the Moral Majority, Inc. Today Moral Majority, Inc. is made up of millions of Americans, including 72,000 ministers, priests, and rabbis, who are deeply concerned about the moral decline of our nation, the traditional family, and the moral values on which our nation was built. We are Catholics, Jews, Protestants, Mormons, Fundamentalists—blacks and whites—farmers, housewives, businessmen, and businesswomen. We are Americans from all walks of life united by one central concern: to serve as a special-interest group providing a voice for a return to moral sanity in these United States of America. Moral Majority is a political organization and is not based on theological considerations. We are Americans who share similar moral convictions. We are opposed to abortion, pornography, the drug epidemic, the breakdown of the traditional family, the establishment of homosexuality as an accepted alternate lifestyle, and other moral cancers that are causing our society to rot from within. Moral Majority strongly supports a pluralistic America. While we believe that this nation was founded upon the Judeo-Christian ethic by men and women who were strongly influenced by biblical moral principles, we are committed to the separation of Church and State.

Here is how Moral Majority stands on today's vital issues;

1. *We believe in the separation of Church and State.* . . .
2. *We are pro-life.* We believe that life begins at fertilization. . . .
3. *We are pro-traditional family.* We believe that the only acceptable family form begins with a legal marriage of a man and woman. . . .
4. *We oppose the illegal drug traffic in America.* . . .

5. *We oppose pornography.* While we do not advocate censorship, we do believe that education and legislation can help stem the tide of pornography and obscenity that is poisoning the American spirit today. Economic boycotts are a proper way in America's free enterprise system to help persuade the media to move back to a sensible and reasonable moral stand. . . .
6. *We support the state of Israel and Jewish people everywhere.* . . .
7. *We believe that a strong national defense is the best deterrent to war.* . . .
8. *We support equal rights for women.* . . .
9. *We believe ERA is the wrong vehicle to obtain equal rights for women.* . . .
10. *We encourage our Moral Majority state organizations to be autonomous and indigenous.* . . .

## What Moral Majority Is Not

1. *We are not a political party.* . . .
2. *We do not endorse political candidates.* . . .
3. We are *not attempting to elect "born-again" candidates.* We are committed to pluralism. . .
4. *Moral Majority, Inc., is not* a *religious organization attempting to control the government.* . . .
5. We are *not* a *censorship organization.* . . .
6. *Moral Majority, Inc., is not* an *organization committed to depriving homosexuals of their civil rights as Americans.* While we believe that homosexuality is a moral perversion, we are committed to guaranteeing the civil rights of homosexuals. . . .
7. We do *not believe that individuals or organizations that disagree with Moral Majority, Inc., belong to an immoral minority.* . . .

## Out of the Pew and Into the Precinct

. . . The recent emergence of Fundamentalists and Evangelicals in politics in no way violates the historical principles of this nation. The incorporation of Christian principles into both the structure and the basic documents of our nation is a matter of historical fact. The doctrine of the separation of church and state simply means that the state shall not control religion and religion shall not control the state. It does not mean that the two may never work together. . . .

Moral Majority, Inc., does not advocate the abolition of public schools. Public schools will always be needed in our pluralistic society. We are committed to helping public schools regain excellence. That is why we support the return of voluntary prayer to public schools and strongly oppose the teaching of the "religion" of secular humanism in the public classroom. . . .

Christians are now realizing again that governmental actions directly affect their lives. They are questioning the government's right to carry out such programs. They are beginning to realize again that the only way to change the actions of government is to change those elected to govern. We are now beginning to do just that. We must continue to exert a strong moral influence upon America if our children and grandchildren are to enjoy the same freedoms that we have known.

*An Appeal to Fundamentalists*

I have always made it clear that I am a Fundamentalist—big F! A Fundamentalist believes the Bible to be verbally inspired by the Holy Spirit and therefore inerrant and absolutely infallible. . . .

I am also a separatist. We Fundamentalists practice separatism from the world and all of its entanglements. We refuse to conform to the standards of a sinful society. . . .

However, we are not without our weaknesses. We tend to be negative and pessimistic. . . .

We have *just* as *many failures in our ranks* as do *the Evangelicals—maybe* more. *We cannot* be *blinded* by *our* tendency to use *our people* to *build our churches,* instead of using *our churches* to build our people.

## Document 2: Another Leader of the Religious Right Makes His Case[12]

*Charles W. Colson was a member of the Nixon administration who was caught up in the Watergate affair and spent some time in prison. When he was released he was a "born-again" Christian, and he began a new prison ministry. A few years after the beginning of the Moral Majority, he had some comments on the nature of religious leaders and politics.*

The debate over religion and politics has so far failed to clarify one very important issue for Christians. The debate has seemed to pose two choices: one side arguing that faith in God and country are inseparable—a position known historically as civil religion; the other side asserting that one's religion is entirely a private matter. The public, including many Christians, has been left believing that religion's proper role in American life has to fall into one of these two politically defined alternatives. But neither of these options has anything to do with historic Christianity—and there is the danger. For example, let us consider the generic civil religion advocated by one camp. "Religion plays a critical role in the political life of our nation," said one candidate. What kind of religion? "If you practice a religion, whether you are Catholic, Protestant, Jewish, or guided by some other faith, then your private life will be influenced by a sense of obligation and so, too, your public life."

Thus, in the civil religionists' view, America has a "tolerant" society, "open to and encouraging of all religions." . . .

Countering this view is the notion that "faith [is] intensely personal"; there are many "faiths," all of which are "true" for those who hold them. To have religion enter political debates might require that a person defend his religious beliefs! What could be more uncivil? . . .

Of course, we Christians should know that such emptiness and cynicism has nothing to do with blessing. Yet, in the heat of the [1984] presidential campaign, there was a great temptation to quietly opt for one of these false paths as a way to express biblical faith.

For example, ought a candidate to have received a Christian's enthusiastic support because he supports certain religious values? What about prayer in public schools? Prayer is surely a religious act, and religion is surely advanced by such acts. . . .

## The Spiritual Dimension

We Christians, of all people, should see through the political illusion. We should understand that the real problems of our society are, at their root, moral and spiritual. Institutions and politicians are limited in what they can do, and we dare not confuse this limited good with the infinite good of the gospel. The kingdom of God will not arrive on Air Force One. . . .

## Document 3: Another Point of View from the Right[13]

*Paul Weyrich is a founding member of the Moral Majority and the Christian Coalition, the successor to the Moral Majority. In 1999, he shocked and confused many of his followers in an article in* Christianity Today. *He has an interesting take on the success and the future of the conservative movement.*

What many of us have been trying to do for many years has been based upon a couple of premises. First, we assumed that a majority of Americans basically agrees with our point of view. I was the one who suggested to Jerry Falwell that he call his organization the "Moral Majority." The second premise has been that if we could just elect enough conservatives, they would fight to implement our agenda.

In looking at the long history of conservative politics, from the defeat of Robert Taft in 1952 to the nomination of Barry Goldwater to the takeover of the Republican party in 1994, I think it is fair to say that conservatives have learned to succeed in politics. That is, we got our people elected.

But that did not result in the adoption of our agenda. The reason, I think, is that politics itself has failed. And politics has failed because of the collapse of the culture. The culture is becoming an ever-wider sewer. We are caught up in a cultural collapse of historic proportions, a collapse so great that it simply overwhelms politics.

That's why I am in the process of rethinking what it is that we, who still believe in our traditional, Western, Judeo-Christian culture, can and should do under the circumstances. Please understand that I am not quarreling with anybody who pursues politics, because it is important to pursue politics, to be involved in government. It is also important to try, as many people have, to retake the cultural institutions that have been captured by the other side.

But the United States is becoming an ideological state. The ideology of Political Correctness, which openly calls for the destruction of our traditional culture, has so gripped the body politic, has so gripped our institutions, that it is even affecting the church. It has completely taken over the academic community. It is now pervasive in the entertainment industry, and it threatens to control every aspect of our lives.

Those who came up with Political Correctness, which we more accurately call "Cultural Marxism," did so in a deliberate fashion. Suffice it to say that the United States is very close to becoming a state totally dominated by an alien ideology, an ideology bitterly hostile to Western culture. . . .

Cultural Marxism is succeeding in its war against our culture. The question becomes: If we are unable to escape the cultural disintegration that is gripping society, then what hope can we have? . . .

If in Washington State and Colorado, after we have spent years talking about partial-birth abortion, we can't by referendum pass a ban on it, we have to face some unpleasant facts. I no longer believe that there is a moral majority. I believe that we probably have lost the culture war. That doesn't mean the war is not going to continue and that it isn't going to be fought on other fronts. But in terms of society in general, we have lost. This is why, even when we win in politics, our victories fail to translate into the kind of policies we believe are important.

Therefore, what seems to me a legitimate strategy for us to follow is to look at ways to separate ourselves from the institutions that have been captured by the ideology of Political Correctness, or by other enemies of our traditional culture. . . .

What I mean by separation is, for example, what the homeschoolers have done. Faced with public-school systems that no longer educate but instead "condition" students with the attitudes demanded by Political Correctness, they have seceded. . . .

I think that we have to look at what we can do to separate ourselves from this hostile culture. . . .

I am very concerned as I talk to young people when I find how much of the decadent culture they have absorbed without even understanding that they are a part of it. And while I'm not suggesting that we all become Amish or move to Idaho, I do think that we have to look at what we can do to separate ourselves from this hostile culture. What steps can we take to make sure that we and our children are not infected? We need some sort of quarantine. . . .

We care not in the dawn of a new civilization, but the twilight of an old one. We will be lucky if we escape with any remnants of the great Judeo-Christian civilization that we have known through the ages.

Again, I don't have all the answers or even all the questions. But I know that what we have been doing for 30 years hasn't worked, that while we have been fighting and winning in politics, our culture has decayed into something approaching barbarism. We need to take another tack, find a different strategy.

## Documents 4–5: Criticism of the Religious Right Varies

*Much has been written on the Religious Right's influence on American politics in recent years. The critics vary in their approach to the movement. Some bash it without reservation, but others say there are lessons to be learned from the movement. The following two documents reflect this variety.*

### Document 4: Lessons can be learned from the Moral Majority

*Robert McAfee Brown, a leader in the civil rights movement and the struggle against the war in Vietnam, was also a critic of the Religious Right. He summarizes his position in this brief excerpt.*

Some of you may have misread the title "The Need for a Moral Minority," and assumed that I was going to address the Moral Majority. . . .

My overall concern is much more how we can relate religion and politics positively. . . . This whole problem of a religious presence on the political scene which has been highlighted for us in this rather recent emergence of the theological right wing, the problem of religion of the political scene is illustrated for me by a comment from an anonymous 17th century writer, one of my favorite anonymous comments. This writer wrote: "I had rather see coming toward me a whole regiment with drawn swords, than one lone Calvinist convinced that he is doing the will of God." Now that statement illustrates both the glory and demonry of Calvinism, and by a not very difficult extension, the potential glory and potential demonry of all political involvement on the part of religiously minded persons. . . .

But there can be a demonry as well in the invoking of God's support which we find exhibited when individuals or groups decide what they want to impose on others, and then claim divine sanction for it. This gives them carte blanche to do whatever they feel is necessary to stop their opponents since their opponents, being opposed to them, are clearly opposed to God as well, and do not finally deserve the right to speak or act or persuade, and Christians have often been guilty of this. . . .

Jerry Falwell, the leader of that movement, states that he knows just what is wrong with our country, and tells us: "God has called me to action. I have a divine mandate to go into the halls of Congress and fight for laws that will save America." As this position develops, it turns out that those who disagree with him are really by definition disagreeing with God, since he, and not they, have access to God's will. . . .

I do not for a moment challenge Mr. Falwell's right or anybody's right to get into the American political process, to work for change, to support candidates, urge people to vote and all the rest. That is the way the American system works, and the more people that are doing that, the better for the health of the system. And it would be a very perverse logic to claim that only people with whom I agree ought to be engaging in political activity, and I want no part of such an argument. I have taken my own political stands in the past; I intend to keep doing so in the present and in the future. So can and should everyone, whether named Billy Graham or Bill Coffin, whether named Jerry Falwell or Robert Drinan.

In Christian terms, and I think in terms with which all Jews could also agree, my real complaint about the Moral Majority's intrusion of the Bible into American politics, is that they are not biblical enough.

So let me illustrate that in two ways. First of all, it seems to me that the Moral Majority's biblically inspired political agenda involves a very selective, very partial, and therefore very distorted use of the Bible. They have isolated a set of concerns that they say get to the heart of what is wrong with America—homosexuality, abortion, and pornography. These are the things that are wrong and that are destroying our nation. We need to be for prayer in public schools, and for more bombs. Jesus wants our kids to pray and he wants the Pentagon to be able to kill more people if necessary. . . .

Take the issue of homosexuality. If one turns to the scriptures as a whole, to try to come up with their central concerns, homosexuality is going to be very low on such a list even if indeed it makes the list at all. The Moral Majority creates an agenda and then proceeds to impose that agenda on scripture by developing little strings of unrelated verses to give divine sanction to the position. As those who work with the Bible know, one can prove absolutely anything that way.

So let me suggest very briefly five characteristics that I think would be appropriate to the moral minority.

A moral minority might be called a remnant within the remnant. By and large, institutional Christianity is going to reflect the culture around it more than it will challenge it, but there could be a remnant within that remnant to define some ways to offer a different model. . . .

Secondly, what would be the resources such a group could employ? Here I think we have a couple of very good things going for us. One of them is the Bible. If we could break out of the kind of "culturally-conditioned" ways we have read the Bible, we would find it an explosive arsenal of materials for creative change. . . .

The third thing the moral minority could stress, perhaps the most important thing in the time in which we live, would be the necessity of a global perspective. This world is now just too small to allow for anything else. And to look at the world simply in terms of what is good for the United States, is ultimately going to be self-defeating. . . .

That suggests a fourth thing the moral minority might become; it could become that group in our society which is genuinely committed to the powerless and the voiceless. . . .

Fifth, and finally, a moral minority must set its own agendas. You may not like the ones that I have been suggesting so far. Certainly there can be others. Moral minority agendas must not be set by the Moral Majority movement. We must not fall into a trap of single-issue politics, or politics narrowly conceived on a tiny set of issues. I find it kind of morally oppressive to be told, again and again, some kind of obsession about other people's sex life is the burning issue of the day, when the majority of the human family went to bed hungry every night or to be told to rally around getting prayers back into schools when millions of people are unable to find jobs, or get minimal help if they are unemployed and disadvantaged. So I hope we can find ways to begin to rally around the problems, for the whole human family is hurting from the mad escalation of the arms race, the need for more equitable distribution of food, coming to terms with denials, both abroad and at home, of basic human rights, such as education and medical care and jobs and all the rest.

I think we need to create a moral minority that could propose convictions without arrogance, insight without absolutism, commitment but without coercion, and democracy without demagoguery.

### Document 5: A humanist reacts to Weyrich[15]

*In the debate over the Moral Majority, many people took different positions. On the Internet, an organization called "Progressive Humanism" talked about a New Moral Majority and reacted to Weyrich's comments quoted earlier.*

It's as official as it needs to be, and about as official as it's likely to get. The so-called moral majority, the group that backed the congressional coup effort to "get" Clinton, is by its own admission no longer a majority. One of the group's leading ayatollahs, Paul Weyrich, recently said so in a well-publicized statement. He suggested, in effect, a reversion to guerrilla tactics, since the frontal assault had been a costly failure. . . .

It's hard to describe the new moral majority, for it's a lot more varied than the old one. One of the interesting things about a democracy is that it tolerates moral diversity. The Christian right does not. That's one of the principal reasons this nation of ours has rejected it. We value our freedom to choose our own ideas and ideals over their doctrine. . . .

But meantime, we have to cope with that guerrilla warfare that is even now being fought by the newly demoted Christian right. They are infiltrating school boards all over the country and will intensify their efforts, aimed at instilling their "morality" in our children. To the extent that doesn't work, they will try to get the state to subsidize their own schools, so that at least they can try to ward off the modernizing of their own younger cadres. The rest of us must resist these efforts. The bottom line is that there must be a new moral majority that strongly supports and constantly reaffirms the principle of separation of church and state.

The abortion issue will continue to dominate the larger controversy. Everybody who opposes future hegemony by the Christian right needs to recognize this battle for what it is, one that transcends the immediate issue of the status of a human embryo, and goes to the heart of whether a determined minority can be allowed to dictate moral choices to the rest of us.

The Christian Right is also launching a detailed, long-term effort to provide a respectable theistic alternative to modern theories of evolution. . . .

So there is indeed a new moral majority on some issues, or there had better be. On the rest of the issues, let's ignore the static from the right as best we can and work things out. Actually, aren't we seeking to achieve a society where there really is no moral majority any more, and where every new issue that comes up is decided on its own merits by a pragmatic, informed, non-doctrinaire public?

### Document 6: A Foreign View[16]

*During the debate over the Religious Right in politics, a British observer took a close look at what was happening. An abbreviated version of his comments follows. Menachem refers to the prime minister of Israel in the 1980s, Menachem Begin.*

Hello Jerry. This is Menachem. Remember me?

Of course. Prime Minister, I'm deeply honoured that you should have called.

"Now, Jerry, I think you realise that things may be rather difficult for my country over the next few days. Can I count on your support?"

"You can bet your life on it, sir. We regard it as our privilege to do all we can for you."

A telephone conversation very much like this did take place in 1981. After the Israelis bombed the Iraqi nuclear power station at Osirak on the 8th of June, they contacted their friends around the world, urging them to defend the raid. The first person whom Begin phoned in the US was a small-town fundamentalist minister by the name of Jerry Falwell. But what was a hard-bitten politician doing talking to a hell-fire preacher during such a crisis?

The phone call was a carefully calculated move: because the Rev. Jerry Falwell is also the host of a TV programme which reaches millions of Americans and the founder of *Moral Majority,* a right-wing pressure group which had shot to prominence during the 1980 presidential election. Begin knew that Falwell could be relied on to rally a great deal of support for Israel. By contacting him he was acknowledging what many political commentators already knew to be true: the Christian Right was a formidable force in American politics. But what is the Christian Right? Is it a continuing force in 1984, and is it possible that a similar movement will gather strength elsewhere?

*Moral Majority* is only one of a number of groups which have come into being over the last five or six years proudly proclaiming themselves to be "pro-America, pro-Family, pro-God." Their aim is to mobilise the 20 per cent of US citizens who are born-again Christians to crusade against what they see as the moral decline of their nation, as evidenced by the break-up of the family, pornography, violence on TV, abortion and homosexuality. . . .

The Christian right-wingers are almost pathologically anti-communist. Falwell has called for the registration of all communists—"we should stamp it on their foreheads"—and sees little value in arms talks with the "godless, not-to-be-trusted Russians." When Reagan recently described Russia as the "focus of evil in the modern world," he was only expressing a view that fundamentalists have held for years. . . .

Along with the anti-communism goes an intense patriotism. This, of course, is not restricted to the fundamentalists. Americans of all political persuasions have seen their country in something approaching messianic terms and accepted its "manifest destiny." But the combination of Christianity and ultra-nationalism, always dangerous, is particularly frightening in a nuclear age.

How is it that *Moral Majority* and groups like it have been able to gain so much influence in the States? Two factors are important.

The first of these is technological. "The electronic church" is a huge industry in the States. Out of America's 8,000 radio stations, 1,400 are religious and the annual revenue of the Christian TV stations is around half a billion dollars. The big name preachers each raise about twice as much money every year as the Republicans and Democrats spend on their presidential campaigns. . . .

The second factor is social. Ronald Reagan won the 1980 presidential election because of a profoundly conservative mood that swept the country. After the chaotic 1960s, when everything seemed to be called into question, and the traumatic 1970s, when America lost faith in itself, there was a widespread longing for strong leadership and the reassertion of traditional American values. Flag-burning and breast-beating gave way to national assertiveness and apple-pie. Reagan was the man for the moment. . . .

Criticism of the Christian Right has come from many quarters. The TV preachers have been likened in the press to "mad mullahs" who are intent on establishing a regime of "holy terror." Car stickers are being sold which proclaim that "The *Moral Majority* is neither." The liberal National Council of Churches has condemned them bitterly for cloaking conservative politics in lofty rhetoric about morality and religion. Coming from a group who've made it their business to baptise the trendy left, this is rather rich. Sociologist Peter Berger points out that "the religio-political extravaganza on the right was preceded by" that on the left. . . . One must ask by what criterion one deems good the pronouncements of left-of centre geese, while condemning the preachments of right of centre ganders. . . .

What of the future of the Christian Right? In America it owes its success in large measure to "Prime Time Religion" and the sociological pressures of a society seeking certainties in a bewildering world. It remains to be seen whether the mood of an America buoyed up by economic recovery and demonstrations of military muscle will be amenable to further growth in its political influence. Returning confidence in the merits of America must well breed a smug self-satisfaction that is less responsive to the messianic rhetoric of the TV crusaders. . . .

## Notes

1. Wisconsin Women's Network Declaration of American Women, 1977, read at the National Women's Conference Houston November 1977, online at www.wiwomens network.org/1977declaration.html.

2. Betty Friedan, *The Feminine Mystique* (New York: W.W. Norton, 1963), 15, 18, 19, 25, 30–31. From THE FEMININE MYSTIQUE by Betty Friedan. Copyright ©

1983, 1974, 1973, 1963 by Betty Friedan. Used by permission of W.W. Norton & Company, Inc.

3. "A Personal Report From *Ms.*," *Ms.*, July 1972, 4–7. Reprinted by permission of *Ms.* magazine, © 1972.

4. Equal Rights Amendment, online at www.now.org/issues/economic/eratext .html.

5. Mary Burke, "The Church and the Equal Rights Amendment," *America*, May 17, 1975, 374–78. Reprinted by permission of *America* © 1975. All rights reserved.

6. James M. Wall, "New Wisdom From Rosie the Riveter," *The Christian Century*, March 4, 1981, 210–20. Copyright © 1981 by the *Christian Century*. Reprinted by permission from the March 4, 1981, issue of the *Christian Century*.

7. J. M. Wall, "The Real Issue for Women is Power," *The Christian Century*, October 27, 1982, 1067. Copyright © by the *Christian Century*. Reprinted by permission from the October 27, 1982, issue of the *Christian Century*.

8. "Equal Rights for Women," *National Review*, April 14, 1972, 383. © 1972 by National Review, Inc., 215 Lexington Avenue, New York, NY 10016. Reprinted by permission.

9. "What Do Women Want?" *National Review*, August 8, 1980, 943. © 1980 by National Review, Inc., 215 Lexington Avenue, New York, NY 10016. Reprinted by permission.

10. Fran Eaton, "In the Spotlight: Phyllis Schlafly," *Illinois Leader*, November 12, 2004, online at www.illinoisleader.com/printer/article.asp?c=20869. Reprinted by permission.

11. Jerry Falwell with Ed Dobson and Ed Hindson, *The Fundamentalist Phenomenon* (New York: Doubleday & Company, Inc., 1981), 186–95. Reprinted by permission of Falwell Estate.

12. Charles W. Colson, "The Lures and Limits of Political Power," *Pastoral Renewal*, January 1986. Originated in *Pastoral Renewal*, January 1986. Reprinted by permission of Charles Colson.

13. Paul Weyrich, *Christianity Today*, September 6, 1999. Reprinted by permission of Paul Weyrich.

14. Robert McAfee Brown, "The Need for a Moral Minority," in *Speak Out Against the New Right*, ed. Herbert F. Vetter (Boston: Beacon Press, 1982). Reprinted by permission of Robert McAfee Brown Estate.

15. Carleton Coon, "The New Moral Majority," March 18, 1999, online at www .progressivehumanism.com/morlmaj.html. Reprinted by permission of Carleton Coon.

16. Iwan Russell-Jones, "Give Me That Prime Time Religion," *New Internationalist*, March 1984. Reprinted by permission of the *New Internationalist*.

# 8

# American Society in Flux

$W$*ITH THE "BABY BOOMERS" COMING of age in the 1960s, society continued to change. Older Americans were caught off guard and did not know how to react to the changes in society, especially those occurring among the young. The "counterculture" was at once frightening and exciting. Most of the "boomers" later became mainstream Americans and looked back on their own activities with either pride or regret.*

*During this same period, American involvement in Vietnam increased. Supported at first as a part of the Cold War, the venture in Southeast Asia soon became controversial, especially after the massive troop buildup after 1964. The fact that young men were being drafted to serve in a war that they opposed made the war more controversial.*

## Part A: Counterculture and Protest

### Background

*The period thought of as the 1960s—roughly from about 1964 or 1965 to 1973 or 1975—was a period of great cultural upheaval. By the early 1960s, the first wave of those people born after World War II—the "baby boomers"—were beginning to reach maturity. This generation of young people looked on the world so differently that their parents and grandparents had little point of reference and were at a loss as to how to react to them.*

*This cultural shift is often referred to as the "counterculture," a term that in some ways defies definition. It included increasing drug use as that practice moved out of the slums and the lower classes into the neighborhoods and homes of the middle and upper classes. It also included an attitude that the major purpose in life was to have fun, to do "what feels good," and to eschew the values—including the work and business ethics—of older generations. The young of the 1960s had more disposable income than at any time in the past, and they could live much as they wanted to. Some of the young moved into communes and experimented with everything—drugs, promiscuous sex, rock and roll, and anything else that met their fancy. They became known as "hippies" or "flower children," people characterized by their bizarre lifestyle, dress, and behavior.*

*As the decade progressed, the counterculture ran headlong into the growing protest movements of the era—civil rights, women's rights, and, especially, the opposition to the war in Vietnam. Some of the hippies became antiwar protesters, while others tried to withdraw farther from society and not to participate in the ways of the world.*

*There is no single characterization of the counterculture of the 1960s. At the time, it meant whatever its participants wanted it to mean, and the confusion still exists today. Most of the documents regarding this period of history are to be found in the memoirs of people who lived through it. Not many of the hippies or others from this period wrote anything coherent at the time.*

## Questions

In reading these documents, the student should ask and answer several questions to put these activities in the proper context.

1. What was the "summer of love"? Was it significant or just a passing fancy?
2. How accurate is "Curse of Hippie Parents" regarding the "sexual revolution"?
3. Was the Students for a Democratic Society (SDS) really a revolutionary group, or was it merely another example of Americans expressing their opposition to government policy?
4. Why was Timothy Leary popular and considered the father of the drug culture?
5. Was Rennie Davis a true representative of the young in the 1960s?

## Document 1: The Summer of Love[1]

*The summer of 1967 was often referred to as the "summer of love." This expression meant different things to different people, but in retrospect it seems to symbolize the youth culture of the 1960s and is remembered either fondly or with*

*disgust by the people who lived through it and participated in it. Below is a brief*
*memoir that gives a good flavor of the time. Haight Ashbury is a section of the*
*city of San Francisco.*

Yes, it is 28 years ago since San Francisco's biggest concern was how many
of America's youth, now known as baby boomers, would descend upon the
Haight Ashbury in search of the holy grail of sex, drugs and rock and roll. In
the spring of '67 one of the members of the Board of Supervisors considering
whether to allow the expected hoards to sleep in Golden Gate Park said,
"Would you let thousands of whores waiting on the other side of the Bay
Bridge into San Francisco."

Of course, in the Haight Ashbury we referred to this holy grail as free love,
expanded consciousness and the ecstatic experience. We looked upon that
summer as the beginning of a children's crusade that would save America and
the world from the ravages of war, and the inner anger that brings it forth, and
materialism. We had already identified our lives with the world as a political
and social entity, and the planet as a unified environment, an earth household.
Love, we believed, would replace fear and small communal groups would replace the patriarchal family and mass alienation.

There were two aspects to the experience of the 60s: the resistance to the war,
and the "psychedelic experience," personified as political activists and hippies.
For the most part these two vectors overlapped in the same individuals, so that
many of those who actively resisted the Vietnam war had used LSD and
smoked marijuana. As a society we have tried to understand the sixties mostly
as political resistance to the war, but have mostly ignored and denied the
changes in values and culture brought about by "psychedelic experiences." It is
difficult to estimate how many people used LSD between 1965 and 1975 when
the war finally ended. One chemist, who wasn't as productive as some, told me
he produced and sold seven million doses. My off the cuff estimate would be
that from 10 to 30 million people took LSD on the average of six times.

"Tripping" was common in every area of society from the wealthy and politically powerful to the arts, and sciences and the media. LSD was trendy, ex-
otic, ecstatic, messianic and dangerous. It promised psychological healing and
spiritual transcendence and often delivered. It should be acknowledged that it
could also cause pain ("bad trips") and psychotic breaks, and even suicides,
and in the case of the Manson Family, it was an accomplice to murder. There
was an aura of living dangerously on a psychological frontier that was part of
its mystique. But given the amount of its use, I would say it was the one of our
least destructive national obsessions.

Why did so many people take this dangerous voyage? What have been its
effects? To understand this we have to reconsider the Haight Ashbury, the

Hippies and the Summer of Love. The predominant feeling among the Hippies from about 1965 through the summer of '67 was that they were agents and witnesses of a dawning of a new age. An age in which the warrior spirit, that had vaulted western man to the domination and potential destruction of creation, would be dissolved in the spiritual transcendence of the saint. Ghandi [sic] and Martin Luther King were our heroes and we had turned to the rich heritage of Asian mysticism and metaphysics for our inspiration and our practice. We leaped across oceans and through time to pre-Christian mythologies like the American Indian, the Egyptian and the occult and pagan philosophies of Europe. We studied with Buddhists and Indian gurus, native shamans, witches and yogis. We turned from Aristotelian and Christian dualism to the four pronged logic of Vedanta philosophy. We studied the Upanishads, the Tao Te Ching, Alan Watt's books on Zen Buddhism, and Hermann Hesse's novels, especially Siddhartha. We wouldn't leave the house without consulting the I Ching, or our Tarot cards or our astrological charts.

Were we being naive or superstitious? No, I think this was the most important and long lasting aspect of the 60s despite the backlash of the 80s. It was the beginning of a renaissance in thought and culture similar to the Renaissance that brought Greek and Roman images and ideas back to Europe in the middle ages. Ideas that eventually led to the end of the domination of the Catholic Church, the rise of the nation state, the rebirth of democracy and the development of science.

We were becoming world citizens. Peace and love weren't just slogans but states of mind and experiences that we were living and bearing witness to. Living in harmony with the earth was an ideal that we felt and perceived as real experience. We were bringing forth a second Renaissance that would change human culture.

In the face of the Cold War and nuclear weapons these changes in philosophical and spiritual orientation would slowly displace the Warrior Spirit and bring us to a new stage of evolution. The transformation of the inner warrior has had its outer effect in the end of the Cold War. Gorbachev said to an American reporter, "I'm going to do a terrible thing to you. I'm going to take your enemy from you."

The Summer of Love was the peak of the Haight Ashbury experience. Over 100,000 youth came to the Haight. Hoards of reporters, movie makers, FBI agents, undercover police, drug addicts, provocateurs, Mafioso and about 100,000 more tourists to watch them all followed in their wake. It was chaotic and wonderful and "heavy" as we used to say and the experience was shared and spread throughout the world. The police and Tac Squad raided the street every weekend gradually driving most of the originators to all parts of the world to plant the seeds of change. . . .

## Document 2: Growing Up Hippie[2]

*Sexual freedom was a large part of the counterculture. Whether this had any-thing to do with the liberation of women is open to interpretation, but many peo-ple believed it was merely the exploitation of women in a period that supposedly supported more equality. The following selection is by a young woman who grew up in the hippie culture. The language of this selection might offend some, but it is a good example of the extreme hippie lifestyle that was so prevalent at the time and was feared by many.*

One summer when I was 10 or 11, a boy I'll call Jackson befriended my brother and came over to our house frequently to play in our pond. After a few hours of splashing around, naked as usual, we went up to the house to dry off and have something to eat. Jackson plopped down on my mom's platform rocker, grabbed his penis and started to masturbate.

"Hey!" I yelled, and threw a pillow at him. "Don't do that right in front of everybody!"

"My mom says, 'If it feels good, do it,'" he said, whacking away.

If it feels good, do it: a rallying cry of the '60s and the root of a lot of really awful parenting. Jackson may have been admirably comfortable with his body, but like many children of hippie parents, he was in the dark about some very basic social rules, such as the one that says don't jack off in public.

Growing up with no boundaries will do that to you. In their effort to raise children without inhibitions, my parents and their peers eschewed the teach-ings of Benjamin Spock and went for a more anarchic, Fellini-esque parent-ing approach. . . . But there was a dark side to this intoxicating rejection of rules and boundaries. With everyone embracing spontaneity and the man-dates of the id, there was no one left to assume the adult role. People like my parents may have had the best of intentions, but in a wide-eyed quest for so-cial change, they became children. And their actual children suffered as a re-sult.

Sure, the benign neglect of hippie parenting had some side benefits. If you wanted to stay home from school, you could—as long as you had a really good excuse, such as, "I just can't get behind school today, Mom." Hippie kids also got to run around in the woods a lot, without being overly burdened by Es-tablishment concepts like sunscreen or mosquito repellent. My mom took me on long walks, taught me to find wild huckleberries and to weave baskets out of sticks. She woke us up at midnight for impromptu waffle feasts. If we found something cool, like a dead dragonfly or a weird mushroom, she would be just as curious and amazed as we were. She was convinced magic existed, and since she was our mom, we absolutely believed it. That was wonderful.

However, the hippie creed of "no rules, no limits" combined with a horror of hypocrisy sent groovy parents skidding down a dangerously slippery child-rearing slope. If you smoke pot, what are you going to do when your kids ask to try it? It would be hypocritical not to let them. And if pot's OK, why not mushrooms or acid? If you tell your kids sexual expression is great, and you yourself frequently "ball" (to use the mot juste) with abandon, how do you explain to your daughter that it's not OK for some crusty old guy at a Grateful Dead show to feel her up in the child-care tipi? The old standby "It's wrong because I said so" was out, because they'd taught us from birth that such a statement is fascistic. So, to avoid the hypocrisy of potentially arbitrary limits, hippie parents placed few or none.

And kids need limits. Someone in the family unit has to take the adult role, preferably the adults themselves. On the commune, I actually begged my mom for rules. "Let's have a rule where kids have to go to bed at a certain time every night!" I said. Or, "Let's have a rule that says children should be seen and not heard!" . . . I longed for discipline, for someone to tell me, "That's quite enough of that, young lady!"

But in the hippie days, discipline was out, and wild Dionysian revelry was in. I can't remember the first time I smoked pot, though I do remember getting a joint for my 7th birthday, all wrapped up in a pink ribbon. And the love was certainly what they called "free." My mom tells me it was considered impolite not to sleep with someone when they asked politely. People would pair up, naturally, but relationships were strained by the constant lure of extracurricular screwing. The repression and conservatism of the '50s were rejected with a vengeance, and people coupled and separated and regrouped like pornographic square-dancers.

This was presented to the children as the natural order of things, but we knew there was something wrong. For one thing, a dizzying number of people were always coming and going. Sometimes they'd say goodbye to the kids who had grown attached to them, sometimes not. We were terribly hurt when people we loved just up and left, and we were embarrassed by all the unfettered humping. Adults seemed so ridiculous with their balling and their toking and their weird wiggly dancing to the Grateful Dead. One evening at the commune, the grownups took Quaaludes or mescaline or something, and they all ended up in a big horny, writhing, drugged-out mass on the living room floor. At some point, my mom says, they heard an angry little throat-clearing sound. They looked up, and I was standing in the doorway, fists on my hips, glaring at them. "What exactly do you think you are all DOING?" I yelled.

Things weren't much better when my brother and I visited our father in San Francisco. Despite fairly clear evidence of some early heterosexuality, Dad had always had homosexual leanings. Just as the hippies violently rejected social norms at least partly in response to straitlaced convention, my father exploded out of the closet like a rocket fueled by repressed yearning. With the gay sexual revolution in San Francisco, he was finally free to express that side of himself openly. This was a wonderful thing, but the effects of it were confusing and bizarre for my brother and me. With him, the Love That Dare Not Speak Its Name became the Love That Would Not Shut Up.

My father marched, he swung, he went to bars, he talked incessantly about his sexual experiences, and he left copies of Torso and Honcho strewn liberally about his Victorian house in the Haight. At first, my brother and I thought they were just some kind of new mainstream magazine. Certainly, they weren't any more male-centric than Time or Life. . . .

Confusingly enough, Dad also had some straight porn as well. I can kind of track his acceptance of his gayness over time by the dwindling ratio of Penthouses to Honchos. By the time I was 9 or 10, he was full-strength, concentrated, half-a-cup-does-the-whole-load gay, and living with a really nice guy named—I'm not making this up—Randy.

On arriving at his house for a visit, after months of cultural deprivation up in the boonies, my brother and I would drop our duffel bags at the door and head for the television like patients in an obsessive/compulsive ward. We had lots of cultural reference catching-up to do, and devoured the subtleties of "The Brady Bunch" and "Speed Racer."

The trouble really started when Dad got a VCR. He quickly amassed a large collection of movies, most of them pirated and hand-labeled, and he didn't bother to segregate the porn. Some, like "The Young and the Hung," were easy to avoid. Others were more worrying. My brother and I would consult each other over ambiguous titles like "12 Angry Men." We finally got up the courage to watch that one, but no way were we going near "The 400 Blows." We loved "Arsenic and Old Lace," but it was kept right next to "Run, Little Sailor Boy, Run." Once we put in the wrong tape, and were treated to the sight of a guy being fellated in an alley. "I don't think that's Alec Guinness," said my brother.

The open sexuality and lack of boundaries of the hippie era, which many parents thought would encourage their children to be happy little free spirits, often had diametrically opposite results. At age 8, I had a big crush on a commune guy I'll call Bill. That crush included sexual fantasies. I had just learned about rape, by overhearing someone tell a joke about it. They made it sound like a fun game, and I decided I wanted to try it with Bill. I went and found him, and told him I wanted to rape him. "OK," he said.

I took him into the kids' building. He took off all his clothes and lay down. He had an erection. I took mine off too and lay down on top of him. He kissed and fondled me. After a while, he got up, kissed me on the top of the head and thanked me. I felt confused and embarrassed.

Over the years, I had many inappropriate sexual experiences, with different partners and levels of interest on my part. The confusion and embarrassment were a constant. Even in less ambiguous situations in which I was exploited by predatory adults, I blamed myself for what happened. I had been raised to think that saying no was uncool, and that my body was up for grabs. . . .

Our parents wanted to raise a happy, sexually liberated free spirit. I took the "free" part to heart, anyway. By the time I hit puberty I was already sexually jaded. I can't remember not knowing what went where, complete with variations and sub-routines. From age 11 until I whipped up a new batch of self-esteem in my late 20s, I slept with so many people that I lost count at around 150. To this day, I can be standing at the sink washing a dish, woolgathering, and something will trigger a memory of a long-forgotten sexual encounter: the guy I slept with in the bathroom of a Greyhound bus, or the taxi driver I screwed for the sole reason that he had a cute Irish accent and I had no money for a tip. I slept with my friends' boyfriends, or their fathers, just because they asked. I alienated a lot of people, mostly women. I was lucky to dodge the scarier of the venereal diseases, but I got a lot of urinary tract infections and had a few unplanned pregnancies. Hey, man—love the one you're with. Right. I'm pretty sure that an overfamiliarity with Bactrim and cannulae is not the beautiful expression of sexuality the hippies had in mind when they rejected traditional parenting.

But all this has a happy ending. Paradoxically, the dangerous freedom I was raised with was the thing that allowed me to rebuild my self-esteem and set boundaries for myself. I had been told for so long I could be anything I wanted to be that I finally figured out I could, by that same token, get over the anger I had for my parents. They had no childraising instruction manual, and they lived through one of the most turbulent, strange times in our country's history.

In the course of working on this, I finally found ways to shock my mother. At one point I decided to become a lawyer, and when I told Mom, she looked stricken. "Oh, no! Anything but that!" she said. "Honey, be a painter or a poet or something else instead!" I felt like a tax-payin', job-havin' James Dean. All I have to do to freak out my Mom is work too hard, or mention my 401K. . . .

So this is a cautionary tale. Go ahead, eat carob. Weave your own dashiki. Get off the grid. Open your mind to new experiences. But when your microbus pulls into the festival lot, don't drop acid and ditch your daughter at the child-care tipi. Sometimes your mind can be so open, your brain falls out.

## Document 3: Students Organize[3]

*In 1962, a group of students organized the Students for a Democratic Society and issued what was known as the Port Huron Statement. Written primarily by Tom Hayden, this document became to many Americans the radical embodiment of the counterculture and the antiwar protest. This document blends Marxism, liberalism, and religious idealism. It is easy to see how many people saw this as a call to revolution.*

We are people of this generation, bred in at least modest comfort, housed now in universities, looking uncomfortably to the world we inherit.

When we were kids the United States was the wealthiest and strongest country in the world; the only one with the atom bomb, the least scarred by modern war, an initiator of the United Nations that we thought would distribute Western influence throughout the world. Freedom and equality for each individual, government of, by, and for the people—these American values we found good, principles by which we could live as men. Many of us began maturing in complacency.

As we grew, however, our comfort was penetrated by events too troubling to dismiss. First, the permeating and victimizing fact of human degradation, symbolized by the Southern struggle against racial bigotry, compelled most of us from silence to activism. Second, the enclosing fact of the Cold War, symbolized by the presence of the Bomb, brought awareness that we ourselves, and our friends, and millions of abstract "others" we knew more directly because of our common peril, might die at any time. We might deliberately ignore, or avoid, or fail to feel all other human problems, but not these two, for these were too immediate and crushing in their impact, too challenging in the demand that we as individuals take the responsibility for encounter and resolution. . . .

Not only did tarnish appear on our image of American virtue, not only did disillusion occur when the hypocrisy of American ideals was discovered, but we began to sense that what we had originally seen as the American Golden Age was actually the decline of an era. The worldwide outbreak of revolution against colonialism and imperialism, the entrenchment of totalitarian states, the menace of war, overpopulation, international disorder, supertechnology—these trends were testing the tenacity of our own commitment to democracy and freedom and our abilities to visualize their application to a world in upheaval.

Our work is guided by the sense that we may be the last generation in the experiment with living. But we are a minority—the vast majority of our people regard the temporary equilibriums of our society and world as eternally functional parts. In this is perhaps the outstanding paradox: we ourselves are imbued with urgency, yet the message of our society is that there is no viable alternative to the present. Beneath the reassuring tones of the politicians, beneath the common opinion that America will "muddle through," beneath the stagnation of those who have closed their minds to the future, is the pervading feeling that there simply are no alternatives, that our times have witnessed the exhaustion not only of Utopias, but of any new departures as well. Feeling the press of complexity upon the emptiness of life, people are fearful of the thought that at any moment things might be thrust out of control. They fear change itself, since change might smash whatever invisible framework seems to hold back chaos for them now. For most Americans, all crusades are suspect, threatening. . . .

Values

. . . We regard men as infinitely precious and possessed of unfulfilled capacities for reason, freedom, and love. In affirming these principles we are aware of countering perhaps the dominant conceptions of man in the twentieth century: that he is a thing to be manipulated, and that he is inherently incapable of directing his own affairs. We oppose the depersonalization that reduces human beings to the status of things—if anything, the brutalities of the twentieth century teach that means and ends are intimately related, that vague appeals to "posterity" cannot justify the mutilations of the present. . . .

We would replace power rooted in possession, privilege, or circumstance by power and uniqueness rooted in love, reflectiveness, reason, and creativity. As a *social system* we seek the establishment of a democracy of individual participation, governed by two central aims: that the individual share in those social decisions determining the quality and direction of his life; that society be organized to encourage independence in men and provide the media for their common participation.

In a participatory democracy, the political life would be based in several root principles:

> that decision-making of basic social consequence be carried on by public groupings;
>
> that politics be seen positively, as the art of collectively creating an acceptable pattern of social relations;
>
> that politics has the function of bringing people out of isolation and into community, thus being a necessary, though not sufficient, means of finding meaning in personal life;
>
> that the political order should serve to clarify problems in a way instrumental to their solution; it should provide outlets for the expression of personal grievance and aspiration; opposing views should be organized

so as to illuminate choices and facilitate the attainment of goals; channels should be commonly available to relate men to knowledge and to power so that private problems—from bad recreation facilities to personal—alienation—are formulated as general issues. . . .

## Document 4: Timothy Leary Testifies[4]

*In 1968, the Democratic National Convention was a lightning rod of protest. Today, students of history look back to that event as a turning point in modern history. Protesters of all sorts came to Chicago to oppose the war in Vietnam, and others came just to participate in the promised spectacle. The result was an urban riot that an investigating committee later called a "police riot." Eight people from the counterculture and antiwar groups were arrested and tried for their part in the disturbances. The case of one of the accused was later severed, and the remaining seven defendants became known as the "Chicago Seven." Their trial in Chicago was a circus of the first order. Five of the seven were convicted of the charges and were sentenced to a prison term of five years.*

*Dr. Timothy Leary was a psychologist who became known to many as the father of the drug culture. He had been dismissed from Harvard University for his experiments with hallucinogenic and psychedelic drugs. He spent the rest of his life promoting the benefits of such drugs. Although he was not in Chicago at the time of the violence, he was called as a defense witness for the Chicago Seven. The following portions of his testimony explain, from his perspective, what the demonstrations were about and offer his defense of the drug culture.*

THE WITNESS: I will try. Psychedelic drugs are drugs which speed up thinking, which broaden the consciousness, which produce religious experiences or creative experiences, or philosophic experiences in the person who takes them.

These psychedelic drugs, of course, are the opposite of the nonpsychedelic drugs like heroin, or alcohol, and barbiturates which slow down thinking, as opposed to psychedelic drugs which expand and accelerate the consciousness.

MR. KUNSTLER: Now, there came a time, did there not, Dr. Leary, when you left Harvard University?

THE WITNESS: Yes, I was dismissed from Harvard University in 1963. There were two reasons for my dismissal. One was a dispute over schedule of classes, and the other was because I was continuing to do research on the effects of psychedelic drugs which was politically risky for Harvard University to sponsor. . . .

MR. KUNSTLER: Now, Dr. Leary, do you recall when your first met Jerry Rubin?

THE WITNESS: Yes, I do. I met Jerry Rubin at the love-in at San Francisco, which was January 1967. . . .

MR. KUNSTLER: . . . All right, Dr. Leary, when did you first meet Abbie Hoffman?

THE WITNESS: The first time I met Mr. Hoffman was at the LSD Shrine and Rescue Center in New York City. That would be November or December of 1966.

MR. KUNSTLER: Now, lest there be any confusion, what does LSD stand for?

THE WITNESS: It was the League of Spiritual Discovery. That was a religion incorporated in the State of New York and we had a rescue center in New York where hundreds of people taking drugs could be rehabilitated.

MR. KUNSTLER: Dr. Leary, I call your attention to late January of 1968 and ask you whether you met with Jerry and Abbie during that month at that time?

THE WITNESS: Yes, I did. I met with Mr. Hoffman and Mr. Rubin and with other people and we formed and founded the Youth International Party.

MR. KUNSTLER: Now, with reference to the founding of the Youth International Party, which we will refer to as Yippie, can you state what was said by the people attending there with reference to the founding of this party?

THE WITNESS: Well, Julius Lester said that the current parties are not responsive to the needs of black people, particularly young black people. Allen Ginsberg said that the Democrat and Republican Parties are not responsive to the creative youth and to college students and high school students who expect more from society.

Abbie Hoffman, as I remember, was particularly eloquent in describing the need for new political tactics and techniques. . . . Abbie Hoffman said that new political methods were needed because the conventions of the Democrat and Republican Parties were controlled by machine politics which had nothing to do with the needs of the people.

Mr. Hoffman continued to say that we should set up a series of political meetings throughout the country, not just for the coming summer but for the coming years. Mr. Hoffman suggested that we have love-ins or be-ins in which thousands of young people and freedom-loving people throughout the country could get together on Sunday afternoons, listen to music which represented the new point of view, the music of love and peace and harmony, and try to bring about a political change in this country that would be nonviolent in people's minds and in their hearts, and this is the concept of the love-in which Mr. Hoffman was urging upon us.

MR. KUNSTLER: Now, at any time during this discussion did anyone make any reference to the Democratic National Convention?

THE WITNESS: Mr. Hoffman said it was important to have a large group of young people and black people and freedom-loving people come to Chicago during the Democratic Convention the following August. That it was important that people that were concerned about peace and brotherhood, come to Chicago and in a very dignified, beautiful way meet in the parks and represent what Mr. Hoffman called the politics of life and politics of love and peace and brotherhood.

Mr. Rubin, I remember, pointed out that since the Democratic Party was meeting here, there was great concern about having police and having National Guard and they were bringing in tear gas. Mr. Rubin pointed out that it could possibly be violent here, and both Mr. Rubin and Allen Ginsberg said that they didn't think that we should come to Chicago if there was a possibility of violence from the soldiers or the police. . . .

MR. KUNSTLER: Dr. Leary, did you speak at that press conference? [March 1968]

THE WITNESS: Yes. I described in great detail the harassment that we had suffered in our religious center at Millbrook, New York, by the police. I described how for the preceding two or three months there had been a police blockade around this young people's center in upstate New York and that our houses had been ransacked at night by sheriffs and policemen and how our young children were being arrested on their bicycles on the roads outside of our houses because they didn't have identification.

And I described how helicopters had been coming over to observe our behavior and I raised the possibility that we did not want this to happen in Chicago and we hoped that Chicago would be free from this sort of unpleasant encounter, because at Millbrook we were living very peaceably, bothering nobody until we were harassed and surrounded by the police.

MR. KUNSTLER: Now, during the month of March did you have occasion to speak with Jerry Rubin?

THE WITNESS: Yes, I called Jerry to tell him about the results of the Yippie meeting in Chicago.

MR. KUNSTLER: All right. Will you tell the jury and the Court what you told Jerry and what he told you, if anything, in that phone conversation?

THE WITNESS: I told Mr. Rubin that I had never experienced such fear on the part of the young people as I did in the young people of Chicago, that they were literally trembling about the possibility of violence in August. And I raised the issue to Jerry as to whether we should reconsider coming to Chicago. . . .

MR. KUNSTLER: Now, Dr. Leary, I call your attention to April of 1968 and ask you if you recall a meeting with Jerry Rubin and Abbie Hoffman?

THE WITNESS: Yes, I met with Jerry Rubin and Abbie Hoffman.

MR. KUNSTLER: What did you say?

THE WITNESS: Mr. Hoffman pointed out that since our last meeting, President Johnson had retired from office. Therefore, President Johnson would not be coming to Chicago. Therefore, the meaning of a celebration of life on our part as opposed to Mr. Johnson was lost since the man we were attempting to oppose was not going to come to Chicago.

Both Mr. Hoffman and Mr. Rubin at that time said to me before I left that they were not sure whether we should come to Chicago, and that we would watch what happened politically. At that time, Jerry Rubin pointed out that Robert Kennedy was still alive, and many of us felt that he represented the aspirations of young people, so we thought we would wait. I remember Mr. Rubin saying, "Let's wait and see what Robert Kennedy comes out with as far as peace is concerned. Let's wait to see if Robert Kennedy does speak to voting people, and if Robert Kennedy does seek to represent the peaceful, joyous, . . . feelings of young people—"

THE WITNESS: So Mr. Rubin suggested that we hold off the decision as to whether we come to Chicago until we saw how Mr. Kennedy's campaign developed, and at that point, I think most of us would have gladly, joyously called off the Chicago meeting. . . .

THE COURT: Cross-examination.

MR. FORAN: Dr. Leary, will you name the drugs that you said speeded up thinking?

THE WITNESS: Yes, psychedelic or mind-expanding drugs include LSD, mescaline, peyote, marijuana, and I could go on. There is a list of perhaps thirty or forty chemical compounds and natural vines and herbs. Do you want more?

MR. FORAN: No, that is enough. Now, when you talked to Jerry Rubin in late March over the telephone from Chicago, you had a long discussion with him at that time about your fears of violence that would occur in Chicago at the Democratic Convention, did you not?

THE WITNESS: Yes, I had been told this by the young people in Chicago.

MR. FORAN: And you expressed your concern?

THE WITNESS: Well, I am always concerned about the possibility of violence anywhere at any time. I am against violence. . . .

MR. KUNSTLER: I have just one further question. Dr. Leary, in answer to Mr. Foran's question about the young people, did you tell Jerry Rubin from where the young people in Chicago expected violence to come, from what source?

THE WITNESS: Well, from the militia, the National Guard. The sheriff was fighting with the police chief of Chicago at the time, and the sheriff, I believe, was enlisting vigilantes and just people off the street to be deputy sheriffs.

MR. KUNSTLER: But it was violence from the police?

THE WITNESS: And the National Guard, police, and sheriff.

MR. KUNSTLER: And not from the young people themselves?

THE WITNESS: There was no possibility of that.

MR. KUNSTLER: Thank you.

THE COURT: No further questions? You may go.

## Document 5: A Protester Remembers[5]

*Rennie Davis was a prominent American leader against the Vietnam War in the 1960s. He traveled to Hanoi to draw attention to U.S. policy and bring back American prisoners of war (POWs). He became the national director of the community organizing program of the Students for a Democratic Society (SDS), and was one of the "Chicago Eight" (later "Chicago Seven"), charged with conspiracy to incite riots during the 1968 Democratic National Convention. Davis granted this telephone interview specifically for this volume on February 23, 2009.*

**Donald Whisenhunt (DW):** I want to know your reflections this many years later on the counterculture and the 1960s.

**Rennie Davis (RD):** I don't believe it has been ever been written about, but one of the fascinating aspects about the millions of activists in the 1960s was their sudden appearance virtually overnight. In January 1960, who could tell the difference with the Cold War political culture of the 1950s and the new decade coming? One decade merged with another with little or no apparent difference in January 1960. Then four students from North Carolina A&T College sat down at the Woolworth's lunch counter in Greensboro, North Carolina, at a white-only lunch counter. That was February 4, 1960. The impact of that sit-in was an overnight sensation covered by *Life* magazine and other national media. Suddenly there were hundreds of thousands of activists on campuses in the North in just a one-month period. I was in college in Ohio and felt surrounded by a new student culture that appeared seemingly overnight. Many were political and many were just simply free spirits wanting to create a new American culture. It felt like a cultural flip that had occurred in one to two months. Some have said this sudden shift was a new generation coming into the world to make change together. It was a bit mysterious and certainly had the edge of inexplicable. The shift from a goodie-two-shoe, fear-based political culture that characterized the 1950s and the vast sixties counterculture happened in a flash.

**DW:** Do you think the sit-ins in North Carolina were the motivation for that?

**RD:** I think they were the trigger. There were historic protest events before that February sit-in such as Rosa Parks refusing to go to the back of the bus, but the change from the fifties to the sixties with the resulting large public movement for change was something that turned on a dime.

*After the United States became deeply involved in the war in Vietnam, a significant anti-war movement developed in the United States. Most of the leaders were college-age young people. One of the early demonstrations against the war was the March on the Pentagon in 1965, a demonstration in which Rennie Davis was deeply involved. Lyndon Baines Johnson Library, photo by Frank Wolfe.*

In February 1960, I was a student at Oberlin College. I suddenly found myself interested in politics. My new interest in the world seemed to turn on a dime too. Suddenly I was passionate about civil rights, participatory democracy, and the enduring principles of the Declaration of Independence. By the spring of 1960, Tom Hayden, who was a student at the University of Michigan, came to Oberlin to visit. He was traveling to various campuses, wanting to organize a new national student organization. A political party had already been formed at Oberlin. Political parties on college campuses were a new phenomenon. Instead of individual candidates running for student government on dorm issues, a political party ran a slate of candidates on a political platform with positions on America's role domestically and internationally. I helped organize a campus political party at Oberlin College while Tom and others at the University of Michigan had done the same. We didn't plan it that way; these political parties just popped up around the country. As Tom traveled here and there trying to see what was going on at other places, he saw the same thing. There was suddenly a student movement out there that hadn't been there before. It was still at the early stage, but the student movement first appeared somewhat spontaneously after that first Greensboro sit-in. I joined Tom and other founders of Students for a Democratic Society (SDS) in the spring of 1960. At the same time, the Student Nonviolent Coordinating Committee (SNCC) was forming in the South. SDS evolved into the dominant national student organization in the North, and SNCC became the leading student organization in the South. By the summer of 1962, there was a national SDS convention that adopted the Port Huron statement and with that convention, student activism on campuses took off. Maybe we all got together before we were born to do this thing, who can say?

DW: Do you see the presidential election of 1960 having any impact on that?

RD: Yes, I think the election of John Kennedy generated hope, energy, and a new positive mood into the country. At the same time, SNCC and SDS didn't immediately embrace Kennedy. The SDS viewpoint was that the change needed in the country required more than electing one candidate to replace another. We called on the corporations, universities, and other institutions to look at their own democratic process. We called for participatory democracy and invited democracy to spread beyond the two-party system of electoral politics. We felt that "people power" was essential to get the vote for black people in Mississippi and other Southern states. Kennedy needed us, was our view. The movement grew in stages. In 1965, SDS organized the first antiwar march in Washington. There were 25,000 people in attendance. By 1967, we had 150,000 protesting the war in Washington. Now there was a coalition of about 150 national organizations forming the National Mobilization Committee against the war. The public awareness of the anti-war movement was certainly visible by 1967, but its beginning was like an overnight sensation back in 1960.

DW: Would you say that the dramatic change in just one year or so represented the coming of age of the baby boom generation?

RD: Yes but again, the movement developed in stages. In 1968, at the Democratic National Convention, we didn't bring as many anti-war people to Chicago as we planned, but the Chicago event was watched by more people on television than watched the first man landing on the moon. When we went to Chicago, we weren't the majority of the country's public opinion but after Chicago, our position to end the war was now the opinion of the majority of the country according to public opinion polls. Then came the Chicago 7 trial, indicting the organizers of the Chicago protests. The trial was yet another building stage. Now the public was focused every day on what was happening at our trial.

DW: You stated earlier that you didn't know some of the other defendants until the trial began.

RD: I'd never met Bobby Seale until the trial began. He was called by the government one of the "co-conspirators." I had invited Eldridge Cleaver to speak in Chicago. At the last minute, something came up, and Eldridge sent Bobby instead. Bobby made two speeches in Chicago and left. In the midst of everything going on, we never even connected while he was in Chicago. I knew he was in the city, but he just came and went. You could say the trial was politically driven. Johnson, who was still president, had appointed a commission headed by the former governor of Illinois to study who caused the riots. The commission published a report that may have been the most positive public profile of me I ever had. The commission labeled the Chicago demonstration a "police riot," and the report went to the top of the *New York Times* best-seller list. I think Nixon saw the opportunity to divide and conquer the conservative "law and order" element of the Democratic party. Besides Mayor Daley from Chicago, there were other "law and order" conservative representatives in the Democratic Party. By indicting us, Nixon reached out to them. We thought the trial was pretty fabulous, giving us a chance to present our views about the war to a large national and world stage. The choice of the trial judge was probably cast in heaven. He was so extreme in his prejudices about us that he built public support for us.

After the trial, ninety percent of the students in the country walked out of class, ending the school year early in the spring of 1970. Then *Time* magazine came out with a cover story called "The Cooling of America." By the fall of 1970, no one wanted to come to an anti-war meeting. Everyone on the campus felt, what else can we do? Where do we go from here? That time marked the beginning of the movement's winding down.

Since the war was escalating, I wanted to increase the public pressure with a large scale civil disobedience. I went to the coalition and proposed that we organize non-violent civil disobedience like Martin Luther King had done in the South but this one in Washington, D.C. The coalition rejected the proposal on the basis that it couldn't be done. I was so certain that we could do it that I went forward for a while on my own. Wherever I spoke on a campus, 5,000 people filled the room, with standing ovations. The coalition came around and got behind the demonstration for May 1971. It began April 15, with 350,000 people, followed by Vietnam veterans camped in front of the Capitol led by John Kerry. When it came time to count heads to see who was prepared to be arrested, there were 100,000 people ready to go. They became the largest arrest in American history. The event had impact, but I knew that we really were also running out of steam.

Just when it seemed the sixties protest was over, John Lennon made his peace statement in Canada. John and I started meeting in his apartment, and he agreed to join an anti-war march on the Republican Convention. We decided together to go to forty-two cities on the way to San Diego. The plan was to bring a million people to the city where the Republicans were going to hold their convention. They had contracts and other arrangements in that city. Our first event was Ann Arbor, Michigan, where we spoke to an indoor stadium of 25,000 people in a venue that sold out in forty-five minutes. The focus of our first event was American political prisoners. John Sinclair had been arrested, convicted, and given a ten-year term for possessing two marijuana joints. Stevie Wonder was the unannounced guest of John Lennon. We proposed closing the city of Detroit if John Sinclair wasn't released in two weeks. He was released in two weeks, never to go back to jail, but deportation proceedings then began against John Lennon, causing John to pull out of the campaign, The Republicans subsequently moved their convention from San Diego to Miami Beach, making it harder for the protest. At Nixon's inauguration, there was one more large anti-war demonstration on the ellipse in front of the White House—100,000 people came—and that basically completed the great sixties American story.

DW: Was the use of drugs a part of the antiwar movement or the hippie culture?

RD: There were two different constituencies in the protest movement. I don't think either one wanted to make a separation with the other. The political types such as the leadership of the National Mobilization were not promoting drugs as a way of life. We were trying to support civil rights and end the war. Others in the coalition like Abbie Hoffman and Jerry Rubin were focused on creating a new culture, and part of the free spirit and experimental journeys of their followers embraced the use of drugs. I personally wasn't a promoter of drugs, but it was a part of the backdrop for that era.

DW: So on the one side you have the Movement—the political side—and on the other you have the social experimentation.

RD: Yes.

DW: What do you see as the legacy of the 1960s?

RD: The sixties decade has had a large continuing influence. One legacy perhaps was the election of Barack Obama. The women's movement, the civil rights movement, and other large social changes were all seeds planted in the 1960s. I would say our legacy was large and breathed new life into the American vision that was set forth in the Declaration of Independence and the Constitution. I respect the people who opposed our approach to change, but in hindsight it would seem we are a better country today for having experienced that unique activist era of American history.

## Part B: Atrocities in Vietnam

### Background

*Beginning about 1964, the American presence in Vietnam increased dramatically, and the war took a decidedly violent turn. Gradually, President Lyndon Johnson agreed with the military's request, eventually increasing American troop strength there to more than 500,000. As the size of the American army increased, so did the opposition to the war. A major part of the opposition had to do with the military draft whereby young men were inducted into the military, some against their will.*

*In 1968, the Tet Offensive launched by the North Vietnamese army and the Viet Cong (the indigenous South Vietnamese resisters) shocked Americans. Even though many people, in government and in the military, considered the Tet Offensive as a major victory for American forces, the public perception was that the Americans had suffered a major defeat. From that point forward, the opposition to the war grew.*

*In that context, one of the most horrifying events occurred shortly after Tet in March 1968. American forces were ordered to attack a group of villages known as Son My, but when the events became known, the attack was usually referred to as My Lai, one of the sub-villages in Son My.*

*When the attack occurred, the military had been assured that any real civilians would be out of the villages by 7 a.m. on their way to market. When American soldiers arrived, they found a large number of old men, women, and children. The events of this attack are still a bit hazy, but the investigation revealed that people of the village were killed indiscriminately by American forces. The number killed ranges between 347 and 504; a memorial at the site today lists 504 names.*

*At first, the reports of the incident treated it as a normal attack on enemy forces, and the "body count" was reported inconsistently by different people. A young man, Warrant Officer Hugh Thompson, Jr., is credited with saving many of the villagers by landing his helicopter between the American troops and the villagers.*

*The first investigations concluded that approximately twenty civilians were inadvertently killed. Eventually another soldier, Ronald Ridenhour, who had not been present but who had heard about the killing of many civilians, began to try to find out the details. Eventually, letters that he wrote to various officials at home resulted in an investigation. In addition to the killing of civilians, there was a massive cover-up of the event. Twenty-six men were eventually charged with some complicity in the affair, but only one, Lt. William Calley, was ever convicted.*

## Questions

In reading these documents, the student should ask and answer several questions to put these activities in the proper context.

1. In reading Thompson's account of his activities, do you conclude that he was honest in his actions, or was he merely trying to get attention?
2. What were Ridenhour's motives in trying to get wider attention to the My Lai incident?
3. Why did it take the army so long to undertake a serious investigation of the incident?
4. What kind of officer was Calley? What does his trial testimony say about his character and the nature of the training of officers at the time?
5. Was the My Lai incident truly an atrocity, or was it merely an accident that happens occasionally during wartime?

## Document 1: Ridenhour's Letter[6]

*Ronald Ridenhour was in Vietnam with the 11th Infantry for almost all of 1968. During this time, he came into contact with numerous soldiers who told him of the My Lai massacre. After he was discharged from the army, he continued to be bothered by the reports he had heard. His conscience bothered him so much that in March 1969 from his home in Phoenix, Arizona, he wrote a detailed letter to Morris Udall, his congressman from Arizona, who had recently become a severe critic of the American action in Vietnam. He sent copies of the letter to other government officials, including the president, the secretary of defense, and more than twenty-five members of Congress. This was the first serious account of the My Lai incident, and it began the exposure of the event, as well as the beginning of the unraveling of the cover-up of the affair.*

Gentlemen:

It was late in April, 1968 that I first heard of "Pinkville" and what allegedly happened there. I received that first report with some skepticism, but in the following months I was to hear similar stories from such a wide variety of people that it became impossible for me to disbelieve that something rather dark and bloody did indeed occur sometime in March, 1968 in a village called "Pinkville" in the Republic of Viet Nam.

The circumstances that led to my having access to the reports I'm about to relate need explanation. I was inducted in March, 1967 into the U. S. Army. After receiving various training I was assigned to the 70th Infantry Detachment (LRP), 11th Light Infantry Brigade at Schofield Barracks, Hawaii, in early October, 1967. That unit, the 70th Infantry Detachment (LRP), was disbanded a week before the 11th Brigade shipped out for Viet Nam on the 5th of December, 1967. All of the men from whom I later heard reports of the "Pinkville" incident were reassigned to "C" Company, 1st Battalion, 20th Infantry, 11th Light Infantry Brigade. I was reassigned to the aviation section of Headquarters Company 11th LIB. After we had been in Viet Nam for 3 to 4 months many of the men from the 70th Inf. Det. (LRP) began to transfer into the same unit, "E" Company, 51st Infantry (LRP).

In late April, 1968 I was awaiting orders for a transfer from . . . when I happened to run into Pfc "Butch" Gruver, whom I had known in Hawaii. Gruver told me he had been assigned to "C" Company 1st of the 20th until April 1st when he transferred to the unit that I was headed for. During the course of our conversation he told me the first of many reports I was to hear of "Pinkville."

"Charlie" Company 1/20 had been assigned to Task Force Barker in late February, 1968 to help conduct "search and destroy" operations on the Batangan Peninsula, Barker's area of operation. . . . Gruver said that Charlie Company had sustained casualties; primarily from mines and booby traps, almost everyday from the first day they arrived on the peninsula. One village area was particularly troublesome and seemed to be infested with booby traps and enemy soldiers. It was located about six miles northeast of Quang Nhai city. . . . It was a notorious area and the men of Task Force Barker had a special name for it: they called it "Pinkville." One morning in the latter part of March, Task Force Barker moved out from its firebase headed for "Pinkville." Its mission: destroy the trouble spot and all of its inhabitants.

When "Butch" told me this I didn't quite believe that what he was telling me was true, but he assured me that it was and went on to describe what had happened. The other two companies that made up the task force cordoned off the village so that "Charlie" Company could move through to destroy the structures and kill the inhabitants. Any villagers who ran from Charlie Company were stopped by the encircling companies. I asked "Butch" several times if all the people were killed. He said that he thought they were, men, women and children. He recalled seeing a small boy, about three or four years old, standing by the trail with a gunshot wound in one arm. The boy was clutching his wounded arm with his other hand, while blood trickled between his fingers. He was staring around himself in shock and disbelief at what he saw. "He just stood there with big eyes staring around like he didn't understand; he didn't believe what was happening. Then the captain's RTO (radio operator) put a burst of 16 (M-16 rifle) fire into him." It was so bad, Gruver said, that one of the men in his squad shot himself in the foot in order to be medivac-ed out of the area so that he would not have to participate in the slaughter. Although he had not seen it, Gruver had been told by people he considered trustworthy that one of the company's officers, 2nd Lieutenant Kally (this spelling may be incorrect) had rounded up several groups of villagers (each group consisting of a minimum of 20 persons of both sexes and all ages). According to the story, Kally then machine-gunned each group. Gruver estimated that the population of the village had been 300 to 400 people and that very few, if any, escaped.

After hearing this account I couldn't quite accept it. Somehow I just couldn't believe that not only had so many young American men participated in such an act of barbarism, but that their officers had ordered it. There were other men in the unit I was soon to be assigned to . . . who had been in Charlie Company at the time that Gruver alleged the incident at "Pinkville" had occurred. I became determined to ask them about "Pinkville" so that I might compare their accounts with Pfc Gruver's.

When I arrived at "Echo" Company, . . . the first men I looked for were Pfc's Michael Terry and William Doherty. Both were veterans of "Charlie" Company, 1/20 and "Pinkville." Instead of contradicting "Butch" Gruver's story they corroborated it, adding some tasty tidbits of information of their own. Terry and Doherty had been in the same squad and their platoon was the third platoon of "C" Company to pass through the village. Most of the people they came to were already dead. Those that weren't were sought out and shot. The platoon left nothing alive, neither livestock nor people. Around noon the two soldiers' squad stopped to eat. "Billy and I started to get out our chow," Terry said, "but close to us was a bunch of Vietnamese in a heap, and some of them were moaning. Kally (2nd Lt. Kally) had been through before us and all of them had been shot, but many weren't dead. It was obvious that they weren't going to get any medical attention so Billy and I got up and went over to where they were. I guess we sort of finished them off." Terry went on to say that he and Doherty then returned to where their packs were and ate lunch. He estimated the size of the village to be 200 to 300 people. Doherty thought that the population of "Pinkville" had been 400 people.

If Terry, Doherty and Gruver could be believed, then not only had "Charlie" Company received orders to slaughter all the inhabitants of the village, but those orders had come from the commanding officer of Task Force Barker, or possibly even higher in the chain of command. Pfc Terry stated that when Captain Medina (Charlie Company's commanding officer Captain Ernest Medina) issued the order for the destruction of "Pinkville" he had been hesitant, as if it were something he didn't want to do but had to. Others I spoke to concurred with Terry on this.

It was June before I spoke to anyone who had something of significance to add to what I had already been told of the "Pinkville" incident. It was the end of June, 1968 when I ran into Sargent [*sic*] Larry La Croix at the USO in Chu Lai. La Croix had been in 2nd Lt. Kally's platoon on the day Task Force Barker swept through "Pinkville." What he told me verified the stories of the others, but he also had something new to add. He had been a witness to Kally's gunning down of at least three separate groups of villagers. "It was terrible. They were slaughtering the villagers like so many sheep." Kally's men were dragging people out of bunkers and hootches and putting them together in a group. The people in the group were men, women and children of all ages. As soon as he felt that the group was big enough, Kally ordered an M-60 (machine-gun) set up and the people killed. La Croix said that he bore witness to this procedure at least three times. The three groups were of different sizes, one of about twenty people, one of about thirty people, and one of about forty people. When the first group was put together Kally ordered Pfc Torres to man the machine-gun and open fire on the villagers that had been grouped together. This Torres did, but before everyone in the group was down he ceased fire and refused to fire again. After ordering Torres to recommence firing several times, Lieutenant Kally took over the M-60 and finished shooting the remaining villagers in that first group himself. Sargent La Croix told me that Kally didn't bother to order anyone to take the machine gun when the other two groups of villagers were formed. He simply manned it himself and shot down all villagers in both groups.

This account of Sargent La Croix's confirmed the rumors that Gruver, Terry and Doherty had previously told me about Lieutenant Kally. It also convinced me that there was a very substantial amount of truth to the stories that all of these men had told. If I needed more convincing, I was to receive it.

It was in the middle of November, 1968 just a few weeks before I was to return to the United States for separation from the army that I talked to Pfc Michael Bernhardt. Bernhardt had served his entire year in Viet Nam in "Charlie" Company 1/20 and he too was about to go home.

"Bernie" substantiated the tales told by the other men I had talked to in vivid, bloody detail and added this. "Bernie" had absolutely refused to take part in the massacre of the villagers of "Pinkville" that morning and he thought that it was rather strange that the officers of the company had not made an issue of it. But that evening "Medina (Captain Ernest Medina) came up to me (Bernie) and told me not to do anything stupid like write my congressman" about what had happened that day. Bernhardt assured Captain Medina that he had no such thing in mind. He had nine months left in Viet Nam and felt that it was dangerous enough just fighting the acknowledged enemy.

Exactly what did, in fact, occur in the village of "Pinkville" in March, 1968 I do not know for *certain*, but I am convinced that it was something very black indeed. I remain irrevocably persuaded that if you and I do truly believe in the principles, of justice and the equality of every man, however humble, before the law, that form the very backbone that this country is founded on, then we must press forward a widespread and public investigation of this matter with all our combined efforts. I think that it was Winston Churchill [*sic*] who once said "A country without a conscience is a country without a soul, and a country without a soul is a country that cannot survive." I feel that I must take some positive action on this matter. I hope that you will launch an investigation immediately and keep me informed of your progress. If you cannot, then I don't know what other course of action to take.

I have considered sending this to newspapers, magazines, and broadcasting companies, but I somehow feel that investigation and action by the Congress of the United States is the appropriate procedure, and as a conscientious citizen I have no desire to further besmirch the image of the American serviceman in the eyes of the world. I feel that this action, while probably it would promote attention, would not bring about the constructive actions that the direct actions of the Congress of the United States would.

Sincerely,
/s/ Ron Ridenhour

## Document 2: Hugh Thompson's Story[7]

*Hugh Thompson, Jr., was a helicopter pilot who witnessed the massacre from the air as he was flying over My Lai. He landed his helicopter between Lt. William Calley and a group of Vietnamese civilians. The next day, he met with Col. Oran K. Henderson, commander of the 11th Infantry Brigade, and told him about his experience. Later in November 1969, General William R. Peers was ordered to investigate the charges and to report on its findings. The Peers Commission was thorough and eventually issued a report that identified 224 serious violations of the military code. In addition to the letter written by Ron Ridenhour, the testimony of the eyewitness, Hugh Thompson, Jr., was crucial to the story's coming out. Here follows a part of Thompson's testimony to the Peers Commission.*

Q: What happened when you put the chopper down?

A: . . . When I saw the bodies in the ditch I came back around and saw that some of them were still alive. So I sat [the helicopter] down on the ground then and talked to—I'm pretty sure it was a sergeant, . . . and I told them there was women and kids over there that were wounded—could he help them or could they help them? And he made some remark to the effect that the only way he could help them was to kill them. And I thought he was joking. I didn't take him seriously. I said, "Why don't you see if you can help them," and I took off again. And as I took off my crew chief said that the guy was shooting into the ditch. As I turned around I could see a guy holding a weapon pointing towards the ditch.

. . . And after that we were still flying recon over the village. The village was smoking pretty good. You couldn't get right over it. And we came around somewhere to the east of the village, and I saw this bunker and either the crew chief or the gunner said that there was a bunch of kids in the bunker, and the Americans were approaching it. There was a little open area, field, shaped sort of like a horseshoe, so I set down in the middle of that horseshoe, got out of the aircraft and talked with this lieutenant, and told him that there was some women and kids in that bunker over there, and could he get them out. He said the only way to get them out was with a hand grenade. I told him to just hold your men right where they are and I'll get the kids out. And I walked over towards the bunker, motioned for them to come out, and they came out. But there was more than women and kids. There was a couple—one or two—old men in there. I'd say about two or three women and then some kids. I got back in the aircraft, didn't take off, just put my helmet on or just plugged my helmet up and I called Mr. Millians who was flying the low gun cover and told him what I had and asked him if he'd come in and get them out of this immediate area back into an area that had not so much firing going on. And he came in and picked up half of them. . . .

A: And I walked the people to him. He could only take about half of them, and flew them out going back to Highway 521. He flew them, I would say, back up to the vicinity of Hoa My . . . because there was a road going off 521 about where he let them out. He came back and got the rest of them and took them up there also. I followed them back. . . .

Q: . . . Did you ever identify the lieutenant?

A: Yes, sir.

Q: Who was he?

A: Lieutenant Calley. . . .

Q: Could you tell us what happened as you best recollect, not from the newspapers, but from the time itself?

A: I just did, sir. I told him to stop his troops after he told me the only way he could get them out, and he stopped them. My crew chief and gunner were outside the aircraft also, and I walked across a rice paddy towards the tree line the bunker was in. I got, oh, I would say within 10 or 15 meters of the tree line and motioned for them to come out. As they came out, I gathered them in a little group, and I called for my low gunship and said: "I got some people down here. Can you come in and take them out for me and get them out of this area?" . . .

Q: Any other actions taken?

A: The gunship came in. The one ship came in, took half of them out, went and dropped them off, and then came back and got the rest of them. And I didn't say anything else to the lieutenant to the best of my knowledge today, sir. . . .

Q: Was there any form of altercation or argument between you and Lieutenant Calley or anybody else there. . . ?

A: When I got out of the helicopter, I told my crew chief and gunner to make sure I was covered real close.

Q: From that, I take it, you expected—you were being covered real close. Were you inferring for protection against VC or protection against something that might have been done to you from the U.S. side?

A: I was worried about getting shot, sir, because when I walked over to where the women and children were if the enemy would have started shooting I would have been in a crossfire from the friendly troops because I was between where the enemy was supposed to have been and where our friendly troops were, sir.

Q: Were you afraid of getting shot by our own forces or by the enemy? . . .

A: They were covering me from both sides, sir. But I'm not saying they were covering me from our troops. Charlie [Viet Cong troops] could have been behind our troops also, sir.

Q: Did Lieutenant Calley threaten you with his M-16 or any other way at this time?

A: No, sir.

Q: Did he point his M-16 at you?

A: No, sir, I didn't have any weapons pointed at me. He might have been standing with the—he didn't have it thrown over his shoulder. I mean, I'm sure he had it in his hand. But it wasn't trained on myself, sir.

Q: Was this PFC Colburn covering you with his M-60?

A:. Yes, sir. Both my crew chief and my gunner both had M-60's.

Q: When you talked to Colonel Henderson in the interview, can you give me your general impression of the interview? . . .

A: He seemed interested, sir.

Q: Did he ask you what happened? Was he asking questions, or how did this all come out?

A: I think he asked me, you know, like what I had seen, and he asked me questions pertaining to a couple of things. You know, it's been a long time, sir, since I was in there, you know. It didn't strike a real great impression on my mind, sir, what I said back then, exactly, you know.

Q: You probably answered this before, but how long did you spend with him?

A: I think it was about 20 to 30 minutes, sir.

Q: You went over it pretty thoroughly with him, did you?

A: What I had seen.

Q: Did he ask you questions about the kind of dead people that you had seen?

A: I believe that I said that I didn't see but two or three draft-age males dead. But I can't just—it was a lot fresher on my mind about how many draft-age persons I saw, but, still, it was fresh on my mind so I feel sure that I probably would have mentioned that to him. But I can't swear that I did. . . .

Q: . . . Did you tell him about the situation with the captain on the ground and the other wounded around the area?

A: I know I told him about the captain. He said, "Do you know who he is?" and I said, "I don't know. How many captains did you have out there today?" I told him I didn't know the man's name, "But I don't know how many captains you had out there that day, but you probably didn't have a lot of them."

Q: Did you tell him about the other wounded that were near there that you had marked with smoke, and that you had seen? The ones you had marked with smoke and then called for help to provide medical assistance, and when you came back they were dead?

A: I can't swear to that, but I think I did.

Q: Yes. Did you tell him about the ditch with the bodies in it?

A: Yes, sir.

Q: Did you tell him about how many bodies you thought were in the ditch?

A: Yes, sir.

Q: Did you tell him that you had returned to the ditch to pick up the one boy at a later time?

A: Yes, sir.

Q: Did you also tell him about the bunker?

A: Yes, sir.

Q: Did you tell him about your conversation with the people near the bunker?

A: No, sir. I didn't tell him my conversation completely. I told him part of it.

Q: Yes. But did you tell him the fact that you had—that they had indicated to you that the only way to get them out was to grenade them out?

A: Yes, sir. I can't say that I feel sure I did, but I can't remember my exact words to this man, sir. But I know that it upset me quite a bit that day. You know, it didn't upset me, it just kind of teed me off, I guess you'd put it. But I know good and well I'd mentioned it to him.

Q: Did you mention to him about your discussion with the sergeant at the ditch?

A: I feel that I did, sir.

Q: Yes. What frame of mind were you in when you talked to him? Did you consider yourself emotionally upset at this point of time? Distraught? Do you think you were clear in presenting the picture?

A: I think I presented it the best I could at that time. I'd say I was upset, or, you know, disturbed or something. . . .


### Document 3: The Viet Cong Tell Their Story[8]

*Shortly after the massacre at My Lai, the Viet Cong began to spread the story of the assault among Vietnamese civilians. This event was a powerful propaganda tool for the Viet Cong. Many leaflets and radio broadcasts were made, many of which told of the massacre in similar fashion. The following is a typical leaflet that put the Viet Cong spin on the event.*

### The Americans Devils Devulge [sic] the Truth

The empire building Americans invade South Vietnam with war. They say that they came to Vietnam to help the Vietnamese people and that they are our friends.

When the US Soldiers first arrived in Vietnam they tried to conceal their cruel invasion. They gave orders to the US soldiers to be good to the Vietnamese people thus employing psychological warfare. They also employed strict discipline which required US soldiers to respect the Vietnamese women and the customs of the Vietnamese people.

When the first US soldiers arrived in Vietnam they were good soldiers and they paid when they made purchases from the people. They would even pay a price in excess of the cost. When they did wrong they gave money to indemnify their deeds. They gave the people around their base camps and in nearby hamlets medical aid. US newspapers often printed pictures of US troops embracing the Vietnamese people and giving candy to children. The American Red Cross also gave medical attention to the Vietnamese. This lead [*sic*] a small group of ARVN's to believe that the American man was a good friend and had continued pity for the people. The Army Republic of Vietnam was happy to have allies which are such good friends and who are rich.

But, it is a play and every play must come to an end and the curtain come down. The espionage was very professional and clever. If the plan is completed it will one day become saucy, because all the people will know what they are trying to hide and what they are really doing to the Vietnamese people.

They continue to produce this play but each year they receive fewer victorious responses. Each year they are attacked by the enemy in the south and they are being defeated more every day. This play lies to the people and will soon be disclosed to them. Today the Americans cannot cover anything. Now they only kill and rape day after day. Their animalistic character has been uncovered even by the American civilians. In Saigon there are some Americans that put their penis outside of their pants and put a dollar on it to pay the girls who sell themselves. The Americans get laid in every public place. This beast in the street is not afraid of the presence of the people.

In the American base camps when they check the people they take their money, rings, watches, and the women's ear rings. . . .

Since the Americans heavy loss in the spring they have become like wounded animals that are crazy and cruel. They bomb places where many people live, places which are not good choices for bombings, such as the cities within the provinces, especially in Hue, Saigon, and Ben Tre. In Hue the US newspapers reported that 70% of the homes were destroyed and 10,000 people killed or left homeless. The newspapers and radios of Europe also tell of the killing of the South Vietnamese people by the Americans. The English tell of the action where the Americans are bombing the cities of South Vietnam. The Americans will be sentenced first by the Public in Saigon. It is there where the people will lose sentiment for them because they bomb the people and all people will soon be against them. The world public objects to this bombing including the American public and that of its Allies. The American often shuts his eye and closes his ear and continues his crime.

In the operation of 15 March 1968 in Son Tinh District the American enemies went crazy. They used machine guns and every other kind of weapon to kill 500 people who had empty hands, in Tinh Khe (Son My) Village (Son

Tinh District, Quang Ngai Province). There were many pregnant women some of which were only a few days from childbirth. The Americans would shoot everybody they saw. They killed people and cows, burned homes. There were some families in which all members were killed.

When the red evil Americans remove their prayer shirts they appear as barbaric men.

When the American wolves remove their sheepskin their sharp meat-eating teeth show. They drink our peoples blood with animal sentimentality.

Our people must choose one way to beat them until they are dead, and stop wriggling.

For the ARVN officer and soldier, by now you have seen the face of the real American. How many times have they left you alone to defend against the National Liberation Front? They do not fire artillery or mortars to help you even when you are near them. They often bomb the bodies of ARVN soldiers. They also fire artillery on the tactical elements of the ARVN soldiers. . . .

Can you accept these criminal friends who slaughter our people and turn Vietnam into red blood like that which runs in our veins?

What are you waiting for and why do not you use your US Rifles to shoot the Americans in the head—for our people, to help our country and your life too?

There is no time better than now

> The American Rifle is in your hands
> You must take aim at the Americans head and

Pull the trigger

### Document 4: The Peers Report[9]

*When the My Lai incident became public knowledge, a more thorough investigation was undertaken by General William R. Peers, but by this time more than a year had passed since the event at My Lai. Peers's report was long and detailed. Below is a portion of the summary in which the major conclusions are reported.*

### D. SUPPRESSION AND WITHHOLDING OF INFORMATION

Within the Americal Division, at every command level from company to division, actions were taken or omitted which together effectively concealed the Son My incident. Outside the division, advisory teams at Province, District and possibly the 2d ARVN Division also contributed to this end. Some of the acts and omissions that resulted in concealment of the incident were inadvertent while others constituted deliberate suppression or withholding of information.

Efforts initiated in 1968 deliberately to withhold information continue to this day. . . .

1. At Company Level

   No reports of the crimes committed . . . during the operation were made by members of the units, although there were many men in both companies who had not participated in any criminal acts. The commander of C/1-20 Inf assembled his men after the operation and advised them not to discuss the incident because an investigation was being conducted, and he advised one individual not to write to his Congressman about the incident. He also made a false report that only 20-28 noncombatants had been killed and attributed the cause of death to artillery and gunships.

   The commander of B/4-3 Inf submitted false reports (possibly without knowing they were false) that 38 VC had been killed by his 1st Platoon and that none of them were women and children.

2. At Task Force and Brigade Levels

   Significant information concerning irregularities in the operation and the commission of war crimes . . . was known to the commanders and staff officers . . . but was never transmitted to the Americal Division. . . . In addition to withholding information, the 11th Brigade headquarters submitted false and misleading reports to Division. . . .

   A reporter and photographer . . . failed to report what they had seen, the reporter wrote a false and misleading account of the operation, and the photographer withheld and suppressed from proper authorities the photographic evidence of atrocities he had obtained. . . .

   In response to a routine division requirement, LTC Barker . . . significantly omitted any reference to noncombatant casualties and other irregularities, falsely depicted a hotly-contested combat action, and appears to have been an outright effort to suppress and mislead.

   Perhaps the most significant action taken to suppress the true facts of the Son My operation was the deception employed by COL Henderson to mislead his commander as to the scope and findings of his investigation of the Thompson allegations. . . .

3. At Division Level

   a. Within Aviation Units

      . . . there were acts and omissions by the commanders of the 123d Aviation Battalion, and Company B of that unit, which contributed to concealment of the facts. One of the principal reasons why the full import of the Thompson Report was probably not appreciated at the division command level can be attributed to these two commanders and their failure to verify or document the serious charges made by WO1 Thompson and others. . . .

A second serious charge against both of these two commanders is that they failed to take any action when they became convinced that the investigation of the incident was a "cover-up." . . .

b. Within Headquarters, American Division

American Division Headquarters was the recipient of much information. . . . Except for routine operational data forwarded on 16 March, none of the reports or allegations concerning irregularities at Son My were transmitted to higher headquarters, . . . While COL Henderson's later reports were false, and the general officers were negligent in having accepted them, they probably believed they were withholding information concerning a much less serious incident than the one that had actually occurred.

Additional information from Vietnamese sources reaching the American Division sometime in April implied that a far more serious event had taken place at Son My. The command response to this information was so inadequate to the situation and so inconsistent with what would ordinarily be expected of officers of the ability and experience of MG Koster and BG Young that it can only be explained as a refusal or an inability to give credence to information or reports which were not consistent with their original, and erroneous, conclusions. . . .

## E. SUMMARY OF FINDINGS
It is concluded that:

1. During the period of 16-19 March 1968, troops of Task Force Barker massacred a large number of Vietnamese nationals in the village of Son My.
2. Knowledge as to the extent of the incident existed at Company level, at least among the key staff officers and commander at the Task Force Barker level, and at the 11th Brigade command level.
3. Efforts at the American Division command level to conceal information concerning what was probably believed to be the killing of 20-28 civilians actually resulted in the suppression of a war crime of far greater magnitude.
4. The commander of the 11th Brigade, upon learning that a war crime had probably been committed, deliberately set out to conceal the fact from proper authority and to deceive his commander concerning the matter.

5. Investigations concerning the incident conducted within the Americal Division were superficial and misleading and not subjected to substantive review.
6. Efforts were made at every level of command from company to division to withhold and suppress information concerning the incident at Son My.
7. Failure of Americal Division headquarters personnel to act on information received from GVN/ARVN officials served to suppress effectively information concerning the Son My incident.
8. Efforts of the Americal Division to suppress and withhold information were assisted by US officers serving in advisory positions with Vietnamese agencies.

### Document 5: Calley Testifies[10]

*Lt. William Calley was the only person convicted of criminal activity in the My Lai case, even though a large number of other people were implicated. Those accused of covering up the event were not prosecuted. Calley was convicted in 1971 of premeditated murder and was initially sentenced to life imprisonment. Two days after the conviction, President Nixon ordered Calley moved from prison to house arrest. After three and a half years, he was freed by a federal judge. Calley was not the most impressive American military officer. A portion of his testimony in his trial indicates the kind of person he was and the type of training he had received. This transcript shows both the prosecution and defense questions.*

### *Direct examination by George Latimer:*

. . . Q: Did you receive any training in any of those places which had to do with obedience to orders?

A: Yes, sir.

Q: What were the nature of the—what were you informed was the principles involved in that field?

A: That all orders were to be assumed legal, that the soldier's job was to carry out any order given him to the best of his ability.

Q: Did you tell your doctor or inform him anything about what might occur if you disobeyed an order by a senior officer?

A: You could be court-martialed for refusing an order and refusing an order in the face of the enemy, you could be sent to death, sir.

Q: Well, let me ask you this: what I am talking and asking is whether or not you were given any instructions on the necessity for—or whether you were required in any way, shape or form to make a determination of the legality or illegality of an order?

A: No, sir. I was never told that I had the choice, sir.

Q: If you had a doubt about the order, what were you supposed to do?

A: If I had—questioned an order, I was supposed to carry the order out and then come back and make my complaint later.

Q: Now, during the course of your movement through the village, had you seen any Vietnamese dead, or dead bodies?

A: Yes, sir.

Q: And how would you classify it as to whether it was a few, many, how would you—what descriptive phrase would you use for your own impression?

A: Many.

Q: Now, did you see some live Vietnamese while you were going through the village?

A: I saw two, sir.

Q: All right. Now, tell us, was there an incident concerning those two?

A: Yes, sir. I shot and killed both of them.

Q: Under what circumstances?

A: There was a large concrete house and I kind of stepped up on the porch and looked in the window. There was about six to eight individuals laying on the floor, apparently dead. And one man was going for the window. I shot him. There was another man standing in a fireplace. He looked like he had just come out of the fireplace, or out of the chimney. And I shot him, sir. He was in a bright green uniform. . . .

Q: Did you at any time direct anybody to push people in the ditch?

A: Like I said, I gave the order to take those people through the ditch and had also told Meadlo if he couldn't move them, to waste them, and I directly—other than that, there was only that one incident. I never stood up there for any period of time. The main mission was to get my men on the other side of the ditch and get in that defensive position, and that is what I did, sir.

Q: Now, why did you give Meadlo a message or the order that if he couldn't get rid of them to waste them?

A: Because that was my order, sir. That as the order of the day, sir.

Q: Who gave you that order?

A: My commanding officer, sir.

Q: He was?

A: Captain Medina, sir.

Q: And stated in that posture, in substantially those words, how many times did you receive such an order from Captain Medina?

A: The night before in the company briefing, platoon leaders' briefing, the following morning before we lifted off and twice there in the village. . . .

Q: Did you form any impression as to whether or not there were children, women, or men, or what did you see in front of you as you were going on?

A: I never sat down to analyze it, men, women, and children. They were enemy and just people.

Q: Did you consciously discriminate as you were operating through there insofar as sex or age is concerned?

A: The only time I denoted sex was when I stopped Conti from molesting a girl. That was the only time sex ever entered the—my whole scope of thinking.

Q: In this instance, when you saw a group being supervised or guarded by Meadlo, how did you visualize that group? Did you go in the specifics in any way?

A: No, sir. It was a group of people that were the enemy, sir.

Q: And were you motivated by other things besides the fact that those were the enemy? Did you have some other reason for treating them that way altogether? I am talking now about your briefings. Did you get any information out of that?

A: Well, I was ordered to go in there and destroy the enemy. That was my job on that day. That was the mission I was given. I did not sit down and think in terms of men, women, and children. They were all classified the same, and that was the classification that we dealt with, just as enemy soldiers.

Q: Who gave you that classification the last time you got it?

A: Captain Medina, sir. . . .

Q: Now, I will ask you this, Lieutenant Calley: Whatever you did at My Lai on that occasion, I will ask you whether in your opinion you were acting rightly and according to your understanding of your directions and orders?

A: I felt then and I still do that I acted as I was directed, and I carried out the orders that I was given, and I do not feel wrong in doing so, sir. . . .

## Cross examination by Daniel:

Q: What did Captain Medina say when you had the group of people, when you told him—

A: He told me basically to get rid of the people, to get moving.

Q: He told you that basically?

A: To the best of my knowledge. I can't remember his exact words.

Q: You described the people to him?

A: No, sir. I didn't.

Q: How did you describe them to him?

A: Vietnamese. VC.

Q: Which?

A: Either one. I don't know, sir.

Q: You don't know how you described them?

A: In that area, I could have used either term.

Q: Do you know if there were women in that group?

A: No, sir.

Q: Do you know if there were children in that group?

A: No, sir.

Q: Do you know if there were men in that group?

A: No, sir.

Q: What did he say?

A: He told me to give—to get rid of the people and get moving.

Q: What did you do?

A: I rogered . . .

Q: How did you interpret that?

A: As getting rid of them if I couldn't move them fast enough. . . .

Q: What did you say to him, then, on that occasion?

A: If he couldn't move the people, to waste them, sir.

Q: What did he say?

A: He said, roger. . . .

Q: What did you find when you got there?

A: My men were shooting men in the ditch, sir.

Q: What men?

A: Vietnamese men, sir.

Q: They were all men?

A: I don't know, sir.

Q: Did you look?

A: I looked into the ditch, yes, sir.

Q: What did you do when you got there?

A: I fired into the ditch, told my men to hurry up and get on the other side and get into position. . . .

Q: How long did you fire into the ditch?

A: I have no idea, sir.

Q: How many shots did you fire?

A: Six to eight, sir.

Q: One burst or semi-automatic?

A: Semi-automatic, sir.

Q: Who did you fire at?

A: Into the ditch, sir.

Q: What at in the ditch?

A: At the people in the ditch, sir.

Q: How many people were in the ditch?

A: I don't know, sir.

Q: Over how large an area were they in the ditch?

A: I don't know, sir.

Q: Could you give us an estimate as to how many people were in the ditch?

A: No, sir.

Q: Would you say it was a large group?

A: No, sir. . . .

Q: What were these people doing as they were being fired upon?

A: Nothing sir.

Q: Were they being hit?

A: I would imagine so, sir. . . .

## Notes

1. Allen Cohen, "Additional Notes on the S.F. Oracle," *The San Francisco Oracle/ The Psychedelic Newspaper of the Haight Ashbury*, CD-rom, the Regent Press. regent-press.net. Reprinted by permission.

2. Sarah Beach, "Curse of the Hippie Parents," *Salon*, August 22, 2001, online at www.salon.com/mwt/feature/2001/08/22/hippie_parents/index2.html. Reprinted by permission of Salon.com.

3. Port Huron Statement of the Students for a Democratic Society, 1962. Reprinted by permission of Tom Hayden.

4. Testimony of Timothy Leary in the Chicago Seven Trial, online at www.law.umkc.edu/faculty/projects/ftrials/Chicago7/Leary.html.

5. Interview with Rennie Davis, February 23, 2009, granted specifically for this book. Used by permission of Rennie Davis.

6. Letter from Mr. Ronald Ridenhour to Secretary of Defense, March 29, 1969, in William R. Peers, *Report of the Department of the Army Review of the Preliminary Investigation into the My Lai Incident*, vol. 1. *The Report of the Investigation* (Washington, D.C.: U.S. Government Printing Office, 1979), 7–11.

7. Hugh Thompson, "Testimony to the Peers Commission," Peers, *Report*, vol. 2, bk. 8, 10–12, 49–52, 43–46.

8. "The Americans Devils Devulge [*sic*] the Truth," Peers, *Report*, vol. 4, 264–65.

9. Peers, *Report*, Summary.

10. William Calley Court-Martial Transcripts, National Archives Complex, College Park, Maryland.

# 9

# Continuing Crises

*A*FTER THE END OF WORLD WAR II, *the United States seemed to be involved in one crisis after another. That condition reflected the changed nature of the world and the existence of weapons of mass destruction. In addition, the preeminent role in the world of the United States made world crises more important to average Americans. In pre-World War II times, many crises went virtually unnoticed by average Americans, but that could be the case no longer.*

*Two of the most important crises were twelve years apart, but they both represented challenges to the future of the United States. One was in foreign policy, and the other was in domestic politics.*

### Part A: Cuban Missile Crisis—How Close to War?

#### Background

*In 1962, the world came as close to nuclear war as it ever did during the days known as the Cold War. The confrontation that could have led to war concerned the island nation of Cuba.*

*On January 1, 1959, Fidel Castro overthrew the dictator of Cuba, Fulgencio Batista, and proclaimed that his democratic revolution had succeeded. At first, most Americans hailed Castro's victory as a solid gain for democracy, but it soon became clear that Castro was not the leader of democratic forces as they had assumed. Within a year and a half, the Soviet Union had recognized the Cuban government, and not long after, Castro proclaimed himself to be a Marxist.*

*Sorely disappointed by the turn of events in Cuba, the United States in August 1960 imposed a trade embargo against Cuba, hoping that the pressure would either cause Castro to change his position or that Castro would be forced out of power. When John F. Kennedy became president in January 1961, he found that an invasion of Cuba, primarily involving Cuban refugees and supported by the American CIA, was planned. After giving his approval for it to go forward, Kennedy then had second thoughts and withheld some of the support he had promised. The failed invasion became known as the "Bay of Pigs" fiasco.*

*In 1961, Kennedy met in Vienna with Premier Nikita Khrushchev of the Soviet Union. Khrushchev was not impressed with the young president and thought him to be weak and indecisive. The Soviet leader's future actions until the missile crisis were based on this assessment of Kennedy.*

*By January 1, 1962, American intelligence sources provided the first reliable evidence that the Soviet Union was sending arms to Cuba. By the summer of 1962, more shipments were leaving Soviet Bloc nations heading for Cuba. By late August, conclusive evidence showed that missile sites were being built in Cuba, and Soviet troops began to arrive in Cuba by the end of the month.*

*In the fall of 1962, President Kennedy was informed that "hard photographic evidence" now showed the missiles in Cuba. Kennedy immediately established a working group of about fourteen close advisers known as ExComm (Executive Committee of the National Security Council) to meet with him on a regular basis to review developments in Cuba. American monitoring of Cuba continued, and the Soviet Union was aware of the surveillance that was taking place.*

*The following documents are only a small sampling of those available showing the tension that existed during the crisis that came close to engulfing the world in nuclear war.*

## Questions

In reading these documents, the student should ask and answer several questions to put this event into the proper perspective.

1. How serious a threat to the United States were the Soviet missiles in Cuba?
2. Did Kennedy unnecessarily endanger the United States with his quarantine of Cuba?
3. Were there other actions Kennedy could have taken to avert the crisis?
4. Did Khrushchev suffer from mental or emotional instability during this period?
5. Why did Khrushchev back off from his position after acting so provocatively?

6. What was the long-term impact of the missile crisis on Soviet–American relations?

### Document 1: Khrushchev Reacts to American Surveillance[1]

*On October 16, 1962, Soviet Premier Khrushchev met with the American ambassador Foy Kohler in a three-hour meeting to express his concerns about American actions regarding Cuba as well as American missile placement in other parts of the world. The following document is part of Kohler's report to the Department of State.*

Moscow, October 16, 1962, 7 p.m.

Khrushchev said he wanted to express his disappointment at one thing that adds fuel to fire of the cold war, namely, that US now is trying to stop Soviet airplanes from flying to Cuba. After I interjected confirmation, he said they regard this as unfriendly act. This is not wartime. We should be developing trade and culture between our countries. He could not understand why we were acting this way. Perhaps we were frightened and our leaders' nerves were bad. If we were going to start a war, then he could understand it. US was boycotting trade with Cuba and appealing to all countries to stop their ships from going there. US is great country with population 183 million, while Cuba has only seven million. Could it really be that US was afraid of Cuba? Who would believe that Cuba was a nightmare for US? It was too small; even if it wanted to gobble up US, it couldn't.... What did US want? To start war? If not, what was happening? "Are you too afraid? Do you want to commit suicide?" ...

I said I should of course report his remarks to President. At Vienna, President had spoken very frankly to him about Cuba. Chairman was misinterpreting Castro regime. Not only US, but all Western Hemisphere countries, feel Castro has let Cuban people down. US and other Western Hemisphere states are not going to help Cuba. We are certainly not afraid of them but we don't intend to help them. Of course, we have different views than Chairman about situation. Speaking as frankly as he had, I felt I must add that size of Soviet shipments to Cuba has increased feeling in US on this problem.

Khrushchev said we must be responsible, since our countries are great powers. We cannot demand that other countries live as we like or there would be war. US has bases in countries neighboring USSR, such as Turkey, as well as in Greece, Italy, France, West Germany and Pakistan. But USSR does not attack these countries. If US thinks it has right to do as it likes about Cuba, why hasn't USSR right to do as it likes about these countries? ... It was one thing when US was very powerful, but now there is a force as great as yours. We will never agree to your capitalistic way of thinking. Our policy is, let us live in peace. Let us have our socialism and you can have your capitalism. Let's respect internal affairs of other countries and not interfere with life of other countries. . . .

Khrushchev [said] . . . saying he also understood President that way but must still express his disappointment about blockade, which is inimical action. Let the people choose their own system. As a result of blockade, Cuban people are suffering and will become more embittered against US. You should trade with Cuba, as we do with Turkey and other of your allies. Why are you not trading with us? You want to strangle us. But you've lost any real understanding of history.

### Document 2: Kennedy Announces Quarantine[2]

*When Kennedy announced a quarantine against Cuba, the speech was a shock to the American people. The Cold War was serious, most people understood, but until this moment, they were unaware of how close to war the United States was. Below is a portion of Kennedy's remarks.*

This Government, as promised, has maintained the closest surveillance of the Soviet military buildup on the island of Cuba. Within the past week, unmistakable evidence has established the fact that a series of offensive missile sites is now in preparation on that imprisoned island. The purpose of these bases can be none other than to provide a nuclear strike capability against the Western Hemisphere.

Upon receiving the first preliminary hard information of this nature last Tuesday morning at 9 A.M., I directed that our surveillance be stepped up. And having now confirmed and completed our evaluation of the evidence and our decision on a course of action, this Government feels obliged to report this new crisis to you in fullest detail.

The characteristics of these new missile sites indicate two distinct types of installations. Several of them include medium range ballistic missiles, capable of carrying a nuclear warhead for a distance of more than 1,000 nautical miles. Each of these missiles, in short, is capable of striking Washington, D.C., the Panama Canal, Cape Canaveral, Mexico City, or any other city in the southeastern part of the United States, in Central America, or in the Caribbean area. . . .

This urgent transformation of Cuba into an important strategic base—by the presence of these large, long-range, and clearly offensive weapons of sudden mass destruction—constitutes an explicit threat to the peace and security of all the Americas, . . .

But this secret, swift, and extraordinary buildup of Communist missiles—in an area well known to have a special and historical relationship to the United States and the nations of the Western Hemisphere, in violation of Soviet assurances, and in defiance of American and hemispheric policy—this sudden, clandestine decision to station strategic weapons for the first time outside of Soviet soil—is a deliberately provocative and unjustified change in the status quo which cannot be accepted by this country, if our courage and our commitments are ever to be trusted again by either friend or foe. . . .

Acting, therefore, in the defense of our own security and of the entire Western Hemisphere, and under the authority entrusted to me by the Constitution as endorsed by the Resolution of the Congress, I have directed that the following *initial* steps be taken immediately:

*First:* To halt this offensive buildup, a strict quarantine on all offensive military equipment under shipment to Cuba is being initiated. . . .

*Second:* I have directed the continued and increased close surveillance of Cuba and its military buildup. . . .

*Third:* It shall be the policy of this Nation to regard any nuclear missile launched from Cuba against any nation in the Western Hemisphere as an attack by the Soviet Union on the United States, requiring a full retaliatory response upon the Soviet Union.

*Fourth:* As a necessary military precaution, I have reinforced our base at Guantanamo, evacuated today the dependents of our personnel there, and ordered additional military units to be on a standby alert basis.

*Fifth:* We are calling tonight for an immediate meeting of the Organ of Consultation under the Organization of American States, to consider this threat to hemispheric security and to invoke articles 6 and 8 of the Rio Treaty in support of all necessary action. . . .

*Sixth:* Under the Charter of the United Nations, we are asking tonight that an emergency meeting of the Security Council be convoked without delay to take action against this latest Soviet threat to world peace. . . .

*Seventh and finally:* I call upon Chairman Khrushchev to halt and eliminate this clandestine, reckless, and provocative threat to world peace and to stable relations between our two nations. I call upon him further to abandon this course of world domination, and to join in an historic effort to end the perilous arms race and to transform the history of man. He has an opportunity now to move the world back from the abyss of destruction—by returning to his government's own words that it had no need to station missiles outside its own territory, and withdrawing these weapons from Cuba—by refraining from any action which will widen or deepen the present crisis—and then by participating in a search for peaceful and permanent solutions. . . .

Finally, I want to say a few words to the captive people of Cuba, to whom this speech is being directly carried by special radio facilities. I speak to you as a friend, as one who knows of your deep attachment to your fatherland, as one who shares your aspirations for liberty and justice for all. And I have watched and the American people have watched with deep sorrow how your nationalist revolution was betrayed—and how your fatherland fell under foreign domination. Now your leaders are no longer Cuban leaders inspired by Cuban ideals. They are puppets and agents of an international conspiracy which has turned Cuba against your friends and neighbors in the Americas—and turned it into the first Latin American country to become a target for nuclear war—the first Latin American country to have these weapons on its soil. . . .

My fellow citizens: let no one doubt that this is a difficult and dangerous effort on which we have set out. No one can foresee precisely what course it will take or what costs or casualties will be incurred. Many months of sacrifice and self-discipline lie ahead—months in which both our patience and our will will be tested—months in which many threats and denunciations will keep us aware of our dangers. But the greatest danger of all would be to do nothing. . . .

### Documents 3–4: The Soviets React

*As expected, the Soviet Union was not happy with the announcement of the quarantine. The Soviets continued to insist that the armaments they were sending to Cuba were totally defensive in nature.*

### Document 3: Khrushchev writes to Kennedy[3]

*The first response to Kennedy was a brief letter from Khrushchev to Kennedy delivered to the American ambassador. Khrushchev was outraged and insisted the weapons in Cuba were defensive ones.*

Moscow, October 23, 1962, 5 p.m.

Mr. President.

. . . I should say frankly that measures outlined in your statement represent serious threat to peace and security of peoples. United States has openly taken path of gross violation of Charter of United Nations, path of violation of international norms of freedom of navigation on high seas, path of aggressive actions both against Cuba and against Soviet Union.

Statement of Government of United States America cannot be evaluated in any other way than as naked interference in domestic affairs of Cuban Republic, Soviet Union, and other states. Charter of United Nations and international norms do not give right to any state whatsoever to establish in international waters control of vessels bound for shores of Cuban Republic.

It is self-understood that we also cannot recognize right of United States to establish control over armaments essential to Republic of Cuba for strengthening of its defensive capacity.

We confirm that armaments now on Cuba, regardless of classification to which they belong, are destined exclusively for defensive purposes, in order to secure Cuban Republic from attack of aggressor.

I hope that Government of United States will show prudence and renounce actions pursued by you, which would lead to catastrophic consequences for peace throughout world.

Viewpoint of Soviet Government with regard to your statement of October 22 is set forth in statement of Soviet Government, which is being conveyed to you through your Ambassador in Moscow.

/s/ N. Khrushchev.

### Document 4: Robert Kennedy reports[4]

*At the president's suggestion, Attorney General Robert Kennedy, the president's brother, met with the Soviet ambassador to the United States, Anatoly Dobrynin, in his office at the Soviet embassy. Dobrynin said that, as far as he knew, there were no missiles in Cuba. This is probably true since evidence suggests that he had not been informed of their deployment to Cuba. The document below is a portion of the written report that Robert Kennedy made to the president.*

Washington, October 24, 1962.

I met with Ambassador Dobrynin last evening . . . and . . . made the following points:

I told him first that I was there on my own and not on the instructions of the President. I said that I wanted to give him some background on the decision of the United States Government and wanted him to know that the duplicity of the Russians had been a major contributing factor. When I had met with him some six weeks before, I said, he had told me that the Russians had not placed any long-range missiles in Cuba and had no intention to do so in the future. He interrupted at that point and confirmed this statement and said he specifically told me they would not put missiles in Cuba which would be able to reach the continental United States. . . .

I pointed out . . . that the President felt he had a very helpful personal relationship with Mr. Khrushchev. Obviously, they did not agree on many issues, but he did feel that there was a mutual trust and confidence between them on which he could rely. . . .

I said that with the background of this relationship, plus the specific assurances that had been given to us, and then the statement of Dobrynin from Khrushchev to Ted Sorensen and to me that no incident would occur before the American elections were completed, we felt the action by Khrushchev and the Russians at this time was hypocritical, misleading and false. I said this should be clearly understood by them as it was by us.

Dobrynin's only answer was that he had told me no missiles were in Cuba but that Khrushchev had also given similar assurances through TASS and as far as he (Dobrynin) knew, there were still no missiles in Cuba.

Dobrynin in the course of the conversation made several other points. The one he stressed was why the President did not tell Gromyko the facts on Thursday. He said this was something they could not understand and that if we had the information at the time why didn't we tell Gromyko.

I answered this by making two points:

Number one, there wasn't anything the President could tell Gromyko that Gromyko didn't know already and after all, why didn't Gromyko tell the President this instead of, in fact, denying it. I said in addition the President was so shocked at Gromyko's presentation and his failure to recite these facts that he felt that any effort to have an intelligent and honest conversation would not be profitable. . . .

Dobrynin seemed extremely concerned. When I left I asked him if ships were going to go through to Cuba. He replied that was their instructions last month and he assumed they had the same instructions at the present time. He also made the point that although we might have pictures, all we really knew about were the sites and not missiles and that there was a lot of difference between sites and the actual missile itself. I said I did not have to argue the point—there were missiles in Cuba—we knew that they were there and that I hoped he would inform himself also.

I left around 10:15 p.m. and went to the White House and gave a verbal report to the President.

### Document 5: Another Exchange of Letters Between Khrushchev and Kennedy[5]

*Following the imposition of the quarantine, no one knew what would happen next, either in the Soviet Union or in the United States.*

*On October 24, Soviet ships reached the quarantine line but did not cross it. On that day, Khrushchev wrote Kennedy again more fully objecting to the American action. The outrage in his letter is apparent. Following Khrushchev's letter is Kennedy's answer.*

Dear Mr. President,

. . . Imagine, Mr. President, what if we were to present to you such an ultimatum as you have presented to us by your actions. How would you react to it? I think you would be outraged at such a move on our part. And this we would understand.

Having presented these conditions to us, Mr. President, you have thrown down the gauntlet. Who asked you to do this? By what right have you done this? Our ties with the Republic of Cuba, as well as our relations with other nations, regardless of their political system, concern only the two countries between which these relations exist. . . .

You, Mr. President, are not declaring a quarantine, but rather issuing an ultimatum, and you are threatening that if we do not obey your orders, you will then use force. Think about what you are saying! And you want to persuade me to agree to this! What does it mean to agree to these demands? It would mean for us to conduct our relations with other countries not by reason, but by yielding to tyranny. You are not appealing to reason; you want to intimidate us.

No, Mr. President, I cannot agree to this, and I think that deep inside, you will admit that I am right. I am convinced that if you were in my place you would do the same.

. . . We firmly adhere to the principles of international law and strictly observe the standards regulating navigation on the open sea, in international waters. . . .

You want to force us to renounce the rights enjoyed by every sovereign state; you are attempting to legislate questions of international law; you are violating the generally accepted standards of this law. All this is due not only to hatred for the Cuban people and their government, but also for reasons having to do with the election campaign in the USA. What morals, what laws can justify such an approach by the American government to international affairs? Such morals and laws are not to be found, because the actions of the USA in relation to Cuba are outright piracy. . . . Unfortunately, people of all nations, and not least the American people themselves, could suffer heavily from madness such as this, since with the appearance of modern types of weapons, the USA has completely lost its former inaccessibility.

Therefore, Mr. President, if you weigh the present situation with a cool head without giving way to passion, you will understand that the Soviet Union cannot afford not to decline the despotic demands of the USA. When you lay conditions such as these before us, try to put yourself in our situation and consider how the USA would react to such conditions. I have no doubt that if anyone attempted to dictate similar conditions to you—the USA, you would reject such an attempt. And we likewise say—no.

The Soviet government considers the violation of the freedom of navigation in international waters and air space to constitute an act of aggression propelling humankind into the abyss of a world nuclear-missile war. Therefore, the Soviet government cannot instruct captains of Soviet ships bound for Cuba to observe orders of American naval forces blockading this island. . . . To be sure, we will not remain mere observers of pirate actions by American ships in the open sea. We will then be forced on our part to take those measures we deem necessary and sufficient to defend our rights. To this end we have all that is necessary.

Respectfully,      /s/ N. Khrushchev

## Kennedy Responds

I have received your letter of October 24, and I regret very much that you still do not appear to understand what it is that has moved us in this matter.

The sequence of events is clear. In August there were reports of important shipments of military equipment and technicians from the Soviet Union to Cuba. In early September I indicated very plainly that the United States would regard any shipment of offensive weapons as presenting the gravest issues. After that time, this Government received the most explicit assurance from your Government and its representatives, both publicly and privately, that no offensive weapons were being sent to Cuba. If you will review the statement issued by TASS in September, you will see how clearly this assurance was given.

In reliance on these solemn assurances I urged restraint upon those in this country who were urging action in this matter at that time. And then I learned beyond doubt what you have not denied—namely, that all these public assurances were false and that your military people had set out recently to establish a set of missile bases in Cuba. I ask you to recognize clearly, Mr. Chairman, that it was not I who issued the first challenge in this case, and that in the light of this record these activities in Cuba required the responses I have announced.

I repeat my regret that these events should cause a deterioration in our relations. I hope that your Government will take the necessary action to permit a restoration of the earlier situation.

## Document 6: America and the Soviet Union Exchange Insults at the United Nations[6]

*During the missile crisis, one of the most famous confrontations took place at the Security Council of the United Nations between American ambassador Adlai*

*Stevenson and Soviet delegate V. A. Zorin. While Stevenson was claiming that the United States had positive proof that missiles existed in Cuba, Zorin continued to insist that there were no offensive weapons there.*

*In response, Ambassador Stevenson provided the photographic evidence gathered by United States intelligence services. In the process of this presentation, he made one of the most famous remarks of his career about waiting "until hell freezes over." This shocked people watching on television because words such as "hell" were not used at that time on television.*

### Zorin's Statement

But now that Mr. Stevenson has tried today to accuse the Soviet Union of being the prime cause of these aggressive actions by the United States, I should like to draw the attention of all members of the Council to the fact. . . . In the statement of President Kennedy of the 22nd of October, Mr. Kennedy said that during the last week unmistakable evidence has established the fact that a series of offensive missile sites is now in preparation on that island. . . .

On 16 October the President of the United States had in his hands unmistakable evidence. What happened then? On 18 October the President of the United States received the representative of the Soviet Union—A.A. Gromyko, the Minister for Foreign Affairs. Why, it must be asked, did the President of the United States, when receiving the Minister of another Power which the Government of the United States now accuses of sending to Cuba offensive weapons directed against the United States, not say a word about this "unmistakable evidence" to the Minister of Foreign Affairs of the Soviet Union? Why? Because there is no such evidence. The Government of the United States possesses no such evidence, except fake evidence, produced by the Intelligence Service of the United States, which is exhibited [in the] halls for inspection and is distributed to the press. That is what the United States has in its hands—fake evidence. . . .

But world politics cannot be carried on in this way. Such reckless adventuring can lead to catastrophic consequences for the whole world. The Soviet Government has issued a warning to the United States and to the world of this fact. . . .

The Soviet Government considers that the United States Government should show restraint and refrain from carrying out its piratical threats, which are fraught with the most serious consequence. . . .

### Stevenson's Response

I want to say to you, Mr. Zorin, that I do not have your talent for obfuscation, for distortion, for confusing language, and for doubletalk—and I must confess to you that I am glad that I do not.

But if I understood what you said, you said that my position had changed; that today I was defensive because we did not have the evidence to prove our assertions, that your Government had installed long-range missiles in Cuba. Well, let me say something to you, Mr. Ambassador: We do have the evidence. We have it, and it is clear and it is incontrovertible. And let me say something else: Those weapons must be taken out of Cuba. . . .

But let me also say to you, sir, that there has been a change. You—the Soviet Union has sent these weapons to Cuba. You, the Soviet Union, have upset the balance of power in the world. You, the Soviet Union, have created this new danger—not the United States. . . .

And while we are asking questions, let me ask you why your Government, your Foreign Minister, deliberately, cynically deceived us about the nuclear build-up in Cuba.

Finally, Mr. Zorin, I remind you that the other day you did not deny the existence of these weapons. Instead, we heard that they had suddenly become defensive weapons. But today—again if I heard you correctly—you now say that they do not exist, or that we have not proved they exist—and you say this with another fine flood of rhetorical scorn. All right, sir, let me ask you one simple question: Do you, Ambassador Zorin, deny that the U.S.S.R. has placed and is placing medium and intermediate-range missiles and sites in Cuba? Yes or no? Do not wait for the interpretation. Yes or no? . . .

You are in the courtroom of world opinion right now, and you can answer "Yes" or "No." You have denied that they exist—and I want to know whether I have understood you correctly. . . .

I am prepared to wait for my answer until hell freezes over, if that's your decision. And I am also prepared to present the evidence in this room.

### Document 7: The Press Gets Involved[7]

*On October 25, the press inadvertently became involved in the crisis. ABC television reporter John Scali was contacted by Alexander S. Fomin, a counselor at the Soviet Embassy, and invited to lunch. Right after the meeting, Scali reported the meeting to the director of the Bureau of Intelligence and Research at the State Department. Fomin was apparently acting on his own initiative, and the meeting did not have any substantial results. It does show, however, how serious the situation was and how some people were trying to find a solution to keep the world from going to nuclear war.*

Washington, undated.

Alexander S. Fomin, Sov Emby Counselor, at lunch which he sought urgently, asks if State would be interested in settlement of Cuban crisis along these lines:

Bases would be dismantled under United Nations supervision and Castro would pledge not to accept offensive weapons of any kind, ever, in return for US pledge not to invade Cuba.

I said I didn't know but that perhaps this is something that could be talked about. He said if Stevenson pursued this line, Zorin would be interested. Asked that I check with State and let him know. He gave me his home telephone number so I could call him tonight, if necessary.

Fomin claimed that Cuban delegate to UN during Security Council debate asked for such no-invasion assurances in return for dismantling but that he got no reply. I told him I'd followed the UN debate very carefully but could not recall any such remarks on Cuba's part.

Fomin also said Russia had been forced "to make some concessions" to Communist China in order to convince them to stop the fighting against India. He declined to say what under my questioning. But he recalled they hadn't helped the ChiComs with nuclear weapons or conventional weapons in the past, even tanks, and hinted it might be aid in the conventional field.

### Document 8: Khrushchev Makes Two Proposals[8]

*On October 26, Premier Khrushchev sent a long, rambling letter to Kennedy that confused Kennedy and everyone around him. The letter wandered into various topics and was somewhat incoherent. Some people believed that Khrushchev was realizing how far he had pushed the situation, was frightened about the prospects, and may have been intoxicated when he wrote it. Most specialists believe that he wrote the letter himself. Despite its rambling nature, there was a specific proposal included.*

*On October 27, Khrushchev sent a second letter to Kennedy with a proposal included. This letter was broadcast on Radio Moscow at the time it was delivered to American officials. In addition to removing the missiles in return for a pledge from the United States that it would not invade Cuba, this letter also proposed the removal of American missiles from Turkey as a condition for ending the crisis.*

*First Letter*

I have received your letter of October 25. From your letter, I got the feeling that you have some understanding of the situation which has developed and a sense of responsibility. I value this. . . .

I think you will understand me correctly if you are really concerned about the welfare of the world. Everyone needs peace: both capitalists, if they have not lost their reason, and, still more, Communists, people who know how to value not only their own lives but, more than anything, the lives of the peoples. . . .

I can, in any case, firmly say this for the peoples of the socialist countries, as well as for all progressive people who want peace, happiness, and friendship among peoples. . . .

In the name of the Soviet Government and the Soviet people, I assure you that your arguments regarding offensive weapons on Cuba are groundless. It is apparent from what you have written me that our conceptions are different on this score, or rather, we have different definitions for these or those military means, indeed, in reality, the same forms of weapons can have different interpretations.

You are a military man and, I hope, will understand me. Let us take for example a simple cannon. What sort of means is this: offensive or defensive? A cannon is a defensive means if it is set up to defend boundaries or a fortified area. But if one concentrates artillery, and adds to it the necessary number of troops, then the same cannons do become an offensive means, because they prepare and clear the way for infantry to advance. The same happens with missile—nuclear weapons as well, with any type of this weapon.

You are mistaken if you think that any of our means on Cuba are offensive. . . .

Consequently, Mr. President, let us show good sense. I assure you that on those ships, which are bound for Cuba, there are no weapons at all. The weapons which were necessary for the defense of Cuba are already there. I do not want to say that there were not any shipments of weapons at all. No, there were such shipments. But now Cuba has already received the necessary means of defense. . . .

Let us normalize relations. We have received an appeal from the Acting Secretary General of the UN, U Thant, with his proposals. I have already answered him. His proposals come to this, that our side should not transport armaments of any kind to Cuba during a certain period of time, while negotiations are being conducted—and we are ready to enter such negotiations—and the other side should not undertake any sort of piratical actions against vessels engaged in navigation on the high seas. I consider these proposals reasonable. This would be a way out of the situation which has been created, which would give the peoples the possibility of breathing calmly. . . .

Why have we proceeded to assist Cuba with military and economic aid? The answer is: we have proceeded to do so only for reasons of humanitarianism. At one time, our people itself had a revolution, when Russia was still a backward country, we were attacked then. We were the target of attack by many countries. . . .

We know how difficult it is to accomplish a revolution and how difficult it is to reconstruct a country on new foundations. We sincerely sympathize with Cuba and the Cuban people, but we are not interfering in questions of domestic structure, we are not interfering in their affairs. The Soviet Union desires to help the Cubans build their life as they themselves wish and that others should not hinder them. . . .

If assurances were given by the President and the Government of the United States that the USA itself would not participate in an attack on Cuba and would restrain others from actions of this sort, if you would recall your fleet, this would immediately change everything. I am not speaking for Fidel Castro, but I think that he and the Government of Cuba, evidently, would declare demobilization and would appeal to the people to get down to peaceful labor. Then, too, the question of armaments would disappear, since, if there is no threat, then armaments are a burden for every people. Then, too, the question of the destruction, not only of the armaments which you call offensive, but of all other armaments as well, would look different. . . .

Let us therefore show statesmanlike wisdom. I propose: we, for our part, will declare that our ships, bound for Cuba, are not carrying any armaments. You would declare that the United States will not invade Cuba with its forces and will not support any sort of forces which might intend to carry out an invasion of Cuba. Then the necessity for the presence of our military specialists in Cuba would disappear. . . .

If you did this as the first step towards the unleashing of war, well then, it is evident that nothing else is left to us but to accept this challenge of yours. If, however, you have not lost your self-control and sensibly conceive what this might lead to, then, Mr. President, we and you ought not now to pull on the ends of the rope in which you have tied the knot of war, because the more the two of us pull, the tighter that knot will be tied. And a moment may come when that knot will be tied so tight that even he who tied it will not have the strength to untie it, and then it will be necessary to cut that knot. And what that would mean is not for me to explain to you, because you yourself understand perfectly of what terrible forces our countries dispose.

Consequently, if there is no intention to tighten that knot and thereby to doom the world to the catastrophe of thermonuclear war, then let us not only relax the forces pulling on the ends of the rope, let us take measures to untie that knot. We are ready for this. . . .

These thoughts are dictated by a sincere desire to relieve the situation, to remove the threat of war.

Respectfully yours,
/s/ N. Khrushchev

*Second Letter*

DEAR MR. PRESIDENT, I have studied with great satisfaction your reply to Mr. Thant concerning measures that should be taken to avoid contact between our vessels and thereby avoid irreparable and fatal consequences. This reasonable step on your part strengthens my belief that you are showing concern for the preservation of peace, which I note with satisfaction.

I have already said that our people, our Government, and I personally, as Chairman of the Council of Ministers, are concerned solely with having our country develop and occupy a worthy place among all peoples of the world in economic competition, in the development of culture and the arts, and in raising the living standard of the people. This is the most noble and necessary field for competition, and both the victor and the vanquished will derive only benefit from it, because it means peace and an increase in the means by which man lives and finds enjoyment. . . .

I therefore make this proposal: We are willing to remove from Cuba the means which you regard as offensive. We are willing to carry this out and to make this pledge in the United Nations. Your representatives will make a declaration to the effect that the United States, for its part, considering the uneasiness and anxiety of the Soviet State, will remove its analogous means from Turkey. Let us reach agreement as to the period of time needed by you and by us to bring this about. . . .

We, in making this pledge, in order to give satisfaction and hope of the peoples of Cuba and Turkey and to strengthen their confidence in their security, will make a statement within the framework of the Security Council to the effect that the Soviet Government gives a solemn promise to respect the inviolability of the borders and sovereignty of Turkey, not to interfere in its internal affairs, not to invade Turkey, not to make available our territory as a bridgehead for such an invasion, and that it would also restrain those who contemplate committing aggression against Turkey, either from the territory of the Soviet Union or from the territory of Turkey's other neighboring states.

The United States Government will make a similar statement within the framework of the Security Council regarding Cuba. It will declare that the United States will respect the inviolability of Cuba's borders and its sovereignty, will pledge not to interfere in its internal affairs, not to invade Cuba itself or make its territory available as a bridgehead for such an invasion, and will also restrain those who might contemplate committing aggression against Cuba, either from the territory of the United States or from the territory of Cuba's other neighboring states. . . .

All of this could possibly serve as a good impetus toward the finding of mutually acceptable agreements on other controversial issues on which you and I have been exchanging views. These views have so far not been resolved, but they are awaiting urgent solution, which would clear up the international atmosphere. We are prepared for this.

These are my proposals, Mr. President.

Respectfully yours,

N. Khrushchev

### Document 9: Khrushchev Ends the Crisis[9]

*American officials finally advised President Kennedy to ignore the second let-ter from Khrushchev and to accept the conditions in the first letter, despite its rambling nature. Kennedy did so, and Khrushchev began removing the missiles without telling Castro at the time of the decision. He wrote Kennedy of his deci-sion, as the following portions of his letter indicate.*

DEAR MR. PRESIDENT: I have received your message of October 27. I express my satisfaction and thank you for the sense of proportion you have displayed and for realization of the responsibility which now de-volves on you for the preservation of the peace of the world. . . .

In order to eliminate as rapidly as possible the conflict which endan-gers the cause of peace, to give an assurance to all people who crave peace, and to reassure the American people, who, I am certain, also want peace, as do the people of the Soviet Union, the Soviet Government, in addition to earlier instructions on the discontinuation of further work on weapons construction sites, has given a new order to dismantle the arms which you described as offensive, and to crate and return them to the Soviet Union. . . .

I regard with respect and trust the statement you made in your mes-sage of October 27, 1962, that there would be no attack, no invasion of Cuba, and not only on the part of the United States, but also on the part of other nations of the Western Hemisphere, as you said in your same message. Then the motives which induced us to render assistance of such a kind to Cuba disappear.

It is for this reason that we instructed our officers—these means as I had already informed you earlier are in the hands of the Soviet officers—to take appropriate measures to discontinue construction of the aforementioned facilities, to dismantle them, and to return them to the Soviet Union. . . .

Although I trust your statement, Mr. President, there are irresponsible people who would like to invade Cuba now and thus touch off a war. If we do take practical steps and proclaim the dismantling and evacuation of the means in question from Cuba, in so doing we, at the same time, want the Cuban people to be certain that we are with them and are not absolving ourselves of responsibility for rendering assistance to the Cuban people. . . .

Respectfully yours,

N. Khrushchev

## Part B: Watergate and the Imperial Presidency

### Background

*What became known as Watergate was the most widespread political scandal in American history. Richard M. Nixon had come back from the political grave-yard after his loss to John F. Kennedy in 1960 and his loss in the California governor's race in 1962 to win the presidency in 1968. The Nixon presidency was known for its clandestine activities. In 1971, a document known as* The Pentagon Papers *was published, despite Nixon's efforts to stop it in the Supreme Court. This document was critical of the United States' activity in Vietnam. Around this time, a special investigative unit was established by the White House known as the "plumbers." This secret organization broke into the offices of the psychiatrist of Daniel Ellsberg, the Pentagon official who had leaked the sensitive document to the* New York Times. *As the reelection campaign of Nixon approached in 1972, Nixon developed what became known as an "enemies list" that included many people in the media and entertainment, as well as various political liberals. Nixon won reelection in 1972 over liberal George McGovern in a landslide victory. During the campaign in the summer of 1972, a break-in occurred at the headquarters of the Democratic Party in the Watergate building in Washington, D.C. At first, it appeared not to be significant, but as the months passed, it became clear that officials in the White House were involved in this criminal activity. Eventually, the break-in and its subsequent cover-up became known as "Watergate" and ended the presidency of Richard M. Nixon.*

### Questions

In reading these documents, the student should ask and answer several questions to put these activities in the proper context.

1. Was the Watergate incident a serious matter, or did it become political football?

2. Were the burglary and the "dirty tricks" just a part of the normal political process?
3. Should President Nixon have resigned from office?
4. Why did President Ford pardon Nixon? Was it the right thing to do?
5. What was the long-range impact of the Watergate affair?

## Document 1: Sirica Comments on the Break-In[10]

*The first report of the break-in at the Democratic headquarters appeared in the* Washington Post *in the summer during the campaign of 1972. It at first appeared to be a routine crime report. The case eventually wound up in the federal district court of John J. Sirica. He later explained how he learned of the break-in and how he reacted to it.*

. . . I had always made it a practice to read the local newspapers carefully to anticipate the work load the court might have and to get a preliminary understanding of the kinds of cases I might have to assign for trial. My interest was immediately aroused on Sunday, June 18, by a little story in the *Washington Post* about a burglary at the Democratic National Committee's headquarters in the Watergate office building.

It wasn't much of a story, but it was a little out of the ordinary. Five men had been arrested inside the headquarters carrying sophisticated electronic equipment and rather large sums of money, mostly in hundred-dollar bills. "Politics," I thought immediately. The average felon doesn't look for money in offices, especially in political offices, so the incident seemed odd even though the Watergate complex was also a popular in-town residence for rich Washingtonians. . . .

The break-in itself occurred early on the morning of June 17. The story of how the burglars were discovered is well known, but I've always wondered what would have happened had Frank Wills, the private security guard at the Watergate offices, not seen the tape covering the locks on the doors inside the office complex. Wills did spot the tape, called the city police, and within minutes, five men were arrested inside the Democrats' office. Their leader was James McCord. . . . It was clear that this was a matter with which I would have more contact.

What wasn't clear, however, and would remain a secret for nearly a year, was just how the five men came to be spying on the Democrats and their chairman, Lawrence F. O'Brien. When the four men from Miami were asked at their arraignment what their occupation was, they answered, "Anti-communist." McCord identified himself as a former CIA agent. There was some thought that the bugging which was found to have occurred was a misguided adventure by a group of superpatriots. But there were suspicious ties between the burglars and President Nixon's re-election committee. McCord was on the payroll of this committee as a security co-ordinator. G. Gordon Liddy, counsel to the fund-raising branch of the committee, and E. Howard Hunt, once an employee of White House aide Charles Colson, were soon tied to the break-in. Officials of the committee, including its leader, John Mitchell, who a few months earlier had resigned as attorney general to run the president's campaign, quickly denied any knowledge of the break-in plans. They blamed Liddy and Hunt for the operation.

Only a few people in Washington that summer knew that the break-in was really just one act in a long series of White House-inspired attempts to circumvent the law. Intense concern about continued protests against the Vietnam War and about leaks of sensitive foreign-policy information embarrassing to the president and to his chief diplomatic adviser, Henry Kissinger, along with the president's own concern about his political future, had led to a series of illegal operations planned inside the White House. In 1969, a group of reporters and administration aides were illegally wiretapped in an attempt to discover the source of leaks about the secret bombing of Cambodia and other unannounced policies. The so-called "Huston plan," which included burglaries, wiretaps, and illegal domestic intelligence gathering by the CIA, was formulated in 1970 in response to the antiwar movement. When Daniel Ellsberg leaked the Pentagon Papers, the White House sent Liddy and Hunt to break into Ellsberg's psychiatrist's office and steal information that would discredit Ellsberg. . . .

Concern for "national security" was the rationale that supported these actions. That concern was matched in the White House by worries about President Nixon's political survival. In 1970 the Republicans did rather poorly across the country, despite, or perhaps because of, hard-hitting and divisive performances by Vice-president Agnew and by the president himself. Senator Edmund Muskie, who had run as the vice-presidential nominee in 1968, appeared to be the Democratic front-runner. By 1971, he was ahead of the president in some public-opinion polls.

In recent presidential contests, the candidates have tended to have only the loosest of relationships with the national party committees, preferring to run their own campaigns. So the Nixon group established the Committee to Reelect the President (CRP). Nixon critics immediately dubbed this committee "CREEP." Attorney General Mitchell, even though still in the Justice Department, was put in charge of the president's political operation. No effort was to be spared. Huge sums of money were raised by Maurice Stans, the finance-committee chairman, who also operated apart from the Republican National Committee. New and stricter campaign-spending rules were coming into effect on April 7, 1972, and Stans and his group made every effort to raise large amounts of money before that date, so that donors could remain anonymous and so that huge individual gifts, many nearly coerced out of corporate leaders by Stans, would not have to be reported fully. . . .

In December 1971, G. Gordon Liddy was named general counsel to the CRP. . . .

In January 1972, Liddy proposed a massive intelligence operation against the Democrats. At a meeting in the attorney general's office, Liddy suggested establishing mugging squads, forming kidnaping [*sic*] teams, procuring prostitutes to compromise delegates to the Democratic convention, and installing a system of electronic bugs to spy on the candidates at the convention. In what John Dean later told the Senate Watergate committee was a "mind-boggling" million-dollar plan, Liddy suggested bugging O'Brien's Watergate office and his headquarters suite at the Democratic convention in Miami that summer. . . . Finally, at a meeting in Florida on March 30, Mitchell, according to Magruder, approved a $250,000 budget for Liddy's plan, which had been dubbed "Gemstone" by its cloak-and-dagger originator.

Liddy wasted no time. He had already enlisted the help of James McCord, then working as a bodyguard for Martha Mitchell and as a security consultant protecting the CRP offices. Hunt, with whom Liddy had worked on the Ellsberg break-in, recruited his friends from Miami.

To pay the recruits and to finance purchase of the necessary equipment, Liddy eventually drew a total of $199,000 in cash from Hugh Sloan, Maurice Stans's deputy in the committee's finance office. . . .

On Sunday, May 28, McCord and the four men from Miami broke into the Democratic headquarters in the Watergate office building and installed electronic bugs in the phones of Larry O'Brien's secretary and of O'Brien's deputy, R. Spencer Oliver. They left undetected. The bugs sent radio signals across the street to the Howard Johnson motel, where they were monitored by Alfred Baldwin III, another former FBI agent. But when the transcripts of these phone conversations reached Magruder and Strachan—and later, by Magruder's account, John Mitchell—they were judged worthless. Liddy and his team planned another break-in, to tap O'Brien's own phone and thereby prove that their operation was worth the extraordinary amount of money the committee was paying for it. That second break-in, on June 17, resulted in the arrest of McCord and the Miamians, and subsequently of Liddy and Hunt. . . .

### Document 2: Nixon Speaks on the Watergate Issue[11]

*Richard Nixon and his administration ignored questions that were raised about the break-in, especially after the burglars' ties to the White House were revealed. Nixon reportedly remarked that the incident was a "third-rate bur-glary" and deserved no comment. As the months passed, more questions were raised about White House involvement and whether the president knew about or authorized the burglary. After some of the Watergate burglars and conspirators pled guilty and others were convicted, the United States Senate created a special committee to investigate presidential campaign activities. Senator Sam Ervin, a Democrat of North Carolina, chaired the committee, and it became known as the Ervin Committee. Gradually, more information began to emerge about the "dirty tricks" activities of the 1972 campaign and the payoff of the Watergate burglars. In April 1973, White House counsel John Dean began cooperating with the Wa-tergate prosecutors. Throughout April, Nixon allowed White House staff to ap-pear before the committee, and the White House announced that Nixon had no prior knowledge of the affair. Finally on April 30, 1973, Nixon made his first of-ficial statement about the whole affair; a portion of the speech is printed below.*

Good evening:

In recent months, members of my Administration and officials of the Com-mittee for the Re-Election of the President—including some of my closest friends and most trusted aides—have been charged with involvement in what has come to be known as the Watergate affair. These include charges of illegal activity during and preceding the 1972 Presidential election and charges that responsible officials participated in efforts to cover up that illegal activity.

The inevitable result of these charges has been to raise serious questions about the integrity of the White House itself. Tonight I wish to address those questions.

Last June 17, while I was in Florida trying to get a few days rest after my visit to Moscow, I first learned from news reports of the Watergate break-in. I was appalled at this senseless, illegal action, and I was shocked to learn that em-ployees of the Re-Election Committee were apparently among those guilty. I immediately ordered an investigation by appropriate Government authorities. On September 15, as you will recall, indictments were brought against seven defendants in the case.

As the investigations went forward, I repeatedly asked those conducting the investigation whether there was any reason to believe that members of my Ad-ministration were in any way involved. I received repeated assurances that there were not. . . .

Until March of this year, I remained convinced that the denials were true and that the charges of involvement by members of the White House Staff were false. . . . However, new information then came to me which persuaded me that there was a real possibility that some of these charges were true, and suggesting further that there had been an effort to conceal the facts both from the public, from you, and from me.

As a result, on March 21, I personally assumed the responsibility for coordinating intensive new inquiries into the matter, and I personally ordered those conducting the investigations to get all the facts and to report them directly to me, right here in this office. . . .

At the same time, I was determined not to take precipitate action and to avoid, if at all possible, any action that would appear to reflect on innocent people. I wanted to be fair. But I knew that in the final analysis, the integrity of this office—public faith in the integrity of this office—would have to take priority over all personal considerations.

Today, in one of the most difficult decisions of my Presidency, I accepted the resignations of two of my closest associates in the White House—Bob Haldeman, John Ehrlichman—two of the finest public servants it has been my privilege to know.

I want to stress that in accepting these resignations, I mean to leave no implication whatever of personal wrongdoing on their part, and I leave no implication tonight of implication on the part of others who have been charged in this matter. . . .

Whatever may appear to have been the case before, whatever improper activities may yet be discovered in connection with this whole sordid affair, I want the American people, I want you to know beyond the shadow of a doubt that during my term as President, justice will be pursued fairly, fully, and impartially, no matter who is involved. This office is a sacred trust and I am determined to be worthy of that trust. . . .

For the fact that alleged improper actions took place within the White House or within my campaign organization, the easiest course would be for me to blame those to whom I delegated the responsibility to run the campaign. But that would be a cowardly thing to do.

I will not place the blame on subordinates—on people whose zeal exceeded their judgment and who may have done wrong in a cause they deeply believed to be right.

In any organization, the man at the top must bear the responsibility. That responsibility, therefore, belongs here, in this office. I accept it. And I pledge to you tonight, from this office, that I will do everything in my power to ensure that the guilty are brought to justice and that such abuses are purged from our political processes in the years to come, long after I have left this office. . . .

. . . It is essential that we let the judicial process go forward, respecting those safeguards that are established to protect the innocent as well as to convict the guilty. It is essential that in reacting to the excesses of others, we not fall into excesses ourselves. . . .

We must maintain the integrity of the White House, and that integrity must be real, not transparent. There can be no whitewash at the White House. . . .

### Document 3: Nixon's Troubles Deepen; Sirica Named Man of the Year[12]

*During the rest of 1973, relations between the president and Congress became more and more strained. White House counsel John Dean testified before the Ervin Committee, beginning with a seven-hour opening statement. He provided minute details of his meetings with the president. In preparation for his testimony, Dean told investigators that he discussed the cover-up with President Nixon at least thirty-five times. Various members of the administration appeared and testified before the committee, but the true bombshell came on July 13, 1973, when Alexander Butterfield, a former aide to Nixon, told the committee that, starting in 1971, Nixon had all conversations and telephone calls in his office recorded, a fact that was known to no one in the administration except for the technicians who operated the system.*

*Following this revelation, legal battles began between Nixon, Congress, and a special prosecutor as to who could have access to the tapes. Nixon refused to release them, claiming "executive privilege." After losing several court battles over control of the tapes, Nixon released some of the tapes.*

*At the beginning of January 1974,* Time Magazine *named Judge John Sirica as its Man of the Year. Sirica was the judge in Washington, D.C., who presided over the trial of the Watergate burglars and handed down very stiff sentences when they were convicted. This action probably began the unraveling of the cover-up being conducted by the White House. When a mainstream publication like* Time *took such action, it revealed that Nixon was clearly in trouble throughout the country. Below is an excerpt from Sirica's memoirs regarding his role in the entire episode.*

There were times during the five years I was involved in the Watergate proceedings that I thought the case would never come to an end. On more nights than I now care to remember, I would wake up after only a few hours of sleep, my heart racing, wondering what new stumbling block President Nixon and his associates would throw in front of me the next day.

I have been asked on many occasions why I didn't just quit after the trial of the original Watergate burglars, and how I made the decisions I did at crucial junctures in the case. I've really never had any easy answers for those questions, and now, looking back on the whole ordeal almost seven years after the original burglary, about all I can say is that my instincts wouldn't let me walk away until I had completed the job.

Those who know me well sometimes remark that I keep my worries to myself. That is exactly what I had to do during Watergate. Unfortunately, as the case dragged on, my thoughts became increasingly painful to conceal.

As I have mentioned before, if it had not been for the Republican party, I might never have done much better than my father, who died at sixty of a heart attack after years of trying desperately to build a secure life for my mother, my brother, and me. I traveled to various parts of the country in 1940 and 1948 for Republican presidential candidates like Wendell Willkie and Thomas E. Dewey; I was never willing to admit that Willkie didn't stand much of a chance.

I had no money to speak of, and one of the best ways that I knew to make something of myself was through politics. I stuck with the party long enough to see Dwight Eisenhower and his running mate, Richard Nixon, elected in 1952. Without the backing of President Eisenhower and his attorney general, Herbert Brownell, I would never have realized my dream of becoming a federal judge.

But day after day, from 1972 on, I was confronted with new evidence which showed that the Republican party had fallen into less trustworthy hands since the days when I had been active in politics. And though it saddened me to watch the party being hurt as I sent some of its leading figures off to jail, this was obviously something I had to do.

And now, although I still sometimes marvel that we came through that awful mess with our government intact, Watergate is finally over. My initial suspicions that no one but top party leaders could have authorized the burglary were proved true by President Nixon's own tapes. And although our nation went through a trauma which could easily have led to a severe constitutional crisis, I believe the United States is stronger for having successfully weathered that storm.

Had there been no Watergate, wealthy contributors might still be pumping undisclosed millions into political campaigns in hopes of buying favor with elected officials. Now we have an independent Federal Election Commission and a stronger campaign law, which demands that all candidates for national offices disclose their sources of funding in writing. . . .

Most important, Watergate, unlike any previous scandal in our political history, was both a crisis and a reaffirmation of our constitutional form of government. Unlike past episodes of dishonesty in Washington, it was a product not of greed in the usual sense, but of greed for power.

The bugging itself obviously resulted from an attempt to guard against political surprise and electoral defeat. The stupidity of that endeavor was fully revealed in November 1972, when Nixon rolled up one of the biggest victories any presidential candidate in our history had ever won. Yet, before the election, his staff members were worried that defeat would come, so worried that to guard against that remote possibility, they violated the law.

Nixon and his aides did not view their tenure in the White House as a period of stewardship, a trust granted for a fixed term that could be revoked by the popular will. Rather, Nixon and his people were arrogant enough to believe that they should substitute their own judgments for those of the electorate. Some of them believed it was permissible to short-circuit the electoral process by eavesdropping on their opponents. Their lust for power, their arrogance, their raw disregard of the law, of fairness, and of the very constitutional processes that they had sworn to enforce and protect, led them to break the law in order to keep themselves in office. After the arrests at the Watergate, they knew that if the truth were revealed, they would lose their coveted power. They broke the law in the spring and summer of 1972 to hold onto power. And then they broke the law again and again in the fall of 1972 and the spring of 1973 to protect their offices.

The country should take great pride that this naked attempt to thwart the Constitution of the United States—to substitute the will of a few powerful men for the rule of law which we have struggled so long and so hard to win and to protect—was in the end defeated, with the perpetrators driven from office and brought to justice. Yet I can never forget Senator Sam Ervin's observation that "they almost got away with it." I think it's worth asking, Why didn't they get away with it?

Everyone has a tendency to find heroes, to claim that individual acts of decency or bravery or devotion bring about great historical events. But I think the lesson of Watergate is quite the opposite. I firmly believe it was our system of government and our system of law that ended that crisis and saved the very constitutional form of government that gave us that system and those laws.

Take the role of the press, for example. The two young reporters at the *Washington Post*, Carl Bernstein and Bob Woodward, became popular heroes for a time after their work helped keep the pressure of public scrutiny on the unanswered questions in the Watergate case. They deserve the attention and the acclaim, of course. And so does the owner of the *Post*, Mrs. Katharine Graham, for having the courage to let those two young men pursue the Watergate story even when other news organizations were ignoring it. But as important as the *Post* and its officers and reporters were, what is more important is that the *Post* is part of a free press, protected by the Constitution. *Who* emerged in the press to expose Watergate is less important than the fact that our system allows reporters the freedom to do so.

And consider the role of Congress. Sam Ervin, to my mind, represented in his conduct of the Watergate hearings the best traditions of American political leadership. But I believe that had there been no Sam Ervin from North

Carolina, there would have been someone on Capitol Hill capable of and willing to lead the kind of fair-minded investigation Senator Ervin did manage. It is more important that we have an independent legislative branch than that a particular senator or group of senators be seen as heroes.

In the difficult days of 1974, as the Watergate crisis was reaching some sort of breaking point, many in Washington doubted that the often unruly politicians in the House of Representatives could manage an impeachment inquiry that would be seen as nonpartisan and fair. Peter Rodino and other members of the House Judiciary Committee did just that, despite all the efforts by the White House and other defenders of Nixon to provoke the committee into a partisan fight. Peter Rodino deserves enormous credit for his role. But I think the fact that our constitution gives Congress the remedy of impeachment to use against a chief executive who breaks the law is ultimately more important than any one legislator's role.

I feel the same way about the courts. It is more important that we had a totally independent judiciary than that I, or any other judge or group of judges, happened to be presiding over the case.

Naturally, I have a special feeling about the role of the courts in the whole crisis. I feel that without the courts, without their ability to get to the facts, to compel testimony and the production of evidence, the Watergate case might never have been cracked. The press played a critical role, of course, but the press cannot subpoena witnesses, it cannot demand the truth under any penalty other than temporary embarrassment, it can only help force further public attention and investigation.

Not even Congress, standing as a coequal branch of the government, had the ability in its investigative role to resolve conflicting testimony, to force out the whole truth, to render final and enforceable judgments. The congressmen conducting the impeachment inquiry found themselves nearly powerless to demand the kinds of evidence needed to reach a final decision. It was the courts that demanded and got the evidence on which the Judiciary Committee finally acted. Without this evidence, I do not believe the impeachment inquiry would have gotten off the ground.

The judiciary, standing above politics as the enforcer and arbiter of our laws, was the critical branch of government in the resolution of the Watergate crisis. And it is our faith and trust in the law, our devotion to the notion that ours should be a government of laws and not men, that saved us from this scandal.

It was the courts and the law that throughout this crisis could compel that the truth be told. Despite efforts in our executive branch to distort the truth, to fabricate a set of facts that looked innocent, *the court system served to set the record straight.* When the people involved in Watergate lied to the public, nothing could be done. But when they lied to the grand jury, and I should say the *courageous* grand jury that sat for months and months looking into the matter, they were sent to jail. When the president and his aides lied about their own activities, it was our courts and our law that compelled them to produce the best evidence in the case—the presidential tapes—to test their versions of what happened. And when the most powerful men in our government tried to obstruct the law, to ignore it, to frustrate the process of justice, the law itself penalized them. The law and our faith in that law was too powerful for even those powerful men. . . .

I have always felt that no matter how bitter the experience one endures, and surely Watergate was a bitter experience, there are some beneficial lessons to be learned. Watergate taught us that our system is not invulnerable to the arrogance of power, to misdeeds by power-hungry individuals, and that we must always be on guard against selecting such people as our leaders. It taught us that our system of law is the most valuable asset in this land and that it must be nurtured, protected, and respected. . . .

Most important, I hope we have learned the value of citizens who do their duty, who do the work set out for them by our laws and our system of government. . . .

After my sudden heart attack in February 1976, I awoke from a long period of unconsciousness. One of my doctors, Stephen Nealon, was with me in the hospital as I began to realize how close to death I had come and in how much danger I remained. He told me later that I said to him, "If I go out, I'd like to think that I did something for my country."

I think I did do something for my country. I think I did my job as best I could. I think I did my duty as a citizen and as someone fortunate enough to hold a position of public responsibility in our system of government.

### Document 4: Barbara Jordan's Position[13]

*On May 9, 1974, the Judiciary Committee of the House of Representatives began impeachment hearings of Richard Nixon. The committee's charge was to investigate and report to the full House whether enough evidence existed for the House to impeach the president and send the case to the Senate for trial as the Constitution specifies. This was an emotion-charged three months as the committee considered the case. One of the most emotional and influential speeches made during the hearings was on July 25 by Barbara Jordan, a junior Democratic member of the House. She was from Texas and an African American. Her edited speech follows.*

Mr. Chairman:

. . . Earlier today, we heard the beginning of the Preamble to the Constitution of the United States, "We, the people." It is a very eloquent beginning. But when the document was completed on the seventeenth of September 1787 I was not included in that "We, the people." I felt somehow for many years that George Washington and Alexander Hamilton just left me out by mistake. But through the process of amendment, interpretation and court decision I have finally been included in "We, the people." . . .

Common sense would be revolted if we engaged upon this process for petty reasons. Congress has a lot to do: Appropriations, tax reform, health insurance, campaign finance reform, housing, environmental protection, energy sufficiency, mass transportation. Pettiness cannot be allowed to stand in the face of such overwhelming problems. So today we are not being petty. We are trying to be big, because the task we have before us is a big one.

This morning, in a discussion of the evidence, we were told that the evidence which purports to support the allegations of misuse of the CIA by the President is thin. We are told that that evidence is insufficient. What that recital of the evidence this morning did not include is what the President did know on June 23, 1972. The President did know that it was Republican money, that it was money from the Committee for the Re-election of the President, which was found in the possession of one of the burglars arrested on June 17.

What the President did know on June 23 was the prior activities of E. Howard Hunt, which included his participation in the break-in of Daniel Ellsberg's psychiatrist, which included Howard Hunt's participation in the Dita Beard ITT affair, which included Howard Hunt's fabrication of cables designed to discredit the Kennedy Administration. . . .

At this point, I would like to juxtapose a few of the impeachment criteria with some of the President's actions.

Impeachment criteria: James Madison, from the Virginia ratification convention. "If the President be connected in any suspicious manner with any person and there is grounds to believe that he will shelter him, he may be impeached."

We have heard time and time again that the evidence reflects payment to the defendants of money. The President had knowledge that these funds were being paid and that these were funds collected for the 1972 presidential campaign. We know that the President met with Mr. Henry Petersen twenty-seven times to discuss matters related to Watergate, and immediately thereafter met with the very persons who were implicated in the information Mr. Petersen was receiving and transmitting to the President. The words are, "If the President be connected in any suspicious manner with any person and there be grounds to believe that he will shelter that person, he may be impeached."

Justice Story: "Impeachment is intended for occasional and extraordinary cases where a superior power acting for the whole people is put into operation to protect their rights and rescue their liberties from violations."

We know about the Huston [Houston] plan. We know about the break-in of the psychiatrist's office. We know that there was absolute, complete direction in August 1971 when the President instructed Ehrlichman to "do whatever is necessary." This instruction led to a surreptitious entry into Dr. Fielding's office. . . .

The South Carolina ratification convention impeachment criteria: Those are impeachable "who behave amiss or betray their public trust."

Beginning shortly after the Watergate break-in and continuing to the present time, the President has engaged in a series of public statements and actions designed to thwart the lawful investigation by government prosecutors. Moreover, the President has made public announcements and assertions bearing on the Watergate case which the evidence will show he knew to be false. . . .

James Madison, again at the constitutional convention: "A President is impeachable if he attempts to subvert the Constitution."

The Constitution charges the President with the task of taking care that the laws be faithfully executed, and yet the President has counseled his aides to commit perjury, willfully disregarded the secrecy of grand jury proceedings, concealed surreptitious entry, attempted to compromise a federal judge while publicly displaying his cooperation with the process of criminal justice. . . .

If the impeachment provision in the Constitution of the United States will not reach the offenses charged here, then perhaps that eighteenth century Constitution should be abandoned to a twentieth century paper shredder.

Has the President committed offenses and planned and directed and acquiesced in a course of conduct which the Constitution will not tolerate? This is the question. We know that. We know the question.

We should now forthwith proceed to answer the question.

It is reason, and not passion, which must guide our deliberations, guide our debate, and guide our decision.


### Document 5: Judiciary Committee Approves Impeachment Articles[14]

*Near the end of July 1974, the House Judiciary Committee was nearing the conclusion of its deliberations. On July 27, it voted to recommend to the full House that it impeach Richard Nixon on three counts of violating the Constitution.*

### Article 1

RESOLVED, That Richard M. Nixon, President of the United States, is impeached for high crimes and misdemeanours, and that the following articles of impeachment to be exhibited to the Senate:

## Article 1

In his conduct of the office of President of the United States, Richard M. Nixon, in violation of his constitutional oath faithfully to execute the office of President of the United States and, to the best of his ability, preserve, protect, and defend the Constitution of the United States, and in violation of his constitutional duty to take care that the laws be faithfully executed, has prevented, obstructed, and impeded the administration of justice, in that:

On June 17, 1972, and prior thereto, agents of the Committee for the Re-election of the President committed unlawful entry of the headquarters of the Democratic National Committee in Washington, District of Columbia, for the purpose of securing political intelligence. Subsequent thereto, Richard M. Nixon, using the powers of his high office, engaged personally and through his close subordinates and agents, in a course of conduct or plan designed to delay, impede, and obstruct the investigation of such illegal entry; to cover up, conceal and protect those responsible; and to conceal the existence and scope of other unlawful covert activities. . . .

In all of this, Richard M. Nixon has acted in a manner contrary to his trust as President and subversive of constitutional government, to the great prejudice of the cause of law and justice and to the manifest injury of the people of the United States.

Wherefore Richard M. Nixon, by such conduct, warrants impeachment and trial, and removal from office.

## Article 2

Using the powers of the office of President of the United States, Richard M. Nixon, in violation of his constitutional oath faithfully to execute the office of President of the United States and, to the best of his ability, preserve, protect, and defend the Constitution of the United States, and in disregard of his constitutional duty to take care that the laws be faithfully executed, has repeatedly engaged in conduct violating the constitutional rights of citizens, impairing the due and proper administration of justice and the conduct of lawful inquiries, or contravening the laws governing agencies of the executive branch and the purposed of these agencies. . . .

In all of this, Richard M. Nixon has acted in a manner contrary to his trust as President and subversive of constitutional government, to the great prejudice of the cause of law and justice and to the manifest injury of the people of the United States.

Wherefore Richard M. Nixon, by such conduct, warrants impeachment and trial, and removal from office.

## Article 3

In his conduct of the office of President of the United States, Richard M. Nixon, . . . has failed without lawful cause or excuse to produce papers and

In 1974, President Richard Nixon was forced to resign the presidency, the first president to do so in the nation's history. Nixon was on the verge of being impeached for his involvement in the break-in of the Democratic headquarters during the presidential campaign of 1972. Nixon had always engendered strong reactions—both positive and negative—among the American people. Here he tearfully boards the presidential helicopter as he leaves the White House for the last time. The Nixon Library and Museum, National Archives, photo no. WHPO E3386c-35.

things as directed by duly authorized subpoenas issued by the Committee on the Judiciary of the House of Representatives on April 11, 1974, May 15, 1974, May 30, 1974, and June 24, 1974, and willfully disobeyed such subpoenas. The subpoenaed papers and things were deemed necessary by the Committee in order to resolve by direct evidence fundamental, factual questions relating to Presidential direction, knowledge or approval of actions demonstrated by other evidence to be substantial grounds for impeachment of the President. In refusing to produce these papers and things Richard M. Nixon, substituting his judgment as to what materials were necessary for the inquiry, interposed the powers of the Presidency against the lawful subpoenas of the House of Representatives, thereby assuming to himself functions and judgments necessary to the exercise of the sole power of impeachment vested by the Constitution in the House of Representatives.

In all of this, Richard M. Nixon has acted in a manner contrary to his trust as President and subversive of constitutional government, to the great prejudice of the cause of law and justice, and to the manifest injury of the people of the United States.

Wherefore, Richard M. Nixon, by such conduct, warrants impeachment and trial, and removal from office.

## Document 6: The "Smoking Gun" Tape[15]

*Shortly after the Judiciary Committee voted the three articles of impeachment, Nixon released transcripts of tapes of three conversations he had with his aide, H. R. Haldeman, six days after the Watergate break-in. The conversations reveal clearly that Nixon ordered the FBI to cease investigation of the break-in, and other tapes show that he ordered a cover-up of White House involvement in the burglary. These tapes became known as "The Smoking Gun" because reasonable people could no longer believe Nixon was innocent of the charges against him. The eleven Republican members of the committee who voted against the impeachment resolutions now said they would have changed their votes had they known of these tapes in advance. Portions of one of the taped conversations follow. Like most informal conversations, it is a bit difficult to follow, but it reveals what Nixon was doing.*

**Haldeman:** Okay—that's fine. Now, on the investigation, you know, the Democratic break-in thing, we're back to the—in the, the problem area because the FBI is not under control, because Gray doesn't exactly know how to control them, and they have, their investigation is now leading into some productive areas, because they've been able to trace the money, not through the money itself, but through the bank, you know, sources—the banker himself. And, and it goes in some directions we don't want it to go. Ah, also there have been some things, like an informant came in off the street to the FBI in Miami, who was a photographer or has a friend who is a photographer who developed some films through this guy, Barker, and the films had pictures of Democratic National Committee letter head documents and things. So I guess, so it's things like that are gonna, that are filtering in. Mitchell came up with yesterday, and John Dean analyzed very carefully last night and concludes, concurs now with Mitchell's recommendation that the only way to solve this, and we're set up beautifully to do it, ah, in that and that . . . the only network that paid any attention to it last night was NBC . . . they did a massive story on the Cuban. . . .

Nixon: Right.

Haldeman: That the way to handle this now is for us to have Walters call Pat Gray and just say, "Stay the hell out of this . . . this is ah, business here we don't want you to go any further on it." That's not an unusual development, . . .

Nixon: What about Pat Gray, ah, you mean he doesn't want to?

Haldeman: Pat does want to. He doesn't know how to, and he doesn't have, he doesn't have any basis for doing it. Given this, he will then have the basis. He'll call Mark Felt [later identified as "Deep Throat," the person who was the leak to the *Washington Post*] in, and the two of them . . . and Mark Felt wants to cooperate because. . . .

Haldeman: Ah, he'll call him in and say, "We've got the signal from across the river to, to put the hold on this." And that will fit rather well because the FBI agents who are working the case, at this point, feel that's what it is. This is CIA.

Nixon: But they've traced the money to 'em.

Haldeman: Well they have, they've traced to a name, but they haven't gotten to the guy yet.

Nixon: Would it be somebody here?

Haldeman: Ken Dahlberg.

Nixon: Who the hell is Ken Dahlberg?

Haldeman: He's ah, he gave $25,000 in Minnesota and ah, the check went directly in to this, to this guy Barker.

Nixon: Maybe he's a . . . bum.

Nixon: He didn't get this from the committee though, from Stans.

Haldeman: Yeah. It is. It is. It's directly traceable and there's some more through some Texas people in—that went to the Mexican bank which they can also trace to the Mexican bank . . . they'll get their names today. And (pause).

Nixon: Well, I mean, ah, there's no way . . . I'm just thinking if they don't cooperate, what do they say? They they, they were approached by the Cubans. That's what Dahlberg has to say, the Texans too. Is that the idea?

Haldeman: Well, if they will. But then we're relying on more and more people all the time. That's the problem. And ah, they'll stop if we could, if we take this other step.

Nixon: All right. Fine.

Haldeman: And, and they seem to feel the thing to do is get them to stop?

Nixon: Right, fine.

Haldeman: They say the only way to do that is from White House instructions. . . .

Nixon: . . . You open that scab there's a hell of a lot of things and that we just feel that it would be very detrimental to have this thing go any further. This involves these Cubans, Hunt, and a lot of hanky-panky that we have nothing to do with ourselves. Well what the hell, did Mitchell know about this thing to any much of a degree?

Haldeman: I think so. I don't think he knew the details, but I think he knew. . . .

Nixon: Good. Good deal! Play it tough. That's the way they play it and that's the way we are going to play it.

Haldeman: O.K. We'll do it.

Nixon: Yeah, when I saw that news summary item, I of course knew it was a bunch of crap, but I thought ah, well it's good to have them off on this wild hair thing because when they start bugging us, which they have, we'll know our little boys will not know how to handle it. I hope they will though. You never know. Maybe, you think about it. Good! . . .

Nixon: When you get in these people when you . . . get these people in, say: "Look, the problem is that this will open the whole, the whole Bay of Pigs thing, and the President just feels that" ah, without going into the details . . . don't, don't lie to them to the extent to say there is no involvement, but just say this is sort of a comedy of errors, bizarre, without getting into it, "the President believes that it is going to open the whole Bay of Pigs thing up again. And, ah because these people are plugging for, for keeps and that they should call the FBI in and say that we wish for the country, don't go any further into this case," period!

Haldeman: OK

Nixon: That's the way to put it, do it straight. (Unintelligible).

Haldeman: Get more done for our cause by the opposition than by us at this point.

Nixon: You think so?

Haldeman: I think so, yeah.

## Document 7: Nixon Resigns[16]

*With everything running against him, Richard Nixon decided to resign from the presidency, the first president ever to do so, rather than to face a trial in the Senate, which virtually every friend and advisor told him he could not win. Therefore, on August 8, 1974, he went before the American people on television to tell them of his decision.*

. . . In all the decisions I have made in my public life, I have always tried to do what was best for the Nation. Throughout the long and difficult period of Watergate, I have felt it was my duty to persevere, to make every possible effort to complete the term of office to which you elected me.

In the past few days, however, it has become evident to me that I no longer have a strong enough political base in the Congress to justify continuing that effort. As long as there was such a base, I felt strongly that it was necessary to see the constitutional process through to its conclusion, that to do otherwise would be unfaithful to the spirit of that deliberately difficult process and a dangerously destabilizing precedent for the future.

But with the disappearance of that base, I now believe that the constitutional purpose has been served, and there is no longer a need for the process to be prolonged. . . .

I have never been a quitter. To leave office before my term is completed is abhorrent to every instinct in my body. But as President, I must put the interest of America first. America needs a full-time President and a full-time Congress, particularly at this time with problems we face at home and abroad.

To continue to fight through the months ahead for my personal vindication would almost totally absorb the time and attention of both the President and the Congress in a period when our entire focus should be on the great issues of peace abroad and prosperity without inflation at home.

Therefore, I shall resign the Presidency effective at noon tomorrow. Vice President Ford will be sworn in as President at that hour in this office. . . .

By taking this action, I hope that I will have hastened the start of that process of healing which is so desperately needed in America.

I regret deeply any injuries that may have been done in the course of the events that led to this decision. I would say only that if some of my judgments were wrong, and some were wrong, they were made in what I believed at the time to be the best interest of the Nation. . . .

So, let us all now join together in affirming that common commitment and in helping our new President succeed for the benefit of all Americans. . . .

## Document 8: President Ford Pardons Nixon[17]

*When Richard Nixon resigned from the presidency, the Watergate affair seemed to be over. However, the new president, Gerald Ford, about a month after taking office, shocked the nation by granting Nixon a full pardon. Some observers believed it cost Ford a chance to be elected to the presidency in his own right in 1976.*

Ladies and gentlemen:

I have come to a decision which I felt I should tell you and all of my fellow American citizens, as soon as I was certain in my own mind and in my own conscience that it is the right thing to do. . . .

After years of bitter controversy and divisive national debate, I have been advised, and I am compelled to conclude that many months and perhaps more years will have to pass before Richard Nixon could obtain a fair trial by jury in any jurisdiction of the United States under governing decisions of the Supreme Court. . . .

In the end, the courts might well hold that Richard Nixon had been denied due process, and the verdict of history would even more be inconclusive with respect to those charges arising out of the period of his Presidency, of which I am presently aware. . . .

As President, my primary concern must always be the greatest good of all the people of the United States whose servant I am. As a man, my first consideration is to be true to my own convictions and my own conscience.

My conscience tells me clearly and certainly that I cannot prolong the bad dreams that continue to reopen a chapter that is closed. My conscience tells me that only I, as President, have the constitutional power to firmly shut and seal this book. My conscience tells me it is my duty, not merely to proclaim domestic tranquility but to use every means that I have to insure it. I do believe that the buck stops here, that I cannot rely upon public opinion polls to tell me what is right. I do believe that right makes might and that if I am wrong, 10 angels swearing I was right would make no difference. I do believe, with all my heart and mind and spirit, that I, not as President but as a humble servant of God, will receive justice without mercy if I fail to show mercy.

Finally, I feel that Richard Nixon and his loved ones have suffered enough and will continue to suffer, no matter what I do, no matter what we, as a great and good nation, can do together to make his goal of peace come true.

Now, therefore, I, Gerald R. Ford, President of the United States, pursuant to the pardon power conferred upon me by Article II, Section 2, of the Constitution, have granted and by these presents do grant a full, free, and absolute pardon unto Richard Nixon for all offenses against the United States which he, Richard Nixon, has committed or may have committed or taken part in during the period from July (January) 20, 1969 through August 9, 1974.

In witness whereof, I have hereunto set my hand this eighth day of September, in the year of our Lord nineteen hundred and seventy-four, and of the Independence of the United States of America the one hundred and ninety-ninth.

## Notes

1. "Telegram From the Embassy in the Soviet Union to the Department of State, October 16, 1962," *U.S. Department of State, Foreign Relations of the United States, 1961-1963*, XI, 47–49.

2. "President John F. Kennedy's Speech Announcing the Quarantine Against Cuba, October 22, 1962," *Public Papers of the Presidents: John F. Kennedy, 1962* (Washington, D.C.: Government Printing Office, 1963), 806–9.

3. "Telegram From the Embassy in the Soviet Union to the Department of State, October 23, 1962," *Foreign Relations of the United States*, v. XI, 170–71.

4. "Memorandum From Attorney General Kennedy to President Kennedy about his meeting with Soviet Ambassador Dobrynin, October 24, 1962," *U.S. Department of State, Foreign Relations of the United States, 1961-1963*, XI, 175–77.

5. "Khrushchev Letter to President Kennedy, October 24, 1962," and "Telegram from the Department of State to the Embassy in the Soviet Union, October 25, 1962," *U.S. Department of State, Foreign Relations of the United States, 1961-1963*, XI, 185–87, 198.

6. "Statement by Soviet Ambassador Zorin, United Nations Security Council Meeting, October 25, 1962," and "Statement by Ambassador Stevenson to U.N. Security Council, October 25, 1962," *United Nations, Security Council Official Records*, 25 October 1962 (New York, 1962), 6–11.

7. "Memorandum From ABC Correspondent John Scali to the Director of the Bureau of Intelligence and Research," undated, *U.S. Department of State, Foreign Relations of the United States, 1961-1963*, XI, 227.

8. "Telegram From the Embassy in the Soviet Union to the Department of State, October 26, 1962," and "Message From Chairman Khrushchev to President Kennedy (the Second Letter), October 27, 1962," *U.S. Department of State, Foreign Relations of the United States, 1961-1963*, XI, 235–41, 257–60.

9. "Message From Chairman Khrushchev to President Kennedy, October 28, 1962," *U.S. Department of State, Foreign Relations of the United States, 1961-1963*, XI, 279–83.

10. John J. Sirica, *To Set the Record Straight: The Break-in, the Tapes, the Conspirators, the Pardon* (New York: W.W. Norton & Company, 1979), 43–48. Reprinted by permission of SLL/Sterling Lord Literistic, Inc. Copyright by John Sirica Jr.

11. Richard Nixon, Address to the Nation About the Watergate Investigations, April 30, 1973, *Public Papers of the Presidents of the United States: Richard Nixon, 1973* (Washington, D.C.: Government Printing Office, 1975), 328–33.

12. Sirica, *To Set the Record Straight*, 297–303. Reprinted by permission of SLL/ Sterling Lord Literistic, Inc. Copyright by John Sirica Jr.

13. "A President is Impeachable If He Attempts to Subvert the Constitution," Speech by Representative Barbara Jordan, July 25, 1974, Reprint by permission of Congresswoman Barbara Jordan Archives–Texas Southern University.

14. Articles of Impeachment Adopted by the Committee on the Judiciary, July 27, 1974, Committee on the Judiciary, House of Representatives, *Impeachment of Richard M. Nixon, President of the United States*, 92nd Congress, 2nd session, House Doc. No. 93-339, August 20, 1974, 2–9.

15. The Smoking Gun Tape, June 23, 1972, Richard M. Nixon Watergate Tapes, National Archives and Record Service.

16. Nixon's Resignation Speech, August 8, 1974, *Public Papers of the Presidents of the United States: Richard Nixon, 1974* (Washington, D.C.: Government Printing Office, 1975), 626–30.

17. President Ford's Pardon of Richard Nixon, September 8, 1974, *Public Papers of the Presidents of the United States; Gerald R. Ford, 1974* (Washington, D.C.: Government Printing Office, 1975), 101–3.

# 10

# High Tech

*T*HE LAST QUARTER OF THE TWENTIETH *century brought as much change, espe-cially in technology, as any period in history. The idea of "high tech" became so common that few questioned its origins or its efficacy. Beginning in the late 1970s—but especially in the 1980s—the personal computer (the PC) became available to virtually everyone. With its growing popularity, the Internet became ubiquitous in American society. Virtually any information available in the world was only a few clicks away. The value of all the information on the Internet was questionable, to be sure, but this new resource became a way of life.*

*Other technological developments came in rapid succession, much of it stim-ulated by the information learned from space exploration—the technology of the exploration itself and the knowledge that it brought to the world. By the end of the century, the Internet was only the tip of the iceberg. Cellular phones con-nected people wherever they were. Even in his wildest dreams, Chester Gould, the creator of the* Dick Tracy *comic strip, would never have believed that his "wrist radio" would become so common that even pre-teenage children would have their own phones. Not only did these phones provide voice communication, they also brought pictures and text on a device as small—or smaller—than a deck of cards. Digital cameras muscled out most negative photography. And those photos—from phones or cameras—could be loaded into personal comput-ers and transmitted within nanoseconds to people around the world. Without question, the technology revolution—as well as the 24-hour news cycle discussed later in this chapter—had a worldwide impact and increased American influ-ence abroad.*

## Part A: Personal Computers

### Background

*Computers became pervasive in business after World War II, but they were large and expensive machines available only to the government and the largest corporations. Beginning in the 1970s, the personal computer (PC), including the Apple, burst on the scene and within ten to fifteen years, a small computer suitable for personal or home use had more power than the original giant machines. PCs continued to drop in price until they were within the range of all except the very poor.*

*Once the PC had become ensconced in the home, it was further enhanced by the development of the Internet—the World Wide Web—which could search billions of records and bring up almost any information conceivable. To call the current era an "information age" is an understatement.*

*One of the most remarkable things about computers and the Internet is the age that most of the innovators were when they began. Most of them were still in high school or in their early twenties.*

*This chapter reviews the development of the PC in a few brief documents. Although the Internet is probably just as important, its development is not covered here.*

### Questions

In reading these documents, the student should ask and answer several questions to put these activities in the proper context.

1. What were the features of the personal computer that made it so attractive—even addictive—to the average person?
2. Is it fair to give credit to just a handful of individuals for the development of the PC, or were they just the visible portion of the new technological wave?
3. What was so important about miniaturization to the development of the PC?
4. Which element was more important to the development of the PC, hardware or software?
5. Why did IBM and Microsoft emerge as the dominant producers of hardware and software?

### Document 1: The Emergence of Personal Computers

*In January 1983,* Time *magazine, which usually names a "Man (or Person) of the Year," named the computer the "Machine of the Year" for 1982. One could argue, perhaps, that when such a prestigious magazine recognized its importance, then the PC had really come into its own.* Time *was not the only magazine to comment on the importance of the personal computer. An article in* The Nation *explained that politically left-leaning people were suspicious of the power of computing. This article, published the same year as the* Time *"Machine of the Year" selection, gave its take on the computer.*

Computers, recently apotheosized as "Machine of the Year" by *Time*, would not win any popularity contests on the left, where the prevailing view is that they are the Enemy.

The left's bill of particulars runs along familiar lines. For the most part, computers are manufactured by monopolistic corporations. They accelerate the trend toward centralization of power and authority. Governments use them for surveillance of their citizens—particularly political dissidents—and corporations use them to standardize operations, which often dehumanizes the workplace. A priesthood of systems analysts and engineers speaking an arcane language has grown up to tend these expensive machines. Computers eliminate jobs in the offices of the First World and lead to the creation of sweatshops in the Third World. The domination of computer technology by the industrialized countries raises the specter of a world divided between information haves and have-nots.

All these charges ignore the introduction of cheap microcomputers in the early 1970s, the proliferation of companies making them and their increased availability to home users and small businesses. These developments have radically changed the picture. Most organizations, no matter how small, can now afford computing power. The cost of computing has decreased by 250 times in the past eighteen years. Systems that cost $1 million in 1965 can be had for $4,000 today, and this downward trend will continue.

Even though multinational corporations will acquire ever larger and more powerful machines, because of the availability of small computers they will no longer dominate the information field. The difference between having a computer and not having one is far greater than the difference between having a relatively slow desk-top model and a fast main-frame unit. Furthermore, by joining a computer network, a small computer can gain access to the largest and fastest models in the world.

Microcomputers also provide an impetus toward decentralization. In most large corporate and government bureaucracies, computing is still in the hands of data-processing specialists, but the wider availability of computers to nonspecialists may strip this priesthood of its power. And just as the office photocopier gave rise to document leaks and other breaches of security, so the desk-top computer could provide whistle-blowers with greater access to electronic records.

Most of the technological problems have been solved, and future innovations will be intellectual, involving higher mathematics, logical analysis and linguistics—that is, they will come in the area of programming. And these intellectual products cannot be as easily monopolized as technological improvements.

Most people who buy a home computer will never write a program. Software capable of taking on an increasing range of analytical and administrative tasks is readily available. All anyone has to do is analyze the task at hand—whether it is combing mailing lists for potential contributors or comparing oil-company pricing policies for a journalistic exposé—and find the software most suited to accomplish it.

The left should recognize that computers can help us overcome many of the organizational deficiencies that have bedeviled our efforts to build and control our own institutions. For instance, they can help us improve the operations of publishing, craft and buyers' cooperatives, and they can streamline fund raising and political organizing.

To assess the larger impact of computers on society, however, it is not enough simply to ask what these machines can do, or be made to do. We must also examine the cultural and political reasons for the growth and power of bureaucracies. For example, we should consider the extent to which the necessity of processing large quantities of paper created the high degree of centralization characteristic of modern states and corporations, and the extent to which control of information on a global scale was crucial to the rise of the multinational corporation. It is conceivable that a network of decentralized units will replace the pyramidal form as the dominant organizational model of Western capitalism. If that happens, bureaucratic and political systems of control will be radically different from those that have grown up during the past two centuries in the West.

From the keyboard of my Apple II computer, the benefits of microcomputing look enormous. It enables me to live outside the city, and I can use my computer as a typewriter, a filing system and an accounting system. I can also use it to prepare copy for phototypesetting. I have recently taken up my education in mathematics where it stopped twenty years ago, and am now exploring differential calculus, formal logic and new computer languages. For the first time in my life I feel that I am close to the frontiers of intellectual endeavor. And I am not an expert in electronics or a trained programmer.

No one seems to have foreseen the spread of microcomputers, beginning with hobbyists and kids playing Pac Man, and ending with secretaries using these units instead of I.B.M. typewriters in offices across the land. Although I.B.M. did join the fray with its own home computer 1981, its model relied on hardware and software designs, bought from small companies (in many cases now big companies) that sprouted like mushrooms during the 1970s.

The introduction of the microcomputer has been chaotic and an uncontrolled process. There are now a variety of systems and a ferociously competitive marketplace, more akin to a Middle Eastern bazaar than to orderly markets of advanced capitalist societies. Some people believe that this process will soon be less chaotic, and that I.B.M., Xerox and Digital Equipment will soon be back on top of the heap. That remains to be seen. What interests me is whether an Apple II could ever have been produced either by a major corporation or by a state enterprise.

In my view, it could not have been. The developments that made Apple IIs, TRS-80s and other microcomputers so useful were not, and probably could not have been, centrally planned. They were a result of thousands of separate ideas (including a lot of false starts and blind alleys), not all of which were able to survive in the marketplace.

And, contrary to the hopes of socialist theorists, all attempts at building socialism in this century have been highly centralized and bureaucratic. This is as true for the British and Scandinavian social democracies as it is for the centrally planned economies of Eastern Europe and Asia. Neither the managers of socialism nor the strategists of I.B.M. or Honeywell have any incentive to produce a cheap personal computer. The big producers of consumer electronics are more interested in centralized systems—for example, cable television, which gives consumers choice of output but no control of input—than in personal computing.

The political, sociological and economic factors that made California and New England the nurseries of the microcomputer age are more complex than is generally recognized. They have to do with local entrepreneurial behavior, the emergence of a counterculture in the 1960s, high concentrations of affluent and technically skilled consumers, the proximity of universities and research institutions high levels of defense investment. Not one of these things, on its own, could have produced the microcomputer. But it is possible that the microcomputer would not exist in its present form if any had been missing.

The potential of the microcomputer revolution is not understood. Nor do we know what its full impact will be. There is an urgent need, however, for the left to examine the wide-ranging effects of personal computers, even though that may involve questioning assumptions regarded as Holy Writ. In order to begin this examination, activists on the left must get their hands on computers, familiarize themselves with their uses and limitations and prepare themselves for the inevitable changes ahead.

### Document 2: Dan Bricklin, Inventor[2]

*As indicated in the previous document, many people were involved in the development of the PC. So many of the pioneers of the personal computer revolutions were young people—some, but not all, from privileged backgrounds—who could afford an education at prestigious colleges and universities. Often, just tinkering in their garages they came up with original and innovative ideas that took the PC far down the road to widespread public acceptance. Dan Bricklin, along with his friend Bob Frankston, invented a spreadsheet that would do very extensive calculations in a matter of seconds. It was named VisiCalc (visible calculator), and, while it was not an overnight success, it gradually gained acceptance and did reasonably well. Dan Bricklin explained how he conceived of the idea, and he explains why it was not patented at the time.*

The idea for the electronic spreadsheet came to me while I was a student at the Harvard Business School, working on my MBA degree, in the spring of 1978. Sitting in Aldrich Hall, room 108, I would daydream. "Imagine if my calculator had a ball in its back, like a mouse. . . ." (I had seen a mouse previously, I think in a demonstration at a conference by Doug Engelbart, and maybe the Alto.) And ". . . imagine if I had a heads-up display, like in a fighter plane, where I could see the virtual image hanging in the air in front of me. I could just move my mouse/keyboard calculator around, punch in a few numbers, circle them to get a sum, do some calculations, and answer '10% will be fine!'" (10% was always the answer in those days when we couldn't do very complicated calculations. . . .)

The summer of 1978, between first and second year of the MBA program, while riding a bike along a path on Martha's Vineyard, I decided that I wanted to pursue this idea and create a real product to sell after I graduated.

Eventually, my vision became more realistic, and the heads-up display gave way to a normal screen. The mouse was replaced in the first prototype in the early fall of 1978 by the game paddle of the Apple II. You could move the cursor left or right, and then push the "fire" button, and then turning the paddle would move the cursor up and down. The R-C circuit or whatever in the Apple II was too sluggish and my pointing too imprecise, so I switched to the two arrow keys of the Apple II keyboard (it only had 2) and used the space bar instead of the button to switch from horizontal movement to vertical.

I created that first prototype over a weekend on an Apple II I borrowed for the purpose from Dan Fylstra of Personal Software, later our publisher. I wrote it in Apple Basic. It did not scroll, yet, but it had the columns and rows and some arithmetic.

To design exactly how the program would work, I'd create state diagrams, showing what would happen when you pressed various keys. . . .

Fylstra, being an MBA himself so he appreciated the value of financial forecasting, made a deal with my friend Bob Frankston and me. The basic deal was worked out during dinner at Joyce Chen's Restaurant in Cambridge, MA, near Fresh Pond. Bob and I would create the program, as authors, and Dan's company, Personal Software, would publish it. This "author/publisher" arrangement became popular in the PC industry. Personal Software would pay us 35.7% of their net gross for normal sales, and 50% for OEM [Original Equipment Manufacturer] sales. This was based, as I remember it, on an initial price for the product equivalent to the TI [Texas Instruments] calculator . . . that was popular at Harvard ($34.95, I think), less some costs, and then splitting the profit by some percentage. The OEM sale percentage reflected the difference in costs and other factors.

Bob and I decided to form a company under which to do business. Software Arts, Inc., was born, incorporating on January 2, 1979.

### Document 3: Wozniak Speaks[3]

*Stephen Wozniak, along with his partner Steven Jobs, invented the Apple Computer, which truly revolutionized computing for the average person. They created a simple, affordable personal computer. In 2008, Wozniak recalled some of his early activities and thoughts on the computer revolution. This is from an interview with the Wharton School of Business at the University of Pennsylvania known as Knowledge@Wharton.*

Knowledge@Wharton: What got you originally excited about math and science?

Steve Wozniak: I can't pin it down to an exact date. I wanted to be like my dad. I'd go to where he worked and see him hook up wires and get signals to appear on screen.

But I wasn't sure I was cut out for that. And then about third grade my mom practiced flash cards with me in the kitchen. [In] school, we had a multiplication test and I beat the girls. And the teacher said that was really strange. So I started thinking, "Woah, I'm good at math."

That was probably the first time I can remember thinking, "Hey, there's something I'm good at."

Knowledge@Wharton: From reading *iWoz* one gets the sense that you were an "accidental entrepreneur" rather than someone who set out to found a company.

Wozniak: I was very skilled at a certain kind of computer design. I could just do magic that other people couldn't do. I knew I'd build a computer when it was possible. That year [1975] was the year it was possible.

As far as starting a company—no, I was so happy with my job [as an engineer at Hewlett Packard]. I could have been an engineer for the rest of my life, had enough income to be happy and designed things in my spare time.

That was what drove me. I wanted to show off my design techniques—and help the world get to this big, revolutionary point. . . .

**Knowledge@Wharton:** You mention in the book that you and Steve Jobs "were always different people . . . right from the start." How so?

**Wozniak:** We were very similar in certain ways, like the values [we had] as we grew up in our high school. We were both leaning towards the counter-culture. Steve was more a part of it and I was more mainstream—feet on the ground, none of these drugs and all that.

Steve and I would have conversations and get excited about the same technological possibilities.

I was more the humorist; I was more the expert designer. But we shared common interests. We were friends for eight years [before] we started Apple.

It was after we started Apple that we defined our roles.

Steve's role was to learn how to run every aspect of a company, to be an executive at every level. I had already come to a very non-political point in my life where I didn't want to run a company, because I didn't want to push other people around, act superior to others, tell them what they had [done] was lousy. So I just said: I will do my engineering as well as it can be done, and I'll do that perfectly. I won't tromp into other people's territory.

So we went into two parts of the company. And from then on, we were very much working on different things almost forever.

Steve did an excellent job of melding the marketing, operations and technology. He understood which technology was good and what people would like.

It was a weird situation. He couldn't design a computer—he was never a designer or a programmer—but he could understand it well enough to understand what was good and what was bad.

I think that was more important—having one mind that could put the entire landscape together. Whereas I just did one piece excellently.

**Knowledge@Wharton:** It sounds like the two of you complemented each other in those early years.

**Wozniak:** Yes, I believe that with families and friends it's much better if you're closer in personalities and values. In the case of Steve Jobs and I, we've always remained extremely close in values, with just different personalities.

In a company, you've got so many things that have to come together [that] it's difficult for one person to do it. If you have one person at the top who is very thoughtful, you get the excellence and the integrity of one mind conceiving how the company works.

Steve had the spirit: "We're doing something new. We're going to be doing something great." [He had] the drive [to do] everything from publicity to finding the last part in the world when we desperately needed one and calling stores and talking them into selling our computers. He was excellent at that.

**Knowledge@Wharton:** Looking back, how do you think your life would have been different if you had never met Steve Jobs?

**Wozniak:** I think that I would have been as humorous and happy as I am, and have the good-quality friends and the things that I love in life.

I don't know if I would have ever had the money to have a house. We were in our twenties when we started Apple. We had no savings account. We didn't own a car. We didn't make anything like the money you need to buy a house in California, even then. We didn't have any experience in business. If I got some money, I'd go out and buy some electronic parts and build something.

The company I worked for, Hewlett Packard, was a big part of my life back then. They had such incredible values [that respected] engineering. I wanted to work there forever. Hewlett Packard has changed over time. It's not the same company that makes high quality products that other engineers use like they used to.

So, I probably would have had some ups and downs. But I was so excellent at what I did electronically, I would have always had a job.

**Knowledge@Wharton:** How do you think Steve Jobs' life would have been different if he had never met you?

**Wozniak:** It's hard to guess, because it could be either way.

He had those skills of organization and the drive to start a company. [If he had never met me] he would have done it with somebody else's product.

He might have wound up just exactly where he is: a top, wealthy businessman who created great products. He really wants to move the world forward and not be just another company making the same old thing to earn a buck.

That was exactly what he wanted the day I met him when we were in high school. He admired these top people in the world—the Newtons and the Shakespeares. He thought that there were very few people who had really changed life forever for all of us. He obviously wanted to be one of them.

And me, I wanted to create interesting technical products and write great programs.

I got interrupted more than he did. I mean, Apple's success and the publicity and fame made it very difficult for me to get the time to just work in my own garage and put things together.

**Knowledge@Wharton:** You mentioned that, in the early days, you and the other people in the Homebrew Computer Club were excited about how the computer would benefit humanity. To what extent has that happened?

**Wozniak:** The computer has benefited humanity 10 times more than we ever could have imagined.

We were all loners. We were people who knew technology but didn't have money. We didn't imagine ever owning or even using a computer.

We [saw that] there were silicon parts coming that were going to make it possible to build computers that human beings like us could afford. Those of us who knew how to program a computer would write programs and would solve problems that our company couldn't solve on their huge mainframe computers. And we'd be changing the world more than CEOs.

Look at how inspiring that is.

As we were building these things we didn't really know for sure it would happen, [whether] it would be affordable. Now everything is on a computer. Every desk has a computer doing business stuff all day.

For entertainment, we have all of our movies and music [on the computer]. Whoever thought a song would fit on a computer back when we started the Homebrew Computer Club? Entertainment is a huge part of our life that the computer has taken over.

And communication—I don't even have to say anymore—from instant messaging to e-mail and video chats.

The blending of your computer and the cell phone is so amazing. There weren't cell phones back then. When we started Apple, in the United States you still could not legally own your own telephone.

It's difficult to think too far into outer space and be correct.

*The emerging personal computer was so pervasive at the end of the twentieth century that it almost dominated American life. One of its most practical uses was as a way for more and more people to work from home. This photo is an example of a contemporary home office with a desktop personal computer. Photo provided by author.*

Knowledge@Wharton: Are there ways in which you think the progress has fallen short? Are there things that the computer ought to be doing for us but the technology just hasn't reached there yet?

Wozniak: Yes. We keep talking about artificial intelligence: "The computer's going to be like a thinking brain. It's going to be more powerful than our brain." That has not happened.

[The] graphics look real and the voice quality sounds like a real human voice. Computers [have become more] human in that way, but not the way a real human being is.

If you're dealing with a human being, they look at your face, they notice your condition. They know what words to say, when to talk. They get different ideas to [move the conversation] in different directions.

Artificial intelligence hasn't gone to one on a scale of a hundred to represent a real person who's lived a life and knows who you are and wants to ask questions about your family and your pets.

I think we're way, way behind. [In the Homebrew Computer Club] we envisioned that computers were going to be like the intelligence and the behavior of human beings.

Knowledge@Wharton: Any sense about how far off that day is?

Wozniak: I don't see it ever. . . .

## Document 4: The Future of Computers[4]

*In 1986, a book was published with interviews from several of the pioneers of the personal computer revolution. One interview was with Dr. Gary A. Kildall, the man who created CP/M as the first operating system for the new microprocessor. By 1977, CP/M was the most popular operating system in the PC industry. In 1986, he speculated on the future of computers.*

INTERVIEWER: What do you think will be the future role of computers?

KILDALL: Basically, our technology tends to simplify mechanical processes. That's why computers have been so successful: We take things normally done with cogs, wheels, and relays, and do them with vacuum tubes and then with semiconductors. Look at automobiles, for example. More and more of the processes in the automobile, like in the 1984 Corvette, are being turned over to the semiconductor or its equivalent. When semiconductors take the place of speedometer cables and tachometers, they turn the car into a less expensive and more reliable product that is easier to produce. Computer systems are going through identical changes right now; the hard disk drive is a mechanical device. Because it is mechanical, we know it will eventually go away. We don't know how it will go away, but we know it's a prime target.

Some gadgets and processes will continue to function mechanically, such as wheel bearings on cars, because it's pretty hard to make those from a semiconductor. But many other things in our daily lives will go through the transition from mechanical to electronic. The print industry is a good example; CD ROMs and optical storage are becoming important there now. Computers help to get away from the mechanical processes of printing: running printing presses, laying out and pasting up by hand, setting up the cameras. The semiconductor will take over the mechanical process. But computers won't stop there. Right now they control the production of print but not the actual display of information.

Right now, a very big bottleneck—one of the reasons why the personal computer industry is in the doldrums—is that we have a difficult time thinking about what to do with computers once we get past spreadsheets and word processing. We don't know what the next step is. We're stuck.

It goes back to what I was saying about the dependence of programming on beliefs rather than reason. Ultimately the problem is that we, as a society, took the big computers that we understood and applied their underlying architecture, languages, and concepts to the development of microcomputers. As we move toward using computers as controllers, we will find that communication between processors will become more important than the processes they are carrying out. Then we will be forced to change the way we code. That will be a very slow evolutionary process.

INTERVIEWER: So the future really depends on our ability to free ourselves from old patterns of thinking?

KILDALL: I felt strongly in the early days of microprocessors that they should be used primarily as embedded processors, talking to one another and coordinating the transition from mechanical to electronic processes. That's where I felt the computer industry was going. I saw them as replacements for random logic, with engineers being the primary users of these small machines. In fact, someone from Lawrence Livermore Labs suggested I develop a BASIC for the microcomputer—that was probably in 1974. I told him that was the most stupid idea I had ever heard. Who would want to do a BASIC for microprocessors when they were being put into such tools as inventory-control systems, cathode-ray tube displays, and word processors? Obviously, I was wrong about that. It turns out that one of my thesis students, Gordon Eubanks, did very well with C BASIC, as did Paul Allen and Bill Gates.

Somehow we have to break loose from the ways we think about microcomputers if we want to stimulate advances in computers. People at home don't want to buy another computer system. They bought one and there was no real use for it. They don't want to be ripped off again. And we're talking about 95 percent, not 5 percent, of computer users. There are 16 million television sets sold every year; there's no reason why we shouldn't sell 16 million gizmos with embedded microprocessors.

INTERVIEWER: You mentioned CD ROM a minute ago, and its potential impact on the printing industry. Will it have any other role in the evolution of computers?

KILDALL: Optical storage will clearly pull the computer industry in a new direction. When we worked with floppy disks, we were just making little machines out of big machines. And we haven't yet gone a whole lot farther than that today.

Optical storage is completely different. We're not talking about computing anymore; we're talking about putting information into people's hands. People now might buy personal computers because somebody else told them they should, but with optical storage, people will buy computers because they want the information. Computers will be competing more with publishing.

INTERVIEWER: So information could take the form of an electronic encyclopedia, like the one you're putting on CD ROM? How do you envision the design—both the retrieval system and the enhancements?

KILDALL: I take the concept for the initial product, get an overall idea of what I want to do, and start coding right from the nucleus, letting it expand in the direction it flows. As long as I don't limit the fundamental data structures, features can be added. We did a videodisc called the Knowledge Disc, which carried over nicely into CD ROM retrieval systems. All text was done with bit-mapped fonts at the pixel level. A very nice side effect of working with pixels is that pictures go into the whole thing very cleanly and nicely. So we don't have to go back and do total redesigns of anything to add images to text that already exists on the CD ROM.

It's a problem if the design doesn't let you add features at a later date. If you have to redo a program, the hours you spend can cause you to lose your competitive edge. A flexible program demonstrates the difference between a good designer and someone who is just getting a piece of code out.

Right now, we're going full speed ahead just to blast as many people out of the water as we possibly can. We're hoping to be ready by the first part of 1986. Economically, we have no choice but to go fast and to use this technology. It's the best. Then we make sure that we license the rights to it.

INTERVIEWER: Are knowledge systems part of where you see the home market going?

KILDALL: Yes. People don't usually go home to work. Some tasks people do at home are related to work, like keeping track of taxes or running a little home business. But mostly they go home to relax. I think games and entertainment are valuable. We have a lot of trouble figuring out how to entertain people at home. And TV does a good job right now; competing with "Dynasty" is extremely difficult.

One possible computer application is something to help kids study. My fourteen-year-old daughter is taking some hard courses and she needs help studying. Computer applications like that would give me a direct benefit: My child does better and that helps her in the future. That's clearly an important area for development.

Another area for development is providing general information about selected subjects, such as medicine. People go to doctors for many reasons. Some are psychological. But sometimes they only want medical information. It costs a lot to go to the doctor, and if people had less expensive ways to access that data, they would. Here's another example: When I want a car, I try and shop L.A., San Francisco, and San Jose to get the best prices. But it's virtually impossible to get the facts about car dealers because people who don't want you to be able to shop like that are protecting the information. I'd be a candidate for that information because it could save me thousands of dollars, not to mention a lot of time. I'd pay a reasonable amount to get it.

We want to develop applications that will give people a definite economic advantage if they buy them. That's why we went for an encyclopedia as the first CD ROM application. Everyone knows encyclopedias usually cost about $1,000. Someone can rationalize buying a computer that has the encyclopedia, if it's in the same price range as the printed encyclopedia.

INTERVIEWER: How friendly will this machine be?

KILDALL: Well, I don't think it's a matter of friendliness, because ultimately if the program is going to accomplish anything of value, it will probably be relatively complex.

Some people suggest that machines would be friendlier if input could be in a natural language. But natural language is probably the worst kind of input because it can be quite ambiguous. The process of retrieving information from the computer would be so time-consuming that you would be better off spending that time getting the information directly from an expert.

Expert systems will be the ultimate in user friendliness. But we're a long way from having the expert in the box. The doctor-in-a-box, although a phenomenal product, is incredibly complex. It would have to be perfect. Someday, we'll have programs like that. I just don't know how far off they are, and there are lots of problems to solve along the way, but that's the fun part.

## Document 5: The Evolution of Computers[5]

*Born in London, England, in 1944, John Page began working with computers as a teenager. In 1970, he joined Hewlett-Packard (HP). He provided technical support for HP for four years in London, Geneva, and other parts of Europe. In 1974, he moved to Cupertino, California, the headquarters of HP, to manage worldwide technical support for the HP 3000 computer. Later, he moved into research and development in software, where he developed the Image Database Management System. While with HP, Page studied artificial intelligence at Stanford University and did his postgraduate work in computer science.*

*Page left Hewlett-Packard in 1980 and teamed up with Fred Gibbons and Janelle Bedke to start Software Publishing Corporation. Working out of his garage, Page developed Software Publishing's first product, which later became PFS: FILE. He reflected in the interview on how computers have changed.*

INTERVIEWER: In the years you've worked in the computer field, you must have developed some impressions about how computers have changed over time.

PAGE: Computers are stuck in a rut because nothing new has happened in quite a while. The market has sucked us into overly complicated systems and the fault is mostly IBM's. All the "new" features being installed are borrowed from mini-computers and mainframes. Each successive generation of the IBM PC is more complicated and harder to use than the last. The PC is fast regressing to being a minicomputer and IBM may even be successful in turning it back into a main-frame. The old complexities are coming back and the elegance is being washed out. Even the poor old Macintosh is being battered because it doesn't have all the things that managers of management-information systems love. Macintosh designers will probably be forced to put all those complexities into the Mac, too. It's sad that such things will probably happen sooner or later.

The net result is that personal computers are becoming more popular with people in large corporations who used to use mainframes. They're beginning to embrace the personal computer but still trying to treat it as if it were a mini-computer. It's not; it's a giant personal calculator and we've lost sight of that.

INTERVIEWER: Do you think this trend toward complexity will continue?

PAGE: I hope not. I've got a feeling the personal computer will develop in two directions. There will be personal desktop business computers, which use all the same tools the mainframe required, like COBOL and all that horrible stuff. MIS managers are still programming in COBOL, just the way they did twenty years ago. If you try to give them anything at all innovative, they just say, "No. Make life simple. I want my dear old COBOL language."

I'm also optimistic that the industry will return to making proper personal computers that people will be able to use, like the original Apple. They will be lower in price, have more power, and be easier to use. We're derailed right now. Developing that true personal computer will breathe some life into the whole industry.

INTERVIEWER: What role do you think computers will play in the future?

PAGE: They will always play an absolutely central role in everything. Information is a fundamental fabric of the universe. Information about things is almost as valuable as the things themselves, and computers process information. I was reading a very interesting article in Business Week about the power of information. People are beginning to realize how important having good information is. One man who has billions of dollars invested said he honestly believed the information about his investments was more valuable in real dollars than the investments themselves.

Think about it—that means that information is a resource or a raw material as valuable as gold. Think about how careful you would be in using it, processing it, and protecting it. That is just what computers do so well. The prediction that computers will permeate every aspect of society will absolutely come true.

INTERVIEWER: In what particular fields will computers develop?

PAGE: I see two significant areas that are still ripe for development in the next ten to fifteen years. One will be to get personal computers back on track and make them genuinely personal—the size of a book and $300. That will happen within two years.

The second area is communications. Right now, the way information is moved about is crude—slow, cumbersome, and expensive. Better ways are beginning to happen because of the competition and new technology. The breakup of AT&T is interesting from this point of view.

INTERVIEWER: What impact will computers have on communications?

PAGE: Communications will be faster and cheaper. Information is only useful if you can get it, and right now you can't. I don't think people realize how poorly informed they are. Once they realize the many possibilities, they won't believe they ever lived without complete information.

Access to information will make a profound difference in our lives. For example, you will be able to communicate by digitized voice. Remember the messages you left for me the first time you called? You got my answering machine, which is a computer. Your voice was digitized and stored on disk in a computer that serves the entire building. I can forward your message to somebody else, and I can alter those messages and forward them from my home. I just dial into the system using the push-button phones. Without computers, that would not be possible. Soon we'll have a home version that will cost about $300—answering machines will actually be able to talk to each other. That's the scary part.

INTERVIEWER: What kind of information do you think we'll have access to in the future?

PAGE: Let me give you an example of what could be available. Let's say you want to go some place in Europe for your vacation. You want good drinking water, a nice hotel on the beach with a lap pool, and hang gliding nearby. How on earth would you find out all those things? You might find the good hotel near a beach in travel brochures, but they probably don't mention the things that interest you most, like hang gliding and a lap pool. Unless you happen to see a photo, you have virtually no information on which to base your vacation decision. So you end up going back to the same vacation spot each year because you can't find a new place that's any better. There are many other examples and tons of information we don't have about almost every aspect of our lives.

INTERVIEWER: Do some of these information resources exist today?

PAGE: Yes. For example, I'm a flier. My ability to fly has been enhanced 20 to 30 percent because I can log onto the weather service and get briefings off my computer. The other way to get the weather is much less efficient. I call the weather service and I may be put on hold for half an hour. If I do get through, I may not hear the weather correctly or I may make a mistake copying it down. I just type in my request on my computer and there it is—fast and accurate. And funny thing—I have better information than the controllers do. It's actually better because I tap straight into the National Weather Service in Boulder, Colorado, whereas they get their weather information through some antiquated system the federal government can't afford to update. I still have to phone in my flight plans, but that will change soon so I can file them on line.

### Document 6: The Software King[6]

*The other side of the PC revolution is the development of software—the instructions that tell the computer what to do. As a piece of hardware, the computer is useless unless it knows what it should do; software must give it instructions. One of the earliest and most successful of those who recognized this was Bill Gates who, along with his partner, Paul Allen, created the company known today as Microsoft. Gates and Allen, childhood friends, got into the software business early, and through luck and brilliant early insight, got into the development of software that today has made Microsoft the most successful company in the world. In his book of 1995, updated in 1996, Gates tells how he and Allen began to tinker with computers when they were still in high school.*

I wrote my first software program when I was thirteen years old. It was for playing tic-tac-toe. The computer I used was huge and cumbersome and slow and absolutely compelling.

Cutting a bunch of teenagers loose on a computer was the idea of the Mothers' Club at Lakeside School in Seattle. The mothers decided that the proceeds from a big rummage sale should go to installing a terminal and buying computer time for the students. Letting students at a computer was a pretty progressive idea in the late 1960s—and a decision I'll always be grateful for.

The computer terminal didn't have a screen. To play, we typed in our moves on a typewriter-style keyboard and then sat around until the results came chug-chugging out of a loud printing device. We'd rush over to take a look and see who'd won or decide on a next move. A game of tic-tac-toe that would take thirty seconds with a pencil and paper might eat up most of a lunch period. But who cared? There was just something neat about the machine.

I realized later that part of the appeal must have been that here was an enormous, expensive, grown-up machine and we, the kids, could control it. We were too young to drive or do any of the other things adults could have fun at, but we could give this big machine orders and it would always obey.

Computers are great because when you're working with them you get immediate results: You know right away whether your program works. It's feedback you don't get from many other kinds of activity. The feedback from simple programs is particularly unambiguous. To this day it thrills me to know that if I can get the program right it will always work perfectly, every time, just the way I told it to. Experiencing this thrill was the beginning of my fascination with software.

As my friends and I got more confident, we started to mess around with the computer, speeding things up when we could or making the games more difficult. One of my friends at Lakeside developed a program in BASIC that simulated Monopoly play. BASIC (Beginner's All Purpose Symbolic Instruction Code), as its name suggests, is a relatively easy-to-learn programming language we used to develop increasingly complex programs. My friend figured out how to make the computer play hundreds of games really fast. We fed it instructions to test out various methods of play. We wanted to discover what strategies won most. And-chug-a-chug, chug-a-chug-the computer told us. . . .

A whole generation of us computer guys, all over the world, dragged that favorite toy with us into adulthood. We caused a kind of revolution—peaceful, mainly—and now the computer has taken up residence in our offices and in our homes. Computers have shrunk in size and grown in power as they've dropped dramatically in price. And it's all happened fairly quickly. Not as quickly as I once thought it would, but still pretty fast. Inexpensive computer chips now show up in engines, watches, antilock brakes, fax machines, elevators, gas pumps, cameras, thermostats, treadmills, vending machines, burglar alarms, and even talking greeting cards. School kids today are doing sophisticated things with personal computers that are no bigger than textbooks but that outperform the largest computers of a generation ago.

The single shift that has had the greatest effect on the history of communication took place about 1450, when Johann Gutenberg, a goldsmith from Mainz, Germany, invented movable type and introduced the first printing press to Europe. (China and Korea already had presses.) That event changed Western culture forever. Before Gutenberg all books were copied by hand. Monks, who usually did the copying, seldom managed more than one text a year. It took Gutenberg two years to compose the type for his first Bible, but once that was done, he could print multiple copies.

The printing press did more than just give the West a faster way to reproduce a book. Until it came on the scene, life had been communal and nearly unchanging despite the passing generations. Most people knew only what they had seen themselves or been told. Few people strayed far from their villages, in part because without reliable maps it was often nearly impossible to find the way home. As James Burke, a favorite author of mine, put it: "In this world all experience was personal: horizons were small, the community was inward-looking. What existed in the outside world was a matter of hearsay."

The printed word changed all that. It was the first mass medium. For the first time knowledge, experiences, and opinions could be passed on in a portable, durable, easily available form. As the written word extended the population's reach far beyond the village, people began to care about what was happening in the wider world. Printing shops sprang up in commercial cities and became centers of intellectual exchange. Literacy was a significant skill that revolutionized education and changed social structures.

Before Gutenberg there were only about 30,000 books on the entire continent of Europe, nearly all of them Bibles or biblical commentary. By 1500 there were more than 9 million books, on all sorts of topics. Handbills and other printed matter affected politics, religion, science, and literature. For the first time, people outside the canonical elite had access to written information.

The global interactive network will transform our culture as dramatically as Gutenberg's press did the Middle Ages.

Personal computers have already changed our work habits, but it is the evolving Internet that will really change our lives. As information machines are connected on the Internet, people, entertainment, and information services suddenly become accessible. As the Internet's popularity and capability increase, you'll be able to stay in touch with anyone, anywhere, who wants to stay in touch with you and to browse through any of thousands of sources of information, day or night. A little further along, you'll be able to answer your apartment intercom from your office or answer any mail from your home. Your misplaced or stolen camera will send you a message telling you exactly where it is, even if it's in a different city. Information that once was difficult to retrieve will be easier and easier to find.

Computer manufacturers didn't see the microprocessor as a threat, though. They just couldn't imagine a puny chip taking on a "real" computer. Not even the scientists at Intel saw their chip's full potential. To them, the 8080 represented nothing more than an improvement in chip technology. And in the short term the computer establishment was right. The 8080 was just another incremental advance. But Paul and I looked past the limits of that new chip and saw a different kind of computer that would be perfect for us, and for everybody—personal, affordable, and adaptable. It was absolutely clear to us that because the new chips were so cheap they would soon be everywhere.

We saw that computer hardware, which had once been scarce, would soon be readily available and that access to computers would no longer be subject to a high hourly charge. It seemed to us that people would find all kinds of new applications for computing if it was cheap. Then software would be the key to delivering on the full potential of these machines. Paul and I thought that Japanese companies and IBM would likely produce most of the hardware. We believed we could come up with new and innovative software. And why not? The microprocessor would change the structure of the industry. maybe there was a place in the new scheme of things for the two of us.

### Part B: News All the Time—The 24-Hour News Cycle

### Background

*Concurrent with development of personal computers was satellite technology—yet another result of space exploration—that made this instant communication available to all. Television was beamed around the world so that what was happening in Bangkok could be seen in Bangor as it was happening. Live broadcasts were no longer a novelty; instead they were expected.*

*Into this environment stepped an entrepreneur from Atlanta, Georgia, who revolutionized television as we know it. Ted Turner began by beaming a local Atlanta television station to satellites and broadcasting on cable television systems so that everyone in the world with cable access could watch baseball, news, and drama from Atlanta, Georgia. Twenty-five years before, this would have been considered science fiction.*

*In 1980, Turner went one step further and revolutionized television news broadcasts. He envisioned a television station that would broadcast news reports live twenty-four hours per day. Many of his critics thought he was delusional and ridiculed him. Turner had one advantage: he had the resources to put his idea into practice without reliance on the usual financial institutions. His invention, CNN—Cable News Network—within only a few years became the standard that just about everyone was trying to emulate. The story of the creation and the early years of CNN is fascinating, but competition soon developed.*

### Questions

In reading these documents, the student should ask and answer several questions to put these activities in the proper context.

1. Was Ted Turner a visionary or just lucky?
2. Did CNN and its imitators improve news broadcasts, or did they cheapen the news by focusing on the sensational?
3. Has the influence of CNN and other cable news companies been exaggerated, considering that their total viewership is such a small portion of the American—and world—population?

4. Based upon their success in the early years, will 24-hour news broadcasts become "old hat" and fade away—or will their influence continue to grow to the point that the traditional networks may cease broadcasting news altogether?
5. What has been the overall influence of the cable networks?

### Document 1: How CNN Began[7]

*The founding president of CNN, Reese Schonfeld, explained how he became acquainted with Turner and the initial meeting between the two of them that led to the creation of CNN.*

When I first met Ted, he was running this dinky little independent television station in Atlanta. The Superstation was just a dream. I thought, who would ever want to put Ted's station on their cable system? I was just like all the other wise guys, but I should've known better. In 1974, only 35 percent of the country was able to watch any independent television station. Sixty-five percent of the country had nothing to watch but the networks. Ted reached out to the 65 percent, middle America, and freed them from network triopoly.

By the time I saw him in 1976 at the INTV [Independent Television News Association] convention in Vegas, I'd started ITNA. We were struggling, but we knew we had a winner. Ted was in the same place. My ITNA independent station owners were a pretty colorful bunch. . . . They were the guys who got their kicks out of Ted's anti-news rants. I believed Ted's rants, but I had never taken him seriously about anything else.

Therefore, I was doubly surprised when in September 1978 I got a phone call from Ted Turner. "Reese," he says, "I want to do a twenty-four-hour news network. Can it be done, and will you do it with me?" I say, "Sure: It's what I've been waiting for, for twenty years."

People still ask: "Whose idea was CNN? Yours or Ted's?" So far as I know, it was Gerry Levin's. He conceived of it as an opportunity for HBO, the Time-Life division that he ran. The year was 1977. . . .

. . . Regardless of whose idea CNN was, and who wound up owning it, it was Ted Turner who had the balls to start it.

. . . Lots of people were talking about a twenty-four-hour news network, but Ted called me first. He knew me from ITNA, knew what ITNA was doing, and knew it was successful. So he called.

I flew down to Atlanta, paying my own expenses—I would not be beholden to Ted. He met me at the airport in his little Toyota. It was one of his affectations. No limos. No big cars for Ted. He saved money on everything, he even flew coach.

We drove back to the same building where I had visited Ted four years before. The building looked as decrepit as ever, but the office was spruced up. It seemed bigger, more organized. Ted introduced me to Bob Sieber, the head of TBS research and the house intellectual. . . .

Ted opens by saying he is going to call the news company the "Cable News Network." He says, "It will be the only thing I ever own that doesn't have 'Turner' on it." He is making sure that everyone in cable identifies with CNN and that CNN belongs to the cable industry. It will be their thing.

Ted is frank. He still doesn't want to do news, but he says it is the only form of programming left open to him. He would rather do sports, but ESPN has preempted that. He would rather do movies, but HBO has preempted that. He would rather do entertainment programming, sitcoms, dramas, and quiz shows, but the networks own all that. He will settle for news because that's where the opportunity lies. To quote George Washington Plunkett, Ted "seen his opportunities, and he took 'em." . . .

He turns his attention elsewhere. "Do you believe in stars?" Ted asks. He's not talking about astrology, he's talking about "name talent." "Yeah;" I say. "Who do you think we can get?" he asks. "Dan Rather?" I reply. Ted asks, "Who's Dan Rather?" "The CBS anchorman-in-waiting," I tell him. "One of the five top names in TV news." . . .

"How much would he cost?"

"A million dollars a year."

"A million dollars a year just to have a guy read the news?" "A million dollars a year to get a guy away from CBS network."

Ted thinks about it for a minute, or maybe less. Suddenly, he says, "Well, I just offered Pete Rose a million dollars to play baseball, and he only works half a year." (Just a month before, Pete Rose had come into Atlanta with a forty-three-game hitting streak. It was broken on his second night in town. But the hitting streak games had brought in 76,000 people . . .)

Having settled on personnel, Ted moves on to location. "Can we do it in Atlanta?"

Now it's my turn to think for a minute. Traditionally, television news comes out of New York and Washington. Atlanta is just a four-man bureau. I tell Ted that anchoring from Atlanta would add a couple of million dollars a year in costs and require a lot of satellite dishes. Ted ignores the costs.

"How many satellite dishes?"

"Seven."

"Is that all?" Ted's already envisioning the row of satellite dishes outside our headquarters that will immediately grab the attention of the media world. No one, least of all me, would ever undervalue Ted's ability to sense PR possibilities.

Machinery comes next. "What do we need in the way of equipment?" he asks. I tell him eight 1-inch tape machines and twelve 3/4-inch machines, but there's waiting time. "Get Gene Wright up here:" Ted calls to Dee Woods, his secretary. Gene is Ted's chief engineer. "Gene," says Ted, "Reese says we need eight 1-inch tape machines and twelve 3/4-inch tape machines. Order them NOW—they're backed up." Gene turns to leave. Ted stops him. "We can cancel them, can't we Gene?" Gene says, "Yes, Ted. We can cancel them."

The most difficult part of forming a cable network is finding a way to reach an audience. That means getting cable systems to agree to put your network on one of their channels. In fifteen minutes, we've settled personnel, location, and equipment. Now Ted turns to the really important stuff. Ted shouts to Dee, "Get me Gerry Levin and Russ Karp." Levin is the power at Time-Life Cable, Karp the head of Teleprompter. Time-Life and Teleprompter are the two biggest cable companies in the country. He tells me, "I'm going to offer each one of them one-third of CNN, but CNN will be based in Atlanta, we'll control it, and you'll run it."

I know little about obtaining affiliates—that's Ted's business—but I trust him to make the best deals he can. Ted gets through to Karp. Karp's not interested. Gerry's secretary says he'll call back. I ask Ted if CNN is a definite go. He replies he'll be going to the Western Cable Show in December. He'll run it past the cable industry, and then get back to me.

On the plane back, I review the meeting in my mind. Despite the exhilaration, all of Ted's talk, all of Ted's actions, nothing's been settled. Ted has made sure he can cancel the tape machines. Ted has not yet committed to CNN. Beneath the wacky razzle-dazzle, Ted is a cautious man.

## Document 2: "Terrible Ted"[8]

*Ted Turner had always been a colorful and controversial man. When he began CNN, many stories surfaced about his exploits. The following is a typical example.*

Pioneers and innovators are not always outrageous people. But when they are—and Ted Turner is—they can turn progress from an ordinary word in the language into real fun.

Robert Edward Turner III—"Terrible Ted," "the Mouth of the South"—is the 41-year-old brat, genius, internationally acclaimed yachtsman, multimillionaire-owner of the Atlanta Braves (baseball), and the Atlanta Hawks (basketball). He is now revolutionizing the television-news industry with a 24-hour television-news network fed by a man-made space satellite.

"Cable News Network is as significant as anything in this quarter of a century as far as journalism goes," says Reese Schonfeld, president and chief organizer of Turner's new adventure. Schonfeld is a tough-minded news executive who in 1975 founded a news-swapping cooperative among big city independent TV stations called Independent Television News Association.

Ted Turner's Cable News Network (CNN) may, indeed, change America's way of seeing news. For cable subscribers it will immediately mean a reassessment of their present, pleasant suppertime half-hour news habit with Walter Cronkite, Frank Reynolds and John Chancellor. CNN, for example, will put a strong sports report on for that early evening half-hour. Then, for two hours of prime time—from 8 to 10 p.m. in the eastern time zone—Turner's network will present a full in-depth news roundup. The rest of the 21-1/2 hours of the day will crackle with breaking news, special reports headlines, news features.

This is a sort of news-is-entertainment philosophy that comes naturally to Ted Turner, whose public antics have always made lively copy. Reporters usually fall back on Rhett Butler (or Clark Gable) in describing him. Turner does have a glamorous, tousled, *macho* look; a rougish mustache; and Gable's straight-back posture, at once boyish and decadent.

Even before he was a news maker, Turner was outrageous. He was kicked out of Brown University and out of his fraternity for setting fire to a homecoming float. In 1977 Baseball Commissioner Bowie Kuhn suspended him for one year for a cocktail party crack that Kuhn felt violated recruiting rules. It kept Turner from his regular poker games with his players, but he was still conspicuous at Braves games, sitting in his box, feet propped up on the roof of the dugout, swilling beer, chomping on Red Man chewing tobacco.

Actually Turner left in June of that year for the classic series of yacht races off Newport, Rhode Island, which concluded in September with Turner successfully defending the America's Cup as skipper of the 12-meter yacht *Courageous*. His roughneck, four-letter style in the decorous yachting world got him dubbed "Captain Outrageous."

When Terrible Ted bellowed that a recent *Playboy* interview quoted him out of context, the frazzled interviewer threw up his hands: Turner's "context"—a steady stream of tape-recorded comments gathered over many weeks in many places—transcribed out to 800 typewritten pages.

But Turner's rambunctious ways have, in at least three instances, turned failing companies into money makers. The most recent and spectacular example turned out to be a warm-up exercise for CNN. He bought a dying local TV station and turned it into what he calls a superstation by bouncing its programming of old-movie reruns and sports coverage to the nation via satellite. The station, WTBS, has grown and prospered.

Ted Turner's Cable News Network is expected to do much grander things. Its market people project an audience of 3 million viewers out of the nation's 15 million cable subscribers. This is hardly a threat to NBC, CBS and ABC.

CNN is a much smaller operation—roughly a fourth the size of the networks' news operations in terms of budget, manpower and equipment. But CNN has special strengths. Sam Zelman, the CNN executive producer and a former CBS News official, explains: "When something big happens we'll have it on immediately and stay with it instead of just flashing a bulletin and 'back to entertainment.'" He adds: "'News in process.' That's a phrase we've developed around here to indicate the excitement of things happening instead of being stockpiled for the 7 p.m. news roundup."

Atlanta construction crews spent $8 million renovating a former private club. Its 90,000 square feet contain the studios and corporate headquarters of Turner Broadcasting System. The white-columned, red brick facility is located on 21 acres of tree-shaded land adjacent to the Georgia Tech campus, a mile and a half from downtown.

In the meantime, space has been rented and is being readied for bureaus in Washington, D.C., New York City and London, and plans are proceeding for news bureaus in Los Angeles, San Francisco, Chicago and Dallas.

Daniel Schorr, a former star reporter for CBS News, will be chief of Washington correspondents for CNN, and George Watson will head the Washington bureau—the equivalent position he held at ABC when he signed on with Turner. Evans and Novak, Bella Abzug and Dr. Joyce Brothers all have signed on for regular commentary on Cable News Network.

"Every week we get a press release of who they've hired," exclaims a cable-system manager, "and . . . it reads like a *Who's Who* of the industry."

To understand the nature of Turner's insurgence, one needs a simple review of the origins and growth of cable television. It is believed to have begun, quaintly enough, in 1949, when John Walson, an appliance dealer in Western Pennsylvania, stuck a TV antenna on a mountaintop and connected it to his floor-model television set. Would-be customers were impressed by the clear image on his screen, but few had mountaintop antenna sites. Walson is said to have then offered to connect any set purchased from him to his own mountaintop antenna.

And that, legend has it, is how community-antenna television, or CATV was born. Now hundreds of localities have cable systems which pick up big-city TV signals via antenna and microwave and, for a monthly fee, send them by cable into millions of homes. In addition to a clearer signal, subscribers now usually get more channels than many of their city cousins. The talk now is of 40 to 100 possible station selections, including some programs and movies fed directly into cable systems. Indeed, some large cities now have one or more CATV systems.

But the new era for cable TV (CATV is fading as a label) began in November 1975, when Home Box Office—a programming company had been "bicycling" its video-taped programs of movies and sports and specials to the cable systems—started sending its signal to a satellite. The satellite throws the signal back to earth and cable-system operators "catch" it in dish-shaped antennas aimed at the satellite. At present only half of the 4,100 cable systems have use of such antennas. But the number is increasing fast. And so are the number of programs and networks available to cable systems via satellite. A new world of "narrowcasting" has sprung up, consisting of the transmission of special-interest programs from gospel to Spanish language to black ethnic. And new specialized networks are gestating, such as ESPN of Bristol, Connecticut, which will cover live sports on a nonstop, 24-hour basis.

Ted Turner is a pioneer in all this. His destiny has been locked onto this growing stepchild of television—cable TV—since the mid-1970s, when he started beaming cable programs from his local TV station, first by microwave, then by satellite. But when he put his Atlanta TV station on the bird in December 1976, his motive was to get a wider audience for the live coverage of his Hawks and Braves games. Then he discovered that his superstation's audience of some 7 million persons could be sold to national advertisers at rates approaching network charges.

Turner's Cable News Network is an even bolder venture into new territory. And it has already made him a hero to many who feel TV news needs to break into a wider context.

Turner was already a hero to local sports fans—for buying the Braves when they were about to leave town and for telecasting the games live. But his show-off style and loudmouth ways have not always been well received.

"I love the guy for what he has done for sports in Atlanta," said Atlanta lawyer John M. Kelly, hefting a beer at a local tavern in a sort of toast to Cap'n Ted. But just before he quaffed his brew, he muttered, "I just hope I don't ever have to meet the s.o.b."

### Document 3: Turner Remembers[9]

*In the early years of the twenty-first century, Ted Turner wrote an article for a Washington magazine decrying government policy regarding broadcasting, but in the process, he explained some of how he developed and created CNN. Portions of the article follow.*

In the late 1960s, when Turner Communications was a business of billboards and radio stations and I was spending much of my energy ocean racing, a UHF-TV station came up for sale in Atlanta. It was losing $50,000 a month and its programs were viewed by fewer than 5 percent of the market.

I acquired it.

When I moved to buy a second station in Charlotte—this one worse than the first—my accountant quit in protest, and the company's board vetoed the deal. So I mortgaged my house and bought it myself. The Atlanta purchase turned into the Superstation; the Charlotte purchase—when I sold it 10 years later—gave me the capital to launch CNN.

Both purchases played a role in revolutionizing television. Both required a streak of independence and a taste for risk. And neither could happen today. In the current climate of consolidation, independent broadcasters simply don't survive for long. That's why we haven't seen a new generation of people like me or even Rupert Murdoch—independent television upstarts who challenge the big boys and force the whole industry to compete and change.

It's not that there aren't entrepreneurs eager to make their names and fortunes in broadcasting if given the chance. . . . The difference is that Washington has changed the rules of the game. When I was getting into the television business, lawmakers and the Federal Communications Commission (FCC) took seriously the commission's mandate to promote diversity, localism, and competition in the media marketplace. They wanted to make sure that the big, established networks—CBS, ABC, NBC—wouldn't forever dominate what the American public could watch on TV. They wanted independent producers to thrive. They wanted more people to be able to own TV stations. They believed in the value of competition.

So when the FCC received a glut of applications for new television stations after World War II, the agency set aside dozens of channels on the new UHF spectrum so independents could get a foothold in television. That helped me get my start 35 years ago. Congress also passed a law in 1962 requiring that TVs be equipped to receive both UHF and VHF channels. That's how I was able to compete as a UHF station, although it was never easy. (I used to tell potential advertisers that our UHF viewers were smarter than the rest, because you had to be a genius just to figure out how to tune us in.) And in 1972, the FCC ruled that cable TV operators could import distant signals. That's how we were able to beam our Atlanta station to homes throughout the South. Five years later, with the help of an RCA satellite, we were sending our signal across the nation, and the Superstation was born.

That was then.

Today, media companies are more concentrated than at any time over the past 40 years, thanks to a continual loosening of ownership rules by Washington. . . .

In the 1970s, I became convinced that a 24-hour all-news network could make money, and perhaps even change the world. But when I invited two large media corporations to invest in the launch of CNN, they turned me down. I couldn't believe it. Together we could have launched the network for a fraction of what it would have taken me alone; they had all the infrastructure, contacts, experience, knowledge. When no one would go in with me, I risked my personal wealth to start CNN. Soon after our launch in 1980, our expenses were twice what we had expected and revenues half what we had projected. Our losses were so high that our loans were called in. I refinanced at 18 percent interest, up from 9, and stayed just a step ahead of the bankers. Eventually, we not only became profitable, but also changed the nature of news—from watching something that happened to watching it as it happened. . . .

When CNN reported to me, if we needed more money for Kosovo or Baghdad, we'd find it. If we had to bust the budget, we busted the budget. We put journalism first, and that's how we built CNN into something the world wanted to watch. I had the power to make these budget decisions because they were my companies. I was an independent entrepreneur who controlled the majority of the votes and could run my company for the long term. Top managers in these huge media conglomerates run their companies for the short term. After we sold Turner Broadcasting to Time Warner, we came under such earnings pressure that we had to cut our promotion budget every year at CNN to make our numbers. Media mega-mergers inevitably lead to an overemphasis on short-term earnings. . . .

### Document 4: CNN Succeeds[10]

*Even though CNN had a very difficult time getting started, especially because of the lack of a revenue stream and costs that were not anticipated, the new network eventually succeeded. Probably because of the boldness of Tuner, the company spread around the world and became the standard of news in many countries. A leading opinion magazine described this success in 1991.*

The bus shelter ads say, "CNN: NOW MORE THAN EVER." They have a point. Indispensable and omnipresent during the gulf war, Ted Turner's Cable News Network now looks to be the future of TV news. But what kind of future will it be? The answer depends on which of its many identities CNN is inhabiting at a given time (or place).

For Americans with cable, CNN serves as a video wire service, offering constant updates on the news. It's also an instant delivery system for dramatic footage from around the globe. In a crisis it becomes a kind of video bulletin board where key players can post messages to one another in full view of the world. With its growing international presence, especially in the environments traveled by powerful elites, CNN represents a new dimension of an emerging global culture that is already heavily Americanized. And in countries where the media are still government controlled, CNN offers an image of an open society—modeled, of course, on the commercial aesthetic of American TV.

Any reckoning with CNN must begin with the reasons for its rise, first in the United States and then internationally. The essence of CNN is that it is a twenty-four-hour *news* network, meaning that within the organization there is no other competing programming. By giving its undivided attention to news, CNN gains a large advantage over the news divisions of the three major networks, which are just that—divisions within an increasingly hostile corporate climate, where there's constant pressure to cut costs. CNN is now ready to accomplish in news what the Hollywood movie studios have done in entertainment—parlay the huge U.S. market into a revenue source that can fund the leap into an even larger international market. It is now in the process of executing this strategy, but the networks, with far more experience in the news business, are closing bureaus and trimming staff.

As a global news service CNN will soon have competition—from the BBC, for example—but none of its international rivals will be able to count on the two income streams CNN enjoys in the United States: cable fees and advertising revenues. Whether Turner continues to own it (there are rumors of a Time-Warner takeover), CNN is here to stay, and not only here but abroad as well. In one form or another, it reaches more than 100 countries; it has agreements to share footage with broadcasting agencies all over the world. It *is* the global village, as Marshall McLuhan is reported to have told Turner.

During the gulf war, CNN's triumph became clear to everyone. It achieved its highest-ever U.S. ratings, ranging from 4.7 million to 10.9 million homes in prime-time hours (compared with fewer than 930,000 before the crisis). The networks also saw their ratings jump during the war, but not their revenues. For them, war coverage cut into prime-time hours normally reserved for entertainment shows; the advertisers didn't like it and refused to buy ads. War news, they said, was not the right "environment." Given the gravity of events in the gulf and the high ratings their own coverage was getting, ABC, NBC and CBS had no choice but to stick with their news divisions, even though they were losing millions of dollars a day in canceled ads. After the war, a new round of budget cuts, which executives justified by the costs of war coverage, hit CBS News.

CNN, meanwhile, was not only keeping advertisers but raising its rates, from $3,500 before the war to more than $20,000 for a thirty-second spot. This underlines the essential advantage the network enjoys: Those who watch are watching it specifically for news; those who advertise on CNN have already decided they are willing to advertise on the news. The result is that CNN, despite its lower ratings, can invest more in news gathering than any of its competitors, a gap that is certain to grow given the networks' financial losses during the war.

ABC now has twelve foreign bureaus, NBC thirteen and CBS seven. CNN has fifteen, with more to come.

On the first night of the war, CNN stunned the rest of the news business by maintaining a phone link into Baghdad as the bombs began dropping. While CNN's correspondents gave us their version of the U.S. bombing raid, the networks witnessed a vivid sign of their own demise. About 200 local stations that had agreements with CNN switched to the cable network's war coverage, including many network affiliates that would ordinarily be carrying Dan Rather, Tom Brokaw or Peter Jennings. In Los Angeles CNN was on all four independent stations, in New York it was on three. We got a sudden glimpse of the future: Local stations will retain their own highly profitable news operations and rely on CNN for national or international news. Who needs Rather, Brokaw and Jennings?

CNN feels it doesn't. Up to now, it has refused to create what is known in the trade as "anchor monsters," with their outsized egos and outrageous salaries. This is part of Turner's strategy of producing the news at lower cost and spreading those costs over twenty-four hours of programming. Of course, the costs are lower relative only to the U.S. networks. In comparison with the toned-down atmosphere of TV news in other countries, CNN looks rich, glitzy, exciting, "American." The pricey anchors may be absent, but the zooming graphics, high-tech feel and picture-driven pace of a network newscast are important features of CNN. This makes it another vehicle for the spread of American values, disguised this time as production values.

Here, too, the parallel with the Hollywood studios holds. Against the calculated slickness and thrill-a-minute action of the big budget Hollywood feature, the filmmakers of other nations have a hard time competing. The same kind of competition is already occurring in news, as the polished look and up-tempo pace of CNN force home-grown broadcasters in Europe to adopt similar techniques. As CNN producer Bob Furnad told the *Los Angeles Times* last year, "We live in an environment where people are watching a channel for three minutes and then pressing that clicker. We've got to get them watching and keep them watching."

The ethic of "get them watching and keep them watching" is born of the American experience of competing for ratings in a multichannel commercial system. It is an attitude toward the audience, a manipulative way of viewing others, that is highly developed in the U.S. media but still underdeveloped abroad. In setting out to equalize this differential, CNN evinces a one-world-ism that is considerably less admirable than Turner's well-publicized concern for the environment and world peace. The one world implied by the production values of CNN is one in which the viewer's attention can be held in the same manner everywhere: with dramatic visuals deployed for their oomph value rather than their importance in any explanatory scheme.

This frenzy of the visual, in which U.S. television has long specialized, has political consequences, but no politics per se. In the gulf war, for example, it worked to the advantage of the U.S. military in favoring-repeated showings of laser-guided missiles hitting their targets squarely and spectacularly. But it also dictated that CNN would show scenes of what Iraq said was a civilian shelter destroyed by allied bombs. It would be wrong to suggest that CNN has no politics: It acts in an explicitly political manner when it shows defiance in the face of an attempt to prevent it from airing the footage it wants to broadcast. Thus the live coverage it sent from Beijing in the spring of 1989, when Chinese officials were seen ordering the network to shut down its signal.

We can also expect more arresting irrelevance, like the coverage via satellite of American crews extinguishing oil fires in Kuwait. CNN carried it live on April 10, essentially because it was promotable on the air April 9. It's significant that prior to the gulf war, CNN's biggest ratings included its live coverage of the 1987 rescue of a baby trapped in a Texas well and the 1989 San Francisco earthquake. This fetishizing of the live may seem harmless, but when the next baby—or trapped whale—captivates the whole world rather than the nation, the power to create global distractions will perhaps draw greater scrutiny. Of course, the same power can (and no doubt will) be used to focus worldwide attention on various government atrocities and political crimes, as long as they are highly visual and available to the cameras. Any rumbling of tanks into city streets, as in Tiananmen Square, will be costly to the government involved.

As CNN begins to constitute—rather than merely inform—the global public sphere, its limitations will become global as well. Political deeds that lack a visual dimension may tend to escape world notice because they bore the image-hungry producers at CNN (or its competitors). Consider in this connection the savings and loan scandal and other complex maneuvers of finance; they occur in a political field that is fundamentally nonvisual and thus of negligible interest to those whose task is to "get them watching and keep them watching." It's not that the facts of such scandals are suppressed, but they are relegated to financial news segments and therefore escape the continuous cycles of repetition that are the essence of the CNN style.

Still, it would be wrong to assume that CNN is entirely or even predominantly a malignant influence. There are several ways in which its approach to news is a progressive one. For example, its preference for live coverage means that it will often carry important news conferences, announcements and hearings in their entirety, avoiding the tyranny of the soundbite and the TV reporter's breezy, overly facile wrap-up. Granted, what CNN considers "important" is likely to involve government officials, but there's still a net gain for viewers, who can watch, listen and decide for themselves what they think. Similarly, the refusal to build up the on-air people as stars has a welcome effect: They're not tempted to appoint themselves Secretary of State, as Ted Koppel is inclined to do.

In general, the fact that CNN is on all the time reduces the pressure on any particular half-hour to perform in the ratings, which means that the people on air don't have to blow-dry themselves to perfection or edit out every trace of reality's messiness. Among network news traditionalists, CNN is often said to lack "depth." But in a tradition where "depth" means five minutes for a complex subject rather than two, the charge is hard to take seriously. For a standard thirty-minute newscast, CNN is similar enough to the networks to substitute for them, which it is doing and will continue to do.

CNN's shrewdest move to date has been to target the international elite, those who are involved in the news as actors more than audiences. In newsrooms, international airports, foreign ministries and financial houses around the world, CNN is left on all the time, becoming the medium of record for people whose business it is to monitor the globe. For hotels that cater to international elites, CNN is also a must. It is this elite viewer, more than any mass audience in foreign countries, who gives CNN a potent international presence. In Iraq during the war, CNN was received by satellite, but only by a handful of government offices that could bear the expense of rooftop dishes. Saddam Hussein could watch, but not most Iraqis. This international presence gives CNN the cachet it needs to capture interviews with world leaders and key announcements from the players in a crisis. These can be aired in real time, making the network even more valuable to political actors. That is why desk officers at foreign ministries assign someone to watch CNN around the clock.

In countries where television and the press have been rigidly controlled, there is little doubt that the arrival of CNN means a freeing-up of the media system. Solidarity knew what it was doing in the mid-1980s when it got the Polish authorities to concede a half-hour of CNN on the nightly government newscast. Similarly, opponents of the ruling party in Mexico credit CNN's presence with making it harder for the government to manipulate voting results. For U.S. viewers, there's the fact that CNN is more likely to give "outlaw" leaders like Saddam and Col. Muammar el-Qaddafi a chance to be heard. The reason, of course, is more economic than political. If you've got twenty-four hours a day to fill, why not let Qaddafi have his say?

In its often sloppy, seat-of-the-pants reporting during the gulf war, and in presenting Peter Arnett's censored reports from Baghdad, CNN showed a tendency to shift the editing function toward the audience. The right to sort through information and discount what some people say was removed from TV producers and given to viewers. That's progress, at least on my ledger. What isn't progressive about CNN is the implicit nihilism of picture-driven news and the "keep 'em watching" mentality. In these respects, Turner's triumph will do more for the spread of TV culture than for the cultivation intelligent citizenship around the globe. But CNN bears watching, if for no other reason than that a good portion of world is likely to be watching it too.

### Document 5: CNN Gets Praise[11]

*CNN developed a loyal following even among other journalists who had no affiliation with the network. Two wars in Iraq, intervention in places like Somalia and Bosnia, and the fall of the Soviet Union gave large boosts to the ratings. One journalist who is an unabashed fan of CNN discusses the importance of television in wartime.*

It's happened again: I'm a CNN junkie. I watch the news when I get up, at midday in the newsroom, and any time at night when I can get control of the remote and switch off the cartoons.

I'm like a rubbernecker at an accident. And what do I see? A picture of the Baghdad skyline at dark, lit up intermittently by bombs and gunfire. It doesn't tell me much.

It is merely a backdrop for the urgent voices of CNN's anchors. They appear at regular intervals, after the big screen that shouts WAR IN IRAQ—as if we didn't know—disappears. And if it's not the war logo, I see AT THIS HOUR or LIVE FROM.

I REALLY wish they'd drop the glitzy packaging, say hello and tell the story in calm, no-frills fashion. The words filling the screen, the melodramatic music that accompanies them, exist to promote the network, not to facilitate the coverage. War is somber business, not a public relations opportunity, and in this case it's a war unfolding before our eyes.

The presence of a TV camera changes everything. I watched a newsman interview a pilot just in from a bombing run. They both were nonchalant and upbeat. The reporter sounded like a sportswriter asking questions in the locker room. The pilot came off like a ballplayer after a game where he has performed very well. Something was very weird with this picture—or else it reflected the new face of war, in which bombs and missiles are launched miles from their targets, guided not by pilots but by computers, and death is made an oddly clean event.

Clean was how the war sounded, as the reporters traveling with the troops described it in the first few days. On Sunday, when real losses began, and it was clear this would be no stroll in the park, I heard the anchormen and reporters express genuine surprise—as if they somehow believed American troops were special and were immune to the inevitable losses of war.

Like other news organizations, CNN at first cooperated in not showing the videotape of those American POWs. Bad idea. We deserve a chance to see it. Broadcasting the video might even force the Iraqi government to be honest about the POWs' treatment. CNN finally decided to show just still photos or abbreviated clips of the POWs. They were sensitive to the Bush administration's opposition to showing the tape and concerned with the feelings of the POWs' families seeing their loved ones on TV.

But the same worry has not extended to the families of captured Iraqis. This newspaper, for instance, has published a few pictures of captured Iraqi soldiers, their faces plainly visible. The rules are apparently different when the shoe is on the other foot, and the captured man's family is not within receiving distance of the American press.

No matter what I think, I watch the screen. I keep the set on, even as I go about my chores in the house, washing dishes, feeding the dog. CNN has become elevator music for anxious times. . . .

Now and then I wonder if CNN can keep up this breathless pace forever, or whether a time will come when the network will decide to report other stories while pursuing its war coverage. The world really is bigger than the way Americans, and American journalists, see it. There are other stories to tell.

I wonder if the course of the war would be different if it weren't conducted under this vast electronic microscope—and how the coverage will change as the war gets harder for us, and the battle for Baghdad begins. So far, even with all those reporters, all those photographers stationed with the troops, the bleeding and dying have taken place off stage. Wait until the bloodshed is front and center on the screen. We may lose some of our taste for this invasion then.

### Document 6: Coverage Expands[12]

*Immediately following the launching of CNN, other broadcasters decided to jump on the bandwagon. Eventually, quite a number of news channels (such as MSNBC, CNBC, Headline News, Fox News Channel, and several others), some very specialized, became a part of the broadcasting landscape. The growth of competition for CNN was not always good news for Turner's brainchild, but the proliferation did provide more coverage and more choice for viewers. War clearly was a source of ratings for all of them.*

This time CNN has competition, and the war is boosting CNN, Fox News and MSNBC: Average cable viewership has tripled. Network news is flat.

Significantly, young viewers (18 to 34) are watching cable: a sixfold increase for MSNBC, fivefold for CNN and nearly fivefold for Fox in the past three weeks. Network newscasts are either flat in that demographic or, as in the case of CBS' *Evening News,* down 16%.

That young viewers are turning to cable bodes well for the industry, says Turner networks ratings chief Jack Wakshlag. . . .

While Fox, CNN and MSNBC all have something to brag about, the flag-waving Fox News Channel, viewed as in step with the Bush administration, has benefited the most in overall viewership. "The numbers speak for themselves," Fox News spokeswoman Irena Steffen says. . . .

In the first 19 days of the war, Fox averaged 3.3 million viewers, a 236% increase from the weeks preceding the war. CNN: 2.7 million, up 313%. MSNBC: 1.4 million, up 360%.

By comparison, the Big Three newscasts still draw millions more total viewers than cable news, but only NBC can boast. *NBC Nightly News'* war average is 11.4 million viewers, up 3%. ABC's *World News Tonight:* 9.9 million, down 6%. CBS: 7.5 million, down 15%.

CNN, hoping that a repeat of its glory days would catapult it ahead of top-rated Fox during the war, remains stuck in second place. But executives say that after months of trying to figure out what it is, CNN has re-established itself in war as the pre-eminent cable source of hard news and a clear alternative to Fox. . . .

MSNBC, viewed before the war as the on-the-ropes also-ran, got big sampling but is third. War "is a shot in the arm," MSNBC's Erik Sorenson says. "But it's not a panacea."

### Documents 7–8: Fox Pulls Ahead

*The greatest competition for CNN came from Fox News Channel. FNC was controversial because many critics accused it of being right-wing and virtually a spokesman for Republican leaders. These charges were vehemently denied by Fox executives, but they persisted. Despite the critics, Fox continued to grow at the expense of CNN and MSNBC.*

#### Document 7: Why Fox won[13]

*After more than twenty years of 24-hour news channels, a professional and scholarly journal analyzed the growth of cable news, especially the Fox Channel.*

In a windowless, sprawling newsroom the size of a football field below street-level in Manhattan's Rockefeller Center, scores of youngish writers, editors, producers, and technicians are scurrying about amid a warren of workstations. The pace quickens as prime time in the East, 7 to 11 P.M., approaches. . . .

Three floors above, forty-nine-year-old John Moody sits in a smallish office at an impeccably neat desk before three muted television screens, tuned to CNN, MSNBC, and Fox. Moody is the former Time bureau chief in Eastern Europe and Latin America . . . who runs Fox's day-to-day news coverage. He is pondering the question: How did the upstart and reviled (in many quarters) FNC, which came on the air in late 1996, so quickly and unpredictably triumph in the ratings over its two competitors: CNN, the granddaddy of cable news networks, begun in 1980; and MSNBC, which arrived (early 1996) with a silver spoon in its mouth, put there by its parents, two of the richest companies in U.S. business history (General Electric and Microsoft), and having NBC News (also owned by GE) as a sibling?

Few in the press gave FNC much of a chance in that field of three, Moody recalls, but they hadn't counted on the resourcefulness of Roger Ailes, the network's chairman—named by Electronic Media magazine as the most powerful figure in TV news for the last two years—or on Rupert Murdoch's determination to mount a successful cable news operation. . . . "We had a message," says Moody. "More than a slogan, it's a way of looking at the news business 'fair and balanced' and it rang a chord with American viewers who were tired of being lectured to, of being told that snail darters are more important than jobs. If there's a reason for our success, it's that we speak to people, not down to them."

Despite all evidence to the contrary, Fox executives resent the charge (or pretend to) that Fox is unequivocally a politically conservative network. ("I absolutely, totally deny it," Ailes roared to Brill's Content in 1999. In November, Ailes drew hostile fire when it came to light that he had volunteered policy advice to President George W. Bush.) . . .

The matter of FNC's political orientation or lack of it is, in fact, a sideshow issue in the fierce rivalry raging between CNN and Fox, with MSNBC a distant third. In January 2002, FNC for the first time began attracting larger audiences than CNN. . . . Fox's emergence as the most watched cable news network is the more remarkable because CNN reaches 9 million more homes. (Fox's viewers are also more affluent, with $64,500 average income among 25- to 54-year-olds, versus $62,000 for CNN and $59,500 for MSNBC. And CNN's viewers are a lot older: 61.1 years on average, to Fox's 57.4 and MSNBC's 52.3.) . . .

Robert Lichter, president of the Washington-based Center for Media and Public Affairs and a paid consultant to Fox, says: "I've never been able to figure out how competition makes cars better and television news worse." He means that the struggle to grab viewers is currently dragging the whole cable news environment down. "In other industries, competition creates new and different products. In television, it makes all the products look the same. That's weird."

Weird or not, TV watchers are showing up in ever greater numbers for the nightly circuses on cable news. Phenomenally, the average audience has doubled just in the last two years from 1.1 million to 2.2 million, according to Nielsen Media Research figures. . . .

So how come Fox's schedule is the big crowd-pleaser? The network's success is arguably more the result of packaging and personalities than right-wing politics. "They're fast, they're funny, and they're furious," says Reese Schonfeld, the founding president of CNN. "They're also very slick and beautifully produced." He thinks that Ailes—former adviser to Nixon, Reagan, and Bush One—performed remarkably in overtaking an established brand like CNN in just six years.

### Document 8: Fox evaluated[14]

*Internet sites offered a forum for both supporters and critics of cable news. On the twenty-fifth anniversary of CNN, one of the "bloggers" evaluated the role of Fox News.*

When FOX overtook CNN in the ratings early in this decade, CNN continued to put forth the notion that they were still the network to go to when news really mattered. In the run up to the Iraq war CNN was angling to own the coverage as they had during the first Gulf War, only it turned out that FOX showed that it could indeed mount a credible overseas operation for an extended period. While MSNBC, CNN, and FOX each brought their own unique tools to the table and to get the best coverage one had to be a channel hopper . . . FOX maintained its dominance in the ratings.

It's no great surprise anymore that FOX is the number one cable news channel in terms of total viewers. . . . FOX now dominates the perception that they are the go to network for news. CNN has not only lost the ratings lead, they have also lost the perception lead. . . .

There can be no other conclusion. FOX News is not just the ratings leader but also the channel more people will now turn to first to get a story—any story. They'll turn to FOX before they'll turn to anybody else. A majority of viewers now believe that FOX News is where the news is happening. More viewers have come to identify FOX with News than CNN or MSNBC. That's why they turn to FOX first. FOX News has won the perception war and stolen the title from CNN as *the* name in news. The ramifications of this are huge.

FOX now truly sits in the catbird seat. Their dominance affords them the luxury of having a bad outing and not getting hurt because the viewers believe that FOX is the place to go to for news. For FOX to be dethroned they would have to have a lot of bad outings versus the competition to make viewers think about looking elsewhere for their news. Don't bet on that happening any time soon. This allows them to try new and different things and take chances (like sending Greta to Aruba) because viewing patterns have now been firmly established because the perception has shifted. The title is not for FOX to lose but for someone else to steal.

For CNN and MSNBC matters are worse. They not only have to fight the raw numbers of FOX's lead in the ratings but also the perception that FOX is the place for news. And they have to prove to the viewer that their offerings are better. Even then, as evidenced by what happened April 24th, they'll have to do it consistently for a long time before they can even make a dent in FOX's dominance. FOX can afford to have a bad day. Its competition can't. Perception is very tough to overcome and right now, and most likely for the foreseeable future, more people perceive FOX as the leader in news than they do CNN or MSNBC. . . .

## Notes

1. Christopher Roper, "Microcomputers and the Left," *The Nation*, February 5, 1983, 141–43.

2. "The Idea" and "Why Didn't We Patent the Spreadsheet?" www.bricklin.com. Used by permission of Dan Bricklin.

3. "Steve Wozniak on Apple, Steve Jobs and the Value of a Good Prank," interview online at knowledge.wharton.upenn.edu/article.cfm?articleid=1903. Reprinted with permission from Knowledge@Wharton http://knowledge.wharton.upenn.edu—the online research and business analysis journal of the Wharton School of the University of Pennsylvania.

4. Interview with Dr. Gary A. Kildall, in Susan M. Lammers, *Programmers at Work* (Redmond, Wash.: Microsoft Press, 1986), 57–69. Reprinted by permission from Susan M. Lammers.

5. Interview with John Pages, in Lammers, *Programmers at Work*, 93–109. Reprinted by permission from Susan Lammers.

6. Bill Gates, *The Road Ahead*, rev. ed. (New York: Penguin, 1996), 1–3. "A Revolution Begins," from THE ROAD AHEAD by Bill Gates, copyright © 1995, 1996 by William H. Gates III. Used by permission of Viking Penguin, a division of Penguin Group (USA) Inc.

7. Reese Schonfeld, *The Unauthorized Story of the Founding of CNN* (New York: Cliff Street, 2001), 13–17, from ME AND TED AGAINST THE WORLD by REESE

SCHONFELD. Copyright © 2000 by Reese Schonfeld. Reprinted by permission of HarperCollins Publishers.

8. Joseph B. Cumming, Jr. "Ted Turner: 'Captain Outrageous,'" *The Saturday Evening Post*, October 1980, 67–69. Reprinted by permission of Joseph B. Cumming, Jr.

9. Ted Turner, "My Beef with Big Media," *Washington Monthly*, July/August, 2004. Reprinted with permission from *The Washington Monthly*. Copyright by Washington Monthly Publishing LLC, www.washingtonmonthly.com.

10. Jay Rosen, "The Whole World Is Watching CNN," *The Nation*, May 13, 1991, 622–25.

11. Mary Jo Melone, "Live From Iraq: CNN Filters War's Grim Reality," *St. Petersburg Times*, March 25, 2003.

12. Peter Johnson, "For Cable News, Iraq War is a Clear Victory," *USA Today*, April 9, 2003. From USA TODAY, a division of Gannett Co., Inc. Reprinted with permission.

13. Neil Hickey, "In a Desperate Race for Ratings, the Public Falls Behind," *Columbia Journalism Review* (Jan./Feb. 2003). Reprinted from *Columbia Journalism Review*, January/February 2003 © by Columbia Journalism Review.

14. "In Depth: FOX News Has Won the Perception War (For Now)," June 23, 2005, Inside Cable News, online at http://insidecable.blogsomc.com/2005/06/23/in-depth-fox-news-has-won-the-perception-war-for-now/. Reprinted by permission of insidecablenews.com.

# 11

# The Culmination of the Cold War

<br>

*A*S THE TWENTIETH CENTURY WAS *moving toward its end, the Cold War contin-*
*ued until, abruptly, the Soviet Union collapsed, and the Cold War ended be-*
*fore most people realized what was happening. During the Reagan administra-*
*tion in the 1980s, the Cold War had been re-intensified. In the mid-1980s, the*
*focus was on the Middle East and the revolutions developing in Latin America.*
*While Americans were trying to stop Marxist revolutions in Latin America,*
*changes were occurring in the Soviet Union with the emergence of Mikhail Gor-*
*bachev. After a few years of trying to keep the Soviet Union afloat, the govern-*
*ment was dissolved almost without warning. Few people who had lived through*
*the twentieth century ever expected to see that happen.*

## Part A: Iran Contra

### Background

*Once the Cold War was in full swing after World War II, American foreign and*
*domestic policies were dominated by concern about the Soviet Union's intentions*
*vis-à-vis America and the rest of the world. This concern led to hot wars in Korea*
*and Vietnam and numerous other incidents in the world that appeared to*
*threaten the United States, either directly or indirectly. Fidel Castro's success in*
*bringing a Marxist revolution to Cuba caused various American presidents to be*
*especially alarmed about unrest and revolutionary activity in other Latin Amer-*
*ican countries. In 1979, the Sandinistas, a left-wing organization, toppled the*

government of Nicaragua and began to nationalize various industries in the country, proclaiming it a Marxist state. This was too much for most Americans; it appeared to be another Cuba in the making. A guerilla organization known as the Contras resisted the Sandinistas and was supported by some American groups.

When Ronald Reagan became president in 1981, he was confronted with the problems in Nicaragua and the fundamentalist revolution in Iran, among many other problems. The Iranian radicals had taken more than fifty Americans hostage; this situation contributed to the election of Reagan over Jimmy Carter, who seemed unable to free the hostages. Even after the hostages were released shortly after Reagan's inauguration, other Americans were regularly taken hostage in various Middle Eastern countries.

The combined situations in Iran and Nicaragua were the catalysts for the Iran-Contra Affair. The Reagan administration was determined to aid the Contras in Nicaragua and to assist the "moderates" in Iran who might be able to help free American hostages and bring about a more moderate government in Iran.

As a result of the Democratic-controlled Congress's concern about Reagan's aid to the Contras, the Congress passed legislation known as the Boland Amendment that made it illegal for government agencies to provide aid to the Contras.

The Reagan administration used the National Security Council (NSC) to get around the law, since it was not explicitly covered by the Boland Amendment. Robert McFarlane and John Poindexter raised money from both private and foreign sources to aid the Contras. Marine Lt. Col. Oliver North directed the Contra operation.

A plan was devised to sell arms to Iran even though the United States had a trade and arms embargo against that country. The money raised from these sales was then redirected to bank accounts in Switzerland to which the Contras in Nicaragua had access.

The Iran-Contra Affair became public knowledge in November 1986 when reports, first from Lebanon newspapers and then in other papers, revealed the activities of the members of the NSC. This very complex affair took months to unravel. McFarlane, Poindexter, and North were indicted and convicted of criminal activity. Poindexter and North had their convictions overturned on appeal, even though few doubted their involvement.

More troublesome was determining the involvement of President Reagan and Vice President George H. W. Bush. They were never charged in this case, but the shadow of Iran-Contra remained for years to come. After former State Department and CIA officials pleaded guilty in 1991 to withholding information from Congress, Caspar Weinberger, secretary of defense under Reagan, was charged in 1992 with the same offense. By this time, Vice President Bush had become president. In 1992, he pardoned Weinberger and others who had been indicted or convicted for withholding information or obstructing justice.

The Iran-Contra Affair showed how much the worldwide struggle against Marxism and various unstable governments dominated American affairs. It also raised serious questions, questions that have not yet been answered, about the power of the executive branch in foreign affairs and Congress's role in foreign policy.

The documents in this case are voluminous. The few documents here provide a glimpse into the complexity of the case.

## Questions

In reading these documents, the student should ask and answer several questions to understand the significance of this event.

1. Was the Boland Amendment a constitutional use of congressional authority?
2. Were the actions of the NSC group involved in Iran-Contra a violation of the Boland Amendment, or were they merely a violation of the *spirit* of the amendment?
3. Was the Bush pardon of Weinberger merely an attempt to stop the investigation, or was it truly to pardon a person caught up accidentally in the affair?
4. What was the role of the special prosecutor in this matter?
5. Did the special prosecutor carry out his duties, and was he reasonable in the conclusions he reported?

## Document 1: The Boland Amendment[1]

*The Boland Amendment specifically prohibited government agencies from assisting the Contras. The Reagan administration argued that the National Security Council was not covered by this congressional action.*

### Joint Resolution

Making continuing appropriations for the fiscal year 1985, and for other purposes.

*Resolved by the Senate and House of Representatives of the United States of America in Congress assembled,*

### TITLE I

That the following sums are hereby appropriated, out of any money in the Treasury not otherwise appropriated, and out of applicable corporate or other revenues, receipts, and funds, for the several departments, agencies, corporations, and other organizational units of the Government for the fiscal year 1985, and for other purposes, namely:

*    *    *

SEC. 8066. (a) During fiscal year 1985, no funds available to the Central Intelligence Agency, the Department of Defense, or any other agency or entity of the United States involved in intelligence activities may be obligated or expended for the purpose or which would have the effect of supporting, directly or indirectly, military or paramilitary operations in Nicaragua by any nation, group, organization, movement, or individual.

## Document 2: Reagan Admits to the Arms Deal[2]

*President Ronald Reagan went public on November 25 to announce that he was appointing a special review board to examine the role of the National Security Council in the arms deal. He was clearly bothered and defensive in this brief appearance.*

The President. Last Friday, after becoming concerned whether my national security apparatus had provided me with a security or a complete factual record with respect to the implementation of my policy toward Iran, I directed the Attorney General [Edwin Meese III] to undertake a review of this matter over the weekend and report to me on Monday. And yesterday Secretary Meese provided me and the White House Chief of Staff [Donald T. Regan] with a report on his preliminary findings. And this report led me to conclude that I was not fully informed on the nature of one of the activities undertaken in connection with this initiative. This action raises serious questions of propriety.

I've just met with my national security advisers and congressional leaders to inform them of the actions that I'm taking today. Determination of the full details of this action will require further review and investigation by the Department of Justice. Looking to the future, I will appoint a Special Review Board to conduct a comprehensive review of the role and procedures of the National Security Council staff in the conduct of foreign and national security policy. I anticipate receiving the reports from the Attorney General and the Special Review Board at the earliest possible date. Upon the completion of these reports, I will share their findings and conclusions with the Congress and the American people.

Although not directly involved, Vice Admiral John Poindexter has asked to be relieved of his assignment as Assistant to the President for National Security Affairs and to return to another assignment in the Navy. Lieutenant

Colonel Oliver North [Deputy Director for Political-Military Affairs] has been relieved of his duties on the National Security Council staff.

I am deeply troubled that the implementation of a policy aimed at resolving a truly tragic situation in the Middle East has resulted in such controversy. As I've stated previously, I believe our policy goals toward Iran were well founded. However, the information brought to my attention yesterday convinced me that in one aspect implementation of that policy was seriously flawed. While I cannot reverse what has happened, I'm initiating steps, including those I've announced today, to assure that the implementation of all future foreign and national security policy initiatives will proceed only in accordance with my authorization. Over the past 6 years we've realized many foreign policy goals. I believe we can yet achieve—and I intend to pursue—the objectives on which we all agree: a safer, more secure, and stable world.

And now, I'm going to ask Attorney General Meese to brief you.

Reporter. What was the flaw?

Q. Do you still maintain you didn't make a mistake, Mr. President?

The President. Hold it.

Q. Did you make a mistake in sending arms to Tehran, sir?

The President. No, and I'm not taking any more questions. And in just a second, I'm going to ask Attorney General Meese to brief you on what we presently know of what he has found out.

Q. Is anyone else going to be let go, sir?

Q. Can you tell us—did Secretary Shultz—

Q. Is anyone else going to be let go? There have been calls for—

The President. No one was let go. They chose to go.

Q. What about Secretary Shultz, Mr. President?

Q. Is Shultz going to stay, sir?

Q. How about Secretary Shultz and Mr. Regan, sir?

Q. What about Secretary Shultz, sir?

Q. Can you tell us if Secretary Shultz is going to stay?

Q. Can you give Secretary Shultz a vote of confidence if you feel that way?

The President. May I give you Attorney General Meese?

Q. And who is going to run national security?

Q. What about Shultz, sir?

Q. Why won't you say what the flaw is?

## Document 3: The Reagan Administration Responds[3]

*The Reagan administration appeared in disarray as the Iran-Contra revela-*
*tions continued to mount. Various officials tried to put a good face on the events.*
*The incident was covered throughout the country, as this report shows.*

WASHINGTON - President Reagan's national security adviser resigned yesterday and a major figure in secret arms sales to Iran was fired as the administration disclosed that up to $30 million of the money the Iranians paid for
U.S. arms was diverted to U.S.-backed Nicaraguan rebels.

Reagan, nonetheless, continued to defend his Iranian policy while admit-
ting one element of its implementation "was seriously flawed" and saying he
was not kept fully informed of his own aides' activities.

Vice Adm. John M. Poindexter resigned. Marine Lt. Col. Oliver North, a
principal aide to Poindexter on the National Security Council, was fired.

Meanwhile, Attorney General Edwin Meese III revealed the first U.S.-sanc-
tioned arms shipment to Iran took place in 1985 without Reagan's knowledge
and was approved by the president only after the fact. And administration
sources, speaking on condition they not be identified, said North gave Israeli
officials the go-ahead for that shipment on his own authority.

Reagan said he would name a commission to examine the role of his National Security Council staff, which directed the operation and has come
under direct fire from the State Department for its operations. The Justice Department will launch a full-scale probe of how the money was handled, to determine whether federal crimes were committed in funneling money to the
Contras at a time when Congress had banned direct U.S. military aid to them.

In a bizarre twist to the tale that already has enveloped Reagan in his most
severe crisis as president, Reagan appeared in the White House briefing room
on short notice to announce he was permitting Poindexter, his chief national
security adviser, to resign to return to the Navy. He said North had been "relieved of his duties on the National Security Council staff."

A knowledgeable source who declined to be identified by name said North
was questioned personally by Meese on Sunday in the attorney general's office.

The day before, sources said, North was questioned by a group of Justice
Department lawyers for about 12 hours at his office in the Old Executive Office Building across the street from the White House.

A White House aide close to North said North was in good spirits despite his dismissal. "He's going to take his hits and support the president," said the aide, who insisted on anonymity.

Meese, following Reagan to the lectern, [*sic*] told reporters that, with North's knowledge, $10 million to $30 million collected from the Iranians for U.S.-shipped weapons was siphoned by Israeli middlemen and transferred to bank accounts set up by Contra rebels fighting the leftist Sandinista regime in Nicaragua.

House Majority Leader Jim Wright, D-Texas, said Meese told congressional leaders at a private White House briefing that negotiations were carried out by Israel and the Iranians to reach a price, which was greater than the cost to the U.S. government. Wright said Meese described at least one of the transactions this way: Arms were sold to the Iranians for $19 million, after which the CIA reimbursed the Pentagon $3 million, covering its costs.

Of the $16 million "residue," Wright said, some $12 million was deposited in a numbered Swiss bank account for the Contras, and Adolfo Calero, a Contra leader, drew out the money.

In Miami, Jorge Rosales, a spokesman for the United Nicaraguan Opposition, an umbrella group for Contra organizations, was asked about the Iranian-Contra money connection.

"We have no information on that," he replied. "This is an internal problem of the United States. We have nothing to do with it."

First lady Nancy Reagan told CBS News she thought her husband had effectively dealt with the situation.

"If there are more steps to be taken, he will take them immediately," she said.

Meese, in an interview with CBS, said he did not think the Iranian controversy had put Reagan "in a bind."

"He's in the lead on this thing . . . and he's already taken remedial action . . . to make sure this kind of thing doesn't happen again," Meese said of Reagan.

Vice President George Bush was described by his spokesman, Marlin Fitzwater, as "very disturbed about the disclosures."

Bush "feels we need to get on very quickly with the Meese investigation and the review of the National Security Council staff," Fitzwater said.

"The vice president feels we need absolute integrity in the decision-making process, . . . that this cannot be allowed to happen again," the spokesman added. . . .

### Document 4: Reagan Charges the Review Board[4]

*Shortly after announcing the special review board, President Reagan appointed former senator John Tower, former senator Edmund Muskie, and General Brent*

*Scowcroft to serve on the new body. On December 1, 1986, Reagan met with the*
*committee and gave the members the charges they were to carry out.*

The President. Well, Senator Tower, Secretary Muskie, General Scowcroft, I'm
grateful to all of you for agreeing to serve on this Board. I know it'll take a lot
of your time, but your experience and expertise in this inquiry are extremely
important in evaluating the National Security Council's staff operations and
providing recommendations on how it should operate.

The purpose of your undertaking is to review past implementation of administration policies and to conduct a comprehensive study of the future role
and procedures of the National Security Council's staff in foreign and national security policy. I would like you to focus on that staff and, one, develop
policy; two, coordinate with other agencies; and, three, implement the President's policies; and, four, oversee the implementation of these policies by others. I hope that you would take particular care to look into the question of
whether and under what circumstances the National Security Council staff
was and should be directly involved in the operational aspects of sensitive
diplomatic, military, or intelligence missions, such as the Achille Lauro, the
TWA hijacking, and Grenada and Iran.

In addition, I have directed the National Security Council staff not to participate in the actual operations associated with such activities pending the
outcome of the report by the Special Review Board. You'll have the full cooperation of all agencies of the executive branch and the White House staff in
carrying out your assignment. And I want to assure you and the American
people that I want all the facts to come out about learning of a possible transfer of funds from the sale of arms to Iran to those fighting the Sandinista government. We acted to learn the facts, and we'll continue to share the actions
we take and the information we obtain with the American people and the
Congress.

The appointment of this Board and the stature of its membership are a
demonstration of a commitment to learn how this happened and how it
can be prevented in the future. The Department of Justice investigation is
continuing with my full support and cooperation. And if they determine an
independent counsel is called for, I would welcome that appointment. If
we're to maintain confidence in our government's foreign policy apparatus,
there must be a full and complete airing of all the facts. And I am determined to get all the facts out and take whatever action is necessary. The
work of this Board and the Department of Justice investigation will do just
that. Just as soon as your findings and recommendations are complete, they
will be shared with the American people and the Congress. So, with that, I
say, go to it!

Reporter. Mr. President, when the Attorney General said you were not fully informed and you said you were not fully informed, did that mean that you never knew anything about contra funding with Iran sales money?

The President. Helen [Helen Thomas, United Press International], I've answered that question. I'm not going to take—we have a meeting now to go into, but I answered that question a couple of times.

Q. Well, does that mean that you had no knowledge at all?

The President. That's what I said.

Q. Mr. President, are you willing to call Congress back in for a special session?

The President. That is under discussion, and there's been no decision yet. But we want to work with the Congress.

### Document 5: Weinberger's Memo[5]

*In the immediate aftermath of the revelation of the Iran-Contra connection, meetings were held among various groups of administration officials. Caspar Weinberger, the secretary of defense, made his own notes on a meeting to discuss how the government should proceed. This document shows how administration officials, including the president, were trying to decide how to put a good face on the actions and still not release much information. Some portions of this memo were blacked out when they were declassified.*

MEMORANDUM FOR RECORD
SUBJECT: Meeting on November 10, 1986, with the President, Vice President, Secretary Shultz, DCI Casey, Attorney General Meese, Don Regan, Admiral Poindexter, and Al Keel, in the Oval Office

[Almost two lines blacked out] The President said we did not do any trading with the enemy for our hostages. We do need to note that [two words blacked] (Khomeni) will be gone someday, and we want better leverage with the new government and with their military. That is why we felt it necessary to give them some small defensive weapons.

We can discuss that publicly, but no way could we ever disclose it all without getting our hostages executed. (We must make it plain that we are not doing business with terrorists. We aren't paying them or dealing with them.) We are trying to get better relations with Iran, and we can't discuss the details of this publicly without endangering the people we are working through and with in Iran. I pointed out we must bear in mind we have given the Israelies [*sic*] and the Iranians the opportunity to blackmail us by reporting selectively bits and pieces of the total story. I also pointed out that Congress could—and probably would—hold legislative hearings. Admiral Poindexter pointed out that we do want a better relationship with Iran.

In June [Jan] 1985[6] the President approved a formal finding under Section 501 of the Arms Export Control Act which directes [sic] the DCI [Director of Central Intelligence] not to notify Congress until further notice, and authorizes discussion with friendly groups which are trying to get a better government in Iran. I had not known of this finding before—Schultz said he had not known of it either. We needed to help those elements to get a more pro-U.S. government in Iran. We found Israel was sending arms to Iran [blacked words] and also wanted the Iran-Iraq war to end as soon as possible. Admiral Poindexter said that McFarlane went to Iran in May 1986, and that was the only trip he made, and then we started working through [blacked words] of Rasfanjani. Previously we had used an Israeli agent called Gorbanifar. We also used many channels to try to get the hostages back. [blacked words] others proved no good because the Iranians always insisted that the Dakah prisoners held by Kuwait be released. We finally did authorize the release of 500 TOWS sold by Israel to Iran, and another 500 were sent last week. This was all arranged as a result of a meeting with Rasfanjani's [blacked words] came here to show that he was a legitimate representative of the government. Poindexter reported there were several meetings in Europe and elsewhere.

I reminded John that he had always told me that there would be no more weapons sent to Iran, after the first 500 TOWS, until <u>after all</u> of the hostages were returned, but unfortunately we did send a second 500 because it "seemed the only way to get the hostages out," according to Poindexter.

Poindexter pointed out the hostage taking had stopped for a year. I pointed out that they took three more quite recently. Poindexter pointed out that this was not done by the same people or Iranians.

[blacked three or four lines] publicized Rasfanjani's contacts with the U.S. Rasfanjani then felt he had to speak out against the U.S. and the McFarlane trip. Because of the obvious errors in Rasfanjani's speech, Poindexter thinks he is sending a message that he wants to work with us. Colonel North thinks we can get two more hostages out by the weekend. I don't. (We didn't.) We have told all our friends in the Mid-East, and according to Poindexter they agree, they would like a negotiated settlement and the war to end. [several blacked out lines]

The President said this is what you had to do to reward Iran for the efforts of those who could help. Actually the captors do not benefit at all. We buy the support and the oportunity [sic] to persuade the Iranians.

I again pointed out we will have to answer many questions and have Congressional hearings. The President said we need to point out any discussion endangers our source in Iran and our plan, because we do want to get additional hostages released. Mr. Schultz spoke up for the first time, saying that it is the responsibility of the government to look after its citizens, but once you do deal for hostages, you expose everyone to future capture. He said we don't know, but we have to assume the captors will get someone. He said he felt the Isralies [sic] sucked us up into their operation so we could not object to their sales to Iran. He pointed out there will be a lot of questions after any statement, even after a statement such as Mr. Casey proposed to read. The President said we should release the statement, but not take any questions. Mr. Regan said we are being hung out to dry, our credibility is at stake, and we have to say enough. Shortly thereafter the meeting adjourned on the note that revised drafts of the Casey proposed statement will be sent to us.

### Document 6: The Independent Counsel Reports[6]

*On December 19, 1986, the U.S. Court of Appeals for the District of Columbia appointed Lawrence E. Walsh as independent counsel to investigate and report on all aspects of the Iran-Contra matter. After several years of investigation—including indictments and trials of various officials, Walsh submitted a three-volume report. In the Executive Summary, he emphasized the primary findings, none of which made President Reagan and his administration look very good. A small portion of the Executive Summary follows.*

### Overall Conclusions

The investigations and prosecutions have shown that high-ranking Administration officials violated laws and executive orders in the Iran/contra matter.

Independent Counsel concluded that:

—the sales of arms to Iran contravened United States Government policy and may have violated the Arms Export Control Act.

—Independent Counsel is aware that the Reagan Administration Justice Department took the position, after the November 1986 revelations, that the 1985 shipments of United States weapons to Iran did not violate the law. This post hoc position does not correspond with the contemporaneous advice given the President. As detailed within this report, Secretary of Defense Caspar W. Weinberger (a lawyer with an extensive record in private practice and the former general counsel of the Bechtel Corporation) advised President Reagan in 1985 that the shipments were illegal. Moreover, Weinberger's opinion was shared by attorneys within the Department of Defense and the White House counsel's office once they became aware of the 1985 shipments. Finally, when Attorney General Meese conducted his initial inquiry into the Iran arms sales, he expressed concern that the shipments may have been illegal.

—the provision and coordination of support to the contras violated the Boland Amendment ban on aid to military activities in Nicaragua;

—the policies behind both the Iran and contra operations were fully reviewed and developed at the highest levels of the Reagan Administration;

—although there was little evidence of National Security Council level knowledge of most of the actual contra-support operations, there was no evidence that any NSC member dissented from the underlying policy—keeping the contras alive despite congressional limitations on contra support;

—the Iran operations were carried out with the knowledge of, among others, President Ronald Reagan, Vice President George Bush, Secretary of State George P. Shultz, Secretary of Defense Caspar W. Weinberger, Director of Central Intelligence William J. Casey, and national security advisers Robert C. McFarlane and John M. Poindexter; of these officials, only Weinberger and Shultz dissented from the policy decision, and Weinberger eventually acquiesced by ordering the Department of Defense to provide the necessary arms; and

—large volumes of highly relevant, contemporaneously created documents were systematically and willfully withheld from investigators by several Reagan Administration officials.

—following the revelation of these operations in October and November 1986, Reagan Administration officials deliberately deceived the Congress and the public about the level and extent of official knowledge of and support for these operations.

In addition, Independent Counsel concluded that the off-the-books nature of the Iran and contra operations gave line-level personnel the opportunity to commit money crimes. . . .

**The Operational Conspiracy**

The operational conspiracy was the basis for Count One of the 23-count indictment returned by the Grand Jury March 16, 1988, against Poindexter, North, Secord, and Hakim. It charged the four with conspiracy to defraud the United States by deceitfully:

(1) supporting military operations in Nicaragua in defiance of congressional controls;
(2) using the Iran arms sales to raise funds to be spent at the direction of North, rather than the U.S. Government; and
(3) endangering the Administration's hostage-release effort by overcharging Iran for the arms to generate unauthorized profits to fund the contras and for other purposes.

The charge was upheld as a matter of law by U.S. District Judge Gerhard A. Gesell even though the Justice Department, in a move that Judge Gesell called "unprecedented," filed an amicus brief supporting North's contention that the charge should be dismissed. Although Count One was ultimately dismissed because the Reagan Administration refused to declassify information necessary to North's defense, Judge Gesell's decision established that high Government officials who engage in conspiracy to subvert civil laws and the Constitution have engaged in criminal acts. Trial on Count One would have disclosed the Government-wide activities that supported North's Iran and contra operations.

Within the NSC, McFarlane pleaded guilty in March 1988 to four counts of withholding information from Congress in connection with his denials that North was providing the contras with military advice and assistance. McFarlane, in his plea agreement, promised to cooperate with Independent Counsel by providing truthful testimony in subsequent trials.

Judge Gesell ordered severance of the trials of the four charged in the conspiracy indictment because of the immunized testimony given by Poindexter, North and Hakim to Congress. North was tried and convicted by a jury in May 1989 of altering and destroying documents, accepting an illegal gratuity and aiding and abetting in the obstruction of Congress. His conviction was reversed on appeal in July 1990 and charges against North were subsequently dismissed in September 1991 on the ground that trial witnesses were tainted by North's nationally televised, immunized testimony before Congress. Poindexter in April 1990 was convicted by a jury on five felony counts of conspiracy, false statements, destruction and removal of records and obstruction of Congress. The Court of Appeals reversed his conviction in November 1991 on the immunized testimony issue. . . .

### The White House and Office of the Vice President

As the White House section of this report describes in detail, the investigation found no credible evidence that President Reagan violated any criminal statute. The OIC could not prove that Reagan authorized or was aware of the diversion or that he had knowledge of the extent of North's control of the contra-resupply network. Nevertheless, he set the stage for the illegal activities of others by encouraging and, in general terms, ordering support of the contras during the October 1984 to October 1986 period when funds for the contras were cut off by the Boland Amendment, and in authorizing the sale of arms to Iran, in contravention of the U.S. embargo on such sales. The President's disregard for civil laws enacted to limit presidential actions abroad—specifically the Boland Amendment, the Arms Export Control Act and congressional-notification requirements in covert-action laws—created a climate in which some of the Government officers assigned to implement his policies felt emboldened to circumvent such laws.

President Reagan's directive to McFarlane to keep the contras alive "body and soul" during the Boland cut-off period was viewed by North, who was charged by McFarlane to carry out the directive, as an invitation to break the law. Similarly, President Reagan's decision in 1985 to authorize the sale of arms to Iran from Israeli stocks, despite warnings by Weinberger and Shultz that such transfers might violate the law, opened the way for Poindexter's subsequent decision to authorize the diversion. Poindexter told Congress that while he made the decision on his own and did not tell the President, he believed the President would have approved. North testified that he believed the President authorized it.

Independent Counsel's investigation did not develop evidence that proved that Vice President Bush violated any criminal statute. Contrary to his public pronouncements, however, he was fully aware of the Iran arms sales. Bush was regularly briefed, along with the President, on the Iran arms sales, and he participated in discussions to obtain third-country support for the contras. The OIC obtained no evidence that Bush was aware of the diversion. The OIC learned in December 1992 that Bush had failed to produce a diary containing contemporaneous notes relevant to Iran/contra, despite requests made in 1987 and again in early 1992 for the production of such material. Bush refused to be interviewed for a final time in light of evidence developed in the latter stages of OIC's investigation, leaving unresolved a clear picture of his Iran-Contra involvement. Bush's pardon of Weinberger on December 24, 1992 preempted a trial in which defense counsel indicated that they intended to call Bush as a witness.

### Document 7: Bush Pardons the Participants[7]

*George Bush, vice president under Ronald Reagan, succeeded to the presidency in 1989, but he was defeated for reelection by Bill Clinton in 1992. Shortly before he left office, Bush pardoned Weinberger and several other participants in the Iran-Contra affair, the investigation of which had been going on for more than six years. Bush provided an extensive defense of his actions in the pardon proclamation.*

December 24, 1992
By the President of the United States of America
A Proclamation
Today I am exercising my power under the Constitution to pardon former Secretary of Defense Caspar Weinberger and others for their conduct related to the Iran-Contra affair.

For more than 6 years now, the American people have invested enormous resources into what has become the most thoroughly investigated matter of its kind in our history. During that time, the last American hostage has come home to freedom, worldwide terrorism has declined, the people of Nicaragua have elected a democratic government, and the Cold War has ended in victory for the American people and the cause of freedom we championed.

In the mid 1980's, however, the outcome of these struggles was far from clear. Some of the best and most dedicated of our countrymen were called upon to step forward. Secretary Weinberger was among the foremost.

Caspar Weinberger is a true American patriot. He has rendered long and extraordinary service to our country. He served for 4 years in the Army during World War II where his bravery earned him a Bronze Star. He gave up a lucrative career in private life to accept a series of public positions in the late 1960's and 1970's, including Chairman of the Federal Trade Commission, Director of the Office of Management and Budget, and Secretary of Health, Education, and Welfare. Caspar Weinberger served in all these positions with distinction and was admired as a public servant above reproach.

He saved his best for last. As Secretary of Defense throughout most of the Reagan Presidency, Caspar Weinberger was one of the principal architects of the downfall of the Berlin Wall and the Soviet Union. He directed the military renaissance in this country that led to the breakup of the communist bloc and a new birth of freedom and democracy. Upon his resignation in 1987, Caspar Weinberger was awarded the highest civilian medal our Nation can bestow on one of its citizens, the Presidential Medal of Freedom.

Secretary Weinberger's legacy will endure beyond the ending of the Cold War. The military readiness of this Nation that he in large measure created could not have been better displayed than it was 2 years ago in the Persian Gulf and today in Somalia.

As Secretary Weinberger's pardon request noted, it is a bitter irony that on the day the first charges against Secretary Weinberger were filed, Russian President Boris Yeltsin arrived in the United States to celebrate the end of the Cold War. I am pardoning him not just out of compassion or to spare a 75-year-old patriot the torment of lengthy and costly legal proceedings, but to make it possible for him to receive the honor he deserves for his extraordinary service to our country.

Moreover, on a somewhat more personal note, I cannot ignore the debilitating illnesses faced by Caspar Weinberger and his wife. When he resigned as Secretary of Defense, it was because of his wife's cancer. In the years since he left public service, her condition has not improved. In addition, since that time, he also has become ill. Nevertheless, Caspar Weinberger has been a pillar of strength for his wife; this pardon will enable him to be by her side undistracted by the ordeal of a costly and arduous trial.

I have also decided to pardon five other individuals for their conduct related to the Iran-Contra affair: Elliott Abrams, Duane Clarridge, Alan Fiers,

Clair George, and Robert McFarlane. First, the common denominator of their motivation—whether their actions were right or wrong—was patriotism. Second, they did not profit or seek to profit from their conduct. Third, each has a record of long and distinguished service to this country. And finally, all five have already paid a price—in depleted savings, lost careers, anguished families—grossly disproportionate to any misdeeds or errors of judgment they may have committed.

The prosecutions of the individuals I am pardoning represent what I believe is a profoundly troubling development in the political and legal climate of our country: the criminalization of policy differences. These differences should be addressed in the political arena, without the Damocles sword of criminality hanging over the heads of some of the combatants. The proper target is the President, not his subordinates; the proper forum is the voting booth, not the courtroom.

In recent years, the use of criminal processes in policy disputes has become all too common. It is my hope that the action I am taking today will begin to restore these disputes to the battleground where they properly belong.

In addition, the actions of the men I am pardoning took place within the larger Cold War struggle. At home, we had a long, sometimes heated debate about how that struggle should be waged. Now the Cold War is over. When earlier wars have ended, Presidents have historically used their power to pardon to put bitterness behind us and look to the future. This healing tradition reaches at least from James Madison's pardon of Lafitte's pirates after the War of 1812, to Andrew Johnson's pardon of soldiers who had fought for the Confederacy, to Harry Truman's and Jimmy Carter's pardons of those who violated the Selective Service laws in World War II and Vietnam.

In many cases, the offenses pardoned by these Presidents were at least as serious as those I am pardoning today. The actions of those pardoned and the decisions to pardon them raised important issues of conscience, the rule of law, and the relationship under our Constitution between the government and the governed. Notwithstanding the seriousness of these issues and the passions they aroused, my predecessors acted because it was time for the country to move on. Today I do the same.

Some may argue that this decision will prevent full disclosure of some new key fact to the American people. That is not true. This matter has been investigated exhaustively. The Tower Board, the Joint Congressional Committee charged with investigating the Iran-Contra affair, and the Independent Counsel have looked into every aspect of this matter. The Tower Board interviewed more than 80 people and reviewed thousands of documents. The Joint Congressional Committee interviewed more than 500 people and reviewed more than 300,000 pages of material. Lengthy committee hearings were held and broadcast on national television to millions of Americans. And as I have noted, the Independent Counsel investigation has gone on for more than 6 years, and it has cost more than $31 million.

Moreover, the Independent Counsel stated last September that he had completed the active phase of his investigation. He will have the opportunity to place his full assessment of the facts in the public record when he submits his final report. While no impartial person has seriously suggested that my own role in this matter is legally questionable, I have further requested that the Independent Counsel provide me with a copy of my sworn testimony to his office, which I am prepared to release immediately. And I understand Secretary Weinberger has requested the release of all of his notes pertaining to the Iran-Contra matter.

For more than 30 years in public service, I have tried to follow three precepts: honor, decency, and fairness. I know, from all those years of service, that the American people believe in fairness and fair play. In granting these pardons today, I am doing what I believe honor, decency, and fairness require.

NOW, THEREFORE, I, GEORGE BUSH, President of the United States of America, pursuant to my powers under Article II, Section 2, of the Constitution, do hereby grant a full, complete, and unconditional pardon to Elliott Abrams, Duane R. Clarridge, Alan Fiers, Clair George, Robert C. McFarlane, and Caspar W. Weinberger for all offenses charged or prosecuted by Independent Counsel Lawrence E. Walsh or other member of his office, or committed by these individuals and within the jurisdiction of that office.

IN WITNESS WHEREOF, I have hereunto set my hand this twenty-fourth day of December, in the year of our Lord nineteen hundred and ninety-two, and of the Independence of the United States of America the two hundred and seventeenth.

GEORGE BUSH


## Document 8: The Independent Counsel Responds[8]

*On the same day that Bush issued the pardons, Independent Counsel Walsh reacted strongly with a statement of his own. As this statement reveals, he believes there was a conspiracy in the Reagan White House and that the impeachment of Reagan was a good possibility had there not been a cover-up. His statement is quite strong.*

### STATEMENT OF INDEPENDENT COUNSEL LAWRENCE E. WALSH

President Bush's pardon of Caspar Weinberger and other Iran-contra defendants undermines the principle that no man is above the law. It demonstrates that powerful people with powerful allies can commit serious crimes in high office—deliberately abusing the public trust—without consequence.

Weinberger, who faced four felony charges, deserved to be tried by a jury of citizens. Although it is the President's prerogative to grant pardons, it is every American's right that the criminal justice system be administered fairly, regardless of a person's rank and connections.

The Iran-contra cover-up, which has continued for more than six years, has now been completed with the pardon of Caspar Weinberger. We will make a full report on our findings to Congress and the public describing the details and extent of this cover-up.

Weinberger's early and deliberate decision to conceal and withhold extensive contemporaneous notes of the Iran-contra matter radically altered the official investigations and possibly forestalled timely impeachment proceedings against President Reagan and other officials. Weinberger's notes contain evidence of a conspiracy among the highest-ranking Reagan administration officials to lie to Congress and the American public. Because the notes were withheld from investigators for years, many of the leads were impossible to follow, key witnesses had purportedly forgotten what was said and done, and statutes of limitation had expired.

Weinberger's concealment of notes is part of a disturbing pattern of deception and obstruction that permeated the highest levels of the Reagan and Bush administrations. This office was informed only within the past two weeks, on December 11, 1992, that President Bush had failed to produce to investigators his own highly relevant contemporaneous notes, despite repeated requests for such documents. The production of these notes is still ongoing and will lead to appropriate action. In light of President Bush's own misconduct, we are gravely concerned about his decision to pardon others who lied to Congress and obstructed official investigations.


## Part B: The End of the Cold War

### Background

*After more than fifty years of the Cold War with all its tensions and occasional outbursts of "hot war," the rivalry between the Soviet bloc and the United States and its Western allies came to an abrupt end. This startling development caught almost everyone by surprise, and many did not know how to cope with the changes.*

*Ronald Reagan was elected president in 1980 and began to renew some of the tension that had tapered off in earlier years. He began a massive arms build-up that caused the Soviets to respond in kind. He even called the Soviet Union the* "evil empire," an act some people thought was unnecessarily provocative. Some observers believe the renewed arms race essentially drove the Soviet Union into bankruptcy.

When Mikhail Gorbachev became the head of the Soviet Union in the mid-1980s, he began a series of reforms, especially economic, intended to bring the Soviet Union into the modern era and to provide more consumer services to the people. Many people have analyzed the impact of Reagan's efforts and Gorbachev's attempts at reforms, but there is no real consensus on what really caused the change. Most people agree that Gorbachev did not have the stomach for repressive measures that his predecessors had wielded at the slightest provocation in the Soviet Union and satellite countries. Gorbachev began new policies called glasnost (openness) and perestroika (reform) that permitted freer speech than ever before.

Beginning in 1989, the winds of change were evident. Demonstrations in Tiananmen Square in China offered hope of change, but the resistance was crushed by force. Restiveness in Marxist countries was spreading. The Berlin Wall was breached and then was demolished, all without violence. For Americans watching on television, it was an almost surreal event. Then the various countries under Soviet control, such as Poland, began to break away. At the end of 1991, the Soviet Union was officially abolished. All this occurred without violence (aside from the Tiananmen Square military assault). For many, this was an American (at least Western) victory, while others saw it as a natural progression and a failure of socialism rather than a Western triumph. Whatever the case, by the 1990s, the Cold War, which Americans had lived with for more than fifty years, was over.

## Questions

In reading these documents, the student should ask and answer several questions to put these activities in the proper context.

1. Why was the Berlin Wall such a symbol of the Cold War? Why was its end so shocking to Americans?
2. What was President Bush's reaction to the end of the Berlin Wall?
3. What motivated Gorbachev to be more open and less repressive than his predecessors?
4. Analyze Gorbachev's resignation speech. What did it say about his views and those of the Soviet Union?
5. How did Americans react to the end of the Cold War, and how did they foresee the future?

## Document 1: Fall of the Berlin Wall[9]

*As mentioned, the fall of the Berlin Wall was one of the most unexpected and unbelievable events as far as Americans were concerned. Many reports were made about this event. A typical report follows.*

EAST BERLIN - In one week the world changed; the symbol of the cold war disintegrated.

On the night of Nov. 9, East Germany's communist rulers opened the Berlin Wall and told a people penned in for 28 years that they were free to come and go.

It spelled the end of the Cold War era and was a step toward ending the postwar division of Europe.

Events unfolded this way:

At a little after 7 p.m. in East Berlin, Communist Party chief spokesman Guenter Schabowski told a news conference that East Germans were free to travel.

The news burst like a bombshell upon a world resigned to the Berlin Wall since 1961.

The communists, on the ropes after weeks of mass protest and an exodus that saw 250,000 mostly young East Germans flee the country, had just kicked out the Stalinist old guard and revamped the Politburo, hinting at free elections.

Nobody dreamed they would take the ultimate gamble.

"There must be some mistake," said an astonished border guard officer at the wall's Checkpoint Charlie.

At 9 p.m., in mild weather, East Germans of all ages flocked to the main crossing points after hearing the news on television. "Can it be really true?" everyone asked.

Border officials did not know what to tell them.

Shortly before midnight, a rumor swept the crowd at the Bahnhof Friedrichstrasse exit point: Visa stamps would be given out immediately at the state travel office in central East Berlin.

Hundreds ran there, laughing and screaming. It was true. It was chaos. They streamed over into West Berlin in the thousands, gulping down freedom.

In the West German capital, Bonn, officials braced for the unimaginable. "No one will be turned back," one said.

That night, and over the next two days, Berlin witnessed a massive, joyful East-West invasion. Strangers embraced in tears. West Berliners stood on top of the concrete wall cheering and waving.

Two million East Germans, many without visas, set foot on the "other side" in the 48 hours after East Berlin opened the gates.

A million more followed by nightfall Monday, creating 40-mile border traffic jams.

On Nov. 10, visiting West German Chancellor Helmut Kohl broke off a historic reconciliation trip to Poland to rush to Berlin.

Western leaders and the world's press hailed what was happening in East Germany. The Soviet Union said it approved of the wall's opening. Stock prices on the Frankfurt exchange surged in what dealers called a "Germany rally."

As day dawned in East Berlin, thousands waited patiently for exit and multiple entry visas that belied a generation of mines, attack dogs, watchtowers, barbed wire and machine guns. East German guards began dismantling sections of the wall.

"We are and remain one nation and we belong together," Kohl told a West Berlin rally.

Sunday, it began to emerge that another political miracle was emerging for East Germans. The vast majority of those who flocked to the West just went to take a look—and came back.

"They have discovered they are a people. They have found a new sense of national identity," a pastor said after thanksgiving in an East Berlin Protestant church.

As East Berliners marveled at consumer goods in the west, their rulers expelled hard-liners from key positions and then agreed to call a special Communist Party congress to consider the party's future.

Saturday, Nov. 11, East Berliners began streaming through a new hole in the wall at the Potsdamer Platz, a bustling intersection before World War II but now overgrown with weeds.

They rode the subway to West Berlin from a long-closed ghost station.

East German authorities said 2.7 million visas had been given out, then 3.4 million, then 4.3 million, then 5.7 million, then a week later 8.6 million, or more than half the population of 16.6 million.

The mayors of the two halves of Berlin sealed their reunion with a handshake, and more crossing points were promised to cope with the human tide.

In West Berlin last Monday, the Western allied powers admitted the speed of change had taken their governments by surprise. They had assumed that, despite reforms launched by Soviet President Mikhail Gorbachev, the wall was a fixture.

In Paris, French President François Mitterrand summoned a snap summit of the 12 European Community leaders for yesterday.

The East German Volkskammer (parliament) elected a non-communist speaker in a tight vote—its first secret ballot—and endorsed reformer Hans Modrow as prime minister.

More than a half-million people took to the streets of six East German cities to insist that only free elections would satisfy them.

The pace kept up in other East European countries. Hard-line Czechoslovakia on Tuesday announced it also was giving up exit visa requirements.

Overshadowed by the East German drama, Bulgaria's Communist Party discarded Todor Zhivkov, their leader for 35 years, to join the wave of reform.

On Tuesday Modrow opened coalition talks with former "satellite parties," hoping to make genuine allies out of one-time puppets.

Wednesday there was speculation that East Germany was about to breach the wall at the Brandenburg Gate, the supreme symbol of German unity and—since it lies behind the wall—its division. But the six-columned gate remains shut.

Modrow Thursday won agreement on a coalition deal at the expense of slackening the Communist Party's grip on power, giving 11 posts to non-communists in a 27-member cabinet committed to radical political and economic reforms.

### Document 2: Bush Reacts[10]

*President George H. W. Bush reacted to the fall of the Berlin Wall in a surprisingly calm way. Some criticized Bush for not reacting more strongly to this and other events hailing the end of the Cold War. He seemed to have been caught off guard as much as anyone else. The question was raised in a press conference, a portion of which is reproduced here.*

**President George Bush:** We just wanted to make a brief statement here. I've just been briefed by the secretary of state and my national security adviser on the latest news coming out of Germany. And of course, I welcome the decision by the East German leadership to open the borders to those wishing to emigrate or travel. And this, if it's implemented fully, certainly conforms with the Helsinki Final Act, which the GDR [German Democratic Republic] signed. And if the GDR goes forward now, this wall built in '61 will have very little relevance. And it clearly is a good development in terms of human rights. And I must say that after discussing this here with the secretary of state and the national security adviser, I am very pleased with this development.

**Question:** Mr. President, would the United States now consider doing more to help West Germany to take care of some of these East Germans coming into that country? Is there more that you could do now to help West Germany accommodate ...

**President George Bush:** Well, we have such a close relationship with the Federal Republic that if Chancellor Kohl asks us to be of some assistance I'm certain we would give it serious consideration. I mean, I don't know what it is they'd have in mind, because I think with a truly open border it is hard to predict how many will be trying to leave. And so, it's a dynamic development, and we just have to wait and see. But our relationship with the Federal Republic is such that we would want to be of the maximum help if it was needed. So far, Germany has done a magnificent job in handling those who have preceded this new exodus.

Question: Have you assured Mr. Kohl that if he does need help that we'll be there for them?

President George Bush: Well, I haven't talked to him . . . since this development because he just went off to Poland. I talked to him about this last week and made very clear to him that we thought—I think it was last week—made very clear to him that we thought they were handling it with great sensitivity. It's an enormous burden on the Federal Republic. And I don't remember in that conversation if I said if we can be of any help, please let me know; but I'm sure he knows that's the case.

Question: Did he give any indication of how far he'd be able to go to accommodate this influx of refugees? I think the number stands at about 110,000 now. Did he say if it hits a million we're going to have real problems?

President George Bush: No, he didn't go into numbers at all, but he demonstrates a quiet confidence that the Federal Republic can cope. As I say, they have done a good job. And here's a new development in this rapidly changing part of the world that we can salute. And it's a dramatic happening for East Germany and, of course, for freedom.

Question: Is this the end of the Iron Curtain, sir?

President George Bush: Well, I don't think any single event is the end of what you might call the Iron Curtain, but clearly this is a long way from the harshest Iron Curtain days—a long way from that.

Question: Mr. President, what do you think the implications are for the Warsaw Pact now? I mean, can we say that this may be an indication that they're headed toward a loosening or even a dismantling of the Warsaw Pact?

President George Bush: I think you have to say what you mean by Warsaw Pact. I mean, it seems to me that it's certainly a loosening up in terms of travel. It concurs with the Helsinki Final Act, and it is a very good development. Our objective is a Europe whole and free. And is it a step towards that? I would say yes. Gorbachev talks about a common home. Is it a step towards that? Probably so. . . .

Question: What's the danger here of events just spinning out of control? Secretary [of State James] Baker commented earlier about how rapid the pace of change has been in Eastern Europe. Nobody really expected this to happen as quickly as it did. Is there a danger here that things are accelerating too quickly?

President George Bush: I wouldn't want to say this kind of development makes things to be moving too quickly at all. It's the kind of development that we have long encouraged by our strong support for the Helsinki Final Act. So, I'm not going to hypothecate that anything goes too fast.

Question: So, you don't see . . .

President George Bush: But we are handling it in a way where we are not trying to give anybody a hard time. We're saluting those who can move forward with democracy. We are encouraging the concept of a Europe whole and free. And so, we just welcome it. But I don't like to go into a lot of hypotheses about too much change or too rapid change or what I'd do, what our whole team here would do, if something went wrong. I think it's been handled by the West very well; and certainly we salute the people in East Germany, the GDR, whose aspirations for freedom seem to be a little further down the road now.

Question: Mr. President, do you think, now that East Germany appears to be moving in the direction of Poland and Hungary, that the rest of the Eastern bloc can continue to resist this? I'm thinking of Czechoslovakia, Bulgaria, Romania—will they be the next?

President George Bush: No, I don't think anyone can resist it, in Europe or in the Western Hemisphere. . . .

Question: Did you ever imagine anything like this happening?

Question: On your watch?

President George Bush: We've imagined it, but I can't say that I foresaw this development at this stage. Now, I didn't foresee it, but imagining it—yes. When I talk about a Europe whole and free, we're talking about this kind of freedom to come and go, this kind of staying with and living by the Helsinki Final Act, which gives the people the rights to come and go.

Question: In what you just said, that this is a sort of great victory for our side in the big East-West battle, but you don't seem elated. And I'm wondering if you're thinking of the problems.

President George Bush: I am not an emotional kind of guy.

Question: Well, how elated are you?

President George Bush: I'm very pleased. And I've been very pleased with a lot of other developments. And, as I've told you, I think the United States' part of this, which is not related to this development today particularly, is being handled in a proper fashion. . . .

And so, the fact that I'm not bubbling over—maybe it's getting along towards evening, because I feel very good about it.

**Question:** Well, what I wanted to ask is—the second part of that was, is your second thought: What are we going to do if it really does explode over there—coming into play here? I mean, obviously, if they just flood into West Germany, they're handling it now, but they've only gotten 200,000. What if they get a million? What if they get 2 million?

**President George Bush:** Well, what I'd like to think is that the political change in the GDR would catch up very fast with this liberation, if you will. You may remember that before I went to Poland . . . I was asked by a Polish journalist if I were a young Pole, what would my advice be. And what I said is I think you ought to stay there and participate in this dramatic change in your country. . . . These are Germans, and Germans love their country. And at some point, I think a lot of Germans who had felt pent-in and unable to move are going to say, look, we can move. But wouldn't it be better to participate in the reforms that are taking place in our own country? So, I think it's too early to predict that because these openings are there that that means everybody is going to take off. . . .

## Document 3: Gorbachev Faces Parliament[11]

*By 1991, the crisis of the Soviet Union was growing worse. Boris Yeltsin had become president of the Russian Federation, and Mikhail Gorbachev was trying to hold the Soviet Union together. Gorbachev made an extraordinary appearance before the parliament of the Russian Federation. He appeared with Yeltsin and faced a barrage of questions and heckling. A portion of the comments was provided by the Public Broadcasting System (PBS).*

ROBERT MacNEIL: We begin our analysis of the Soviet story with an extended excerpt from Mikhail Gorbachev's extraordinary appearance before the parliament of the Russian Federation. He had to share top billing with Russian President Boris Yeltsin and he faced a barrage of questioning and heckling.

After his opening speech, Mr. Gorbachev was first asked why he would not outlaw the Communist Party in the USSR.

PRES. GORBACHEV: A question has been asked in such a clear way that I can only answer it equally clearly and definitely. If you set the task before the Supreme Soviet and the government of the Russian federation and even before other Supreme Soviets of driving socialism from the territory of the Soviet Union we will never succeed in accomplishing such a task. This is just another way of carrying on a crusade or religious war at the present time.

Socialism, as I understand it, is a type of conviction which people have and we are not the only ones that have it. But it exists in other countries, not only today but at other times. And we have declared here freedom of conviction, freedom of belief. And if we start to do what I say—no, no, no, you just listen to what I have to say.

LEGISLATOR: Mikhail Sergeivich, we haven't heard about any practical measures other than some new appointments. We haven't heard anything about the question of property or other matters.

PRES. GORBACHEV: First of all I do not agree with you. I sense that the whole point was that at this stage we now directly realize what goals we have to pursue to reach a new life. We have to sign the union treaty. We have to have an anti-crisis program, a food program, a fuel program. The finances have to be stabilized. We have to do all of these things. In order to do this, we must have a major regrouping of forces, a new legislator and executive which will take on themselves responsibility which would have confidence, who will solve all these problems.

BORIS YELTSIN, President, Russia: The question of property was raised. I'd like to remind you that we during these events have agreed that if you do not take a decision on conveying the property on the territory of Russia to the Russian jurisdiction that the President of Russia would do that by issuing a decree to that effect. I on the 20th of this month did sign such a decree, but you today said that you would sign a decree confirming all of my decrees. [applause]

PRES. GORBACHEV: I do not think that you have tried to put me in a trap by bringing me here, no, I do not think that. Let me confirm once again that the Supreme Soviet of the Russian Federation and the President and its government in these extremely difficult situations acted the way they did and what they did was dictated by the situation and therefore has the force of law and has to be confirmed by the President even post facto everything that concerns the question of carrying out the union treaty or implementing the union treaty, as we have discussed this with Boris Nikolaivich, and I hereby confirm this.

BORIS YELTSIN: Comrades, how about the decree on cessation of activity of the Russian Communist Party? [Applause] And the decree is hereby signed.

PRES. GORBACHEV: Wait a minute. It was not the whole Communist Party of record that participated in this plot and supported it. Therefore, if it is determined that the Russian Committee or some other provincial committee were in solidarity with this committee, the coup plotters, then I would support such a decree. But to prohibit the Communist Party, I have to tell you, would be a mistake for such a democratic Supreme Soviet or such a democratic president of Russia.

BORIS YELTSIN: It is not a proposition. It is a decree on cessation of the activity of the Communist Party until this can be dealt with by the courts. It's a law. [applause] The party will not be registered any longer in Russia.

PRES. GORBACHEV: Let's remain democrats to the end, remain democrats to the end, and then everybody will be with you.

## Document 4: Gorbachev Resigns[12]

*Later in 1991, Gorbachev took the unprecedented step of resigning as president of the Commonwealth of Independent States (CIS), the successor to the Soviet Union.*

Dear fellow countrymen, compatriots. Due to the situation which has evolved as a result of the formation of the Commonwealth of Independent States, I hereby discontinue my activities at the post of President of the Union of Soviet Socialist Republics.

I am making this decision out of considerations based on principle. I have firmly stood for independence, self-rule of nations, for the sovereignty of the republics, but at the same time for preservation of the union state, the unity of the country.

Events went a different way. The policy prevailed of dismembering this country and disuniting the state, with which I cannot agree. And after the Alma-Ata meeting and the decisions taken there, my position on this matter has not changed. Besides, it is my conviction that decisions of this caliber should have been made on the basis of popular will. . . .

Fate had it that when I found myself at the head of the state, it was already clear that all was not well in the country. We had a lot of everything—land, oil and gas, other natural resources—and there was intellect and talent in abundance. Yet we lived much worse than developed countries and keep falling behind them more and more. The reason was obvious even then. This country was suffocating in the shackles of the bureaucratic-command system, doomed to serve ideology and bear the terrible burden of the arms race. It had reached the limit of its possibilities. All attempts at partial reform—and there had been many—had suffered defeat, one after another. We could not go on living like that.

Everything had to be changed radically.

That is why not once—not once—have I regretted that I did not take advantage of the post of [Communist Party] general secretary to rule as czar for several years. I considered it irresponsible and amoral. I realized that to start reforms of such a scale in a society such as ours was a most difficult and even a risky thing. But even now, I am convinced that the democratic reform that we launched in the spring of 1985 was historically correct. The process of renovating this country and radical changes in the world community turned out to be far more complicated than could be expected.

However, what has been done ought to be given its due.

This society acquired freedom, liberated itself politically and spiritually, and this is the foremost achievement—which we have not yet understood completely, because we have not learned to use freedom. However, work of historic significance has been accomplished.

The totalitarian system that deprived the country of an opportunity to become successful and prosperous long ago has been eliminated. A breakthrough has been achieved on the way to democratic changes. Free elections, freedom of the press, religious freedoms, representative organs of power, a multiparty [system] became a reality. Human rights are recognized as the supreme principle.

Movement has been started toward a multi-tier economy, and the equality of all forms of ownership is being established. Within the framework of land reform, peasantry began to reemerge as a class. Farmers have appeared, billions of hectares of land are being given to urbanites and rural residents alike. Economic freedom of the producer has been legalized, and entrepreneurship, shareholding, privatization are gaining momentum. In turning the economy toward a market, it is important to remember that all this is done for the sake of the individual. At this difficult time, all should be done for his social protection, especially for senior citizens and children. . . .

We opened ourselves to the rest of the world, abandoned the practices of interfering in others' internal affairs and using troops outside this country, and we were reciprocated with trust, solidarity and respect. We have become one of the main foundations for the transformation of modern civilization on peaceful democratic grounds.

The nations and the peoples [of this country] gained real freedom of self-determination. The search for a democratic reformation of the multi-national state brought us to the threshold of concluding a new union treaty. All these changes demanded immense strain. They were carried out with sharp struggle, with growing resistance from the old, the obsolete forces: the former party-state structures, the economic elite, as well as our habits, ideological superstitions, the psychology of sponging and leveling everyone out.

They stumbled on our intolerance, low level of political culture, fear of change. That is why we lost so much time. The old system collapsed before the new one had time to begin working, and the crisis in the society became even more acute. . . .

But once again I'd like to stress: Radical changes in such a vast country, and a country with such a heritage, cannot pass painlessly without difficulties and shake-up.

The August coup brought the overall crisis to its ultimate limit. The most dangerous thing about the crisis is the collapse of statehood. And today I am worried by our people's loss of the citizenship of a great country. The consequences may turn out to be very hard for everyone.

Sept. 30

'I CAN'T BELIEVE MY EYES!'

Valtman '91

When the Soviet Union began to totter in 1989, most adults were stunned. Few Americans could ever have believed that the Soviet Union would simply disintegrate. The Soviets had been the enemy for so long that most Americans could not imagine a world without a Cold War. This cartoonist imagines the reaction that Karl Marx might have had. Library of Congress, Prints & Photographs Division, drawing by Edmund S. Valtman, LC-USZ62-130438.

I think it is vitally important to preserve the democratic achievements of the last years. They have been paid for by the suffering of our whole history, our tragic experience. They must not be given up under any circumstances or any pretext, otherwise all our hopes for the better will be buried. I am telling you all this honestly and straightforwardly because this is my moral duty.

Today I'd like to express my gratitude to all citizens who supported the policy of renovating the country, got involved in the implementation of the democratic reforms. I am grateful to statesmen, public and political figures, millions of people abroad, those who understood our intentions, gave their support and met us halfway. I thank them for their sincere cooperation with us.

I am leaving my post with apprehension, but also with hope, with faith in you, your wisdom and force of spirit. We are the heirs of a great civilization, and its rebirth into a new, modern and dignified life now depends on one and all. I wish to thank with all my heart all those who have stood together with me all these years for the fair and good cause. Some mistakes could surely have been avoided. Many things could have been done better. But I am convinced that sooner or later our common efforts will bear fruit, our nations will live in a prosperous and democratic society. I wish everyone all the best.

### Document 5: America's Place in the New World[13]

*Various news agencies analyzed what the fall of the Soviet Union meant and what the United States' role in the new world order would be.*

This was the year that didn't make sense. Mikhail Gorbachev's Soviet Union collapsed. The United States won a smashing victory in the Persian Gulf. Just a few months ago, as the year unfolded, it looked like a world where decades of dreams were coming true.

And what did we get? A deep recession.

It would be understandable, indeed, if Americans might ask: What went wrong? What happened to the dreams?

The dreams, of course, were that triumph in the Cold War, and triumph in the Persian Gulf, would produce some sort of nirvana. The resources long pledged to war could be turned to health and education and the environment and all those good things we've put off so long.

And now there's no money. George Bush doesn't look like Scrooge, as some have suggested. He looks like a panhandler. . . .

All the polls show it. Bush himself has fallen below a 50 percent approval rating for the first time. Something like 70 percent of those polled say he is mismanaging the economy.

It would be easy to draw a simplistic and wrongheaded conclusion from this train of events, the conclusion that much of our prosperity has been built on a military economy in the Cold War.

Certainly trillions of dollars have been poured into that economy, creating whole industries and thousands of jobs. And it is true that this economy must be, and will be, slowly dismantled.

But to conclude that to sustain our prosperity we as a people must build weapons that will never be used is a giant leap.

Our real problem, and real challenge, is the transition. How do we go from a semi-warfare economy to a peacetime economy? How do we devote our intelligence and our energies to more productive enterprises than building weapons?

Right here is where both George Bush and his presumptive Democratic challengers in 1992 are failing us.

We face a new world, a different world, a world with totally new problems of a type we haven't had to deal with in the last 45 years. We've got to start over from Square 1 and devise a system for dealing with a far more peaceful, less threatening world.

We haven't done that yet, and our political leaders have not been much help.

Christopher Layne, who teaches international politics at UCLA, has got it right. He has argued that what is needed is a sweeping review of U.S. foreign policy and a reassessment of national priorities.

"The questions at issue go to the heart of national policy," he has written. "What are America's vital interests? What military forces are needed to defend those interests? How much can America afford to spend on security without endangering its economic health?"

Pointing out that we have spent some $6 trillion prosecuting the Cold War, he has sought to point the way, suggesting that a lot more emphasis could be put on tax cuts, education, deficit reduction and civilian research and development. "Americans should not continue to bear Cold War economic burdens when there is no compelling reason to do so," he writes.

Bush, he argues, "clings to Cold War relics such as NATO" and has resisted the development of an independent European defense capability, which could save Americans billions.

Most of the Democratic aspirants for the presidency haven't done much better than Bush. With the exception of Gov. Bill Clinton, of Arkansas, they have talked generalities, not specifics.

Clinton has called for "a new vision" in "a new era," based on sharper defense cuts and more active support of democratic regimes, but his program falls somewhat short of a clarion call. He at least is trying, however.

This is a time for New Year's resolutions, pledges to do better in the coming year.

The best New Year's resolution we could get from Bush and from his potential opponents for the presidency would be promises to focus on the real issue in 1992.

The real issue is: How do we start over, with a new kind of world, and make America work?

## Notes

1. U.S. Congress, "Public Law 98-473" (Boland Amendment II), October 12, 1984.

2. Remarks Announcing the Review of the National Security Council's Role in the Iran Arms and *Contra* Aid Controversy, November 25, 1986, *Public Papers of the Presidents of the United States: Ronald Reagan, 1986* (Washington, D.C.: Government Printing Office, 1987), Pt. 2, 1587–88.

3. "Iran, Contra Aid Link Ousts 2 Advisers: Kept in Dark, Reagan Says, but Still OKs Policy," *The Patriot News* (Harrisburg, Pa.), November 26, 1986. Reprinted by permission of the Associated Press.

4. Remarks at a Meeting With the President's Special Review Board for the National Security Council, December 1, 1986, *Public Papers, 1986*, Pt. 2, 1591.

5. Caspar Weinberger, Memorandum for the Record, "Meeting on November 10, 1986, with the President, et. al.," in Peter Kornbluh and Malcolm Byrne, *The Iran-Contra Scandal: The Declassified History* (New York: The New Press, 1993).

6. Lawrence E. Walsh, *Final Report of the Independent Counsel for Iran/Contra Matters* (Washington, D.C.: Government Printing Office, 1993), xiii–xviii.

7. George Bush, Presidential Pardon of Caspar Weinberger, et al., December 24, 1992, in Kornbluh and Byrne, *Iran-Contra Scandal,* 374–76.

8. Lawrence Walsh, Response to Presidential Pardon, December 24, 1992, in Kornbluh and Byrne, 377–78.

9. Douglas Hamilton, "Fall of the Berlin Wall: A Week That Changed the World," *Seattle Times,* November 19, 1989. Reprinted by permission of Reuters.

10. "Remarks and a Question-and-Answer Session With Reporters on the Relaxation of East German Border Controls, November 9, 1989," *Public Papers of the Presidents of the United States: George H.W. Bush* (Washington, D.C.: Government Printing Office, 1990), II, 1488–90.

11. "Gorbachev, Yeltsin in Public," August 23, 1991, online at www.pbs.org/news hour/bb/europe/russia/1991/gorb-yelt_8-23-91.html.

12. Mikhail Gorbachev, Resignation. December 25, 1991. Original Source: Broadcast on Central Television, December 25, 1991; printed in Rossiiskaia Gazeta, December 26, 1991, Seventeen Moments in Soviet History, online at http://soviethistory.org/index.php?action=L3&ArticleID=1991resign1&SubjectID=1991end&Year=1991.

13. James McCartney, "America's Place in a New Kind of World," *Chicago Tribune*, December 29, 1991. © McClatchy-Tribune Information Services. All Rights Reserved. Reprinted with permission.

# Postscript

## Crises at Century's End: The Clinton Impeachment and the 9/11 Attacks

### Background

*T*HE TWENTIETH CENTURY BEGAN *with the United States flexing its muscles and acquiring foreign territory—becoming an empire. During the century, as the documents here show, the United States continued to grow, despite periodic set-backs, in wealth, power, and influence around the world. By the end of the century, the Cold War had ended, and the United States was the sole remaining "super power." The relief felt at the collapse of the Soviet Union was soon replaced by anxiety regarding small conflicts all around the world. The United States had replaced Great Britain as the world's most powerful country and often found it-self in a situation similar to ones faced by the British by trying to maintain the peace around the world while serving as the protector of the balance of power.*

*At century's end and the beginning of a new century, the nation's crises did not end. Two events symbolize the changed role for the United States—the impeachment and trial of the president of the United States and the first attack on American soil by foreign enemies since the attack on Pearl Harbor in 1941.*

### Part A: The Impeachment of President Clinton

#### Background

*President William Jefferson Clinton was elected president in 1992. From the very beginning of his emergence on the national scene, rumors and charges swirled about him for all sorts of personal failings, but the one that had the longest life was the one that accused him of having a series extramartial affairs while he was governor of Arkansas. He was able to weather the charges and was elected as one of the youngest presidents in American history.*

*After becoming president, Clinton was possibly the most attacked president in American history. He was hated by Republicans and various right-wing organizations. They dug around in his past trying to find something they could blame him for and bring down his enormous possibilities. He was even accused of being involved—or at least complicit—in the death of Vince Foster, one of his friends from Arkansas who committed suicide probably due to the pressures of his work in Washington. His opponents were able to get an independent counsel appointed to investigate the activities of Clinton and his wife in a land deal in Arkansas, known as Whitewater, in which they lost money.*

*In 1995 the government shut down almost completely due to a belief on the part of the Republicans, who had regained control of Congress in 1994 under the leadership of Newt Gingrich, that Clinton could be intimidated in approving some of their measures. During this partial shutdown, when few people were at work in the White House, Clinton had a sexual encounter with a young, unpaid intern, Monica Lewinsky. There were several of these episodes before Clinton broke it off.*

*In 1997 and 1998 the attacks on Clinton continued unabated—increased, in fact—even after he had won reelection in 1996 by a comfortable majority. Kenneth Starr, the independent counsel, seemed obsessed with Clinton and in finding something incriminating in his past or current actions.*

*The whole issue came to a head when the Lewinsky affair became known. Clinton categorically denied on television that he had "had sexual relations" with her. From this point forward, the case gained momentum. It is so complex that it cannot be explained in a few pages. Suffice it to say that the case, originating with the Lewinsky affair, eventually became a national scandal that almost brought down the Clinton presidency.*

*Clinton was impeached in the House of Representatives in 1998 on two charges: perjury and obstruction of justice. A trial in the Senate, as required by the Constitution, failed to get the two-thirds majority that is required. Thus, Clinton was acquitted and remained in office. Unfortunately, the attention of the country was distracted for more than a year with this issue, and the Clinton presidency, which had accomplished several significant things, was tarnished because of his personal behavior.*

## Questions

In reading these documents, the student should ask and answer several questions to put these activities in the proper context.

1. In looking at the impeachment charges, do they appear to be "high crimes and misdemeanors" as required by the Constitution?
2. Did Clinton actually lie to the Grand Jury? Why would he do that and take the risk it involved?
3. Was Clinton's denial of "sexual relations" true, or was he just creating definitions of words for his own benefit?
4. Why was Clinton acquitted? What would have been the consequences for the country if he had been convicted and removed from office?

## Document 1: The Starr Report[1]

*Kenneth Starr, the independent counsel appointed to investigate the president's activities, made a sensational report on his conclusions about President Clinton's activities. It was widely discussed because of its content about the president's behavior, but it was also read widely because of the salacious language used in the report. Below are a few of the summary arguments that Clinton had committed impeachable acts.*

Substantial and credible information demonstrates that the President made three false statements under oath in his civil deposition regarding whether he had been alone with Ms. Lewinsky.

First, the President lied when he said "I don't recall" in response to the question whether he had ever been alone with Ms. Lewinsky. The President admitted to the grand jury that he had been alone with Ms. Lewinsky. It is not credible that he actually had no memory of this fact six months earlier, particularly given that they were obviously alone when engaging in sexual activity.

Second, when asked whether he had been alone with Ms. Lewinsky in the hallway in the Oval Office, the President answered, "I don't believe so, unless we were walking back to the back dining room with the pizza. That statement, too, was false: Most of the sexual encounters between the President and Ms. Lewinsky occurred in that hallway (and on other occasions, they walked through the hallway to the dining room or study), and it is not credible that the President would have forgotten this fact.

Third, the President suggested at his civil deposition that he had no specific recollection of being alone with Ms. Lewinsky in the Oval Office, but had a general recollection that Ms. Lewinsky may have brought him "papers to sign" on certain occasions when she worked at the Legislative Affairs Office. This statement was false. Ms. Lewinsky did not bring him papers for official purposes. To the contrary, "bringing papers" was one of the sham "cover stories" that the President and Ms. Lewinsky had originally crafted to conceal their sexual relationship. The fact that the President resorted to a previously de-signed cover story when testifying under oath at the Jones deposition con-firms that he made these false denials in a calculated manner with the intent and knowledge that they were false.

The President had an obvious motive to lie in this respect. He knew that it would appear odd for a President to have been alone with a female intern or low-level staffer on so many occasions. Such an admission might persuade Judge Wright to deny any motion by Ms. Lewinsky to quash her deposition subpoena. It also might prompt Ms. Jones's attorneys to oppose efforts by Ms. Lewinsky not to be deposed and to ask specific questions of Ms. Lewinsky about the times she was alone with the President. It also might raise questions publicly if and when the President's deposition became public; at least parts of the deposition were likely to become public at trial, if not at the summary judgment stage.

Because lying about their sexual relationship was insufficient to avoid rais-ing further questions, the President also lied about being alone with Ms. Lewinsky—or at least feigned lack of memory as to specific occurrences.

**B. There is substantial and credible information that the President lied under oath in his civil deposition about gifts he exchanged with Monica Lewinsky.**

During his civil deposition, the President also was asked several questions about gifts he and Monica Lewinsky had exchanged. The evidence demon-strates that he answered the questions falsely. As with the questions about being alone, truthful answers to these questions would have raised questions about the nature of the relationship. Such answers also would have been in-consistent with the understanding of the President and Ms. Lewinsky that, in response to her subpoena, Ms. Lewinsky would not produce all of the gifts she had received from the President.

**1. The President's Civil Deposition Testimony About His Gifts to Monica Lewinsky**

During the President's deposition in the Jones case, Ms. Jones's attorneys asked several questions about whether he had given gifts to Monica Lewinsky.

Q: Well, have you ever given any gifts to Monica Lewinsky?

WJC: I don't recall. Do you know what they were?

Q: A hat pin?

WJC: I don't, I don't remember. But I certainly, I could have.

Q: A book about Walt Whitman?

WJC: I give—let me just say, I give people a lot of gifts, and when people are around I give a lot of things I have at the White House away, so I could have given her a gift, but I don't remember a specific gift.

Q: Do you remember giving her a gold broach?

WJC: No.

## 2. Evidence that Contradicts the President's Civil Deposition Testimony

(i) Just three weeks before the President's deposition, on December 28, 1997, President Clinton gave Ms. Lewinsky a number of gifts, the largest number he had ever given her. They included a large Rockettes blanket, a pin of the New York skyline, a marble-like bear's head from Vancouver, a pair of sunglasses, a small box of cherry chocolates, a canvas bag from the Black Dog, and a stuffed animal wearing a T-shirt from the Black Dog. Ms. Lewinsky produced the Rockettes blanket, the bear's head, the Black Dog canvas bag, the Black Dog stuffed animal, and the sunglasses to the OIC on July 29, 1998.

(ii) The evidence also demonstrates that the President gave Ms. Lewinsky a hat pin as a belated Christmas gift on February 28, 1997. The President and Ms. Lewinsky discussed the hatpin on December 28, 1997, after Ms. Lewinsky received a subpoena calling for her to produce all gifts from the President, including any hat pins. In her meeting with the President on December 28, 1997, according to Ms. Lewinsky, "I mentioned that I had been concerned about the hat pin being on the subpoena and he said that that had sort of concerned him also and asked me if I had told anyone that he had given me this hat pin and I said no." The President's secretary Betty Currie also testified that she had previously discussed the hat pin with the President.

(iii) Ms. Lewinsky testified that the President gave her additional gifts over the course of their relationship, such as a brooch, the book *Leaves of Grass* by Walt Whitman, an Annie Lennox compact disk, and a cigar.

## 3. President's Civil Deposition Testimony About Gifts from Monica Lewinsky to the President

When asked at his civil deposition in the Jones case whether Monica Lewinsky had ever given him gifts, President Clinton testified as follows:

Q: Has Monica Lewinsky ever given you any gifts?

WJC: Once or twice. I think she's given me a book or two.

Q: Did she give you a silver cigar box?

WJC: No.

Q: Did she give you a tie?

WJC: Yes, she has given me a tie before. I believe that's right. Now, as I said, let me remind you, normally when I get these ties, I get ties, you know, together, and then they're given to me later, but I believe that she has given me a tie.

## 4. Evidence that Contradicts the President's Testimony
## (i) Monica Lewinsky's Testimony

The evidence reveals that Ms. Lewinsky gave the President approximately 38 gifts; she says she almost always brought a gift or two when she visited.

a. Ms. Lewinsky testified before the grand jury that she gave the President six neckties.

b. Ms. Lewinsky testified that she gave the President a pair of sunglasses on approximately October 22, 1997. The President's attorney, David E. Kendall, stated in a letter on March 16, 1998: "We believe that Ms. Lewinsky might have given the President a few additional items, such as ties and a pair of sunglasses, but we have not been able to locate these items."

c. On November 13, 1997, Ms. Lewinsky gave the President an antique paperweight that depicted the White House. Ms. Lewinsky testified that on December 6, 1997, and possibly again on December 28, 1997, she saw this paperweight in the dining room, where the President keeps many items of political memorabilia. The President turned over the paperweight to the OIC in response to a second subpoena calling for it.

d. Ms. Lewinsky gave the President at least seven books: . . .

e. Ms. Lewinsky gave the President an antique cigar holder, on December 6, 1997.

f. Ms. Lewinsky testified that she gave the President a number of additional gifts.

### Document 2: Clinton Speaks to the Nation[2]

*In August 1998, Clinton testified before the Independent Counsel and the Grand Jury. Following that event, and before the Independent Counsel released his report, Clinton spoke to the nation and tried to explain his actions and offered an apology for his actions. This was an unprecedented action by a sitting president.*

Good evening.

This afternoon in this room, from this chair, I testified before the Office of Independent Counsel and the grand jury.

I answered their questions truthfully, including questions about my private life, questions no American citizen would ever want to answer.

Still, I must take complete responsibility for all my actions, both public and private. And that is why I am speaking to you tonight.

As you know, in a deposition in January, I was asked questions about my relationship with Monica Lewinsky. While my answers were legally accurate, I did not volunteer information.

Indeed, I did have a relationship with Ms. Lewinsky that was not appropriate. In fact, it was wrong. It constituted a critical lapse in judgment and a personal failure on my part for which I am solely and completely responsible.

But I told the grand jury today and I say to you now that at no time did I ask anyone to lie, to hide or destroy evidence or to take any other unlawful action.

I know that my public comments and my silence about this matter gave a false impression. I misled people, including even my wife. I deeply regret that.

I can only tell you I was motivated by many factors. First, by a desire to protect myself from the embarrassment of my own conduct.

I was also very concerned about protecting my family. The fact that these questions were being asked in a politically inspired lawsuit, which has since been dismissed, was a consideration, too.

In addition, I had real and serious concerns about an independent counsel investigation that began with private business dealings 20 years ago, dealings, I might add, about which an independent federal agency found no evidence of any wrongdoing by me or my wife over two years ago.

The independent counsel investigation moved on to my staff and friends, then into my private life. And now the investigation itself is under investigation.

This has gone on too long, cost too much and hurt too many innocent people.

Now, this matter is between me, the two people I love most—my wife and our daughter—and our God. I must put it right, and I am prepared to do whatever it takes to do so.

Nothing is more important to me personally. But it is private, and I intend to reclaim my family life for my family. It's nobody's business but ours.

Even presidents have private lives. It is time to stop the pursuit of personal destruction and the prying into private lives and get on with our national life.

Our country has been distracted by this matter for too long, and I take my responsibility for my part in all of this. That is all I can do.

Now it is time—in fact, it is past time—to move on.

We have important work to do—real opportunities to seize, real problems to solve, real security matters to face.

And so tonight, I ask you to turn away from the spectacle of the past seven months, to repair the fabric of our national discourse, and to return our attention to all the challenges and all the promise of the next American century.

Thank you for watching. And good night.

## Document 3: Impeachment Resolutions[3]

*In the Congressional elections of 1998, the Democrats regained some of the losses they had suffered in 1994, but the Republican Party still retained control of both houses of Congress. During the lame-duck session after the November 1998 elections, impeachment proceedings against President Clinton began. This was done partly because the Republican Party had a larger majority in the House of Representatives that it would have when the new Congress convened. Four impeachment resolutions were considered. The full House approved two and rejected two of the resolutions. The resolutions that went before the Senate for trial follow.*

### RESOLUTION

Impeaching William Jefferson Clinton, President of the United States, for high crimes and misdemeanors.

*Resolved,* That William Jefferson Clinton, President of the United States, is impeached for high crimes and misdemeanors, and that the following articles of impeachment be exhibited to the United States Senate:

Articles of impeachment exhibited by the House of Representatives of the United States of America in the name of itself and of the people of the United States of America, against William Jefferson Clinton, President of the United States of America, in maintenance and support of its impeachment against him for high crimes and misdemeanors.

### Article I

In his conduct while President of the United States, William Jefferson Clinton, in violation of his constitutional oath faithfully to execute the office of President of the United States and, to the best of his ability, preserve, protect, and defend the Constitution of the United States, and in violation of his constitutional duty to take care that the laws be faithfully executed, has willfully corrupted and manipulated the judicial process of the United States for his personal gain and exoneration, impeding the administration of justice, in that:

On August 17, 1998, William Jefferson Clinton swore to tell the truth, the whole truth, and nothing but the truth before a Federal grand jury of the United States. Contrary to that oath, William Jefferson Clinton willfully provided perjurious, false and misleading testimony to the grand jury concerning one or more of the following: (1) the nature and details of his relationship with a subordinate Government employee; (2) prior perjurious, false and misleading testimony he gave in a Federal civil rights action brought against him; (3) prior false and misleading statements he allowed his attorney to make to a Federal judge in that civil rights action; and (4) his corrupt efforts to influence the testimony of witnesses and to impede the discovery of evidence in that civil rights action.

In doing this, William Jefferson Clinton has undermined the integrity of his office, has brought disrepute on the Presidency, has betrayed his trust as President, and has acted in a manner subversive of the rule of law and justice, to the manifest injury of the people of the United States.

Wherefore, William Jefferson Clinton, by such conduct, warrants impeachment and trial, and removal from office and disqualification to hold and enjoy any office of honor, trust, or profit under the United States.

## Article II

In his conduct while President of the United States, William Jefferson Clinton, in violation of his constitutional oath faithfully to execute the office of President of the United States and, to the best of his ability, preserve, protect, and defend the Constitution of the United States, and in violation of his constitutional duty to take care that the laws be faithfully executed, has prevented, obstructed, and impeded the administration of justice, and has to that end engaged personally, and through his subordinates and agents, in a course of conduct or scheme designed to delay, impede, cover up, and conceal the existence of evidence and testimony related to a Federal civil rights action brought against him in a duly instituted judicial proceeding. The means used to implement this course of conduct or scheme included one or more of the following acts:

(1) On or about December 17, 1997, William Jefferson Clinton corruptly encouraged a witness in a Federal civil rights action brought against him to execute a sworn affidavit in that proceeding that he knew to be perjurious, false and misleading.

(2) On or about December 17, 1997, William Jefferson Clinton corruptly encouraged a witness in a Federal civil rights action brought against him to give perjurious, false and misleading testimony if and when called to testify personally in that proceeding.

(3) On or about December 28, 1997, William Jefferson Clinton corruptly engaged in, encouraged, or supported a scheme to conceal evidence that had been subpoenaed in a Federal civil rights action brought against him.

(4) Beginning on or about December 7, 1997, and continuing through and including January 14, 1998, William Jefferson Clinton intensified and succeeded in an effort to secure job assistance to a witness in a Federal civil rights action brought against him in order to corruptly prevent the truthful testimony of that witness in that proceeding at a time when the truthful testimony of that witness would have been harmful to him.

(5) On January 17, 1998, at his deposition in a Federal civil rights action brought against him, William Jefferson Clinton corruptly allowed his

attorney to make false and misleading statements to a Federal judge characterizing an affidavit, in order to prevent questioning deemed relevant by the judge. Such false and misleading statements were subsequently acknowledged by his attorney in a communication to that judge.

(6) On or about January 18 and January 20-21, 1998, William Jefferson Clinton related a false and misleading account of events relevant to a Federal civil rights action brought against him to a potential witness in that proceeding, in order to corruptly influence the testimony of that witness.

(7) On or about January 21, 23, and 26, 1998, William Jefferson Clinton made false and misleading statements to potential witnesses in a Federal grand jury proceeding in order to corruptly influence the testimony of those witnesses. The false and misleading statements made by William Jefferson Clinton were repeated by the witnesses to the grand jury, causing the grand jury to receive false and misleading information.

In all of this, William Jefferson Clinton has undermined the integrity of his office, has brought disrepute on the Presidency, has betrayed his trust as President, and has acted in a manner subversive of the rule of law and justice, to the manifest injury of the people of the United States.

Wherefore, William Jefferson Clinton, by such conduct, warrants impeachment and trial, and removal from office and disqualification to hold and enjoy any office of honor, trust, or profit under the United States.

Passed the House of Representatives December 19, 1998.

## Document 4: Hyde Testimony in the Senate[4]

*Once the impeachment resolutions were approved in the House of Representatives, the trial was held in the Senate after the new Congress took office. The trial lasted from January 7 to February 12, 1999. In the final vote, the resolution regarding perjury was defeated by a vote of 45 in favor and 55 opposed. The obstruction of justice vote failed with a tie vote of 50–50. Neither of the votes came close to passing because the Constitution requires a two-thirds vote of the Senate to convict.*

*Henry Hyde, a member of the House from Illinois, was one of the managers (similar to a prosecutor) from the House to make the case against President Clinton in the Senate. During his closing arguments in the Senate, he tried to refute some of the public perception that the impeachment was about President Clinton's sexual adventures. Hyde tried to put the argument on a more legal basis, but his argument did not sway enough Senators to get a guilty verdict on either charge. This is a portion of his closing argument.*

Mr. Manager HYDE. Mr. Chief Justice, counsel for the President, distinguished Members of the Senate, . . .

This controversy began with the fact that the President of the United States took an oath to tell the truth in his testimony before the grand jury, just as he had on two prior occasions sworn a solemn oath to preserve, protect, and defend the Constitution and to faithfully execute the laws of the United States.

One of the most memorable aspects of this proceeding was the solemn occasion wherein every Senator in this Chamber took an oath to do impartial justice under the Constitution.

But I must say, despite massive and relentless efforts to change the subject, the case before you Senators is not about sexual misconduct, infidelity or adultery—those are private acts and none of our business. It is not even a question of lying about sex. The matter before this body is a question of lying under oath. This is a public act.

The matter before you is a question of the willful, premeditated deliberate corruption of the Nation's system of justice, through perjury and obstruction of justice. These are public acts, and when committed by the chief law enforcement officer of the land, the one who appoints every United States district attorney, every Federal judge, every member of the Supreme Court, the Attorney General—they do become the concern of Congress.

That is why your judgment, respectfully, should rise above politics, above partisanship, above polling data. This case is a test of whether what the Founding Fathers described as "sacred honor" still has meaning in our time: two hundred twenty-two years after those two words—sacred honor—were inscribed in our country's birth certificate, our national charter of freedom, our Declaration of Independence. . . .

The Presidency is an office of trust. Every public office is a public trust, but the Office of President is a very special public trust. The President is the trustee of the national conscience. No one owns the Office of President, the people do. The President is elected by the people and their representatives in the electoral college. And in accepting the burdens of that great office, the President, in his inaugural oath, enters into a covenant—a binding agreement of mutual trust and obligation—with the American people.

Shortly after his election and during his first months in office, President Clinton spoke with some frequency about a "new covenant" in America. In this instance, let us take the President at his word: that his office is a covenant, a solemn pact of mutual trust and obligation—with the American people. Let us take the President seriously when he speaks of covenants: because a covenant is about promise-making and promise-keeping. For it is because the President has defaulted on the promises he made—it is because he has violated the oaths he has sworn—that he has been impeached. . . .

Today, we see something else: that the fundamental trust between America and the world can be broken, if a Presidential Perjurer represents our country in world affairs. If the President calculatedly and repeatedly violates his oath, if the President breaks the covenant of trust he has made with the American people, he can no longer be trusted. And, because the executive plays so large a role in representing the country to the world, America can no longer be trusted. . . .

Trust, not what James Madison called the "parchment barriers" of laws, is the fundamental bond between the people and their elected representatives, between those who govern and those who are governed. Trust is the mortar that secures the foundations of the American house of freedom. And the Senate of the United States, sitting in judgment in this impeachment trial, should not ignore, or minimize, or dismiss the fact that the bond of trust has been broken, because the President has violated both his oaths of office and the oath he took before his grand jury testimony. . . .

No greater harm can be done than breaking the covenant of trust between the President and the people; among the three branches of our government; and between the country and the world.

For to break that covenant of trust is to dissolve the mortar that binds the foundation stones of our freedom into a secure and solid edifice. And to break that covenant of trust by violating one's oath is to do grave damage to the rule of law among us.

That none of us is above the law is a bedrock principle of democracy. To erode that bedrock is to risk even further injustice. To erode that bedrock is to subscribe, to a "divine right of kings" theory of governance, in which those who govern are absolved from adhering to the basic moral standards to which the governed are accountable. We must never tolerate one law for the ruler, and another for the ruled. If we do, we break faith with our ancestors from Bunker Hill, Lexington and Concord to Flanders Field, Normandy, Iwo Jima, Panmunjom, Saigon and Desert Storm.

Let us be clear: The vote that you are asked to cast is, in the final analysis, a vote about the rule of law.

The rule of law is one of the great achievements of our civilization. For the alternative to the rule of law is the rule of raw power. We here today are the heirs of three thousand years of history in which humanity slowly, painfully and at great cost, evolved a form of politics in which law, not brute force, is the arbiter of our public destinies. . . .

Morally serious men and women can imagine circumstances, at the far edge of the morally permissible, when, with the gravest matters of national interest at stake, a President could shade the truth in order to serve the common good. But under oath, for a private pleasure?

In doing this, the Office of President of the United States has been debased and the justice system jeopardized.

In doing this, he has broken his covenant of trust with the American people.

The framers also knew that the Office of President of the United States could be gravely damaged if it continued to be unworthily occupied. That is why they devised the process of impeachment by the House and trial by the Senate. It is, in truth, a direct process. If, on impeachment, the President is convicted, he is removed from office—and the office itself suffers no permanent damage. If, on impeachment, the President is acquitted, the issue is resolved once and for all, and the office is similarly protected from permanent damage.

But if, on impeachment, the President is not convicted and removed from office despite the fact that numerous Senators are convinced that he has, in the words of one proposed resolution of censure, "egregiously failed" the test of his oath of office, "violated the trust of the American people," and "dishonored the office which they entrusted to him," then the Office of the Presidency has been deeply, and perhaps permanently damaged . . . .

Senators, we of the House do not come before you today lightly. And, if you will permit me, it is a disservice to the House to suggest that it has brought these articles of impeachment before you in a mean-spirited or irresponsible way. That is not true.

We have brought these articles of impeachment because we are convinced, in conscience, that the President of the United States lied under oath; that the President committed perjury on several occasions before a Federal grand jury. We have brought these articles of impeachment because we are convinced, in conscience, that the President willfully obstructed justice and thereby threatened the legal system he swore a solemn oath to protect and defend.

These are not trivial matters. These are not partisan matters. These are matters of justice, the justice that each of you has taken a solemn oath to serve in this trial. . . .


## Part B: The 9/11 Attacks


### Background

*Because of the dependence of the world on the oil reserves of the Middle East, Americans became more involved in the affairs of that part of the world. Since the Middle East, with the exception of Israel, is predominantly Muslim in religion and culture, one would think that Americans would become more knowledgeable and understanding of that culture, but that was not the case. The rise of radical*

*Islamic groups puzzled Americans, many of whom saw no way of dealing with them.*

*The most dramatic event in this regard came just at the beginning of the twenty-first century when a group of Islamic suicide bombers attacked the World Trade Center towers in New York and the Pentagon in Washington. The shock and anger of Americans were understandable. Except for the attack by the Japanese on Pearl Harbor in 1941, the nation had been invincible to attack at home since the British invaded and burned Washington, D.C., during the War of 1812.*

*Therefore, the attack on September 11, 2001, is a good symbol of the status of the United States at the end of the twentieth century. It stands as a good bookend to the acquisition of the Philippines and other possessions that occurred in the last year of the nineteenth century.*

## Document 1: The Attack[5]

*In the aftermath of the attack, a special commission was appointed to investigate the attack and the response. The first few paragraphs of the Executive Summary of the Report provide a good, brief overview of what happened.*

At 8:46 on the morning of September 11, 2001, the United States became a nation transformed.

An airliner traveling at hundreds of miles per hour and carrying some 10,000 gallons of jet fuel plowed into the North Tower of the World Trade Center in Lower Manhattan. At 9:03, a second airliner hit the South Tower. Fire and smoke billowed upward. Steel, glass, ash, and bodies fell below. The Twin Towers, where up to 50,000 people worked each day, both collapsed less than 90 minutes later.

At 9:37 that same morning, a third airliner slammed into the western face of the Pentagon. At 10:03, a fourth airliner crashed in a field in southern Pennsylvania. It had been aimed at the United States Capitol or the White House, and was forced down by heroic passengers armed with the knowledge that America was under attack.

More than 2,600 people died at the World Trade Center; 125 died at the Pentagon; 256 died on the four planes. The death toll surpassed that at Pearl Harbor in December 1941.

This immeasurable pain was inflicted by 19 young Arabs acting at the behest of Islamist extremists headquartered in distant Afghanistan. Some had been in the United States for more than a year, mixing with the rest of the population. Though four had training as pilots, most were not well-educated. Most spoke English poorly, some hardly at all. In groups of four or five, carrying with them only small knives, box cutters, and cans of Mace or pepper

*The attacks on September 11, 2001, were the worst on American soil since the Pearl Harbor attack in 1941. The Twin Towers of the World Trade Center In New York City were a symbol of what America had become. For these towers to be attacked and then to collapse was almost incomprehensible. This view shows the towers in flames from across the East River in Brooklyn. Copyright Mark Smith, www.camazotz.com/wtc/large/1.html. Used by permission.*

spray, they had hijacked the four planes and turned them into deadly guided missiles. . . .

### Documents 2–3: President Bush Reacts

*When the attacks occurred, President George W. Bush was in Florida in an elementary school classroom. When someone came in and whispered in his ear about the attacks, the president did not respond immediately. He seemed befuddled and did not know how to respond, but he later made a more comprehensive speech.*

*Document 2: Bush's comments from Florida[6]*

*Soon after hearing about the attacks, the president did issue a brief statement.*

Ladies and gentlemen, this is a difficult moment for America. I, unfortunately, will be going back to Washington after my remarks. Secretary Rod Paige and the Lt. Governor will take the podium and discuss education. I do want to thank the folks here at Booker Elementary School for their hospitality.

Today, we've had a national tragedy. Two airplanes have crashed into the World Trade Center in an apparent terrorist attack on our country. I have spoken to the Vice President, to the Governor of New York, to the Director of the FBI, and have ordered that the full resources of the federal government go to help the victims and their families, and to conduct a full-scale investigation to hunt down and to find those folks who committed this act.

Terrorism against our nation will not stand.

And now if you [would] join me in a moment of silence.

May God bless the victims, their families, and America.

Thank you very much.

*Document 3: President Bush addresses the Nation[7]*

*Later in the evening of September 11, President Bush addressed the nation. It was a brief presentation meant mostly to reassure the nation regarding its fears and uncertainties.*

THE PRESIDENT: Good evening. Today, our fellow citizens, our way of life, our very freedom came under attack in a series of deliberate and deadly terrorist acts. The victims were in airplanes, or in their offices; secretaries, businessmen and women, military and federal workers; moms and dads, friends and neighbors. Thousands of lives were suddenly ended by evil, despicable acts of terror.

The pictures of airplanes flying into buildings, fires burning, huge structures collapsing, have filled us with disbelief, terrible sadness, and a quiet, unyielding anger. These acts of mass murder were intended to frighten our nation into chaos and retreat. But they have failed; our country is strong.

A great people has been moved to defend a great nation. Terrorist attacks can shake the foundations of our biggest buildings, but they cannot touch the foundation of America. These acts shattered steel, but they cannot dent the steel of American resolve. America was targeted for attack because we're the brightest beacon for freedom and opportunity in the world. And no one will keep that light from shining.

Today, our nation saw evil, the very worst of human nature. And we responded with the best of America—with the daring of our rescue workers, with the caring for strangers and neighbors who came to give blood and help in any way they could.

Immediately following the first attack, I implemented our government's emergency response plans. Our military is powerful, and it's prepared. Our emergency teams are working in New York City and Washington, D.C. to help with local rescue efforts.

Our first priority is to get help to those who have been injured, and to take every precaution to protect our citizens at home and around the world from further attacks.

The functions of our government continue without interruption. Federal agencies in Washington which had to be evacuated today are reopening for essential personnel tonight, and will be open for business tomorrow. Our financial institutions remain strong, and the American economy will be open for business, as well.

The search is underway for those who are behind these evil acts. I've directed the full resources of our intelligence and law enforcement communities to find those responsible and to bring them to justice. We will make no distinction between the terrorists who committed these acts and those who harbor them.

I appreciate so very much the members of Congress who have joined me in strongly condemning these attacks. And on behalf of the American people, I thank the many world leaders who have called to offer their condolences and assistance.

America and our friends and allies join with all those who want peace and security in the world, and we stand together to win the war against terrorism.

Tonight, I ask for your prayers for all those who grieve, for the children whose worlds have been shattered, for all whose sense of safety and security has been threatened. And I pray they will be comforted by a power greater than any of us, spoken through the ages in Psalm 23: "Even though I walk through the valley of the shadow of death, I fear no evil, for You are with me."

This is a day when all Americans from every walk of life unite in our resolve for justice and peace. America has stood down enemies before, and we will do so this time. None of us will ever forget this day. Yet, we go forward to defend freedom and all that is good and just in our world.

Thank you. Good night, and God bless America.

## Documents 4–5: The Liberal Press Responds

*In the aftermath of the attack,* The Nation, *a venerable press representative of liberal Americans, was understandably concerned about the impact the attack would have on the rights of Americans.*

### Document 4: The Nation *urges caution*[8]

*One of the responses from* The Nation, *in an editorial, urged caution in the American response.*

We have taken a great wound, we Americans, and our first task is to rescue survivors if that is still possible, to grieve and to remain alert until we better understand what happened to us. The time will come soon enough to sort out the causes, who delivered this vicious attack and how we hold them accountable, then to assign official blame at home, if the facts require it. We should also begin deeper arguments about the political meanings, the failures in our own leadership and the role our government has chosen to play in the world. . . .

One odd privilege of being American is that we have had very little experience with such blindsiding assaults, at least in modern times. Other countries became the battlegrounds, not ours. Other peoples were schooled in stoical expectations, knowing that the worst can happen and sometimes does, but not Americans.

It is essential now to stick to hard facts, not fearsome shadows or injured hubris (or the xenophobic hatreds already in the air). Yet the intelligence agencies that had not a clue what was coming were claiming within hours to have proof of who organized the attack. . . .

Civil liberties, already under attack, were immediate targets. Legislators talked of granting the FBI and other agencies broad new powers—this despite the fact that the FBI is already intercepting a record number of calls. Some called for wholesale closing of US borders. On Tuesday, only Senator Joseph Biden, himself a key supporter of the noxious Anti-Terrorism and Effective Death Penalty bill of 1996, to his credit stood on the Capitol lawn to suggest that any incursions on civil liberties should be resisted.

After the dead are properly mourned, after we have reliably established how this happened and who was responsible, then we Americans must undertake a most difficult conversation among ourselves. Yes, we should speak with one voice expressing our compassion and outrage, but we need a multiplicity of voices, a true national debate about what sane national security means in the twenty-first century. . . . In the long run, the only way to deal with international terrorism is to build and support international institutions toward that end.

This is a pivotal moment when we should reconsider our posture toward the world and examine the true burdens and obligations of acting like an empire awesomely more powerful than any others and answerable to no one. . . . Yet, as we learned and should have already understood, this great country is vulnerable too, beyond imagination. Whoever planned this vicious attack must have calculated that the United States is at a fragile juncture, its great prosperity sinking and uncertain leaders in power. They probably intended an unraveling, both of financial markets and the national confidence. It may seem trite to say so, but the calamity does test our character. If we are shrewd about ourselves and truly brave, citizens will not yield to hysteria—or accept draconian new laws that undermine civil liberties—but will force these difficult questions into the political debate.

*Document 5: Did the government have advance knowledge?*[9]

*Almost from the beginning, some people wondered if the government had prior knowledge about the possibility of attack. Some wondered if the knowledge was there, why no action had been taken, as one can see in this opinion piece.*

"Faceless cowards." This was mini-President Bush in the first of his abysmal statements on the assault. Faceless maybe, but cowards? Were the Japanese aviators who surprised Pearl Harbor on December 7, 1941, cowards? I don't think so, and they at least had the hope of returning to their aircraft carriers. The onslaughts on the World Trade Center and the Pentagon are being likened to Pearl Harbor, and the comparison is just. From the point of view of the assailants the attacks were near miracles of logistical calculation, timing, audacity in execution and devastation inflicted upon the targets. And the commando units captured four aircraft, armed only with penknives. Was there ever better proof of Napoleon's dictum that in war the moral is to the material as three is to one?

Beyond the installation of another national trauma, there may be further similarity to Pearl Harbor. The possibility of a Japanese attack in early December of 1941 was known to US Naval Intelligence. The day after the September 11 attack, a friend told me that a relative working at the US Army's Picatinny Arsenal in New Jersey said that six weeks earlier the arsenal had been placed on top-security alert. In late August Osama bin Laden, a prime suspect, said in an interview with Abdel Bari Atwan, the editor in chief of the London-based *al-Quds al-Arabi* newspaper, that he planned "very, very big attacks against American interests." On the evening of September 11, Senator John Kerry said he had recently been told by Director of Central Intelligence George Tenet that the agency had successfully pre-empted earlier attacks by bin Laden's people. Maybe the intelligence agencies didn't reckon with the possibility of assaults in rapid succession.

The lust for retaliation traditionally outstrips precision in identifying the actual assailant. The targets abroad will be all the usual suspects. The target at home will be the Bill of Rights. . . .

The explosions were not an hour old before terror pundits like Anthony Cordesman, Wesley Clark, Robert Gates and Lawrence Eagleburger were saying that these attacks had been possible "because America is a democracy," adding that now some democratic perquisites might have to be abandoned. What might this mean? . . .

That dark Tuesday did not offer a flattering exhibition of America's leaders. For most of the day the only Bush who looked composed and controlled was Laura, who happened to be waiting to testify on Capitol Hill. Her husband gave a timid and stilted initial reaction in Sarasota, Florida, then disappeared for an hour before resurfacing at an Air Force base near Shreveport, Louisiana, where he gave another flaccid address. He then ran to ground in a deep shelter in Nebraska, before someone finally had the wit to suggest that the best place for an American President at a time of national emergency is the Oval Office. . . .

The commentators were similarly incapable of explaining with any depth the likely context of the attacks. . . . One could watch endlessly without hearing any intimation that these attacks might be the consequence of the recent Israeli rampages in the occupied territories, which have included assassinations of Palestinian leaders and the slaughter of Palestinian civilians with the use of American arms and aircraft that these attacks might also stem from the sanctions against Iraq, which have killed more than half a million children; that these attacks might in part be a response to US cruise missile destruction of the Sudanese factories that were falsely fingered by US intelligence as connected to bin Laden.

. . . George Bush will have no trouble in raiding the famous lockbox, using Social Security trust funds to give more money to the Defense Department. That about sums it up. Three planes are successfully steered into three of America's most conspicuous buildings, and the US response will be to put more money into missile defense as a way of bolstering the economy.

### Documents 6–7: The Conservative Press Reacts

*The* National Review *is one of the leading conservative magazines, but its positions are not always what one would expect.*

### Document 6: "At war" *says the* National Review

*In its first editorial after the attacks, the* National Review *looked upon the events as an act of war.*

. . . Few wars begin like their predecessors. The wars of the last century opened with thrusts into Belgium or Poland, a surprise attack on battleships, a lurch in Kuwait, a steadily accreting campaign of jungle murder. This war began with four hijacked airplanes targeted at the Pentagon, Camp David, and the two World Trade Towers.

No one should think of this as terrorism, which is the effort to spread death and dismay among civilian populations. . . .

Our enemies have proximate motives, as political and military actors always do. But let no one imagine that any American policy or lack of it, or any change in our ethnic or religious makeup, could have insulated us from such a strike. The United States is hated because we are, indeed, powerful, rich, and good. . . . Our national headquarters and totems excite the fear and wrath of those in the world who feel themselves shortchanged. For this historical moment, anyone who has a quarrel with the status quo will find us, with varying degrees of truth, somehow implicated in his discontents. Our exposure to these emotions is an unavoidable badge of honor.

Because this was an act of war, its agents must not be pursued by resolutions, lawsuits, or any of the other legalistic and diplomatic devices by which we have tried to combat terrorists in the recent past. President Bush's and Secretary of State Powell's early talk of "hunting down" the perpetrators is incomplete. These are not traffic violators to be given a desk ticket at the night court of The Hague. After the time it takes to guess the attackers' commanders, which should not be long, those commanders, and their allies and patrons, should be paved over. If our retaliatory strikes hit a few of the world's warriors who happened not to be involved in this war, that will be no great loss.

News reports showed dancing in the streets of Middle Eastern cities, graphic proof that our enemies are not restricted to cadres of ideologues or leaders. Striking the war-making capacity of hostile nations may involve clearing some of those streets. When that happens, we should not shrink. . . .

The vacation that began with the end of the Cold War ended with the summer of 2001. . . . The first duty of the state is to protect the national security. . . . We need our diplomats, not to attend conferences and solve the world's problems, but to cut deals that are to our advantage and explain the consequences of actions that are not; we need our military resources, not to run elections and perform social work in the BedStuys and Appalachias of the world, but to punish offenses and intimidate enemies.

The September Massacres would not, of course, have been stopped by missile defense. They were not stopped by aircraft carriers. Does that mean we should have none? No great power seems to have been actively involved, but that not mean that a great power might not threaten one day to send four warheads somewhere. We must be prepared to meet that threat, as we prepare to repel further attacks of this kind. Such an operation was not the work of a handful of men; there had to be coordination, planning, support. Our intelligence was woefully lacking; our domestic defense capabilities need to be addressed. . . .

The world, we have been taught, is always full of competing views. In the intellectual pine barrens of the West, there are anarchist and neo-Communist stirrings. Islam harbors a fundamentalist strain, a minority even in the Middle East, a minority worldwide. China is modernizing the Asian road to despotism—a very old road; Confucius warned against it. These options lead to poverty and tyranny. The United States, for all its follies and sins, is the best the world has to offer.

We should therefore be of good cheer. In the darkest early days of World War II Winston Churchill told British diplomats on the European continent to light their windows, hold the usual functions, to conduct themselves with confidence and spirit. No skulking in bunkers or military bases for him, or for us. Schedule the rebuilding of our wasted icons. Our fellow citizens are lost, but the steel and glass will come back. When it does we will hang out a million flags.

### Document 7: The attacks were war, not crimes[11]

*One of the columns in the* National Review *warned the readers not to mistake the attacks as criminal acts. This author suggested that in wartime, one cannot be as careful of the lives of civilians as might be true in other circumstances.*

"Make no mistake: The United States will hunt down and punish those responsible for these cowardly acts." So spoke President Bush in his address to the nation soon after the catastrophic events of September 11.

I agree with the president's sentiments but disagree with two specifics in this statement. First, there was nothing cowardly about the attacks, which were deeds of incredible—albeit perverted—bravery. Second, to "hunt down and punish" the perpetrators is deeply to misunderstand the problem. It implies that we view the plane crashes as criminal deeds rather than what they truly are—acts of war. . . . Occurring with almost predictable regularity a few times a year, assaults on Americans have included explosions on airliners, at commercial buildings, and at a variety of U.S. governmental installations. Before last week, the total death toll was about 600 American lives.

To me, this sustained record of violence looks awfully much like war, but Washington in its wisdom has insisted otherwise. Official policy has viewed the attacks as a sequence of discrete criminal incidents. Seeing terrorism primarily as a problem of law enforcement is a mistake, because it means:

• Focusing on the arrest and trial of the dispensable characters who actually carry out violent acts, leaving the funders, planners, organizers, and commanders of terrorism to continue their work unscathed, prepared to carry out more attacks.

- Relying primarily on such defensive measures as metal detectors, security guards, bunkers, police arrests, and prosecutorial eloquence—rather than on such offensive tools as soldiers, aircraft, and ships.
- Misunderstanding the terrorist's motivations as criminal, whereas they are usually based on extremist ideologies.
- Missing the fact that terrorist groups (and the states that support them) have declared war on the United States (sometimes publicly).
- Requiring that the U.S. government have unrealistically high levels of proof before deploying military force. If it lacks evidence that can stand up in a U.S. court of justice, as is usually the case, no action is taken. The legalistic mindset thus ensures that, in the vast majority of cases, the U.S. government does not respond, and killers of Americans pay little or no price.

The time has come for a paradigm shift, toward viewing terrorism as a form of warfare. Such a change will have many implications. It means targeting not just those foot soldiers who actually carry out the violence but the organizations and governments that stand behind them. It means relying on the armed forces, not policemen, to protect Americans. It means defense overseas rather than in American courtrooms. It means that organizations and governments that sponsor terrorism—not just the foot soldiers who carry it out—will pay the price.

It means dispensing with the unrealistically high expectations of proof so that when reasonable evidence points to a regime's or an organization's having harmed Americans, U.S. military force can be deployed. It means that, as in conventional war, Washington need not know the names and specific actions of enemy soldiers before fighting them.

It means retaliating every single time terrorism harms an American. There is no need to know the precise identity of a perpetrator; in war, there are times when one strikes first and asks questions later. When an attack takes place, it could be reason to target any of those known to harbor terrorists. If the perpetrator is not precisely known, then punish those who are known to harbor terrorists. Go after the governments and organizations that support terrorism.

It means using force so that the punishment is disproportionately greater than the attack. The U.S. has a military force far more powerful than any other in the world: Why spend hundreds of billions of dollars a year on it and not deploy it to defend Americans?

I give fair warning: The military approach demands more from Americans than does the legal one. It requires a readiness to spend money and to lose lives. . . . Going the military route requires a long-term commitment that will demand much from Americans over many years.

But it will be worth it, for the safety of Americans depends ultimately not on defense but on offense; on victories not in the courtroom but on the battlefield. The US-government needs to establish a newly fearsome reputation, so that anyone who harms Americans knows that retribution will be certain and nasty. Nothing can replace the destruction of any organization or government that harms so much as a single American citizen.

To those who say this approach would start a cycle of violence, the answer is obvious: That cycle already exists, as Americans are constantly murdered in acts of terrorism. Further, by baring their teeth, Americans are far more likely to intimidate their enemies than to instigate further violence. Retaliation will reduce violence, not further increase it, providing Americans with a safety they presently do not enjoy.

### Document 8: The Commission Reports[12]

*The 9/11 Commission was appointed to investigate the attacks and make recommendations for future policy and actions. Controversy surrounded the commission, even its creation, a year or more after the September 11, 2001, attacks. The report was issued in July 2004. It is a long report; even its Executive Summary is long. Below is an excerpt of the Executive Summary.*

### EXECUTIVE SUMMARY

We present the narrative of this report and the recommendations that flow from it to the President of the United States, the United States Congress, and the American people for their consideration. Ten Commissioners—five Republicans and five Democrats chosen by elected leaders from our nation's capital at a time of great partisan division—have come together to present this report without dissent.

We have come together with a unity of purpose because our nation demands it. September 11, 2001, was a day of unprecedented shock and suffering in the history of the United States. The nation was unprepared.

### A NATION TRANSFORMED

### A Shock, Not a Surprise

...The 9/11 attacks on the World Trade Center and the Pentagon were far more elaborate, precise, and destructive than any of these earlier assaults. But by September 2001, the executive branch of the U.S. government, the Congress, the news media, and the American public had received clear warning that Islamist terrorists meant to kill Americans in high numbers. . . .

By September 11, 2001, al Qaeda possessed

- leaders able to evaluate, approve, and supervise the planning and direction of a major operation;

- a personnel system that could recruit candidates, indoctrinate them, vet them, and give them the necessary training;
- communications sufficient to enable planning and direction of operatives and those who would be helping them;
- an intelligence effort to gather required information and form assessments of enemy strengths and weaknesses;
- the ability to move people great distances; and
- the ability to raise and move the money necessary to finance an attack.

### 1998 to September 11, 2001. . .

U.S. intelligence frequently picked up reports of attacks planned by al Qaeda. Working with foreign security services, the CIA broke up some al Qaeda cells. The core of Bin Ladin's organization nevertheless remained intact. In December 1999, news about the arrests of the terrorist cell in Jordan and the arrest of a terrorist at the U.S.-Canadian border became part of a "millennium alert." The government was galvanized, and the public was on alert for any possible attack. . . .

During the spring and summer of 2001, U.S. intelligence agencies received a stream of warnings that al Qaeda planned, as one report put it, "something very, very, very big." Director of Central Intelligence George Tenet told us, "The system was blinking red." . . .

### September 11, 2001

The day began with the 19 hijackers getting through a security checkpoint system that they had evidently analyzed and knew how to defeat. Their success rate in penetrating the system was 19 for 19. They took over the four flights, taking advantage of air crews and cockpits that were not prepared for the contingency of a suicide hijacking.

On 9/11, the defense of U.S. air space depended on close interaction between two federal agencies: the Federal Aviation Administration (FAA) and North American Aerospace Defense Command (NORAD). Existing protocols on 9/11 were unsuited in every respect for an attack in which hijacked planes were used as weapons.

What ensued was a hurried attempt to improvise a defense by civilians who had never handled a hijacked aircraft that attempted to disappear, and by a military unprepared for the transformation of commercial aircraft into weapons of mass destruction.

A shootdown authorization was not communicated to the NORAD air defense sector until 28 minutes after United 93 had crashed in Pennsylvania. Planes were scrambled, but ineffectively, as they did not know where to go or what targets they were to intercept. And once the shootdown order was given, it was not communicated to the pilots. In short, while leaders in Washington believed that the fighters circling above them had been instructed to "take out" hostile aircraft, the only orders actually conveyed to the pilots were to "ID type and tail." ...

## Operational Opportunities

We write with the benefit and handicap of hindsight. We are mindful of the danger of being unjust to men and women who made choices in conditions of uncertainty and in circumstances over which they often had little control.

Nonetheless, there were specific points of vulnerability in the plot and opportunities to disrupt it. Operational failures—opportunities that were not or could not be exploited by the organizations and systems of that time—included:

- not watchlisting future hijackers Hazmi and Mihdhar, not trailing them after they traveled to Bangkok, and not informing the FBI about one future hijacker's U.S. visa or his companion's travel to the United States;
- not sharing information linking individuals in the *Cole* attack to Mihdhar;
- not taking adequate steps in time to find Mihdhar or Hazmi in the United States;
- not linking the arrest of Zacarias Moussaoui, described as interested in flight training for the purpose of using an airplane in a terrorist act, to the heightened indications of attack;
- not discovering false statements on visa applications;
- not recognizing passports manipulated in a fraudulent manner;
- not expanding no-fly lists to include names from terrorist watchlists;
- not searching airline passengers identified by the computer-based CAPPS screening system; and
- not hardening aircraft cockpit doors or taking other measures to prepare for the possibility of suicide hijackings.

## GENERAL FINDINGS

Since the plotters were flexible and resourceful, we cannot know whether any single step or series of steps would have defeated them. What we can say with confidence is that none of the measures adopted by the U.S. government from 1998 to 2001 disturbed or even delayed the progress of the al Qaeda plot. Across the government, there were failures of imagination, policy, capabilities, and management. ...

## Capabilities

Before 9/11, the United States tried to solve the al Qaeda problem with the capabilities it had used in the last stages of the Cold War and its immediate aftermath. These capabilities were insufficient. Little was done to expand or reform them. ...

America's homeland defenders faced outward. NORAD itself was barely able to retain any alert bases at all. Its planning scenarios occasionally considered the danger of hijacked aircraft being guided to American targets, but only aircraft that were coming from overseas.

The most serious weaknesses in agency capabilities were in the domestic arena. The FBI did not have the capability to link the collective knowledge of agents in the field to national priorities. Other domestic agencies deferred to the FBI. . . .

## Management

The missed opportunities to thwart the 9/11 plot were also symptoms of a broader inability to adapt the way government manages problems to the new challenges of the twenty-first century. Action officers should have been able to draw on all available knowledge about al Qaeda in the government. Management should have ensured that information was shared and duties were clearly assigned across agencies, and across the foreign-domestic divide. . . .

The U.S. government did not find a way of pooling intelligence and using it to guide the planning and assignment of responsibilities for joint operations involving entities as disparate as the CIA, the FBI, the State Department, the military, and the agencies involved in homeland security.

## SPECIFIC FINDINGS

## Problems within the Intelligence Community

. . . Before 9/11, no agency did more to attack al Qaeda than the CIA. But there were limits to what the CIA was able to achieve by disrupting terrorist activities abroad and by using proxies to try to capture Bin Ladin and his lieutenants in Afghanistan. CIA officers were aware of those limitations.

To put it simply, covert action was not a silver bullet. It was important to engage proxies in Afghanistan and to build various capabilities so that if an opportunity presented itself, the CIA could act on it. But for more than three years, through both the late Clinton and early Bush administrations, the CIA relied on proxy forces, and there was growing frustration within the CIA's Counterterrorist Center and in the National Security Council staff with the lack of results. . . .

## Congress

The Congress, like the executive branch, responded slowly to the rise of transnational terrorism as a threat to national security. The legislative branch adjusted little and did not restructure itself to address changing threats. Its attention to terrorism was episodic and splintered across several committees. . . .

So long as oversight is undermined by current congressional rules and resolutions, we believe the American people will not get the security they want and need. The United States needs a strong, stable, and capable congressional committee structure to give America's national intelligence agencies oversight, support, and leadership.

## Are We Safer?

Since 9/11, the United States and its allies have killed or captured a majority of al Qaeda's leadership; toppled the Taliban, which gave al Qaeda sanctuary in Afghanistan; and severely damaged the organization. Yet terrorist attacks continue. Even as we have thwarted attacks, nearly everyone expects they will come. How can this be?

The problem is that al Qaeda represents an ideological movement, not a finite group of people. It initiates and inspires, even if it no longer directs. In this way it has transformed itself into a decentralized force. Bin Ladin may be limited in his ability to organize major attacks from his hideouts. Yet killing or capturing him, while extremely important, would not end terror. His message of inspiration to a new generation of terrorists would continue.

Because of offensive actions against al Qaeda since 9/11, and defensive actions to improve homeland security, we believe we are safer today. But we are not safe. We therefore make the following recommendations that we believe can make America safer and more secure.

## RECOMMENDATIONS

Three years after 9/11, the national debate continues about how to protect our nation in this new era. We divide our recommendations into two basic parts: What to do, and how to do it.

## WHAT TO DO? A GLOBAL STRATEGY

. . . We propose a strategy with three dimensions: (1) attack terrorists and their organizations, (2) prevent the continued growth of Islamist terrorism, and (3) protect against and prepare for terrorist attacks.

### Attack Terrorists and Their Organizations

- Root out sanctuaries. . . .
- Strengthen long-term U.S. and international commitments to the future of Pakistan and Afghanistan.
- Confront problems with Saudi Arabia in the open and build a relationship beyond oil, a relationship that both sides can defend to their citizens and includes a shared commitment to reform.

### Prevent the Continued Growth of Islamist Terrorism

In October 2003, Secretary of Defense Donald Rumsfeld asked if enough was being done "to fashion a broad integrated plan to stop the next generation of terrorists." As part of such a plan, the U.S. government should

- Define the message and stand as an example of moral leadership in the world. . . .

- Where Muslim governments, even those who are friends, do not offer opportunity, respect the rule of law, or tolerate differences, then the United States needs to stand for a better future.
- Communicate and defend American ideals in the Islamic world, through much stronger public diplomacy to reach more people, including students and leaders outside of government. . . .
- Offer an agenda of opportunity that includes support for public education and economic openness.
- Develop a comprehensive coalition strategy against Islamist terrorism, using a flexible contact group of leading coalition governments and fashioning a common coalition approach on issues like the treatment of captured terrorists.
- Devote a maximum effort to the parallel task of countering the proliferation of weapons of mass destruction.
- Expect less from trying to dry up terrorist money and more from following the money for intelligence, as a tool to hunt terrorists, understand their networks, and disrupt their operations. . . .
- Target terrorist travel, an intelligence and security strategy that the 9/11 story showed could be at least as powerful as the effort devoted to terrorist finance.
- Address problems of screening people with biometric identifiers across agencies and governments, including our border and transportation systems, by designing a comprehensive screening system that addresses common problems and sets common standards. As standards spread, this necessary and ambitious effort could dramatically strengthen the world's ability to intercept individuals who could pose catastrophic threats.
- Quickly complete a biometric entry-exit screening system, one that also speeds qualified travelers.
- Set standards for the issuance of birth certificates and sources of identification, such as driver's licenses.
- Develop strategies for neglected parts of our transportation security system. Since 9/11, about 90 percent of the nation's $5 billion annual investment in transportation security has gone to aviation, to fight the last war.
- In aviation, prevent arguments about a new computerized profiling system from delaying vital improvements in the "no-fly" and "automatic selectee" lists. Also, give priority to the improvement of checkpoint screening.
- Determine, with leadership from the President, guidelines for gathering and sharing information in the new security systems that are needed, guidelines that integrate safeguards for privacy and other essential liberties.
- Underscore that as government power necessarily expands in certain ways, the burden of retaining such powers remains on the executive to

demonstrate the value of such powers and ensure adequate supervision of how they are used, including a new board to oversee the implementation of the guidelines needed for gathering and sharing information in these new security systems.

- Base federal funding for emergency preparedness solely on risks and vulnerabilities, putting New York City and Washington, D.C., at the top of the current list. Such assistance should not remain a program for general revenue sharing or pork-barrel spending.
- Make homeland security funding contingent on the adoption of an incident command system to strengthen teamwork in a crisis, including a regional approach. . . .

## HOW TO DO IT? A DIFFERENT WAY OF ORGANIZING GOVERNMENT

. . . We call for unity of effort in five areas, beginning with unity of effort on the challenge of counterterrorism itself:

- unifying strategic intelligence and operational planning against Islamist terrorists across the foreign–domestic divide with a National Counterterrorism Center;
- unifying the intelligence community with a new National Intelligence Director;
- unifying the many participants in the counterterrorism effort and their knowledge in a network-based information sharing system that transcends traditional governmental boundaries;
- unifying and strengthening congressional oversight to improve quality and accountability; and
- strengthening the FBI and homeland defenders. . . .

## Notes

1. Report of the Office of Independent Counsel (Starr Report), September 19, 1998, online at http://icreport.access.gpo.gov/report/7grounds.htm#L44.

2. "Clinton, William Jefferson, Address to the Nation on Testimony Before the Independent Counsel's Grand Jury, August 17, 1998, *Public Papers of the Presidents: William J. Clinton, 1998* (Washington: Government Printing Office, 1999).

3. Congressional Record, 105th Cong., 2d Sess, December 19, 1998, From the Congressional Record Online via GPO Access [wais.access.gpo.gov].

4. Congressional Record, 106th Cong., 1st Sess, January 16, 1999, From the Congressional Record Online via GPO Access [wais.access.gpo.gov].

5. National Commission on Terrorist Attacks upon the United States, *The 9/11 Commission Report: Final Report of the National Commission on Terrorist Attacks Upon the United States* (Washington, D.C.: Government Publishing Office, 2004), 1–2.

6. George W. Bush, Remarks in Sarasota, Florida, on the Terrorist Attack on New York City's World Trade Center, September 11, 2001, *Public Papers of the Presidents of the United States: George W. Bush, 2001* (Washington, D.C.: Government Printing Office, 2003), 1098.

7. George W. Bush Address to the Nation on the Terrorist Attacks, September 11, 2001, *Public Papers of the Presidents of the United States: George W. Bush, 2001* (Washington, D.C.: Government Printing Office, 2003), 1099–1100.

8. "A Great Wound," *The Nation*, October 1, 2001. Reprinted by permission of The Nation.

9. Alexander Cockburn, "Faceless Cowards," *The Nation*, October 1, 2001, 655. Reprinted by permission of Alexander Cockburn.

10. "At War," *National Review*, October 1, 2001. © 2001 by National Review, Inc. Reprinted by permission.

11. Daniel Pipes, "War, not 'Crimes,'" *National Review*, October 1, 2001, 12. © 2001 by National Review, Inc. Reprinted by permission.

12. *The 9/11 Commission Report*, 1–26.

# Index

# About the Author

Donald W. Whisenhunt is emeritus professor of history at Western Washington University. He has had a long career both as a faculty member and as an administrator at several colleges and universities. He has served on three occasions as a Fulbright Professor of History. His assignments included China in 1995, Korea in 1999, and Belarus in 2004. He has published widely, mostly in the history of the United States in the twentieth century. Some of his most recent books include *The Human Tradition in America Between the Wars, 1920–1945* (Scholarly Resources/Rowman and Littlefield, 2002), *Poetry of the People: Poems to the President, 1929–1945* (Popular Press, 1996), *Tent Show: Arthur Names and His "Famous" Players* (Texas A&M University Press, 2000), and *It Seems to Me: Selected Letters of Eleanor Roosevelt* (University Press of Kentucky, 2001).

Made in the USA
Las Vegas, NV
14 January 2021